SECRET
CITY

THE INSIDER'S GUIDE
TO THE WORLD'S
COOLEST NEIGHBOURHOODS

CONTENTS

© peeterv / Getty Images; © Daniel Fung / Shutterstock; © Yu Chun Christopher Wong / Shutterstock; © Elena Lar / Shutterstock

© Michael Abid / 500px; © f11photo / Shutterstock; © marchello74 / Shutterstock; © lazyllama / Shutterstock

INTRODUCTION

It's easy to fall in love with San Francisco. But to understand what makes the city tick, I needed to do a little sleuthing.

The first time I explored this preening peacock of a city, I dutifully toured its signature attractions. I weaved through crowds on the Golden Gate Bridge, I boarded the ferry to Alcatraz, I queued for big-ticket galleries... but something was missing. My feet were tired, my wallet was emptying fast, yet I was learning little about why locals love the city by the bay.

Following the advice of San Franciscans, I turned my attention to the city's outlying neighbourhoods. And that's when San Francisco truly revealed its gritty, glittering self. Looking down from Potrero Hill as the late-afternoon sunshine painted the skyline gold, the city started to work its magic. Deep in a bar in industrial neighbourhood Dogpatch, to the maracas sound of cocktail shakers, I no longer felt an outsider but like one of the locals.

Seeking out intriguing neighbourhoods continues to enrich my travels. I fell head over heels with Melbourne (p. 284) by brunching my way through Brunswick and bolting into Windsor's hidden bars. Basing myself in Sukhumvit allowed me to dive head-first into the giddy nightlife of Bangkok (p. 38).

It's the joy of exploring neighbourhoods that inspired us to create *Secret City*, a curious traveller's guide to 50 cities around the world. Some are classic destinations like Paris (p. 110), Rome (p. 122) and Istanbul (p. 160), which have long lured travellers to their timeless attractions. Other cities have undergone dramatic changes over recent years, so much so that an insider's recommendations can completely transform a traveller's experience: cities like Havana (p. 318), Austin (p. 216), Lima (p. 314) and Moscow (p. 166). We also included popular cities that travellers think they know well – blonde, beachy Sydney (p. 292); desert-backed glamourpuss Dubai (p. 24); haven of the cashed-up beautiful people, Los Angeles (p. 202) – and asked our in-the-know writers to reveal the hidden scoop.

For each of the 50 cities profiled in the book, we've swung the spotlight onto neighbourhoods where you can feel the rhythms of local life. Sometimes the city's most well-trampled streets are only a short distance away but there's a well-concealed treasure: perhaps a blink-and-you'll-miss-it cafe in Rio de Janeiro's Copacabana (p. 329) or a historic jazz bar in Stockholm's Gamla Stan (p. 151). Elsewhere we profile neighbourhoods you might not know much about but should really consider staying in: Tokyo's grungy Kōenji (p. 76), barnacle-clung Wapping and Rotherhithe in London (p. 98), and Staten Island's North Shore in New York City (p. 266).

Each neighbourhood profile has out-of-the-ordinary recommendations for eating, drinking, partying and delving into local culture. All of them are hand-picked by experts who know these cities inside out, and they're accompanied by maps to orient you in these exciting districts.

Locals might groan that we've divulged some of their best neighbourhood secrets, but we think you'll love our toolkit for travelling deeply.

Happy exploring,

Anita Isalska, Editor

AFRICA & THE MIDDLE EAST

ARTS & CULTURE   **MUSIC & FILM**   **SPORTS & LEISURE**   **EATING**   **DRINKING**   **SHOPPING**

Mouassine & Central Souqs

Marrakesh

Kasbah & Mellah

MARRAKESH

Bold and at times abrasive, Marrakesh is a many-faced metropolis where modern Africa dances with historic monuments, ancient crafts and caravanserai traditions.

The heart and soul of Marrakesh lie in the tangled guts of its medina, an ancient deep-veined city that started life under the Berber Almoravids in 1070. For centuries it prospered as the epicentre of the western Islamic world, plundered and glorified in turn by successive sultans, and later ruled as a French protectorate. Between 2018 and 2019 the souqs, *funduqs* (ancient inns) and shrines of the medina were scrubbed and restored, making it prettier (and more sanitised) than ever.

The central neighbourhood of Mouassine is riding the winds of change with rooftop cafes and achingly hip boutiques that have one eye on Europe and the other on Africa, all wedged between gritty, working souqs. Travellers seeking a pinch more tranquillity should head south to the Kasbah and Mellah, where Marrakesh's first fortresses were erected and the Saadian Sultan Ahmed al-Mansour entombed his dynasty. Wander on foot to feel the city's full sensory slap.

KASBAH & MELLAH

Approaching the medina's southerly Kasbah and Mellah, the streets widen and storks strut on blushing fortified walls. The Kasbah is Marrakesh's oldest quarter and its cluster of ancient sights – the Badi Palace, Bahia Palace and Saadian Tombs – bring floods of visitors. Tour groups rarely linger and it remains a mellow neighbourhood, especially when combined with Marrakesh's old Jewish quarter.

Les Jardins de la Medina

One of the medina's largest palm-fringed pools lies behind the deceptively blank facade of Les Jardins de la Medina riad. When the mercury spikes, there's no better place for a swim. Day access packages (Dh400 to Dh650) include lunch by the pool and graceful colonial bar (and yes, it does serve alcohol). *21 Derb Chtouka, Kasbah; www. lesjardinsdelamedina.com.*

Café Clock

This import from Fez is far more than a cafe famed for its camel burgers. Come for its cultural roster supporting local talents: there are jam sessions, tribal beat music from Gnaoua performers, calligraphy classes, cooking workshops and cinema nights. Moroccan storytelling evenings are particularly poignant, striving to record a fading oral history. *224 Derb Chtouka, Kasbah; www. cafeclock.com; 9am-11pm.*

Lazama Synagogue

Established in 1492 by Jews expelled from Spain, the Lazama Synagogue is an active place of worship and a museum exploring 2000 years of Jewish heritage in Morocco. It offers a window into the history of Marrakesh's Jewish diaspora (there are only 150 left). *Derb Talmud Tora, Mellah; 9am-7pm Sun-Thu, to 6pm Fri; Dh10.*

Kaftan Queen

Good-quality, contemporary kaftans are the lifeblood of this hidden, first-floor fashion boutique. Maxi, bejewelled, patterned or plain – shoppers can take their time trying them on in sumptuous fitting rooms, paired with pastel *babouches* (slippers). *1st fl, 186 Al Fatouki (enter from Rue Riad Zitoun el-Kedim); www. facebook.com/Kaftanqueen; 10am-1pm & 3-7pm Mon-Sat.*

Place des Ferblantiers

Once a hive of metalworkers, this industrious square is gateway to the Mellah. Guarding its perimeter are the Mellah Market, where butchers routinely behead chickens amid the perfume of florists, the Grand Bijouterie jewellers' souq, and an approachable covered spice souq.

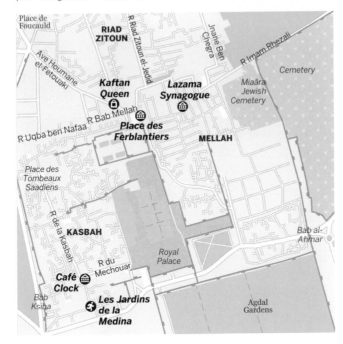

MOUASSINE & CENTRAL SOUQS

Walk due north from the Djemaa el Fna's din of drums and you'll eventually emerge in a clash of inventive boutiques and ancient architecture. This is where many treasures are made and popular museums reside, but it's also the area modernising fastest.

🔒 Al Nour
Hand-stitched cotton kaftans, kids' smocks and elegant scarves are all imagined in uncharacteristically nude and earthy tones at this top-quality textile store run by a cooperative for disabled women. *19 Derb Moulay El Ghali; www. alnour-textiles.com; 9.30am-2pm & 3-7.30pm.*

✖ Ben Youssef Food Stalls
If you can't face the scrum of eating in the Djemaa el Fna, this backstreet maze of charcoal-fired grill stands offers the same local theatre minus much of the hassle. To find them, follow the plumes of smoke that lace the streets just south of the Ben Youssef Mosque around lunchtime. *11am-3pm.*

🏛 Musée Boucharouite
Boucharouites are Morocco's raggedy carpets of the poor, made with strips of discarded clothing, and this private museum in an 18th-century riad is an eloquent celebration of their charms. One of its secret pleasures is the quiet rooftop cafe. *Derb el Cadi; www.facebook. com/musee.boucharouite; 9.30am-6pm Mon-Sat, closed Aug; Dh40.*

🏛 Riad Yima
While the ambience is one of calm, the rooms of this riad gallery and teahouse are a riot of in-your-face pop art and homewares inspired by North African life. Riad Yima is the medina hideaway of acclaimed Moroccan artist and photographer Hassan Hajjaj, chock-a-block with kitsch *babouches* and contemporary photography featuring hijab-cloaked African women. *52 Derb Aajane, Rahba Lakdima; www. riadyima.com; 10am-7pm Sat-Thu, 10am-1.30pm & 2.30-7pm Fri.*

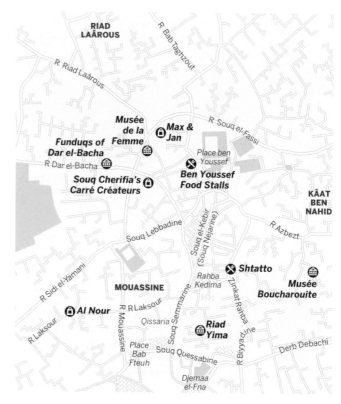

MARRAKESH

✖ Shtatto

Naked bulbs are strung across the whitewashed rooftop, the gravel tone of grinding coffee floats on the breeze, and straw-hatted fashionistas scan the 'gram under palms. Below there's three floors of *très chic* shops, including Amine Bendriouich couture. *81 Derb Nkal, Rahba Lakdima; www.shtattomarrakech.com; 9am-10pm.*

© 2020, Riad Yima

© Monica Wells / Alamy Stock Photo

🔓 Souq Cherifia's Carré Créateurs

The first floor of this makeshift souq is known as the 'artisan square', an exciting collection of independent (mostly female) Moroccan designers. Highlights include Tilila, with its Berber-bling *babouches*, Sisi Morocco's one-off, lino-printed cushions, and hand-embroidered hessian shoes and bags from Khmissa. *Off R Mouassine; 10am-7pm.*

🏛 Funduqs of Dar el-Bacha

Marrakesh's ancient network of caravanserai inns still exists, many of them now converted into rustic artisan workshops, and Dar el-Bacha is a thoroughfare

SPIRITUAL SCRUB

If you want to see behind the veil of Marrakshi life you need to visit the local hammam. Every neighbourhood has one, with different hours or entrances for men and women. They are always single-sex because everybody inside is nearly naked. The one in Mouassine is tourist-friendly. Go armed like the locals – with black olive soap to wash and a mitt to scrub away the dead skin (both of these can be bought in the souqs).

with a large cluster of them. Funduq el Mizane was once used for weighing goods, and a giant pair of scales still stands inside. Funduq El Amir is worth a look for its red ochre, geometric decor.

🔓 Max & Jan

The horseshoe entryway to this concept store is like a Narnia door to contemporary African fashion, super-cool homewares and a rooftop restaurant. One half of the Belgian/Swiss design duo behind the store, Maximilian Scharl, was born in Casablanca. Collections are designed and produced in Morocco. *16 R Amsefah; www.maxandjan.com; 10am-7pm.*

🏛 Musée de la Femme

The little-visited Women's Museum is the first initiative of its kind in North Africa, launched by a group of local men to preserve women's culture. *40 R Sidi Abdelaziz; www.museedelafemme.ma; 9.30am-6.30pm.*

Clockwise from top left: colourful Riad Yima; brimming sacks in Ben Youssef Sq; Max & Jan's chic designs

© Marc Van Vaek / 2020, Max & Jan

CAPE TOWN

Cape Town is like that kid in school who had it all: fun, popular, a little bit quirky and undeniably, indescribably beautiful.

It doesn't matter where you are in Cape Town, Table Mountain provides an endlessly impressive backdrop. For many, Sea Point is the perfect neighbourhood: it has all the energy of the inner city but with the calming addition of the Atlantic Ocean crashing alongside the promenade. You can jump on a bus from here and head east to Woodstock, an industrial suburb that's more gritty than pretty – though it does have a perfect view of Devil's Peak. The neighbourhood is undergoing gradual gentrification, with art galleries and gin distilleries sharing the streets with factories and busy workshops. Board a train to get to Muizenberg, a seaside suburb some 20km south. Here, regeneration has also played a role, with arty stores and cool bars providing a reason to visit beyond the excellent surf and coastal walking path.

SEA POINT

Long and skinny, wedged between ocean and mountain, Sea Point's action is largely found on two very busy strips. So busy, in fact, that you can find local haunts and near-secret spots hiding between more frequented restaurants and bars on Regent Road and Main Road. Sea Point is primarily known for its eating opportunities, with cuisine from every continent bar Antarctica represented.

🏛 Sea Point Contact

Charles Darwin spent 18 days in Cape Town on his homeward-bound journey in 1836. His main interest wasn't animals but rocks, specifically at a point where hot magma had baked onto the sedimentary rock and cooled to form granite. Also known as Charles Darwin's Rocks, a plaque marks the spot, which is a great place to watch the sunset. *Queen's Beach.*

❌ Hesheng

You might well get a lesson in what constitutes 'real' Chinese food when you sit down, but it's worth it for the authentic feast that ends up arriving at your table. It's an unassuming and utterly unfussy place that's rightfully popular with Cape Town's Chinese community. *269 Main Rd; http:// hesheng.co.za; 11am-3pm & 5-9pm Wed-Mon.*

❌ Total Garage

In a neighbourhood known for its dining scene, it seems odd to head to a gas station for breakfast, but Sea Point locals swear by the baked goods here. Pick up some fresh bagels, carrot cake or their legendary cheesecake. The coffee is also excellent. *345 Main Rd; 021 439 4034; 24hr.*

❌ @Seoul

Cape Town's Korean cuisine offering is limited, but this little place would fit right in on a Gangnam side street. All the classics are here: *deok boki* (rice cakes in a spicy sauce), *bibimbap* and excellent soups including *doenjang jjigae* and hearty *samgyetang*. There are only a few tables so book ahead. *72 Regent Rd; 021 439 3373; noon-2pm & 6-10.30pm Mon-Sat.*

🏔 Lion's Head

Hiking up Lion's Head is hardly a secret but few people start their hike from the Sea Point side of the mountain – so for the first section at least, you'll likely have the path to yourself. Look out for the Kramat of Shaykh Mohamed Hassen Ghaibie along the way – this shrine was left remarkably unscathed after a massive wildfire in early 2019. The hike starts at the top of Rhine Road.

Rocklands Bay
Rocklands Beach
Main Rd
❌ Hesheng
Atlantic Ocean
Main Rd
High Level Rd
SEA POINT
Lion's Head
❌ Total Garage
Boat Bay
Beach Rd
Queen's Beach
❌ @Seoul
FRESNAYE
Regent Rd
Kloof Rd
High Level Rd
Table Mountain National Park
🏛 Sea Point Contact
Queens Rd

© Gary Latham / Lonely Planet

WOODSTOCK

One of the hippest neighbourhoods in the city, Woodstock is home to microbreweries, craft distilleries, coffee roasteries and art studios. At heart, it's still an industrial district – after dark you'd be wise to summon a ride-share service to get from A to B. Thanks to its slow gentrification, there are plenty of newly opened attractions and hidden sights to seek out, some even sitting on the main roads.

✕ Altona Fisheries

Clear your dining schedule for the rest of the day. As well as fish and chips, Altona serves Cape Town's home-grown mega-sandwich, the Gatsby. The foot-long rolls are stuffed with chips, salad and a choice of fish, masala steak or Vienna sausages. A magnificent hangover cure. *127 Victoria Rd; 021 447 0735; 7am-7pm Mon-Fri, to 4pm Sat.*

🔒 Dress Me Up

Woodstock is awash with galleries and funky little stores. This friendly place specialises in retro and vintage clothes and is a favourite for revellers heading out to the annual AfrikaBurn, South Africa's answer to Burning Man. As well as fabulous dresses and some wonderfully weird headgear, you'll find retro *objets d'art* and a few vinyl records. *77 Roodebloem Rd; 072 713 8907; 11am-6pm Tue-Sat.*

🍺 Drifter Brewing Company

Drifter embodies the ethos of the global craft beer scene: a bunch of creatives having a mighty good time and producing great beer while they're at it. Seasonal brews are served alongside the core range (ask for a blend of their coconut ale and smoked porter) in the nautically themed taproom. If you're feeling flush, grab a bottle of the ocean-aged tripel to sip with friends on the balcony, which has a great view of Devil's Peak. *156 Victoria Rd; www.drifterbrewing.co.za; 3-10pm Fri, 11am-3pm Sat.*

🍸 Hope on Hopkins

Lucy Beard and Leigh Lisk are at the forefront of Cape Town's gin distilling scene. The tasting room overlooks their distillery, but advance booking is recommended – they're only open on Saturday afternoons and it's a popular spot for locals seeking to sip the latest creations. Tastings are refreshingly relaxed: order

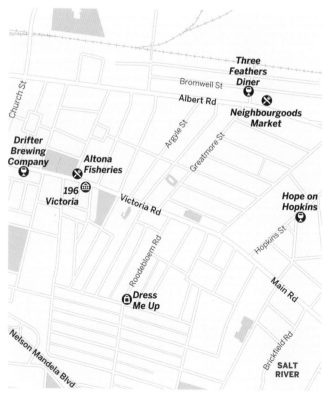

© Moobatto / Shutterstock

a trio of gins and taste at your leisure while lounging on couches. *7 Hopkins St; https://hopeonhopkins.co.za; noon-5pm Sat.*

🏛 196 Victoria

Despite its impressive facade, you could easily pass by the 196 Victoria building without realising you can actually go inside. And you'd probably never guess what you'll find within: a selection of artisans and holistic therapists, a yoga studio and Clay Hands, where ceramicist Natasha Viljoen encourages potters of all ages to play and create. *196 Victoria Rd; www.196victoria.com.*

🚇 Three Feathers Diner

You can enter this 'man cave' diner through the Woodstock Co-op, a store selling art and fashion from local designers. The change from serene shopping experience to atmospheric

© Michelle Parkin Photography / 2020, Hope on Hopkins

BEER & GRAFFITI CRAWL

Local resident Hester Bergh (061 533 6622) combines a love of good ale and good art in these half-day tours around her neighbourhood. Woodstock is rich in street art and you'll get the stories behind these inner city murals as you wander, stopping at a couple of microbreweries on the way.

bar with graffiti-adorned walls, pinball machine and pool table, plus a couple of classic American cars, pretty much sums up everything that is awesome about Woodstock. *78 Bromwell St; https://three-feathers-diner.business.site; 9.30am-5pm Mon-Sat.*

✖ Neighbourgoods Market

Perhaps the best time to visit Woodstock is on a Saturday morning when the enduringly popular and ever-busy Neighbourgoods Market takes place at the Old Biscuit Mill. The market, which mostly specialises in foodstuffs, is about as un-secret as it gets, but the crowds it pulls spill out into the surrounding streets and give Woodstock a buzz it tends to lack during the rest of the week. If you're visiting Cape Town, this market shouldn't be missed. *375 Albert Rd; www.neighbourgoodsmarket.co.za; 9am-3pm Sat.*

Top: food stalls galore at Neighbourgoods Market
Left: Hope on Hopkins

MUIZENBERG

Once a run-down row of boarded-up buildings, Muizenberg's seafront has happily received a massive facelift and now houses some great bars and restaurants. Of course, the main strip is known by all and you'll need to wander the narrow side streets to see the cafes and one-off boutiques the 'Berg's Bohemian residents love so dearly.

🏛 Sobeit Store & Hong Kong Charlie Café

Hidden in plain sight on the main road from Tokai, Sobeit is a self-described 'mayhem space'. Upstairs, artists work on paintings, sculpture and unique pieces of art. Downstairs, the studio's work is sold alongside antiques, locally made jewellery, utterly unique furniture and to quote the studio's literature, 'other cool shit'. It's a marvellous place to browse while waiting for your sushi platter at the in-store cafe. *51 Main Rd; www.facebook.com/ SobeitStudioCapeTown; 8am-9pm Mon-Sat, to 2pm Sun.*

❄ Striped Horse

Although this beachfront bar alongside the train tracks is hardly hidden, most know it as a place for light lunch and a pint of craft beer. But on weekend evenings, the normally chilled pub bursts at the seams with Capetonians coming to watch live local bands. *12-14 York Rd; http://stripedhorsebar. com; 9am-1am Mon, noon-1am Tue-Sat, 11am-9pm Sun.*

❄ Pecks Valley Hiking Trail

It's a steep hike up Pecks Valley to Muizenberg Peak, from where you get great views of the beach and on clear days, right across False Bay. The hike starts from Boyes Dr and can continue all the way to Silvermine, but this is a secluded section of the mountains, so be sure to walk in a group. *Boyes Dr.*

🔒 Blue Priest

It's not far from the beach, but many visitors to the 'Berg never wander into what locals call 'The Village'. The narrow streets here are mostly residential, but Palmer Rd is dotted with cool shops and places to eat. Blue Priest sells one-off streetwear rich in African prints – grab a custom cap or a unique pair of boardies to wear to the beach. *42 Palmer Rd; www. facebook.com/BLUEPRIEST. CO.ZA; 10am-6pm Tue-Thu, to 8pm Fri & Sat, to 2pm Sun.*

Map labels:
Imperial Yacht Club
Rondevlei Nature Reserve 4km (2.5 miles)
Lake Zandvlei
Main Rd
Boyes Dr
Lakeside Sports Ground
MUIZENBERG
Beach Rd
Sobeit Store & Hong Kong Charlie Café
Bean Dreaming
Blue Priest
Palmer Rd
Pecks Valley Hiking Trail
Muizenberg Park
Striped Horse
Atlantic Rd

MADE IN MUIZENBERG

Although their flagship shop has closed, Made in Muizenberg is still striving to celebrate local entrepreneurs, performers and artisans. They organise occasional markets, festivals, classes and workshops all designed to showcase the craftwork and general creativity of the 'Berg's residents. Keep an eye on what they're planning next: www.facebook.com/madeinmuizenberg.

🌀 Imperial Yacht Club

Everyone knows you can surf, stand-up paddleboard and kitesurf in Muizenberg, but only a short distance inland you can also learn to sail on Zandvlei, a lake that's enormously popular with picnicking Capetonians but somehow remains almost undiscovered by visitors. *1 Promenade Ave; http://imperialyachtclub.co.za.*

🍴 Bean Dreaming

Husband-and-wife team Kiam and Stef share this space to each follow their own personal dream. Stef is out front serving great coffee and some seriously decadent pancakes in the cafe, while Kiam works as a tattoo artist in the studio behind. *34 Palmer Rd; www.facebook.com/beandreamingcoffee; 084 232 0537; 7.30am-5pm Mon-Fri, 9am-2pm Sat & Sun.*

🌿 Rondevlei Nature Reserve

Sightings are near-mythical, but there are hippos in the water at Rondevlei, a 10-minute drive from the beach. More often sighted are some of the 200-odd bird species that call the lake home. *Fishermans Walk, Zeekovlei; 7.30am-5pm.*

Top: a row of rainbow-coloured beach huts in seafront Muizenberg Left: Striped Horse bar

Tel Aviv

Neve
Tzedek

Florentin

TEL AVIV

Cosmopolitan, vibrant and ever-changing, Tel Aviv is a heady collision of high tech, glitzy nightlife, Bauhaus architecture and pungent markets.

Tel Aviv is a bit of an urban sprawl, albeit one punctuated by peaceful green spaces and fringed by a strip of fine beaches. While attractions are spread out all over Tel Aviv, many sights worth your time are concentrated in the historic neighbourhoods in the south of the city, squeezed between the ancient port city of Jaffa to the south and the Old North beyond Arlozorov St.

Neve Tzedek is a top choice for travellers who enjoy exploring narrow cobbled lanes and making chance discoveries of characterful cafes and independent boutiques. A short walk south, Florentin is the rough-around-the-edges home of young, on-trend types. It's rich in street art, art studios, fusion restaurants and bars, with the hubbub of Levinsky Market just steps away.

The city centre is easily walkable. If you want to get the most out of Tel Aviv, it's worth renting a bicycle and taking to its many cycle lanes.

TEL AVIV

NEVE TZEDEK

North of Jaffa is Tel Aviv's oldest neighbourhood. It's hemmed by trendy Florentin to the east and borders the historic Yemeni neighbourhood of Karem HaTeimanim and Lev Ha'ir (Tel Aviv's city centre) to the north. Its quiet tangle of narrow streets, lined with pastel-coloured houses, is easily navigated on foot. Its main street, Shabazi St, runs gently downhill to the Tel Aviv Promenade.

🏛 Rokach House-Museum

The full-figured, naked ceramic ladies that greet visitors here are the works of Lea Majaro-Mintz, the great-granddaughter of one of Tel Aviv's pioneers. In 1887, Shimon Rokach and his family were one of 10 families chosen to settle the Neve Tzedek district. Besides an exhibition on early Tel Aviv life, Rokach House doubles as an art gallery. *Shimon Rokach St 36; www.rokach-house.co.il; 10am & 2pm Thu & Sat.*

❌ Alma Café

This cafe has earned itself a loyal local following with its vegetarian and vegan recipes – from hummus omelettes and vegetable shawarma to moreish *shakshuka* (eggs poached in a spiced tomato sauce), imaginative salads and French toast. Popular for brunch. *Shabazi St 55; 03-516-8793; 8.30am-11pm.*

❌ Hummus HaCarmel

A five-minute walk north from Neve Tzedek, this hole-in-the-wall in the middle of bustling Carmel Market is locally renowned for its superlative hummus. The stained-glass entrance and scrolls on the wall remind you that you're dining in a repurposed synagogue. Try the original or the *masabacha*, both served with homemade pickles. *HaCarmel St 11; 7.30am-4.30pm Sun-Fri.*

🏛 Suzanne Dellal Centre

In 1989, an 1890s school was turned into this locally beloved centre for modern dance and drama, breathing new life into the neighbourhood, which was in decline at the time. Catch a performance by the Batsheva or the Inbal Dance Company, or enjoy the tranquillity of the beautifully landscaped courtyards. *Yehieli St 5; www.suzannedellal.org.il; box office 9am-9pm Sun-Thu, to 1pm Fri.*

🏛 Eden Cinema

This handsome art deco building once housed Tel Aviv's first cinema, founded in 1913 and in business until 1975. It originally screened silent movies accompanied by orchestra music. These days it's a beloved cultural landmark. *Lillienblum St 2.*

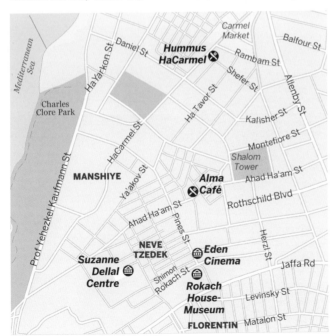

FLORENTIN

Squeezed between the ethnically diverse Shapira and Nave Shaanan neighbourhoods to the east, Jaffa to the west and Neve Tzedek to the north, Florentin is a former industrial zone synonymous with street art – it's also Tel Aviv's trendiest neighbourhood. Having attracted artists and musicians with cheap rent in the '80s, Florentin now draws visitors with fusion restaurants by day, and bars and nightclubs by night.

Pachot M'Elef

Street art has found its natural home in bohemian Florentin. Some argue that bringing an anti-establishment, outdoor form of artistic expression indoors erodes its character, but street artist and photographer Daniel Siboni (co-owner of the gallery) disagrees. Here you can buy reproductions and photos of the art painted on the neighbourhood's buildings. *Arbarbanel St 54; noon-8pm Sun-Thu, 10am-4pm Fri.*

Florentin45

Of Tel Aviv's many art galleries, Florentin45 retains the edge. Its changing exhibitions are a balance between internationally renowned Israeli artists and emerging young talent. Past shows have included the likes of Maya Smira and Adi Oz-Ari. *Florentin St 45; 9am-5pm Mon-Sat.*

ChavShush

Levinsky has been the epitome of a Middle Eastern market since Greek Jews originally set up their stalls in the 1930s: pungent, colourful and full of garrulous customers trying to strike a bargain. Run by the descendants of a Yemeni Jewish trader who settled in Palestine in 1931, ChavShush stands out with its eye-catching bags of fragrant spices, and a friendly and un-pushy manner. *HaChalutzim 18; 7.30am-1pm Sun-Fri.*

Mezcal

This well-loved little neighbourhood bar is responsible for Tel Aviv's most authentic Mexican food, so popular that it expanded to include a fantastic taco joint next door. Have your tacos filled with a sultry, dark *mole* sauce, or spice them up with *salsa de chile ancho* (sauce made with a smoky, pungent chilli), and wash them down with a full range of tequilas and mezcals. *Chayim Vital St 2; www.facebook.com/MezcalTelAviv; 03-518-7925; noon-1am.*

© The Visual Explorer / Shutterstock

🍸 Casbah

With its proliferation of hanging plants, artfully mismatched furniture and works by local artists, Casbah sums up the neighbourhood nicely. It's a welcoming place at any time of the day, whether it's to share a *shakshuka* breakfast with a friend, tap away at your laptop over a coffee or prepare for a night out over a burger and some beers. *Florentin St 3; www.facebook.com/casbah.florentin; 03-518 2144; 8am-2am Sun-Fri, 9am-1am Sat.*

🏛 Hanut Theatre

This unusual little place, sitting unobtrusively between small grocery stores on HaAliya, is hard to pin down. Frequent warm-up acts – from modern dance to object theatre to video

© 2020, Mezcal

TEL AVIV GREETERS

If you want to see Tel Aviv from a local's perspective, it's well worth taking a free walk in the company of a Tel Aviv Greeter (www.telavivgreeter.com). Greeters are enthusiastic local people who are keen to show you the city's hidden corners. Guests and guides are matched according to their interests and age, and bookings are required well in advance.

art – kick off in the shop window, attracting passers-by. The rest of the performance takes place inside the multidisciplinary 'shop', with an intimate audience of up to 30, and you don't need to be proficient in Hebrew to enjoy the show. *HaAliya St 31; www.hanut31.co.il.*

⊗ Ouzeria

Part of the Levinsky Market, this local institution has been going strong for over a decade, merging hearty Greek hospitality with imaginative Mediterranean cuisine. Order a Greek meze or squid ink pasta, or perch at the bar with anise-based firewater. No reservations, so be prepared to queue. *Matalon St 44; www.facebook.com/ouzeria; 03-533-0899; noon-midnight Sun-Fri.*

Clockwise from top left: street art in Florentin; mixology in Mezcal; breakfast time at neighbourly cafe Casbah

© Eyal Granit / 2020, Casbah

Deira

Al Satwa

Dubai

Al Quoz 1

Jumeirah Lakes Towers

DUBAI

Uncover an emirate entrenched in exciting art, multicultural cuisine and global histories brought to life by its vast expat population.

Two days is sufficient to tick off Dubai's bucket-list tourist experiences, including the top trio, Dubai Mall, Dubai Fountain and record-breaking Burj Khalifa. Then what? Beach days can be as endless as Dubai's miles of sandy coastline – but there's so much more to the emirate than sun, sea, shopping and skyscrapers.

Step off the well-trampled tourist path in this compact metropolis and be rewarded with saffron-infused ice cream topped with frozen corn noodles from Iran, or a curiously harmonious hot, sweet cheese-and-rose pie straight from Nablus (just north of Jerusalem). Scale the heights of a hidden rooftop bar in Satwa, kept secret by landscape photographers. Discover the best place to buy vinyl in a reimagined industrial estate in Al Quoz 1 and join the revellers at Jumeirah Lakes Towers' beloved late-night Irish bar, where the *craic* is forever merry. This is the Dubai that the expat population wants to keep to itself – embrace it and you'll realise why.

DUBAI

AL SATWA

'Little Asia', as Satwa's sometimes known, is centrally located between Sheikh Zayed Rd and Dubai's moneyed shoreline neighbourhoods. In stark contrast to the gleaming skyscrapers and eye-wateringly expensive restaurants of DIFC (Dubai International Financial Centre) across the motorway, it's defined by dusty low-rise residential blocks, independent shops and tailors, street art, and authentic food cooked up by its dominant Asian demographic.

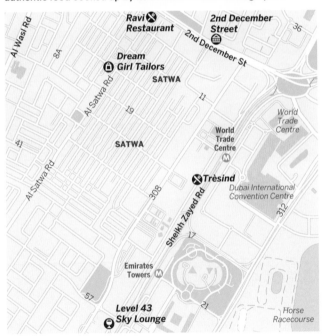

outfit and let them weave their magic. *Al Satwa Rd, nr Satwa Medical Fitness; 10am-1pm & 4-9.30pm Sun-Thu, 6-8pm Fri.*

✖ Ravi Restaurant
Rich, buttery mutton Peshawari is one of the Pakistani specialities Ravi has been dishing up for more than 30 years. Enjoy this spicy tomato-based stew with warm and steamy naans. Totalling Dhs24, it'll cost less than a designer latte in some swanky Dubai cafes. *Shop 245, 2nd December St; 04 331 5353; 5am-3am.*

✖ Trèsind
One of Dubai's most affordable five-star hotel restaurants. Adored for its fine-dining approach to street food, Trèsind (a French-English portmanteau of *'très Indian'*), serves set menus from Dhs110 in maharaja-inspired blue and champagne gold interiors. Don't miss the modernist *chaat* trolley serving the crispy, tamarind-spiked snack with table-side culinary theatre. *Level 2, Voco Hotel, Sheikh Zayed Rd; www.tresind.com; 04 308 0440; noon-3pm & 7-11.30pm.*

🚇 Level 43 Sky Lounge
At dusk, budding photographers set up tripods on this neon-lit rooftop terrace to capture what they try to keep secret: one of Dubai's most atmospheric views. The panorama is complemented by Asian food and cocktails. *Four Points by Sheraton Sheikh Zayed Rd; www.level43lounge.com; 04 316 9888; 2pm-2am.*

🏛 2nd December Street
Sixteen vast murals depict elements of Bedouin culture on buildings lining Satwa's main arterial road, the commissions of 2016's Dubai Street Museum initiative. Known as Al Dhiyafa Rd up until 2011, the street was renamed in honour of the date in 1971 when the United Arab Emirates was founded.

🔒 Dream Girl Tailors
Fashions have changed since this dressmaker opened in the '70s, but Kamal Makhija's team of ladies' tailors are still in demand. Take in a sketch or photo of your desired

DEIRA

Drawn by its souqs, markets and dhow boat-filled creek, tourists briefly dip in and out of Deira, but nowhere else captures the essence of Dubai like this original boom town. Early entrepreneurs sailed in on historic trade routes from neighbouring Arab and Indian lands, bringing their cultures and cuisines with them. They prevail to this day, enhanced with the addition of some Filipino spice.

❌ Frying Pan Adventures

Far more than a four-hour culinary walking tour, FPA's Middle Eastern Food Pilgrimage reminds explorers that, despite the influx of expats, the streets of Deira are still home to many of the Emiratis who grew up here. Find out where they get their Arabian-style pizza, baklava, and iced noodles with saffron ice cream, meeting local characters along the way. *Al Rigga Metro Station; www. fryingpanadventures.com; 056 471 8244; Dhs395.*

🏛 Bait al Banat Women's Museum

In its last life, the 'House of Women' was occupied by an Emirati family with a lot of daughters, hence the nickname. As a young girl, Professor Rafia Obaid Ghubash lived nearby and was inspired in later life to convert the vacated property into a museum charting the history of Emirati women. From early female scholars to current pioneers, you'll find them all honoured here. *Sika 28, off Al Khor St & Al Soor St; www.womenmuseumuae.com; 10am-7pm Sat-Thu; Dhs20.*

🏛 VOX Outdoor at Aloft

On top of funky new four-star Aloft City Centre Deira lies a new kind of Middle Eastern cinema experience. Deira's first fully licensed cinema not only offers drinks and reclining sofas; in the summer months, the roof retracts allowing cinemagoers to watch big-screen stars under the actual stars. Guests must be 21 or over. *Aloft Deira City Centre, Baniyas Rd, 8th St; https://uae. voxcinemas.com; couch package from Dhs137.*

🏛 Deira Clock Tower

Before Burj Al Arab and Burj Khalifa, there was Dubai Clock Tower, the emirate's first landmark, built in 1965 around a timepiece gifted to the Sheikh, and so named because it was at the

DUBAI

The Gulf

Baniyas Rd — Palm Deira — Al Khaleej Rd — Mussallah al-Eid — Al Rasheed Rd — **AL MUTEENA** — Naif Rd — Al Muteena St — **Bait al Banat Women's Museum** — **DEIRA** — Al Sabkha Rd — **NAIF** — Al Maktoum Hospital — Salah Al Din — *Boracay* — Baniyas Square — *Qwaider Al Nabulsi* — **Abra Boats** — **Geewin Café** — Union Square — Union — Al Rigga Rd — Al Rigga — Al Maktoum Rd — **RIGGA** — **Frying Pan Adventures** — **Deira Clock Tower** — Baniyas Rd — Dubai Creek (Khor Dubai) — Sheikh Khalifa Bin Zayed Rd — Al Seef St — **UMM HURAIR** — BurJuman — BurJuman Centre — **MANKHOOL** — Zabeel Rd — **VOX Outdoor at Aloft 500m (0.25 miles)** — Floating Bridge — **KARAMA**

centre of old Dubai. Renamed and overlooked in favour of record-breaking feats of engineering, this icon is back in the spotlight with plans to list it under the Modern Heritage programme protecting iconic '60s buildings. *Al Maktoum Rd, Umm Hurrair Rd & Rte D89.*

✕ Qwaider Al Nabulsi

An unusual dessert comprising molten cheese and noodle-like pastry soaked in sugar syrup, seasoned with pistachio and rose water, *kunafa* has various spellings and many countries claiming it as their own invention. After tasting the hot, gooey, crunchy cake at Palestinian restaurant Qwaider Al Nabulsi, where it's perfectly balanced with just the right amount of salt in the cheese, you might concur with them that the Palestinian Territories probably slam-dunked it. *Murraggabat St, next to Kings Park Hotel; www. facebook.com/pages/qwaider-ql-nabulsi; 8am-2am.*

ABRA-CADABRA!

Magical trips across Deira Creek cost from as little as Dhs1 in the transport system's modernised motorised abra boats (www.rta.ae). Don't let the opportunity of this historical sailing trip pass you by, even if you simply cross the water and come straight back again. These boat trips are among Dubai's simplest – and cheapest – pleasures.

✕ Geewin Café

At this long-standing kiosk, sample luxurious ice cream made from protein- and mineral-rich camel's milk, naturally low in sugar (until flavourings are added). Middle Eastern-inspired flavours include saffron, pistachio and date, but classic chocolate is most popular. *Baniyas Rd, nr Deira Old Souq Abra Station; 9am-5pm.*

♪ Boracay

Named after the Filipino party island, this is the place to meet Dubai's Pinoy population. The nightclub's theatrical neon premises bear a resemblance to the set of *Pinoy Idol* (the Philippine edition of *Pop Idol*). Each night, acts take to the stage to perform covers while audiences look on from tables, hopefully less disparagingly than infamous show judge Simon Cowell. *6th fl, Asiana Hotel, Salah Al Din St; www.boracayclubdubai.com; 8pm-3am; free.*

Above: boats cruising Dubai Creek
Left: the striking silhouette of Deira Clock Tower

JUMEIRAH LAKES TOWERS

Directly across the Sheikh Zayed Rd from tourist magnet Dubai Marina, the high-rise residential development of JLT, wrapped around series of urban lakes, has been causing a stir in culinary circles. Complemented by concealed licensed bars, humble and authentic multicultural neighbourhood diners have been knocking it out of the park. And yes, there's a park here too, hosting an eclectic flea market.

McGettigan's JLT

Dubai expats want to keep this sprawling Irish pub, hidden under the Bonnington Hotel, all to themselves. It's already heaving most nights, with live bands, on-screen sport, pool tables and pub grub like pork belly popcorn. *Bonnington Jumeirah Lakes Towers, Cluster J; www. mcgettigans.com/jlt-dubai; noon-3am.*

Vietnamese Foodies

Restaurants like this one are giving JLT its newfound reputation as a foodie haven. With a focus on southern Vietnamese health food, the pho noodle soup, made with stock that's nurtured for 14 hours, fills benches at this little spot. *PL-04 Lake Terrace Tower, Cluster D; www.vietnamesefoodies.com; 04 565 6088; 11am-10.30pm Sun-Thu, 11am-11pm Fri-Sat.*

Pitfire Pizza

Hand-tossed dough receives the indulgent toppings of New York and the crispy charring of Naples. Deliciously fresh mozzarella is produced and delivered to the cosy lakeside pizzeria every day by Dubai-based Italian artisan cheese makers. *Lake Terrace Tower, Cluster D; www.pitfiredubai.ae; 800 748 3473; 11am-11pm.*

9Round

This small but perfectly formed gym offers a simple way to burn off calories. Unlike most Dubai gyms, membership isn't needed, which is handy for travellers. *Unit 1, Al Seef Tower 3, Cluster U; https://uae.9round.com; 6am-1pm & 3-10pm Sun-Thu, 8am-noon Fri, 8am-noon & 5-9pm Sat; Dhs85.*

JLT Flea Market

Manned by a community of committed 'car booters', JLT's lively flea market, held monthly outside of summer, is a trove of jewellery, second-hand clothing and books. *Jumeirah Lakes Towers Park; www.dubai-fleamarket.com.*

DUBAI

AL QUOZ 1

What was once a dusty industrial estate is now a fashionable block of commercial warehouse-galleries. Open for viewing, they present ever-evolving perspectives on Middle Eastern and Asian art. Community spaces and cafes offer places to congregate for organic coffee and conversation between exhibitions; otherwise, join a craft workshop, take a stretch class or catch critically acclaimed world cinema.

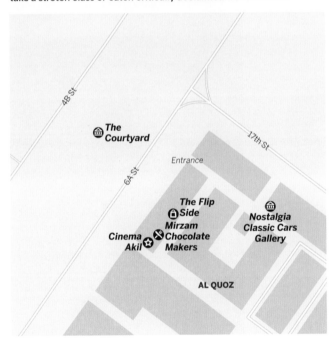

🏛 The Courtyard
The pretty stone-paved namesake of this community centre leads to Total Arts gallery, which showcases contemporary Middle Eastern work; the Courtyard Playhouse, hosting regular improv performances; and Tribe, a craft workshop. Grab a flat white at on-site bistro Boston Lane, then learn to paint, sculpt or make your own dream catcher. *St 4b/St 6; www. courtyard-uae.com; 8am-7pm.*

🏛 Nostalgia Classic Cars Gallery
Open to the public, this luxury showroom is home to some of the region's most Bond-worthy vintage vehicles. The company buys, sells and restores classic cars and artfully displays them here. A place to shamelessly ogle steel curves. *Warehouse 88-89, Alserkal Ave; www.nostalgiaclassiccars.ae; 10am-7pm Sat-Thu.*

🔒 The Flip Side
Vintage vinyl is on the menu at Dubai's only old-school independent record store. It hosts music documentary screenings and DJ-hosted gatherings against Alserkal's grey steel backdrop of warehouses-turned-art galleries. *Warehouse 71, Alserkal Ave; www. facebook.com/theflipsidedxb; noon-9pm Sun-Sat.*

✖ Mirzam Chocolate Makers
Named after the star that guided sailors along the Spice Route, Mirzam welcomes visitors in its aromatic factory-cafe. Single-origin cocoa-based confections come loaded with ingredients from the ancient east-to-west trade path. The Emirati collection is emboldened with honey, dates and Arabian coffee. *Warehouse 70, Alserkal Ave; 04 333 5888; https://mirzam.com; 10am-7pm Sat-Thu.*

✪ Cinema Akil
Dubai's only art-house cinema presents an antidote to the American box office hits at the region's mall-based theatres: expect vintage wallpaper, cosy armchairs and cups of masala chai. Brave world cinema, often subtitled, tackles subjects many might assume would be censored here. *Warehouse 68, Alserkal Ave; www.cinemaakil.com.*

ASIA

Versova

Dadar

Mumbai

Byculla

MUMBAI

India's greatest economic centre, Mumbai has always been a shifting skein of commerce, cultures and peoples. It has some of Asia's biggest slums, and the largest tropical forest in an urban zone.

I n central Mumbai sits musty, gritty Byculla, which once held the glories of the Portuguese and British empire in its wealthy palms. Slightly north is Dadar, the great, green, throbbing Maharashtrian heart of the city, built between 1899 and 1900, and the city's most important railway station on the Western line. Meanwhile the northern suburb of Versova is where bus-loads of aspiring Bollywood stars jockey for their patch of space under the silver-screen sun.

You can footslog your way through each neighbourhood, but vanishing footpaths may push you to use Mumbai's excellent local transport. As well as buses and trains, there are black-and-yellow cabs, which are ubiquitous but they don't have air-con – that means they're often cheaper than air-conditioned Uber and its local counterpart, Ola. Just avoid the rush hours, if you can.

MUMBAI

DADAR

When the city was felled in 1896 by the ferocious Bombay plague, the government created Dadar. The city's first planned neighbourhood, Dadar is now a haven for cricketers, thanks to the vast expanse of Shivaji Park. It has since grown into a serene residential Maharashtrian area, home to the Mayor's bungalow, unfussy eateries and a grubby stripe of beach.

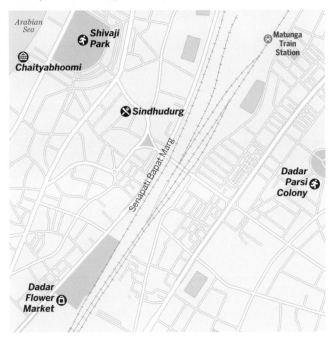

🔒 Dadar Flower Market

Early mornings outside clangorous Dadar Station, you'll find a sea of flowers down a little lane under Dadar Bridge. Here is the origin of most of Mumbai's floral arrangements: roses, gerberas, lilies, marigolds, chrysanthemums, carnations, tulips and orchids are all available at wholesale rates. Go at 5am, before the heat and before the flowers sell out. *Phool Galli, Senapati Bapat Marg; 4am-9am.*

❌ Sindhudurg

A meal at Sindhudurg is an excellent way to shoehorn your way into Mumbai's coastal Malvani food: think fried clams and prawns mantled in a vivid masala, local fish fried to cornflake-crispness, and a ruddy gravy to dunk it all into. Steer yourself towards the fish, chicken and mutton *thalis* (set meals). *Sita Sadan, Rk Vaidya Road; 2430 1610; 11.30am-11.30pm.*

✈ Shivaji Park

Shivaji Park has a long pre-Independence history of hosting political rallies. Nowadays you're more likely to spot younglings playing cricket or practising *mallakhamb* (an ancient Indian martial art). Some of India's best cricketers trained here, from Sachin Tendulkar to Sunil Gavaskar and Ajit Wadekar. *www.shivajipark.com.*

🏛 Chaityabhoomi

A serene Buddhist shrine honouring the memory of Dr Ambedkar, pioneering Dalit (the lowest rung of Hindu caste hierarchy) scholar-reformer and architect of the Indian constitution. On 6 December, the anniversary of his death, hundreds of thousands of Dalits converge at the monument to pay respects. *Dadar Chowpatty, off Cadell Road, Sant Dyaneshwar Marg.*

✈ Dadar Parsi Colony

In a city where most heritage structures get short shrift, Dadar Parsi Colony – home to Zoroastrian immigrants to India from Iran – is an anomaly. Take a long walk down its capillaried lanes, which meander through a 25-acre maze of neoclassical and art deco buildings. Picturesque DPC, as its residents call it, has featured in many Bollywood films (and on Instagram; see @dadarparsicolony_dpc).

BYCULLA

Once home to the city's elegant gentry, bustling and dog-eared Byculla is today a distillation of Mumbai. It's brightly chequered with Jewish, Catholic, Hindu, Muslim, Parsi and British influences, including stately mansions, art deco cinemas, walled Parsi colonies, a Jewish cemetery, and cheap but superb Muslim eating. Its easy accessibility to touristy south Mumbai is fast transforming it into hipster paradise.

🏛 Bhau Daji Lad Museum
Byculla is home to arguably the city's most resplendent museum, the Bhau Daji Lad (formerly the Victoria & Albert). It often hosts special exhibitions, art shows and lectures, though it's fringed by a zoo where animal welfare standards are abysmal. *Rani Baug, Dr Baba Saheb*

Ambedkar Rd, Byculla; www. bdlmuseum.org; 2373 1234; 10am-5.30pm Thu-Tue.

🏛 Magen David Synagogue
Built in 1861, this cerulean jewellery box of a building – with a soaring clock tower and stained glass windows – was once home to a religious school, a free

medical dispensary, a hostel for travellers, and a ritual bath area. *340 Sir J Jijibhoy Rd, Police Colony, New Nagpada; 2300 6675; hours vary.*

🏛 Gloria Church
The neo-Gothic Gloria Church began life in the 16th century as a private chapel belonging to a Portuguese Franciscan family. It experienced growth, destruction and rebuilding more than once, and was finally rebuilt in 1911 at its current location. *Sant Savata Mali Marg, Byculla East; 2372 6630; open for mass only.*

✖ Regal Restaurant & Bakery
Zoroastrian Iranians settled in Mumbai in the 19th century and this place has all the trappings of a typical Irani cafe: bentwood chairs, chequerboard flooring, antique cupboards brimming with grocery items, old fans stirring the soupy Mumbai air, and an upstairs 'family' section that is open to all. Try the chai, the *brun maska* (buns slathered with yellow butter), the *kheema* (mince) and the omelette. *Opposite Byculla Railway Station; 2372 3270; 6am-10pm.*

✖ American Express Bakery
Born in 1908, this bakery offers flaky, gold-domed croissants, buttery chicken and mutton puffs, *pattice* (a hybrid of a small pie and a patty), and macaroons flecked with almond. There's a little cafe at the back. *66A Mirza Ghalib Marg; www.americanexpressbakery. com; 2380 4441; 9am-8.30pm Mon-Sat.*

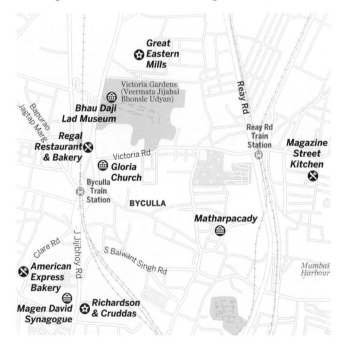

MUMBAI

© Dinodia Photos / Alamy Stock Photo

✖ Magazine Street Kitchen

Though it's tucked inside a vast mill compound in the scrum of Byculla lanes, the hunt for Magazine Street Kitchen is worth it. There's an open-kitchen dining space, it hosts cooking workshops and community meals, and serves tasting menu-style dinners by chefs from around India and the world. Its beating heart is its bakery, Mag St Bread Co, that delivers fresh-baked bread and pastry around the city via the food delivery app, Scootsy (tip: the croissant is legendary). *Gala No 13, Devidayal Compound, Magazine St, Gupta Mills Estate, Darukhana; 2372 6708.*

© 2020, American Express Bakery

☆☆ MAGEN DAVID SYNAGOGUE ☆☆

MATHARPACADY

A tiny facsimile of Goa sits squarely in nearby Mazgaon. In this small, time-worn heritage village, the homes are painted dazzling coral and sea blue, their sloping roofs sheathed in old Mangalore tiles. Already the juggernaut of development has razored much of Matharpacady – go before the rest of it succumbs. Find the entrance near Village Villa in Mazgaon.

✪ Richardson & Cruddas

It doesn't look like much on the outside, but Richardson & Cruddas is perhaps Mumbai's coolest performance venue. Built in 1972, it is an immense industrial warehouse that has hosted performances by musical acts as diverse as alt-J, Megadeth, The Wailers and Dutch EDM outfit Yellow Claw. *Sir Jamshedji Jeejeebhoy Rd; 2379 4006; 9.30am-5.30pm.*

✪ Great Eastern Mills

There is something enormously fitting about situating an antiques showroom and a posh art gallery, Nine Fish, inside the Great Eastern Mills compound. Outside is constant construction and destruction, while inside there is only calm. The Far Out Left EDM Festival was hosted here, but most famously, renowned Indian fashion designer Manish Malhotra debuted his Lakme India Fashion Week collection here. *Dr Ambedkar Rd, near Rani Baug; www.ninefish.in.*

**Top: American Express Bakery
Left: sky-blue stunner Magen David Synagogue in Byculla**

VERSOVA

One of the city's most easily accessible northern suburbs, Versova is home to Mumbai's oldest inhabitants but also to the shiny cosmos of Bollywood. Fitness studios, cafes and malls have sprung up but Versova holds something far deeper and older: a crumbling Portuguese fort and a fishing village that predates the rest of Mumbai.

Versova Beach
Versova beach has shot into the limelight thanks to the ardent efforts of one man, Afroz Shah, who mobilised thousands of residents to help clean it up. As a result of one of India's largest ever beach clean-ups, olive ridley turtle hatchlings now waddle their way onto the sands, while a platoon of volunteers spends nights watching over them.

Yoga 101
Versova's beautiful people congregate here to learn various types of yoga, sometimes in the company of the owner's canine companions. Yoga 101 is also rented out to artists, performers, even flea markets. *Cottage 101, Aram Nagar part 2, Machhlimar, JP Rd, Versova; 8am-9.15pm.*

Harkat Studio
This is a sunlit co-working space for freelancers as well as an alternative space for performances. What do you get when you sign up? Endless cups of tea and coffee, wi-fi, a printer, a library, and delivery personnel who will whisk that urgent parcel delivery across town or bring you sandwiches from the cafe next door. *Bungalow No. 75, Aram Nagar 2, Versova; www.harkat.in.*

Versova Koli Village
The city's overwhelming population surge forced Mumbai's first inhabitants, the Koli fisherfolk, into a tiny spit of land at the very tip of Versova. Up until builders swallow the village, some of Mumbai's freshest fish is available in the Koli fish markets. You can book a meal with Authenticook, a home chef aggregator that partners with the community for an enriching coastal dining experience inside a Koli home. Expect spicy prawns, clams and the catch of the day. *www.authenticook.com.*

Jamjar Diner
Versova's favourite hipster haunt sits in a quaint bungalow by the

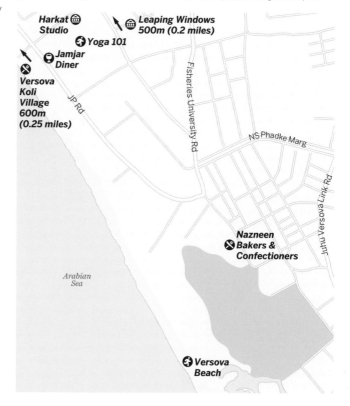

MUMBAI

sea – perfect for watching the world go by, drink in hand. There are board games, a jukebox stacked with retro music, and a vast menu that encompasses everything from comforting carbs to keto and vegan dishes. *JP Rd, Aram Nagar, Versova; 9am-1am.*

🪟 Leaping Windows

A small sanctuary for superheroes with a library packed top to toe with comics. Upstairs is a little cafe hawking salads, sandwiches, burgers, nachos and other comfort foods. If you're lucky, you'll spot some of Bollywood's indie darlings hunched over a cup

KOLI SEAFOOD FEST

When January rolls around, Versova girds its loins for a massive Koli seafood festival, complete with folk musicians and dancers, chilled beer and seafood. Who in their right mind could say no to grilled king crab, clams in a bath of coconut-streaked masala, and bombil fish draped in a wafer-crisp cloak of semolina and fried? See www.facebook.com/Versova-Village.

of coffee. *3 Corner View, off Yari Rd; 10am-midnight.*

✖ Nazneen Bakers & Confectioners

One beauty remains of Versova's formerly abundant bungalows: Shanti Niwas, home to Nazneen Bakery, purveyors of perhaps the city's best *nankhatai* (shortbread-style biscuits). *Shanti Niwas, near Nananani Park, 7 Bungalows, Versova; 9am-7pm Mon-Sat.*

Clockwise from top: retro stylish Jamjar Diner; hip Harkat Studio; Versova Koli Village's fresh seafood

BANGKOK

Sweaty, raucous and indulgent – and these days cosmopolitan, sophisticated and cool – Bangkok lives up to all the clichés and more.

BANGKOK

A decade ago, most travellers dreaded Bangkok, seeing it as little more than an obligatory transit point before heading to an island or a trek. Now people love the city, and it's easy to see why. Divide Bangkok up – like the segments of a mangosteen – and there's a neighbourhood appealing to just about everybody. And recent extensions of the BTS (the elevated train system) and the MRT (the underground) mean that nowadays it's simple to reach any of these areas.

A good starting point is Ko Ratanakosin, Bangkok's historical centre. Head south along the Chao Phraya River to Chinatown, another old district that's undergoing change. Contemporary Bangkok begins next door at Silom, which has a dual role both as Bangkok's financial district and its 'gaybourhood'. Just north is the flashy commercial district known colloquially as Siam, home to several megamalls. And east of here is Sukhumvit, probably the city's most eclectic 'hood.

KO RATANAKOSIN

Most people come to this neighbourhood, hit Bangkok's most famous temples, and retreat to their air-conditioned hotel rooms. But with charming architecture, a breezy riverside atmosphere, and a handful of up-and-coming restaurants, Ko Ratanakosin warrants more extensive foot-bound exploration. River taxi was previously the most efficient way to reach this area, but the extension of the MRT has made things much easier.

⊗ Err

The Thai colloquialism 'err' is roughly equivalent to 'yep,' which is what you'll say when presented with the menu of tasty Thai-style drinking snacks at this playful restaurant. Think sour sausages, a salad of slippery watermelon seeds, a 'dry' curry, and fruity, fragrant cocktails. *Off Th Maha Rat; www.errbkk.com; 02 622 2292; 11am-4pm & 5-9pm Tue-Sun.*

⊗ Tonkin Annam

Tired of Thai food but don't want to stray too far? Consider a Vietnamese meal at this tiny, trendy, shophouse-based restaurant. The menu reveals dishes that are often not found outside of the homeland. A perfect pit-stop on a day of temple touring. *69 Soi Tha Tien; www.facebook.com/tonkinannam; 093 469 2969; 11am-9.30pm Wed-Mon.*

🔒 Mowaan

This hidden, fourth-generation apothecary makes oils, smelling salts, analgesic balms (we had to look that one up, too) and other products rooted in Thai traditional medicine. The lost-in-time showroom is not unlike a museum, and the products feature beautifully retro packaging, making them excellent candidates for one-of-a-kind gifts. *9 Soi Thesa; https://mowaan.com; 9am-5pm.*

🔒 Nightingale-Olympic

Dating back more than nine decades, this is Bangkok's oldest department store. Today more museum than emporium, Nightingale-Olympic still holds cosmetics dating from the 1950s, boxes of pantyhose from the '60s, and sporting goods from the '70s and '80s. *70 Th Triphet; 9am-5.30pm Mon-Sat.*

🏛 Museum Siam

Forget dusty dioramas and gilt-framed portraits; this forward-thinking museum is a lively introduction to the people of Thailand and their culture. Many displays have elements that you're encouraged to touch or tweak. *4 Th Sanam Chai; www.museumsiam.org; 10am-6pm Tue-Sun; 200 baht.*

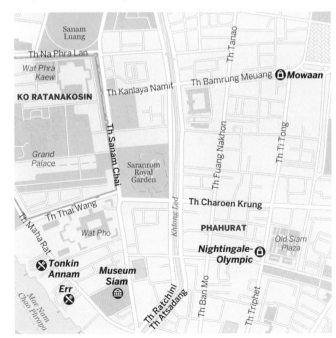

© CC7 / Shutterstock

SUKHUMVIT

This long road is where much of Bangkok comes to party and eat – especially its vast expat community. People from the Middle East, Japan and Korea, in addition to *farang* (foreigners of European descent), give the area a distinctly cosmopolitan feel. The BTS runs along much of the road, so getting to and around here is a snap.

WTF

Ostensibly a bar, WTF (Wonderful Thai Friendship) also hosts thought-provoking art exhibitions in its upstairs gallery, occasional dinner pop-ups, storytelling events, poetry slams and the like. Think of it as a cultural centre that also happens to serve really excellent cocktails. Check the website to see what's on when you're in town. *7 Soi 51, Th Sukhumvit; www.wtfbangkok. com; 5pm-1am Tue-Fri.*

The Commons

Could this hit venue signal a shift away from the often characterless, typically mall-based Bangkok food court? It certainly feels like it. Enter the spacious, contemporary-feeling structure to encounter a cafe and craft beer bar, as well as outlets of some of the city's better restaurants, with options ranging from Neapolitan-style pizza to Mexican. *335 Soi 17, Soi 55 (Thong Lo), Th Sukhumvit; https://thecommonsbkk.com; 8am-1am.*

Sri Trat

The people of Bangkok are finally taking notice of their country's diverse regional cuisines, and one of the more exciting places to eat vicariously in the provinces is Sri Trat, dedicated to the cuisine of Thailand's eastern seaboard. Expect dishes packed with fragrant herbs, subtle influences from Cambodia, pleasantly sweet flavours and lots of seafood. *90 Soi 33, Th Sukhumvit; www.sritrat.com; 02 088 0968; noon-11pm Wed-Mon.*

Tuba

Wacky is probably the best term to describe the interior design theme here, which incorporates over-the-top furnishings from the '60s and '70s, gaudy paintings and life-sized superhero statues. Order a cocktail the size of your head (really) and some very tasty bar snacks (don't miss the deep-fried *laap*, a 'salad' of minced meat), and try to make sense of it all. *34 Room 11-12 A, Soi 63*

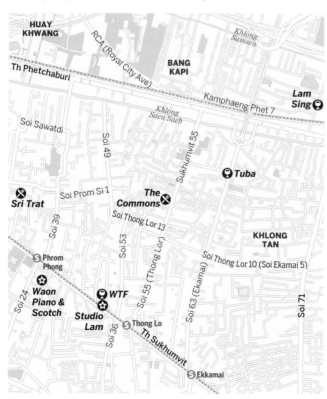

(Ekamai), Th Sukhumvit; www.
papaya55.com/tuba-bkk.html;
noon-2am.

⭐ Studio Lam

Most Bangkok clubs are
staunchly of the boom-boom,
pfff-pfff variety and you could be
mistaken for being in any large
city. But Studio Lam is resolutely
Thai, which makes it a lot more
fun. The DJs here spin vintage
vinyl, much of it local, but from
virtually any time or place people
recorded music. *3/1 Soi 51, Th
Sukhumvit; www.facebook.com/
studiolambangkok; 6pm-1am
Tue-Sun.*

© Anansing / Shutterstock

🎵 Lam Sing

Given that this live music hall is
where taxi drivers go to party
after their shifts are over, there's
hardly any more street cred we
could attribute to it. Inside, the
beer flows freely, there are spicy
Thai-style drinking snacks, and
the performances of songs from
Thailand's rural northeast are
gaudy, loud, raucous, and so
much fun. *57/5 Th Phet Phra Ram;
www.facebook.com/isanlamsing;
9.30pm-4am.*

GLOBAL RESIDENTS

Th Sukhumvit is Bangkok's
most cosmopolitan street.
Soi 3/1 is definitively
Middle Eastern, while
there's a small Korean
enclave at the mouth of
Soi 12. Much of the real
estate between Soi 33
and Soi 55 is dedicated
to the area's Japanese
residents, and many of
the city's *farang* (white)
residents also call the
neighbourhood home.

⭐ Waon Piano & Scotch

Sure, you've karaoked, but have
you ever belted it out to live
accompaniment? If not, consider
this Japanese-run karaoke bar,
where the owner is perched
behind a piano, awaiting your
request. Even the tone deaf can
pitch in via acoustic guitar or
tambourine. *10/11 Soi 26, Th
Sukhumvit; 8pm-1am Mon-Sat.*

**Clockwise from top: street
food stalls in Sukhumvit;
thirst-quenching WTF;
foodie hub The Commons**

© Wison Tungthunya & W Workspace / 2019, The Commons

© Christopher Wise / 2020, WTF

SILOM

As the base for several banks, Th Silom is, approximately, Bangkok's Wall Street. But this is Bangkok, and the eastern extent of the street doubles as the city's gay nightlife zone. This means that there's a bit of everything here – shopping, eating and nightlife. Whatever you're looking for, it's easy to get here, as both the MRT and BTS have stops here.

⭐ Bangkok Screening Room

The sweltering heat means that movie theatres are an essential part of life. Consider a flick at this cosy independent house. Films come from virtually every era and part of the globe, and you can couple your screening with domestic craft beer from the bar. *2nd fl, Woof Pack building,*

3-7 Soi 1, Th Sala Daeng; www. bkksr.com; 3.30-11pm Tue-Fri, 11am-11pm Sat-Sun.

🚇 Smalls

It's a cliché, but this bar is where locals – both domestic and foreign – actually hang out. And it's easy to see why. The atmosphere's eclectic (yes, that's a zinc bar from Paris and

a giant Ultraman on the ceiling), and Smalls hosts a variety of music and food events. *186/3 Soi Suan Phlu; www.facebook.com/ smallsbkk; 7pm-2am Wed-Mon.*

❌ Kad Kokoa

Thailand is home to a burgeoning chocolate industry, and this new cafe is the best place to taste its progress. Choose from rich chocolate drinks, desserts, and single-origin chocolate bars from different parts of the country. If he's in, the chocolatier will show you the steps from bean to bar. *Soi 17, Th Narathiwat Ratchanakarin; www.kadkokoa.co; 081 265 5611; 11am-7pm Tue-Sun.*

🚇 Soi 4

The lower part of Th Silom is Bangkok's unofficial gaybourhood, and this frenetic, dead-end street is its ground zero. Come to people-gawk from the streetside tables at Telephone Pub and Balcony, catch a raucous cabaret show at The Stranger, or belt out some karaoke tunes at Hugs. All are welcome. *Soi 4, Th Silom; approx 5pm-1am.*

🔒 Karmakamet

Want to buy a gift but dismayed by the tat sold on the streets? Pop in to this store – easily Bangkok's most fragrant – for scented candles, aroma diffusers, oils and other olfactory delights. With sophisticated scents and packaging, you'll probably end up buying something for yourself as well. *Yada Building, 56 Th Silom; www.karmakamet.co.th; 10am-10pm.*

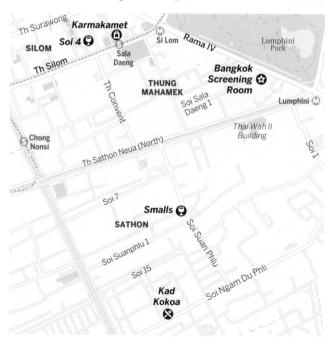

BANGKOK

SIAM

Bangkok's Siam district is synonymous with shopping. Easily accessed via the BTS train network, the area is home to several mega malls, which in recent years have become meeting places for the people of Bangkok. If burning *baht* isn't your thing, the malls all have food courts, and the area also has a handful of visit-worthy cultural institutions.

🔒 Siam Discovery

After a recent makeover, one of Bangkok's oldest malls is now one of its coolest. There's an artsy edge to the venue and wares here, and outlets such as Objects of Desire and Ecotopia are places to pick up a domestically designed keepsake or souvenir you're unlikely to find elsewhere. *Cnr Th Rama I & Th Phayathai; www.siamdiscovery. co.th; 10am-10pm.*

🏛 Bangkok Art & Culture Centre (BACC)

This vast, contemporary-feeling art space has hosted a variety of exhibitions by both local and foreign artists; check the website to see what's on. It's also home to worthwhile cafes (try Gallery Drip for domestic beans) and shops (hit It's Going Green for a retro Thai souvenir). *Cnr Th Rama I & Th Phayathai; http://en.bacc.or.th; 10am-9pm Tue-Sun; free.*

❌ After You Dessert Cafe

Want to eat like a true Bangkokian? Forget the *phat thai* on the street and head to this exceedingly popular dessert venue. Take a queue number (really) and order the bible-sized honey toast or the *kakigōri*, the latter a virtual mountain of finely shaved, seasoned ice. *Ground fl, Siam Paragon, 991 Th Rama I; www.afteryoudessertcafe.com; 10am-10.30pm.*

⭐ Scala Theatre

For a trip back to when movie theatres had only one screen and wonky sound, consider a flick at this retro cinema. If the aesthetic appeals, we suggest pre-gaming at the basement-level Chinese restaurant, which brazenly (and successfully, we think) combines design elements of the Maya Empire, imperial China, and the 1970s. *Soi 1, Siam Sq, 218/3-4 Th Rama I; www.apexsiam-square. com; noon-10pm.*

❌ Eathai

Mall-based food courts are everywhere, but Eathai ups the game by sticking to Thai food and hosting some of the most lauded vendors, with stalls doing dishes from across the country. *Basement, Central Embassy, 1031 Th Phloen Chit; www. centralembassy.com/store/eathai; 10am-10pm.*

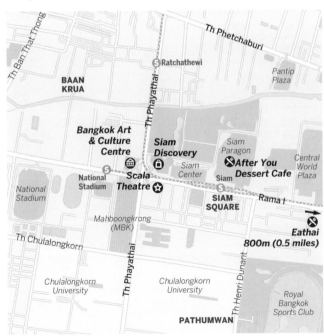

CHINATOWN

Even as recently as a few years ago, nobody went to Bangkok's Chinatown to drink. Sure, the area's street food is the city's best, but drinking was reserved for other parts of town that, well, actually had bars. Today, Chinatown is home to some of the most unique drinking venues and restaurants in Bangkok, most of which are easily accessed via the MRT.

✖ 100 Mahaseth

This restaurant excels at taking Thai flavours, ingredients and techniques and pushing them just to the edge of what's considered traditional. Vegetarians beware, there's hardly a leaf in sight here, and dishes often centre around ingredients such as bladder, tripe and bone marrow. If you're open to the nose-to-tail approach, the result is delicious. *100 Th Mahaseth; www.facebook.com/100Mahaseth; 02 235 0023; 11.30am-11pm.*

🚇 Ba Hao

Housed in a beautifully refurbished shophouse, this Shanghai-in-1935 themed bar also serves some of the tastiest and most unique drinking snacks in town. Think crunchy bits of deep-fried dough seasoned with chilli and garlic, or soft, rich, cold tofu served with a salty, savoury dressing, in addition to more substantial dishes, craft beers, and Chinese-themed signature cocktails. *8 Soi Nana; www.ba-hao.com; 6pm-midnight Tue-Thu, 6pm-1am Fri-Sat, 6pm-midnight Sun.*

🅰 Warehouse 30

Finally, somebody opted to take advantage of this string of former godowns (warehouses) located next the Chao Phraya River. Inside you'll find linked shops, cafes and restaurants; in one visit you can down an espresso macchiato, browse vintage French work jackets, pick up a silk scarf, and gaze at beautiful old slabs of teak. *52-60 Soi 30 (Captain Bush Lane), Th Charoen Krung; www.facebook.com/TheWarehouse30; 11am-8pm.*

✖ Jua

This contemporary-feeling, casual Japanese restaurant serves some of the tastiest non-Thai food in town – don't miss the tomato salad with shiso pesto, the corn butter bacon or just about anything grilled. But for many, the draw is the chummy vibe and its dual function

(map)

Th Luang · ✖ **Nay Hong**
POM PRAP SATTRU PHAI
Th Luang
Th Suapa
Th Matrichit
Th Mittraphan
Th Krung Kasem
Rama VI
Th Charoen Krung
Wong Wian 22 Karakada
Th Yaowarat
CHINATOWN
Th Ratchawong
Th Song Sawat
SAMPHAN THAWONG
Th Charoen Krung
🚇 **Ba Hao**
🚇 **Tep Bar** · Hualamphong Train Station
Ⓜ Hua Lamphong · Rama IV
Mae Nam Chao Phraya
TALAT NOI
Th Maha Phrutharam
Th Maha Nakhon
Th Somdet Chao Phraya
River City · ✖ **Jua** · Th Si Phraya
Milennium Hilton
✖ **Someday Everyday**
100 ✖ **Mahaseth**
🅰 **Warehouse 30** · **BANGRAK**

as a bar, one with an infectious enthusiasm for sake. *672/49 Soi 28, Th Charoen Krung; www.juabkk. com; 02 103 6598; 6pm-midnight Mon-Sat, 6-10pm Sun.*

❎ Someday Everyday

Enter the light-filled, modern building, and point and choose from a selection of pre-made curries, soups, stir-fries and Thai-style dips, which will be loaded on a tray for you to carry upstairs. Oh, and even if you've felt 'meh' about Thai sweets before, don't neglect dessert. *78/38 Soi 30, Th Charoen Krung; www.facebook. com/somedayeverydayrestaurant; 11am-6pm Wed-Sun.*

❎ Nay Hong

If you can find it, Nay Hong serves one dish: *kuaytiaw khua kai*, wide, flat rice noodles fried in lard with egg, chicken and preserved squid. It's a truly Bangkok dish, and eating it in this tiny alley, with cats walking between your legs and sweat dripping down your back, is a truly Bangkok experience. *Off Th Yukol 2; 4-10pm.*

STREET FOOD

Mention Chinatown, and Bangkokians reflexively think of fried noodles, deep-fried snacks, durians and won ton soup. Most restaurants and stalls are found along Th Yaowarat, Chinatown's main drag. But its side streets are also a good place to scout for tasty eats. Visit at night, but not on a Monday when many street stalls take the day off.

🍸 Tep Bar

Come to this renovated shophouse in a narrow lane, from Thursday to Sunday, and be treated to a wild, and frankly, loud, performance of traditional music. Come any night for surprisingly potable Thai-style herbal (some say medicinal) booze and grilled snacks. *69-71 Soi Nana; www.facebook.com/TEPBARBKK; 5pm-midnight Tue-Thu, 5pm-1am Fri-Sat, 5pm-midnight Sun.*

Top: Someday Everyday
Below: Jua's Japanese eats

SINGAPORE

Singapore's centre is slick, shiny and a little showy, but step out of the Central Business District bubble and discover a totally different side to the Lion City.

Singapore's well-worn tourist trail takes in the city's grand colonial architecture, sci-fi gardens, meticulously curated museums and a plethora of temples, shrines and monuments. Deviate to the fringe of the city centre, however, and you'll enjoy a deeper understanding of this island city-state. Heritage neighbourhoods like the charming art deco public housing estate Tiong Bahru, and under-the-radar creative hot-spot Jalan Besar, are just a few MRT stops away from the downtown core.

Slightly further afield, west of the city centre, is Singapore's southwest coast. It's known for its wild urban jungle trails, but scratch a little deeper and you'll find a few well-hidden cultural experiences and a number of great drinking spots, too. To completely decompress, travel to sleepy Changi Village, in the island's far east. Here, you can partake in outdoor adventures, as well as sample craft beers and delectable grub by the sea.

SINGAPORE

JALAN BESAR

Sandwiched between frenetic Little India and uber-cool Kampong Glam is the laid-back heritage district of Jalan Besar. Its quaint streets are lined with beautiful Peranakan shophouses and peppered with on-trend cafes, bars, and some of the island's best local eats. Easily reached from the Lavender, Farrer Park and Jalan Besar MRT stations.

🚇 Apartment Coffee

The new kid on the caffeine block in Jalan Besar, Apartment Coffee is making a name for itself for its dedication to creating the perfect cup. The 10-seat coffee bench is ideal for striking up a conversation with baristas. The coffee, a touch pricey due to it being sustainably sourced, is oh-so-good. *01-12, 161 Lavender St; www.apartmentcoffee.co; 9am-6pm Thu-Tue.*

🏛 Petain Road Terrace Houses

Marvel at the riot of colours and ornate cornices on display at this row of wonderfully ostentatious Chinese-baroque shophouses. Built in 1930 by local landowner Mohamad bin Haji Omar, this strip of heritage buildings has traditional Malay fretted eaves, Chinese symbols and motifs in the plaster relief, and hundreds of glazed floral ceramic tiles. *Petain Rd.*

🔒 Onlewo

Take a slice of Singapore home with you in the form of a quirky keepsake by local brand Onlewo. Known for its patterned fabric designs, inspired by Singaporean culture, the studio sells fun fashion, homewares and gift items. The silk twill scarves are exceptionally lovely. *129 Jln Besar; www.onlewo.com; 11am-4pm Tue-Sat.*

❌ The Tiramisu Hero

This kitsch cat-adorned cafe is known for...well, its tiramisu! The original is sublime but if you're feeling adventurous, order the somewhat polarising durian flavour. Each fluffy dessert is served in its own glass jar, perfect for sharing. *121 Tyrwhitt Rd; www.thetiramisuhero.com; 11am-10pm.*

❌ Hong Kong 88 Roast Meat Specialist

Roast pork fans should not miss the *sio bak* (Chinese roast pork belly) at this hawker stall. Chef-owner Martin has honed his recipe over many years, which includes a two-hour varied temperature cooking process. The result? Melt-in-your-mouth tender pork, topped with shatteringly crunchy skin. It's best eaten straight from the oven so try to get there when the stall opens at 11am, and beat the lunchtime hordes while you're at it. *153 Tyrwhitt Rd; 11am-9pm Mon-Fri, to 10pm Sat & Sun.*

TIONG BAHRU

Just a short stroll from Tiong Bahru MRT Station, this 1930s public residential estate is touted as one of Singapore's hippest 'hoods thanks to its wonderful mixture of old-school charm and new-school cool. Start at the bustling wet market and hawker centre, the neighbourhood's beating heart, before exploring surrounding streets lined with art deco buildings, indie boutiques, cafes and street art.

Bird Singing Corner Mural

Celebrated local heritage artist Yip Yew Chong gives viewers a peek back into Singapore's past with his life-sized 3-D heritage scenes. Here, four gossiping uncles enjoy a cup of *kopi* (coffee) while listening to their songbirds, a once-common ritual. Head up the alley next to it to discover the *Pasar and the Fortune Teller* mural. *61 Seng Poh Ln; www.yipyc.com.*

Qi Tian Gong (Monkey God Temple)

Dedicated to Sun Wu Kong, the Monkey King from the 16th-century literary classic *Journey to the West*, this temple claims to be Singapore's oldest that worships the Monkey God. Ensconced on the ground floor of a corner shophouse, and shrouded in incense smoke, the entrance pillars are wrapped with impressive dragons motifs and inside there are no fewer than 10 Monkey God statues! *44 Eng Hoon St; www.qitiangong.com; 7am-5pm.*

Bincho

First impressions aren't always what they seem...otherwise, you might never discover this sleek yakitori bistro hidden in plain sight behind Hua Bee, a 75-year-old *mee pok* (fish ball noodles) restaurant. Gain entry via the service door in the car park behind and then settle in to be delighted by some of Singapore's best Japanese cuisine – the set menu is the way to go. *01-19, 78 Moh Guan Tce; www.bincho. com.sg; noon-3pm & 6pm-late Tue-Sun.*

BooksActually

Literature enthusiasts will be in wordsmith heaven perusing the titles at this charming indie bookshop. You'll find everything from the classics to works by emerging local authors, poetry to essays, new releases and out-of-print gems. Make sure to say hello to the store's three famed feline

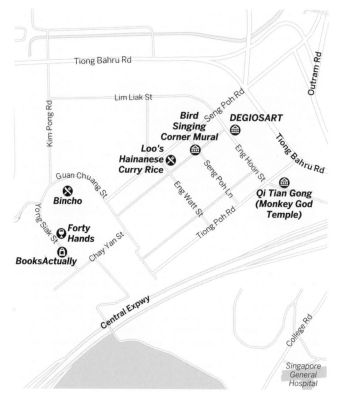

Map labels: Tiong Bahru Rd; Lim Liak St; Kim Pong Rd; Tiong Bahru Rd; Outram Rd; Seng Poh Rd; Bird Singing Corner Mural; DEGIOSART; Loo's Hainanese Curry Rice; Eng Hoon St; Seng Poh Ln; Guan Chuang St; Eng Watt St; Qi Tian Gong (Monkey God Temple); Bincho; Yong Siak St; Forty Hands; Tiong Poh Rd; Chay Yan St; BooksActually; Central Expwy; College Rd; Singapore General Hospital

assistants and don't miss the back room – it's a trove of trinkets and obscure curios. *9 Yong Siak St, www.booksactuallyshop. com; 9am-7pm Tue-Sat, to 6pm Sun & Mon.*

🟤 Forty Hands

This hole-in-the wall coffee joint is famed for being one of the forerunners in Singapore's trendy cafe revolution. They do indeed serve a great cup of joe, the beans freshly roasted by Common Man Coffee Roasters, but it's the hearty all-day breakfast menu that has foodies salivating – the banana bacon French toast is the perfect mix of sweet and savoury. *01-12, 78 Yong Siak St; www.40handscoffee.com; 7am-6pm Mon-Fri, 7.30am-7pm Sat & Sun.*

🏛 DEGIOSART

Gallery founder Giuseppe de Giosa's passion for antiques

WHAT'S IN A NAME?

The name Tiong Bahru translates to 'new cemetery' and is a mixture of Hokkien ('*tiong*' meaning 'to die') and Malay ('*bahru*' meaning 'new'). Before the construction of the public housing development began in the 1920s, this area had been a burial ground for the Hakka Peranakan community since 1859.

and Asian art is reflected in his immaculately curated art space, which is filled with antiques, paintings, furniture and lighting from Asia and around the world. He's also turned his hand to designing and fashionistas will be mesmerised by the one-of-a-kind vintage textile clothing and accessories created by in-house label DGA Threads. *01-82, 57 Eng Hoon St; www.degiosart.com; 10am-7pm.*

✖ Loo's Hainanese Curry Rice

Located in Tiong Bahru since 1946, this simple curry rice stall is a firm local favourite. Pick and choose from the various ready-made dishes, but don't miss the pork chop, encased in a traditional cream cracker crust, and the tender curry *satong* (squid). The curry recipe takes three days to prepare, and queuing is totally worth it. *01-49, 71 Seng Poh Rd, 8am-2.30pm Fri-Wed.*

**Top: shelves of indie offerings at BooksActually
Left: plate of chicken hearts at yakitori bistro Bincho**

SOUTHWEST SINGAPORE

This quiet pocket west of Singapore's downtown area is well known by nature and exercise fanatics, who rave about the popular 10km (6-mile) Southern Ridges trail. Dig deeper and you'll find plenty more to explore, like the city's first gin distillery, art galleries, a foodie hot spot in a reinvented military camp, and a slightly off-putting cultural park. Some locations have an MRT station, but taxis are more convenient.

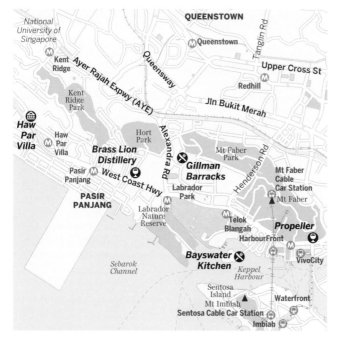

🍺 Brass Lion Distillery
At Singapore's first gin micro-distillery, the magic happens in a gleaming copper still, handcrafted in Germany. The signature Singapore Dry Gin features herbs and spices that represent Singapore, while the Butterfly Pea Gin unveils a colour-changing surprise. Tours are available. *40 Alexandra Tce; www. brassliondistillery.com; 5pm-* midnight Tue-Fri, from 2pm Sat, 2pm-7pm Sun.

🏛 Haw Par Villa
The brainchild of Aw Boon Haw, founder of Tiger Balm ointment, the park is filled with colourful dioramas that depict scenes from Chinese legends and mythology. The most famous, and most gruesome, is the 'Ten Courts of Hell'. *262 Pasir Panjang Rd; www.hawparvilla.sg; 9am-7pm, last entry 6pm.*

🍸 Propeller
This rooftop bar's panoramic vista over Keppel Bay and Sentosa is picturesque. Drinks are substantially cheaper than at city centre rooftop bars. *Bay Hotel, 50 Telok Blangah Rd; www.bayhotelsingapore.com; 5pm-midnight Sun-Thu, to 2am Fri & Sat.*

✖ Gillman Barracks
You could easily spend a whole day wandering the 11 galleries dotted around this disbanded barracks. Come hungry, as this lush enclave is also home to delectable eating. Don't miss seafood powerhouse The Naked Finn but for a rocking good time head to Handlebar, Singapore's only biker bar. *9 Lock Rd; www.gillmanbarracks.com.*

✖ Bayswater Kitchen
In-the-know locals who like fresh seafood and cool breezes frequent this place on the marina. Happy hour is between 4pm and 8pm. *2 Keppel Bay Vista; www.bayswaterkitchen.com.sg; 11.30am-11pm Tue-Thu, to 2am Fri, 6pm-1am Sat, 11am-11pm Sun.*

CHANGI VILLAGE

Compared to the frenetic energy of the city centre, the pace in Changi Village is practically glacial – and that's just one of its charms. There's plenty to explore, including biking on Pulau Ubin (an island just a 10-minute bumboat ride away), a seaside craft brewery and plenty of gastronomic delights. It's a 20-minute taxi journey from the city, but well worth the effort.

🍺 Little Island Brewing Co

Beer connoisseurs flock to this warehouse-style microbrewery for its thirst-quenching craft suds. Pour your own at the neat pay-by-volume taps before settling in to enjoy live bands (Friday through Sunday) and perfectly paired beer eats – wood-fired pizzas and smoked meats. *6 Changi Village Rd; www.libc.co; noon-11pm Mon-Thu, to midnight Fri, 11am-midnight Sat, 11am-11pm Sun.*

🦑 Smith Marine Floating Restaurant

Set sail on a nautical adventure to a floating *kelong* (offshore hut) off the coast of Palau Ubin. The bumboat trip costs S$100 return for up to 12 guests. Once there, fish for your lunch in the 'sure catch' ponds. If you come up empty-handed there's plenty of seafood at the restaurant. *Changi Point Ferry Terminal; www.smithmarine.com.sg; 10am-7pm, reserve at least 3 days in advance.*

✈ Changi Point Coastal Walk

Meander along this 2.2km (1.4-mile) boardwalk that hugs the Singapore coastline and offers calming views across the Strait of Johor to Malaysia. Keep your eyes peeled for the blue-backed Pacific swallow, as well as historical landmarks the Changi Sailing Club and Changi Beach Club. *6 Changi Village Rd; www.nparks.gov.sg.*

🦑 Ho Guan Satay Bee Hoon

Changi Village Hawker Centre is known for two highly competitive *nasi lemak* (coconut rice with fried anchovies, peanuts and a curry dish) stalls (01-03 and 01-26). However, it's the nutty satay *bee hoon* (rice noodles) that sets taste buds singing. The sauce is simmered for hours over a slow flame. *01-61 Changi Village Hawker Centre, 2 Changi Village Rd; 11am-9pm Thu-Mon.*

✈ Ketam Mountain Bike Park

Singapore's concrete pathways are excellent for cruising by bike. If you're after an adrenaline-inducing ride, this bike park is the place. You'll need to take a 10-minute bumboat ride to nearby Pulau Ubin for these challenging trails through quarries and mangroves. *Pulau Ubin; www.nparks.gov.sg.*

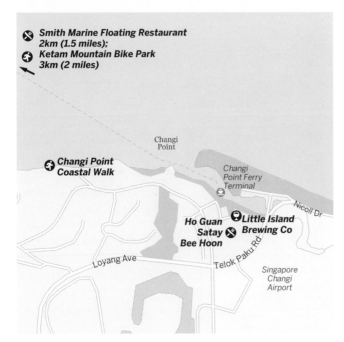

🦑 **Smith Marine Floating Restaurant** 2km (1.5 miles); ✈ **Ketam Mountain Bike Park** 3km (2 miles)

✈ **Changi Point Coastal Walk**

Changi Point

Changi Point Ferry Terminal

Nicoll Dr

🦑 **Ho Guan Satay Bee Hoon** 🍺 **Little Island Brewing Co**

Loyang Ave

Telok Paku Rd

Singapore Changi Airport

798
Art
District

Beijing

Xisi

Dashilan

BEIJING

With a tumultuous history going back centuries, it's no wonder the capital of China is a city of secrets. Venture beyond the centre to unlock its charms and local life.

S ince the Ming dynasty, Beijing was the very definition of a secret city. The gilded palaces of the Forbidden City, and the walled Imperial City enclosing it, were entirely off-limits to mere mortals. Ordinary folk had barely an inkling of what the emperor looked like. Today, Beijing has sprawled miles beyond its old walled limits, with peripheral neighbourhoods like the 798 Art District offering a fascinating counterpoint to the historic inner city and its faded imperial grandeur.

Beijing's antique districts are characterised by *hutong*, grid-like residential alleyways with their roots here in Kublai Khan's Yuan dynasty capital. Along these grey-walled lanes, courtyard homes conceal authentic places to eat, boutique hotels and edgy cocktail bars.

Beijing is as flat as a *bing* (a local street-food pancake), which makes cycling the perfect way to get around the inner neighbourhoods. For far-flung districts, Beijing's subway network is the one of the world's biggest and cheapest.

798 ART DISTRICT

On the edge of Beijing lies a rusting hulk of a factory complex, once the gold standard of Communist industrial power. When the last production line juddered to a halt in the early 1990s, artists moved in. The district was named after one of the factory's East-German designed Bauhaus workshops, now edgy art studios and high-ceilinged, post-industrial exhibition spaces.

🏛 BTAP
The first international gallery to open in 798, Beijing Tokyo Art Projects is a collaboration between Tokyo and Beijing, helping to champion rising Chinese artists. Glance up above the artworks to the ceiling and you'll see a faded red slogan put there to motivate the workers. It says: 'Mao Zedong is the red sun in our hearts!' *2 Jiuxianqiao Lu; www.tokyo-gallery. com; 10am-5.30pm Tue-Sun.*

❌ Fodder Factory
A nostalgic shrine to the 1980s, this industrial-chic restaurant is decked out in wall displays of old rotary dial telephones and television sets – a nod to 798's former life as an electronics factory. The spicy Sichuan and Hunan stir-fries here will soon jolt you out of your reverie. *Qilingliu Beiyijie; 11am-10pm.*

🏛 Mansudae Art Studio
One of the most intriguing galleries is this one from North Korea, exhibiting official propaganda art commissioned by the hermit kingdom itself in Pyongyang. Paintings depict heroic miners and soldiers in strident, socialist realist style. You can also buy North Korean stamps, pin badges and state-run magazines with tractors on the cover. *2 Jiuxianqiao Lu; 10am-6pm Tue-Sun.*

☕ Voyage Coffee
Carved out of an old warehouse is this third-wave coffee roaster and cafe, serving 798's most precise pour-overs and espresso drinks. Just outside is a headless statue of Chairman Mao, all that remains of the now-closed Xin Dong Cheng Space for Contemporary Art. *7 Qixing Zhongjie; 10am-6pm.*

🏛 D-Park Walkway
Go past the galleries and cafes to D-Park in the west of 798 and you'll find a startling display of Communist industrial architecture: soaring brick chimneys, boilers, hissing pipes and gargantuan metal structures at every turn. Slicing through these retro-futurist relics is a raised walkway affording Instagram-worthy views through what resembles the ultimate steampunk movie set. *751 D-Park; 8am-8pm.*

XISI

Defined by temples and tumbledown *hutong* lanes, Xisi feels like the last true bastion of old Beijing, a place where it's still possible to lose yourself in untouristed alleyways and spy local life unfolding: a game of *xiangqi* (Chinese chess) here, a roving fruit seller there... The name (literally 'West Four') refers to four ornate *paifang* (decorative Chinese gates) that once marked a busy commercial crossroads here.

🚇 Bear Brew
Arty third-wave coffee is the draw at this hip, gay-friendly *hutong* gem. Its name refers to the two personable Chinese bears in charge of the place. Best of all is the tiny rooftop terrace, with a scatter of tables facing what must be Beijing's most unheralded view: the Miaoying Temple White Dagoba, standing proud over a sea of grey *hutong* rooftops. *6 Baitasi Dongjiaodao; 10am-8pm.*

🏛 Miaoying Temple White Dagoba
The crowning glory of Xisi is this curvaceous, chalk-white stupa lording it over the ash-grey *hutong* around it. Aesthetically un-Chinese, it was designed by a Nepali architect for Kublai Khan, the Mongol founder of the Yuan dynasty, in 1271. At 51m (167ft) high it remains the tallest Tibetan-style pagoda in China. Today, it forms part of the gorgeously ornate Miaoying Temple complex, constructed around it during the Ming dynasty. *171 Fuchengmennei Dajie; 9am-5pm Tue-Sun.*

🏛 Wansong Laoren Tower
There are few (if any) pagodas left in Beijing, which makes this nine-tiered brick tower in a quiet Xisi courtyard such a thrilling find. Set in a walled garden of tangled grape vines, there are old stone carvings and *hutong* timbers scattered about like an open-air museum. The bookshop sells pots of jasmine tea to be enjoyed at tables under the pomegranate trees. *43 Xisi Nandajie; 9am-9pm.*

✖ Yufunan
This obsessively stylish, white-walled restaurant specialises in sweat-inducing fare from Hunan province. Delectable stir-fries are charged with the sour spiciness of pickled chillies and the earthy smokiness of cured pork belly, resulting in some of the tastiest food in Beijing. Make sure you order Yufunan's 'secret beef' (*mizhi niurou*), where the meat is first slow-cooked until juicy and tender and then stir-fried on a high heat with dried chillis and cumin. Yum! *49 Gongmenkou Toutiao; 11am-9pm.*

Háidiàn & Xichéng · Guanyuan Park · XĪCHÉNG · Huguosi Jie · Chegongzhuang · Ping'anli Xidajie · Ping'anli · Xisi Beidajie · Xihuangchenggen Beijie · Dengyu Lu · Miaoying Temple White Dagoba · Yufunan · Bear Brew · Cathedral of Our Saviour · Royal Palace Crisp Beef Pies · Fuchengmen · Xisi · 1901 Cafe · XĪDĀN · Wansong Laoren Tower · Xi'anmen Dajie

Saviour, it served as Beijing's centre for Catholic Action until 1949. *101 Xi'anmen Dajie; 9am-midnight.*

❌ Royal Palace Crisp Beef Pies

One of the tastiest (and hardest to find) snacks in the capital are these puck-shaped pies filled with beef and leek, said to date all the way back to the Tang dynasty (7th to 10th century). There's always a line at this tiny hole-in-the-wall, so join the queue and watch the pie makers working their magic as you wait your turn. It's definitely worth it. *341 Fuchengmen Nei Dajie; 9am-7pm.*

🏛 Cathedral of Our Saviour

Stumbling upon this sizeable Gothic cathedral tucked away in a quiet side road is a serendipitous Xisi surprise. Another surprise lies within. A stone bearing the dates '13 June – 16 August 1900' is the sole memorial to a bloody siege that took place here during the Boxer Rebellion, costing the lives of 400 churchgoers. Reopened as a Catholic church in 1985, it has a 2pm Sunday service conducted in English and French. *33 Xishiku Dajie; 5am-6pm.*

🍺 1901 Cafe

One the few surviving Qing-era townhouses in Beijing, this baroque-style, three-storey gem is home to a whimsical cafe with attached library, where you can find a quiet corner and soak up the historic ambience over a cappuccino and a good book. Donated to the Cathedral of Our

GETTING LOST IN XISI'S *HUTONG MAZE*

The winding alleyways overlooked by the gorgeously bulbous Miaoying Temple White Dagoba reward the wanderer with slices of local life seldom seen elsewhere in the city. Forgotten temple facades, pigeon lofts, residents decked out in blue Mao caps and suits, storefronts toasting sesame *shaobing* bread, and fine old China parasol trees, so called for the way they spread their leafy canopy over the grey rooftops. Take the alleyway just east of the Miaoying Temple to begin your wanderings.

Top: a game of Chinese chess
Right: Wansong Laoren Tower

© Luoxi / Shutterstock

© Thomas O'Malley / Lonely Planet

DASHILAN

Once a boisterous enclave of theatres, opium dens, boutiques and brothels, the district of Dashilan in central Beijing was thoroughly scrubbed and sanitised by the new Communist government in the 1950s. After decades in the doldrums, a recent reawakening has taken place and *joie de vivre* is returning to this increasingly appealing neighbourhood.

🔒 Beijing Postcards

The history buffs behind this atmospheric *hutong* shop have been collecting old Beijing photographs and maps for years, which you can purchase framed or printed on to cushions, tote bags, jigsaws and calendars. The store is also the starting point for historic walking tours conducted by Danish founder Lars, journeying deep into the surrounding alleys and even the Forbidden City. *97 Yangmeizhu Xiejie; www. bjpostcards.com; noon-6pm Wed-Sun.*

❌ Deyuan Roast Duck

A humble purveyor of authentic Peking duck, the beautifully bronzed birds here are roasted in hung ovens over fruitwood then carved, theatrically, at the front of the restaurant. Deyuan is also a fine spot to sample two other famous Beijing meats, mutton and donkey, best washed down with an ice-cold bottle of Yanjing, Beijing's local beer. *57 Dazhalan Xijie; 10am-9pm.*

🔒 Caicifang Porcelain Workshop

This innovative boutique upcycles broken fragments of vases smashed during the Cultural Revolution into unique jewellery pieces, boxes, sculptures... even fridge magnets! Note the wonderful floor display in the shape of a Buddhist swastika, its glass recesses inset with coloured shards from different dynasties. *5 Yangmeizhu Xiejie; www. caicifang.com; 10am-7pm.*

☕ Soloist Coffee

Housed in a decades-old building said have been a public bathhouse, this third-wave roaster and cafe is one of the city's best-kept secrets. Innovative coffee-based cocktails include an Espresso Old Fashioned and Cold Brew Gin Tonic, best enjoyed out on the terrace with views over the historic *hutong* alley. *9 Yangmeizhu Xiejie; www. soloistcoffee.com; noon-7pm.*

🔒 Taciturnli

This vintage-inspired clothing brand born in Beijing has converted a historic *hutong* house into an obscenely stylish boutique. A modern Chinese success story,

Map labels:
Qianmen Xiheyan Jie
Meishi Jie
DASHILAR
Sanjing Hutong
Caicifang Porcelain Workshop
🔒 Taciturnli
Ruifuxiang
Soloist Coffee
Suzuki Kitchen
Dazhalan Jie
Meishi Jie
Dazhalan Xijie
Liangshidian Jie
Beijing Postcards
Deyuan Roast Duck
Yingtao Xiejie
Meishi Jie

Taciturnli started life as an online store on Taobao, China's biggest e-commerce platform, gaining instant fame for its workwear-inspired pants, shirts and dresses. *27 Yangmeizhu Xiejie; noon-8pm.*

✖ Suzuki Kitchen

Zen minimalism meets *hutong* cool at this Japanese restaurant opened by a team of arty Beijingers. Great-value, beautifully presented dishes include pork cutlet curry, beef rice bowls and Japanese-style hot pot. The garden is just as beautiful as the interior, and also houses a secret boutique selling designer Japanese clothes and ornaments. *10-14 Yangmeizhu Xiejie; www.suzukikitchen.com; 11.30am-9pm.*

🔒 Ruifuxiang

Trading at this spot since 1893, this is one of China's most famous silk sellers, stocking top-quality Shandong silk, brocade and satin. The Ruifuxiang chain was founded by a descendant of the Confucian philosopher Mencius way back in the early Qing dynasty. The first flag of the People's Republic, raised triumphantly above Tiananmen Square in 1949, was made of Ruifuxiang silk. *5 Dazhalan Jie; 9.30am-8pm.*

© zhao jiankang / Shutterstock

© maoyunping / Shutterstock

© 2020, Caicifang Porcelain Workshop

Clockwise from top: kaleidoscopic Dashilan; Caicifang Porcelain Workshop; a tram in Dashilan

ARTS & CULTURE   MUSIC & FILM   SPORTS & LEISURE   EATING   DRINKING   SHOPPING

HONG KONG

This glittering global city of glass, steel, skyscrapers and neon sitting at the edge of the South China Sea is overwhelming in the best way.

Taken by the British as the spoils of the Opium Wars, Hong Kong transformed from a sleepy fishing port into a heaving metropolis. It was handed back to China in 1997 but the city still has an international feel, with English widely spoken and food, art and music from around the world.

While most visitors stick to central Hong Kong Island and the Kowloon peninsula, the city is much more than that. A short tram, bus or MTR (subway) ride from the city centre is Eastern District, a largely residential and industrial area dotted with postage stamp-sized eateries and hidden artists' studios. North of Kowloon's main sights is Sham Shui Po, a manufacturing area where everything you can imagine and more is for sale. Further north, Tai Po has been a market town for centuries. And on a largely rural eastern peninsula, Sai Kung is a fun-loving multicultural village surrounded by the sea.

HONG KONG

SHAM SHUI PO

The working-class manufacturing neighbourhood of Sham Shui Po is the place Hong Kongers come when they need something: a drill bit, a yard of satin, 100 bunny-shaped erasers for a kid's birthday party... Each market teems with gimlet-eyed bargain hunters. Old-school cafes and shops offer respite from the chaos. It's easily accessible by MTR.

🏛 Jockey Club Creative Arts Centre

This former factory building has been converted into studio spaces and galleries. Come to watch artists at work, visit shops and galleries, catch some theatre, or hang out in the atmospheric courtyard with a coffee. *30 Pak Tin St, www.jccac.org.hk.*

🛍 Vinyl Hero

Vinyl connoisseurs make pilgrimages to this shop, on the fifth floor of an obscure residential building, to geek out with owner Paul over his floor-to-ceiling used record collection. Poring over the boxes takes hours. *239 Cheung Sha Wan Rd, Wai Hong Building, 5th Fl, Flat D; 9841 7136; call for hours.*

🛍 Fuk Wing Street

Almost every street in central Sham Shui Po is a market dedicated to a different type of goods; Fuk Wing Street is all about toys and school supplies. Fun browsables include reams of cute Japanese stickers, miniature toy foods, and knockoff Lego. *Approx 10am-6pm.*

🏛 Man Fung Building

Spanish artist Okuda San Miguel transformed this humble residential building, painting it with multicoloured geometric shapes to resemble a kind of psychedelic fox. It's a favourite photo op for the Instagram set. The district is home to several dozen other colourful murals – take a street art treasure hunt! *180 Tai Nan St.*

✖ Garden Café

Garden Company Limited has been supplying Hong Kong supermarkets with bread and packaged pastries for nearly 100 years, making it a local icon. The ground floor of the company's retro-looking HQ has a gift shop and cafe, which fills up at teatime with locals looking for a cheap nostalgic treat. *58 Castle Peak Rd; 2720 1055; 8.30am-6pm.*

✈ Garden Hill

Hike up this small hill for postcard-worthy views of the urban canyons below. At sunset it's a magnet for tripod-toting photographers. The stairs behind Mei Ho House on Berwick St lead to the summit.

EASTERN DISTRICT

Encompassing the highly developed northeast of Hong Kong Island, including North Point, Quarry Bay, Sai Wan Ho and Chai Wan, Eastern gets little glory. It's largely residential, and lacks the atmospheric old alleys of Central and Western Hong Kong Island. But the diligent will find cheap eats, peaceful hiking trails and secret art studios.

Quarry Bay Park and Promenade

Watch local life unfurl in this well-loved waterfront park. Strollers along the promenade watch junks and fishing boats bob across Victoria Harbour, kids scramble up the stairs of the historic fireboat-turned-museum, elderly men practise tai chi and Instagrammers hunt for blossoming cherry trees. *Hoi Tai St; 7am-11pm.*

Chun Yeung Street Market

The tram tracks run through this lively open-air food market, so fruit vendors, fishmongers and butchers regularly jump aside when the 'ding ding' (as locals call the tram) rolls by. It's the place to come for speciality items from Fujian Province, the ancestral homeland of many neighbourhood residents. *Chun Yeung St, North Point; 9am-7pm.*

Eslite Spectrum

In the high-end Cityplaza mall, this Taiwanese bookstore chain has opened a two-storey, 4650-sq-metre (50,000-sq-ft) megastore selling books, clothes, gifts and 'lifestyle items'. Look for handmade Taiwanese herbal soaps, organic French ginger candies, luxury German fountain pens, shelves of cute Japanese washi tape and way more. *18 Tai Koo Shing Rd, 1st Floor, Tai Koo; 3419 1188; 10am-10pm.*

Sunbeam Theatre

A mostly elderly crowd of Cantonese opera fans keep this retro 1970s-era theatre alive. Opera performances can clock in at well over three hours, with elaborate costumes and plots often based on Chinese legends. *423 King's Rd, North Point; most performances 7.30pm.*

VICTORIA HARBOUR

Chun Yeung Street Market

Sunbeam Theatre

YAU TONG

Qinghai Tibetan Noodles

Quarry Bay Park & Promenade

Lei Yue Mun Channel

MOM Livehouse

TIN HAU

Eslite Spectrum

On Lee Noodle Soup

SHAU KEI WAN

Mt Parker Hike

Tai Tam Country Park

MingCha Tea House

CHAI WAN

Tai Tam Reservoir

Shek O Country Park

© Bima Adhitya / Shutterstock

✖ Qinghai Tibetan Noodles

Huge bowls of oil-slicked beef noodles, cumin-rubbed lamb chops and skewers of garlicky roasted veggies are hot ticket items at this always-crowded alleyway spot. There's no English on the sign; it's the last restaurant on the alley. *27 Kam Ping St, North Point; 2151 0506; noon-3pm & 6-10pm.*

✖ On Lee Noodle Soup

Lunchtime is a zoo at this humble *cha chaan teng* (Hong Kong greasy spoon), beloved for classic Cantonese bites: fish ball noodles, milk tea, white toast with butter and condensed milk. *22 Shau Kei Wan Main St E, Shau Kei Wan; 2513 8398; 9am-7pm Fri-Wed.*

✚ Mt Parker Hike

Several trails lead from Eastern neighbourhoods to the top of this peak. The narrow, leafy path from Tai Koo is peaceful, while the straight climb up Mt Parker Road from Quarry Bay is most straightforward. Summit views are especially glittery and gorgeous at night.

EASTERN'S DISTRICT DIVERSITY

Eastern has long been a magnet for immigrants from mainland China. In the post-WWII era the North Point area was nicknamed 'Little Shanghai', and is still known for its Shanghainese barber shops, now dwindling in number. It's now more often called 'Little Fujian' for its immigrants from the southeastern Chinese province – look for Fujianese food in Chun Yeung Street Market.

⚲ MingCha Tea House

In-the-know tea-lovers head to this hidden shop in industrial Chai Wan for bags of fragrant jasmine and earthy pu'er. Despite its unassuming location, MingCha is consistently rated one of the world's best tea houses. English-language tea-tasting workshops will send you home sounding like an expert. *Room 901-902, 9/F Cheung Tat Centre, 18 Cheung Lee St, Chai Wan; www.mingcha. com; 10am-7pm Mon-Sat.*

✿ MOM Livehouse

This rare spot to catch live indie music, in the basement below a shopping centre, attracts music geek 20-somethings and the occasional big name. Chatting with the guy or girl head-nodding next to you will likely net you some excellent tips on the local music scene. *B39, Seven Seas Shopping Centre, 117-121 Kings Rd, North Point; 6360 7676.*

**Top: Chun Yeung Market
Left: the dazzling spectacle of the Cantonese opera *Four Beauties* at Sunbeam Theatre, Hong Kong**

TAI PO

This riverside area has been a trading centre since the Ming Dynasty, when the Tang Clan settled here and built a market. Today it's still home to thriving outdoor markets, as well as 1970s high-rise estates and a beautiful, well-used waterfront along Tolo Harbour. Urban Hong Kongers take the MTR here on weekends to ride bikes and eat snacks.

🎯 Fu Shin Street Market
Old Tai Po lives on in this open-air street market, where squid dries in bamboo baskets and market cats wander freely. It's a good place to pick up candied nuts, tiny oranges and cups of fresh-squeezed sugar cane juice. *Fu Shin St; daily.*

🏛 Man Mo Temple
Set back from Fu Shin Street Market, this incense-smoky temple was built in 1892 and dedicated jointly to the gods of literature and war. Their statues rest in a wooden altar in the back hall, in front of tables decked with offerings like pomelos, peanut oil and candy. *Fu Shin St; 6am-6pm.*

🎯 Tai Po Waterfront Park
On sunny days, the sky above this urban park is thick with kites. Visitors also picnic on the (rare in Hong Kong) lawns, climb the lookout tower and take selfies in flower gardens. Rent bikes here to cycle the waterfront promenade. *Directly east of Tai Wo MTR station; 24hr, lookout tower 7am-7pm.*

🎯 Plover Cove Country Park
City stresses dissolve inside this wilderness, a favourite of hikers, cyclists, kayakers and birdwatchers. Trails range from easy family jaunts to serious treks to hidden waterfalls. The reservoir leading into the park is a top photo spot. It's 25 minutes by taxi from Tai Po Market MTR. *Bride's Pool Rd, Shuen Wan.*

✖ Granny's Tofu Pudding
Locals line up for bowls of silky fresh tofu sprinkled with palm sugar. Eat while standing then return your bowl to the counter. Cold fresh soy milk is a treat, too. *2A Tai Kwong Ln; 8am-6pm.*

Top: Man Mo Temple

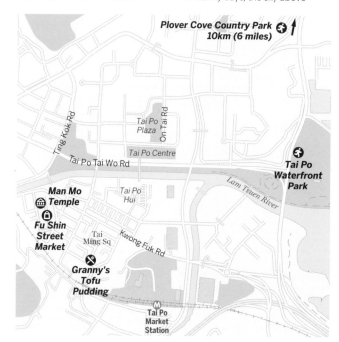

Map labels:
Plover Cove Country Park 🎯 ↑
10km (6 miles)
Ting Kok Rd
Tai Po Plaza
On Tai Rd
Tai Po Centre
Tai Po Tai Wo Rd
Tai Po Waterfront Park 🎯
Lam Tsuen River
Man Mo Temple 🏛
Tai Po Hui
Fu Shin Street Market
Tai Ming Sq
Kwong Fuk Rd
Granny's Tofu Pudding ✖
Tai Po Market Station Ⓜ

HONG KONG

SAI KUNG

The Sai Kung Peninsula is popular with weekend day-trippers, who come to hike its mountain trails, lie on its beaches, and feast on seafood in its traditional fishing villages. The area is only accessible by bus or taxi, which invites a 'getting away from it all' feeling. The main population centre, Sai Kung Town, has global dining options, pubs, and a friendly international vibe.

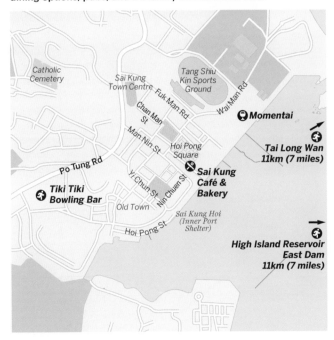

🛫 Tai Long Wan

Most visitors to Hong Kong aren't expecting tropical beaches like Tai Long Wan, cradled by mountains with turquoise water and powdery sand. Beachgoers swim, lounge and sip beers at the rustic food stall, and even camp overnight. Get here via a 1½-hour hike through Sai Kung East Country Park, then hike back or, for a less energetic option, take a *kaito* (motorboat ferry) directly to Sai Kung Town.

🛫 High Island Reservoir East Dam

Part of the Hong Kong Global Geopark, this spectacularly scenic seaside dam is known for its hexagonal rock columns, remnants of the city's volcanic prehistory. The best way to visit is with a guided boat tour of the whole Geopark, but the dam's also accessible by taxi or minibus from Sai Kung Town. *www. geopark.gov.hk.*

🍹 Tiki Tiki Bowling Bar

When the weather turns sour, locals lace up their bowling shoes at this quirky Polynesian-themed bowling alley and restaurant. Slushy drinks and plenty of beer will keep even non-bowlers happy. *1A Chui Tong Road, 4th fl; www.tikitiki.hk/en; 4-10pm Wed-Fri, from 10am Sat & Sun.*

🍹 Momentai

Translating to 'relax, no problem' in English, this waterfront spot is a local favourite thanks to its laid-back vibe (think pool tables, board games, couches), local brews, Sunday afternoon DJ sessions, and global comfort foods like burgers and poke bowls. *Kiosk 1, Sai Kung Waterfront; www.momentai-la. com; noon-11pm Tue-Sat, to 10pm Sun.*

🍴 Sai Kung Café and Bakery

Line up with the locals at this bakery for a classic Hong Kong 'pineapple bun' stuffed with a thick tile of butter. There's no actual fruit in the recipe; the sweet bun's crackled top resembles the skin of a pineapple. *6-7 Kam Po Court, 2 Hoi Pong Square; 2792 3861; 7am-10pm.*

Gwanghwamun

Euljiro

Seoul

SEOUL

Step into the shadows of this city of bright lights, K-Pop and cutting-edge technology and discover Seoul's coolest bars and best eats.

From Joseon Dynasty history to ready-to-wear fashion, Seoul has everything travellers look for in a cosmopolitan city. Yes, there are museums, skyscrapers, malls and more, but the best way to see South Korea's capital isn't hopping from one landmark to another. Instead, stroll down small alleyways and discover the lone crowded bar on otherwise empty streets.

South of the Han River, in the famous Gangnam area, travellers can have extravagant nights out in posh clubs and French restaurants. Further north, in downtown Seoul, adventurers can find bargains in traditional markets on bellies full of street food. Downtown Seoul, between Gwanghwamun and Euljiro, is the perfect neighbourhood to explore by foot. Put on your sneakers and traverse the city's man-made Cheongyecheon Stream as you make your way around from one hole-in-the-wall restaurant to the next. The city's just waiting for you to eat it up!

GWANGHWAMUN

Although Gwanghwamun refers to the Joseon Dynasty gate of Gyeongbokgung Palace, Koreans also use the name to describe its surrounding neighbourhood. Tourists snap photos of the famous General Yi Sun-shin and King Sejong statues, and admire the mountains shadowing the Palace. Locals merrily eat and drink at some of Seoul's finest establishments, tucked into Gwanghwamun's corners.

✖ Gwanghwamun Jip

One of the most famous kimchi stew joints in Seoul, Gwanghwamun Jip only has two main items on its menu – kimchi stew and spicy, pan-fried pork. The restaurant's sign dating back to the '50s and the old-school vibes make it an essential Seoul experience. *12 Saemunan-ro 5-gil; 9am-10pm.*

✖ Gwanghwamun Gukbap

Recognised by Michelin's Bib Gourmand, Gwanghwamun Gukbap's signature dish is a modern take on *gukbap* – a rich, comforting Korean dish of broth and rice. Headed by former journalist Park Chan-il, the restaurant focuses on quality ingredients and transparent flavours. *53 Sejong-daero 21-gil; 11.30am-10pm.*

🍸 Charles H

This speakeasy in the basement of the Four Seasons Hotel pays homage to 20th-century writer Charles H Baker. Ranked the best bar in Korea by The World's 100 Best Bars 2018 list, the cocktails taste even better in its glamorous interior. *97 Saemunan-ro B1; www.fourseasons.com/seoul; 6pm-1am, weekends to 2.30am.*

☕ Namusairo

A pioneer in Korea's coffee world, Namusairo opened in 2002 and was one of the first cafes in Seoul to prioritise coffee flavour over ambience – importing rare beans and serving the illustrious Panama Geisha variety. The cafe, built in a picturesque *hanok* (traditional Korean house), is a true respite from chain cafes. *21 Sajik-ro 8-gil; www.namusairo.com; 10am-10pm.*

✦ Ilmin Museum of Art

This private art museum run by the Ilmin Cultural Foundation focuses on contemporary visual culture and runs the country's only documentary archive. *152 Sejong-daero; http://ilmin.org; 11am-7pm.*

🏛 Emu Artspace

A small movie theatre and cafe in a mostly residential part of Seoul, Emu is especially dear to expats in Seoul as it's one of the few venues that occasionally screen Korean films with English subtitles. *7 Gyeonghuigung 1ga; www.emuartspace.com.*

Map of Gwanghwamun: Sajik Park, DANGJU-DONG, Sajik-ro, Gyeongbokgung, Yulgok-ro, Namusairo, Sajik-ro 8-gil, JONGNO-GU, Saemunan-ro 3-gil, Jong-ro 1-gil, Gwanghwamun Sq, Emu Artspace, Gyeonghuigung Park, Seoul Museum of History, Gwanghwamun Jip, Four Seasons Hotel, Kyobo Building, Seoul Museum of Art Annexe, Saemunan-ro, Charles H, Ilmin Museum of Art, Jong-ro, Gwanghwamun, Gwanghwamun Gukbap, Sejong-daero, Seoul Finance Centre

EULJIRO

Discover noodle dishes and craft brews in this trendy, industrial-chic neighbourhood. Minutes from Seoul's touristy Myeongdong neighbourhood, Euljiro is an industrial quarter filled with printing presses and hardware shops. Men in their 50s reigned supreme here five years ago, but recent gentrification has brought in hidden bars and cafes as well as millennial-aged hipsters.

Coffee Hanyakbang

Housed in a narrow alleyway, Coffee Hanyakbang is a speciality coffee shop with old-school Korean flourishes. Guests can take a peep at the cafe's owner, Kang Yun-seok, as he roasts the beans in a corner near the counter on the first floor, or take their aromatic brews upstairs for a bit more space. *16-6 Samil-daero 12-gil; 8am-10.30pm.*

Seendosi

Located on the fifth floor of a dark, seemingly abandoned warehouse, Seendosi is a bar, lounge and art space decorated with neon lights and bold furniture. Some weekends, the bar hosts indie concerts and during the summer, guests cool off by a digital screen that displays a waterfall on loop on the bar's rooftop. *31 Eulji-ro 11-gil; 6pm-2am Mon-Fri, from 3pm Sat.*

Wooraeoak

Undoubtedly one of Seoul's most famous old restaurants, many of Wooraeoak's customers have been dining here for decades. Both the *naengmyun*, buckwheat noodles in ice broth, and *bulgogi*, marinated, pan-grilled beef, are restaurant signatures but those on a budget can skip the beef – the noodles alone are a knock-out! *62-29 Changgyeonggung-ro; 11.30am-9.30pm Tue-Sun.*

Masun Hof

Eulji-ro 13-gil is lined with *hofs* (beer halls) that serve chicken, dried fish and alcohol. While each *hof* boasts crowds of locals revelling on the storefront plastic furniture, Masun Hof specialises in a garlic fried chicken, making it a notch above the rest. For the quintessential Euljiro experience, pair the culinary delights with cold beers and good friends. *19 Eulji-ro 13-gil; noon-midnight.*

1/10

Take one look at 1/10's threadbare exterior and you'd never guess

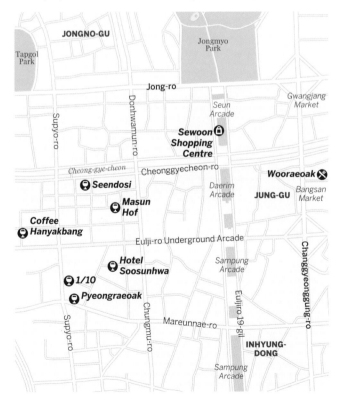

© Take Photo / Shutterstock

that the second-floor bar could feel so much like a Parisian cafe. A unique combination of vintage objects and simple bites, 1/10's short wine menu features a dozen bottles – red, white and sparkling – at prices that are shockingly affordable by Seoul standards. *42-9 Supyo-ro; www.instagram.com/sipboon_il; 6pm-midnight.*

⊗ Pyeongraeoak

This establishment dating back to the 1950s sees lines down the street for their signature *chogyetang*, chilled chicken soup. Although the soup is only available for portions of two or more, solo travellers need not despair – the spicy chicken and cucumber side dish served with every meal is the true star. *21-1 Mareunnae-ro; 11am-9.30pm Mon-Sat.*

🛏 Hotel Soosunhwa

Three designers came together to create this 'hotel' located on the fourth floor of an Euljiro warehouse. Arguably one of the most Instagram-friendly spots in the neighbourhood, Hotel

SEOUL BIKE-SHARING

While the Seoul Metro is a fast and cheap way to get around, travellers who prefer travel on two wheels can take advantage of the public bike-sharing services all over the city. Sign up for an account and find the closest rental location near you on www.bikeseoul.com.

Soosunhwa doesn't actually offer accommodation. The dark cafe, bar and co-working space is brought to life with its Tiffany-style pendant lights and retro china. *17 Chungmu-ro 7-gil; www.facebook.com/hotelsoosunhwa; noon-midnight Mon-Sat.*

🔒 Sewoon Shopping Centre

This is more of a peek into Seoul's history than it is a place to shop. Originally built in 1968, the plaza was Korea's first electronics market. When it was remodelled in 2017, it sparked a nationwide conversation about redevelopment in the city. Today, the plaza is a marriage of stores dating from the 1980s and more recent hipster-run coffee spots. *159 Cheonggyecheon-ro; 9am-7pm Mon-Sat.*

**Top: bike-sharing in Seoul
Below: tropical cocktails at Hotel Soosunhwa**

© 2020, Hotel Soosunhwa

TOKYO

Tokyo is a dazzling city of skyscrapers, neon and crowds. But it has another side, concealed in its residential pockets, each with its own local character.

TOKYO

Tokyo is a sprawling city anchored by several major hubs, from where train lines run outwards through residential districts. In general, the southwest quadrant of the city, connected to Shinjuku or Shibuya, has the trendiest neighbourhoods. This is where you'll find Tomigaya, the current hipster hot spot, and Naka-Meguro, favoured by the fashion crowd. Both have chic dining and coffee scenes. Also out this way is Shimo-Kitazawa, which has more of a hippie vibe (and is particularly good for nightlife).

Kōenji, due west of the city centre (and also accessed via Shinjuku), is purposefully unpolished with a free-wheeling local culture; it's a great spot for budget travellers.

Tokyo's east side is often overlooked: it's older and less developed. The exception is Kiyosumi-Shirakawa, which has some of that and also some cool new spots. The neighbourhoods themselves are compact and easy to get around on foot.

NAKA-MEGURO

Naka-Meguro is a fashionable residential enclave strung out along a leafy canal, the Meguro-gawa, which gives the neighbourhood a laid-back vibe. Many creative-types live here, which accounts for the high concentration of one-of-a-kind boutiques and restaurants. Naka-Meguro is the end of the Hibiya subway line and also a stop on the Tōkyū Tōyoko line (two stops from Shibuya).

♨ Kōmeisen

The local *sento* (bathhouse), run by the same family for three generations, got a contemporary remake a few years ago courtesy of architect Imai Kentarō. Men get the outdoor bath one week; women the next. Both sides have a sauna. *1-6-1 Kami-Meguro; http://kohmeisen.com; hours vary; ¥460.*

✘ Deli fu cious

Gourmet seafood burgers from a former high-end sushi chef. The 'konbu fish burger' is the classic menu item; the fish, chosen seasonally, is pressed with *konbu* (kelp) first before being batter-fried. *1-9-13 Higashiyama; www.delifucious.com; 03-6874-0412; noon-9pm, Thu-Tue.*

☕ Onibus Coffee

A traditional, two-storey shophouse with a big fat roaster taking up much of the ground floor. Sip your latte on a bench out front or at the communal table upstairs. *2-14-1 Kami-Meguro; www.onibuscoffee.com; 9am-6pm.*

🛍 1LDK

This gleaming boutique offers an edited selection of covetable minimalist staples from cult-favourite Japanese brands like Universal Products. For lifestyle goods, check out 1LDK Apartments across the lane (there's a cafe there too). *1-8-28 Kamimeguro, http://1ldkshop.com; noon-8pm.*

🛍 SML

This artisan homeware shop takes a gallery-like approach, featuring works from a changing selection of artists. It's particularly good for earthy pottery. *1-15-1 Aobadai, http://sm-l.jp; noon-8pm.*

🛍 Tsutaya Books

Gorgeous bookstore designed by Klein Dytham architecture under the elevated train tracks. There are art and design tomes in English here, plus other stylish sundries. Bonus: it's open super late. *1-22-10 Kami-Meguro, https://store.tsite.jp/nakameguro/; 7am-midnight.*

🛍 Vase

This tiny shop is the place to source avant-garde items from obscure designers, like androgynous pieces with unconventional silhouettes. *1-7-7 Kami-Meguro, www.vasenakameguro.com; noon-8pm.*

SARUGAKU-CHŌ

Meguro-gawa

Kyū-Yamate-dōri

🛍 SML

✘ Deli fu cious

AOBADAI

Yamate-dōri

🛍 1LDK
♨ Kōmeisen
🛍 Vase

Komazawa-dōri

Ⓢ Naka-Meguro

Naka-Meguro

NAKA-MEGURO

Onibus Coffee ☕

🛍 Tsutaya Books

KAMI-MEGURO

TOMIGAYA

Tomigaya is part of what is sometimes called 'deep Shibuya' – it's within walking distance of the brash, built-up commercial and entertainment hub Shibuya, but couldn't be more different. The buildings here are small, housing chef-owned restaurants and trendsetting cafes that are driving Tokyo's food and drink scene. The nearest subway stop is Yoyogi-kōen on the Chiyoda line.

🏛 Yoyogi Hachiman-gū Shrine

Long before the bistros and cafes, there was Shintō shrine Yoyogi Hachiman-gū, founded in the 13th century. The deity associated with the shrine, which is ensconced in green and up some stone steps, is said to be particularly receptive to prayers for good business and easy childbirth. This is Tomigaya's local shrine, where residents gather for cultural observances like *hatsu-mōde*, the first shrine visit of the new year. *5-1-1 Yoyogi.*

✖ Ahiru Store

A small, casual and often standing-room-only bistro specialising in down-to-earth French food and natural wines. Bread is baked fresh and the sausages are homemade, too. It's very popular and usually has a queue. *1-19-4 Tomigaya; 03-5454-2146; 6pm-midnight Mon-Fri, 3-9pm Sat.*

✖ Camelback

A stand serving tasty sandwiches and coffee. The omelette sandwich is the thing to order – it's the kind of omelette usually served at sushi restaurants (but here on fluffy bread). Great for breakfast. *42-2 Kamiyama-chō; www.camelback.tokyo; 03-6407-0069; 8am-5pm Tue-Sun.*

☕ Fuglen Tokyo

In Tomigaya, all roads lead to Fuglen, a Norwegian import with a mid-century Scandi interior. During the day, it's full of people clicking away on laptops. In the evening it morphs into a cool cocktail lounge, sometimes with music events. Best on a warm day when you can sit outside. *1-16-11 Tomigaya; www.fuglen. no; 8am-10pm Mon & Tue, to 1am Wed & Thu, to 2am Fri, 9am-2am Sat, 9am-midnight Sun.*

☕ Little Nap Coffee Stand

The place to pick up a latte before or after a trip to the park,

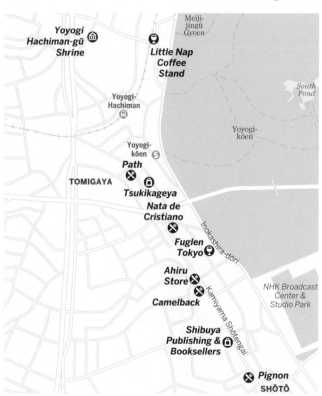

Yoyogi Hachiman-gū Shrine
Meiji-jingū Gyoen
Little Nap Coffee Stand
Yoyogi-Hachiman
South Pond
Yoyogi-kōen
Yoyogi-kōen
Path
TOMIGAYA
Tsukikageya
Nata de Cristiano
Fuglen Tokyo
Inokashira-dōri
Ahiru Store
Camelback
NHK Broadcast Center & Studio Park
Kamiyama Shōtengai
Shibuya Publishing & Booksellers
Pignon
SHŌTŌ

TOKYO

in the company of dog owners and lycra-clad joggers. The beans are roasted at another spot in the neighbourhood. *5-65-4 Yoyogi; www.littlenap.jp; 9am-7pm Tue-Sun.*

❌ Nata de Cristiano
Another little take-away stand, this one serving Portuguese-style pastries like *pastéis de nata* (custard tarts). It's a good bet for amassing picnic supplies to take to nearby Yoyogi-kōen (you can get bottles of wine here, too). *1-14-16 Tomigaya; www.cristianos.jp/nata; 03-6804-9723; 10am-7.30pm.*

❌ Path
Come early for pastries, sandwiches and coffee (made with beans courtesy of either Fuglen or Little Nap, naturally) or in the evening for plates of contemporary Italian-meets-Japanese cuisine (paired with craft sake or wine). Reservations

PARK PICNICS

Yoyogi-kōen isn't Tokyo's prettiest park but it's definitely the most popular. Weekends are full of picnickers, and there are often festivals at the plaza across the street. On weekdays, it's mostly locals taking advantage of all that wide-open space. For Tomigaya residents, the good food and coffee is just a bonus: the park is the reason to live here.

recommended for dinner. *1-44-2 Tomigaya; 03-6407-0011; 8am-3pm, 6pm-midnight Tue-Sun.*

❌ Pignon
This neighbourhood bistro has French and north African flavours, a laid-back atmosphere and an artsy following. On a warm night try to score the outdoor table for a prime people-watching position.

16-3 Kamiyama-chō; www.pignontokyo.jp; 03-3468-2331; 6.30-10.30pm Mon-Sat.

🔒 Shibuya Publishing & Booksellers
Boutique book store with lots on art, travel and food (and always a crowd browsing in the evening). There's some stuff in English, and also stylish totes and tees on sale. *17-3 Kamiyama-chō; www.shibuyabooks.co.jp; 11am-11pm Mon-Sat, to 10pm Sun.*

🔒 Tsukikageya
The shop and studio of designer Natsuki Shigeta whose outré textile designs appear on the *yukata* (cotton kimono) on display here. Also: somewhat kooky accessories. *1-9-19 Tomigaya, Shibuya-ku; www.tsukikageya.com; noon-8pm Thu-Mon, closed irregularly.*

Top: spring in Yoyogi Park
Left: Nata de Cristiano

© Kanokpol Tokumhnerd / Shutterstock

SHIMO-KITAZAWA

Shimo-Kitazawa, with its low skyline and tangled mess of narrow streets, has for decades attracted artists, musicians and students. In other words, people with irregular schedules – which means it has great nightlife any night of the week, plus live music venues and record shops aplenty. The neighbourhood is connected to hubs Shinjuku and Shibuya by train.

Never Never Land
Long-running Shimo-Kitazawa bar that gets going late. Communal vibe and great Okinawan food. *3-19-3 Kitazawa; 6pm-2am Mon-Sat, to midnight Sun.*

Bear Pond Espresso
One of Tokyo's most famous coffee spots, especially known for its rich, viscous 'angel stain' espresso. Come early, the owner will only make a certain number per day. *2-36-12 Kitazawa; www.bear-pond.com; 11am-5.30pm Wed-Mon.*

Shimo-Kitazawa Three
Low-key basement spot for catching local indie musicians and DJs. The line-up is almost always good fun. Keep an eye out for free events. *5-18-1 Daizawa; https://shimokitazawathree.tumblr.com.*

Ghetto
A dark bolthole inside the Suzunari theatre complex, itself a rather dilapidated venue. For when you want to chat with strangers into the night. Cheap drinks. *1-45-16 Daizawa; 8.30pm-late.*

Hiroki
Popular local spot for grilled-in-front-of-you *okonomiyaki* (savoury pancake) and particularly the Hiroshima style of the dish (with added noodles). *2-14-14 Kitazawa; www.teppan-hiroki.com; 03-3412-3908; noon-9.30pm.*

Mother
A neighbourhood landmark with a trippy interior – part treehouse, part grotto – and a groovy 1970s atmosphere. Tasty seasonal cocktails. *5-36-14 Daizawa; www.rock-mother.com; 5pm-2am Sun-Thu, to 5am Fri & Sat.*

Shirube
Boisterous *izakaya* (pub-eatery) with an open kitchen and high-energy chefs. Order house speciality *aburi saba* (blowtorched mackerel). Reservations recommended. *2-18-2 Kitazawa; 03-3413-3785; 5.30pm-midnight.*

Map labels:
Ichiban-gai
Bear Pond Espresso
KITAZAWA
Kamakura-dori
Azuma-dori
Never Never Land
Ghetto
Shimo-Kitazawa
Minami-guchi Shotengai
Chazawa-dori
Shirube
Hiroki
Mother
DAIZAWA
Shimo-Kitazawa Three

KIYOSUMI-SHIRAKAWA

Way over in Tokyo's 'far east'– that is, east of the Sumida-gawa – Kiyosumi-Shirakawa is among the oldest parts of Tokyo, a former industrial centre that's now cast as an alternative to the city's west-side 'hoods. It has easy access to the city centre, via the Hanzōmon Line and the Toei Ōedo subway lines from Kiyosumi-Shirakawa station.

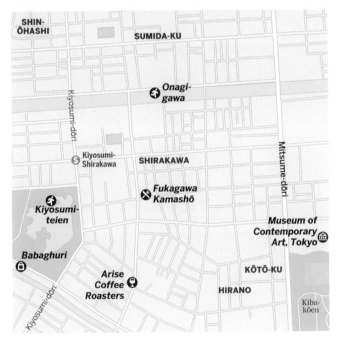

⊕ Kiyosumi-teien
This is one of Tokyo's prettiest gardens and it's rarely crowded. It started out as the grounds of an 18th-century villa (though the building is long gone); the massive stones were brought in from all over the country. Perch on a bench overlooking the central pond or stroll the path along the perimeter. *3-3-9 Kiyosumi; http://teien.tokyo-park.or.jp; 9am-5pm; ¥150.*

⊕ Onagi-gawa
The canal that runs through the neighbourhood, flanked by pedestrian paths is a peaceful spot for a stroll, especially in early April when cherry blossoms bloom here.

☕ Arise Coffee Roasters
A spot for chatting with neighbours (as opposed to flipping open a laptop), with skateboards on the wall and a selection of single-origin brews. *1-13-8 Hirano; http://arisecoffee.jp; 10am-6pm Tue-Sun.*

✕ Fukagawa Kamashō
Fukagawa-meshi is a dish of clams over rice and it's local to this very specific part of Tokyo (which used to be tidal flats). Try it at this small, home-style shop. *2-1-13 Shirakawa; 03-3643-4053; 11am-8pm Wed & Fri-Sun, to 3pm Tue & Thu.*

🔒 Babaghuri
German fashion designer Jurgen Lehl lived in Japan for decades while building the fashion house Babaghuri, known for its use of natural material and dyes. *3-1-7 Kiyosumi; www.babaghuri.jp; 11am-7pm.*

🏛 Museum of Contemporary Art, Tokyo
Visit the permanent gallery for a crash course in contemporary Japanese art, or come to check out the monumental building by architect Yanagisawa Takahiko – especially the sunken stone and water garden. There's a great art book store here, too. Special exhibitions often cover fashion and design. *4-1-1 Miyoshi; www.mot-art-museum.jp; 10am-6pm Tue-Sun; ¥500.*

KŌENJI

Kōenji is proudly grungy with a punk spirit. Its anti-consumerist ethos is evident in its preponderance of second-hand shops, older buildings and cheap, zero-frills restaurants and bars, while its creative streak shows up in its street art and live music venues. It's a stop on the JR Chūō-Sōbu line, the commuter line that connects hub Shinjuku with the western 'burbs.

🏛 Kōenji Hikawa-jinja
This otherwise ordinary neighbourhood has Japan's only shrine devoted entirely to weather. For ¥500, you can purchase a prayer plaque from the shrine office for weather-related requests (like sun on your wedding day). *4-44-19 Kōenji-minami; 9am-5pm.*

🏛 Mural City Project
There are six (and counting!) murals from different artists on buildings around the neighbourhood, part of a project to bring more street art to Tokyo. See the website for locations. *http://mural-city.com.*

✪ SUBStore
On Friday and Saturday nights indie musicians often play on the floor here, but small and cosy SUBStore isn't a conventional venue: it's a used record store that's also an Indonesian restaurant and sometimes an art gallery. *3-1-12 Kōenji-Kita; https://substore.jimdo. com; 3pm-midnight Thu-Mon, 5pm-midnight Wed.*

✪ Kosugi-yu
A rare early-20th-century bathhouse, with a dramatic curving gabled roof. Inside it's clean and modern, with four different bathing tubs on each side (divided by sex). The lounge doubles as a gallery for local artists. *3-32-2 Kōenji-kita; www13.plala.or.jp/Kosugiyu; 3.30pm-1.45am Fri-Wed; ¥460.*

✖ Dachibin
Landmark Okinawan restaurant that nails all the classics, like *goya-champuru* (stir-fried bitter melon) and *rafute* (braised pork belly). A few times a month there's live music too: sometimes Okinawan folk music, sometimes indie rock. *3-2-13 Kōenji-kita; www.dachibin. com; 03-3337-1352; 5pm-5am.*

🍸 Cocktail Shobō
This beautifully maintained, century-old house is both cocktail bar and second-hand bookstore. In keeping with the vintage theme,

Kosugi-yu

KŌENJI-KITA

Cocktail Shobō

Hayatochiri

Nantoka Bar

Dachibin

Naka-dōri

Kōshin-dōri

Junjō Shōtengai

Azuma-dōri

Shimon-ya · SUBStore

Kōenji

Mural City Project (Mural #1)

Sokkyō

KŌENJI-MINAMI

Poem

Kōenji Hikawa-jinja

Pal Shōtengai

Kōnan-dōri

Etoile-dōri

© Akbarmoose / 2020, SUBStore

the crockery and glassware are antiques and cocktails are made with retro soft drinks. At lunch time, come by for a curry and coffee. *3-8-13 Kōenji-kita; http:// koenji-cocktail.info; 03-3310-8130; 11.30am-3pm & 5-11pm Wed-Sun, 5-11pm Mon-Tue.*

Nantoka Bar
Every night a different character runs the show here, setting the menu and mood (*nantoka* means 'something or other'). It's an ad hoc, low-budget operation in a ramshackle old building. For when you want to truly go with the flow. *3-4-12 Kōenji-kita; www.shirouto. org/nantokabar; 7pm-late.*

Poem
Running for over 50 years, Poem is an old-school coffee shop, with low tables, pleather banquettes and pour-over coffee. *4-44-5 Kōenji-minami; 11am-9.30pm.*

Shimon-ya
This is a very pared-back *izakaya* with clear plastic tarps over the entrance, up-turned beer crates for tables and a loyal following (thanks to very budget-friendly

KŌENJI AWA ODORI

Kōenji's biggest event of the year is the Awa Odori (www.koenji-awaodori. com), held in late August. It's a traditional celebration of O-bon (the Japanese Buddhist rite of remembrance) that features a big parade of folk dancers. It's wildly popular, drawing huge crowds of spectators, who also come to enjoy the street food and cracking beers on the street.

prices). There are all sorts of charcoal-grilled skewers on the menu; don't miss the *gyūsuji nikomi* (stewed beef tendon). It's under the elevated train tracks, where there are lots of other restaurants and bars, too. *3-69-1 Kōenji-minami; 03-3330-7273; 5pm-midnight.*

Hayatochiri
Tokyo's most off-the-wall clothing shop, a tiny space crammed with one-of-a-kind remake pieces, pretty much all of which are a pop-art statement. *3-4-11 Kōenji-kita; http://hayatochiri.thebase.in; 3-9pm, closed Thu & irregularly.*

Sokkyō
A trendsetting second-hand boutique where the selection is pared down to the very random and the very cool. There's a discreet 'open' sign out front. *102 Nakanishi Apt Bldg, 3-59-14 Kōenji-minami; www.sokkyou.net; 1-9pm.*

**Top: rock out at SUBStore
Below: folk parade Awa Odori**

© canyalcin / Shutterstock

EUROPE

ARTS & CULTURE   MUSIC & FILM   SPORTS & LEISURE   EATING   DRINKING   SHOPPING

LISBON

There is a Lisbon beyond the postcard-perfect tile facades glistening in the sun, and it's not too far from tourists' favourite neighbourhoods...

Northwestern Campo de Ourique is perfect for tourists eager to explore attractions and restaurants that rarely grace top 10 lists. Mostly a residential neighbourhood, Campo de Ourique is not (yet) reachable by metro but it's served by trams 28 and 25 from Lisbon's downtown; just get off the tram one stop before last.

Madragoa in the southwest, closer to the Tagus River and often sharing the spotlight with neighbouring Design District Santos and nightlife hub Cais do Sodré, is a haven of traditional Portuguese restaurants, family-owned and community-driven shops, and locals' favourite museums. A short tram ride away from the city centre, it's one of the oldest neighbourhoods in Lisbon although not much of it survived the 1755 earthquake. You'll still be rewarded with a fair dose of steep cobblestone streets, tile facades, clotheslines full of laundry hanging to dry, and neighbourly entertainment during the St Anthony's festivities in June.

LISBON

CAMPO DE OURIQUE

At the end of the line of iconic tram 28, Campo de Ourique doesn't feature on most tourist itineraries. The wide streets of modernist-style pastel-coloured buildings aren't full of landmarks, but they're brimming with local shops and family-owned restaurants. This is the Lisbon you'll gloat about to friends and family, never fully unveiling all the spots you found on your wanders.

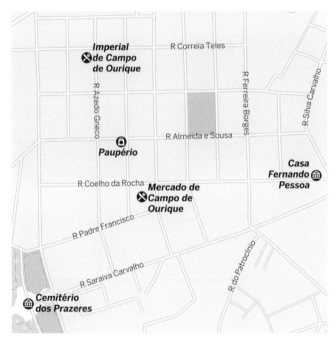

🏛 Casa Fernando Pessoa
The home where poet Fernando Pessoa lived his final years is a treasure trove of the modernist's life. Personal belongings, family photos and a free-access library of his books in different languages shed light on the Lisbon-born literary genius whose work hasn't been completely deciphered yet. *R Coelho da Rocha 16; www.casafernandopessoa.pt; 10am-6pm.*

❌ Mercado de Campo de Ourique
This lively neighbourhood market, frequented by morning grocery shoppers, doubles as lunch haunt for tourists and local workers. Restaurants serve a mix of local cuisine, international novelties and healthy dishes. Grab a signature cocktail at Gin Corner. *R Coelho da Rocha; www.mercadodecampodeourique.pt; 10am-11pm.*

🔒 Paupério
Factory Paupério, based in the north of Portugal, opened this shop in Lisbon and it's as appealing to Lisboans who crave their childhood's biscuits as it is to curious tourists lured in by brightly coloured tins. This corner store sells packaged assortments of the artisanal biscuits made in Valongo for more than 145 years. *R Almeida e Sousa 49A; www.pauperio.pt; 10am-7pm.*

❌ Imperial de Campo de Ourique
This family-owned *tasca* (an inexpensive tavern-like restaurant) serves typical hearty and affordable daily specials. Service is fast but never rushed, always under the sharp eye of the owner Mr João, who says goodbye to regulars and first-timers with the same heartfelt *obrigado, prazer em vê-lo* ('thank you, nice to see you'). *R Correia Teles 67; 213 886 096; 7am-8pm.*

🏛 Cemitério dos Prazeres
Beyond the massive gate of Lisbon's largest cemetery, there's more than elaborate tombs. One of the lesser-known views to Bridge 25 de Abril unveils next to the artists' plot. Free maps of the cemetery at the entrance. *Praça São João Bosco 568; 9am-6pm.*

MADRAGOA

A seven-minute tram ride from the centre, Madragoa is where polished cosmopolitan businesses meet the weathered alleys and tile-facade buildings of a typical Lisbon neighbourhood. A place to escape the tourist crowds, here the authenticity is not contrived and there's a good balance of old and new restaurants, museums and shops, loved and recommended by locals to first-time visitors.

🏛 Museu Nacional de Arte Antiga

The largest and oldest art museum in Lisbon, MNAA has been housed in the same palace since its inception. If you're short on time to visit all four floors, pick the free brochure with one of the suggested guides under the '12 Choices' project: 12 public figures, Portuguese or with a connection to the country, picked 12 must-see works in the museum. *R das Janelas Verdes; www. museudearteantiga.pt; 10am-6pm Tue-Sun; €6.*

🏛 Museu da Marioneta

A well-known spot for several generations of Lisboans, this small museum pays tribute to the history of the art of puppetry and Portuguese artisans. Housed in the old Convento das Bernardas, colourful puppets of all shapes, sizes and origins trace the timeline of this ancient performance art form. *R da Esperança 146; www. museudamarioneta.pt; 10am-6pm Tue-Sun; €5.*

❌ Varina da Madragoa

Known for its *pataniscas* (salted cod fritters) and *peixinhos da horta* (crisp tempura green beans), Varina da Madragoa's bright blue doors open up to a dark but cosy dining room with tiled walls and photos of celebrities, and tables covered in blue-and-white chequered cloths. Food is traditional Portuguese and portions are generous. *R das Madres 34; 213 965 533; 12.30-3pm Tue-Sun.*

☕ Fauna & Flora

A local business with an international vibe in the heart of Madragoa, Fauna & Flora caters to a young, hipster-cool crowd of locals, tourists and expats who appreciate good coffee, eye-catching design and healthy food made with mostly Portuguese ingredients. *R da Esperança 33; 9am-7pm.*

❌ Taberna da Esperança

Don't be fooled by the chaos of mismatched furniture. The decor is a nod to every Lisboan's childhood kitchen, where families sat around the table to share a

Map of Madragoa showing R do Quelhas, Flor da Selva, Varina da Madragoa, R das Praças, Tv do Convento das Bernardas, R dos Remedios, R de São Felix, R Garcia da Horta, MADRAGOA, Museu da Marioneta, R das Madres, Fauna & Flora, Taberna da Esperança, R da Esperança, Mercearia da Mila, R de Santos-O-Velho, Lg de Santos, Av 24 de Julho, Santos Train Station, Museu Nacional de Arte Antiga, Cais da Viscondessa

one-pot meal. The menu honours that tradition with typical ingredients such as *bacalhau* (dried salt-cod) and lamb reimagined as contemporary dishes meant for sharing. Wines either take a Portuguese approach to international varietals or are sourced from small producers. *R da Esperança 112; www.tabernadaesperanca. com; 213 962 744; 7.30pm-2am Tue-Sun.*

🔒 Flor da Selva

The absence of signage might make you doubt if you're walking up the right steep, cobblestone street, but the faint smell of freshly roasted coffee beans confirms you're near Flor da Selva. In business since 1950, it's the only roaster in Lisbon that still uses firewood. A supplier for many cafes and restaurants in the city, Flor da Selva also caters to coffee aficionados. *Tv do Pasteleiro 32; www.flordaselva. com; 9am-6pm Mon-Fri.*

MADRAGOA'S UNSUNG AFRICAN ROOTS

Although locals and tourists know Madragoa as a former fishers' neighbourhood, it was originally founded in the 16th century as a district where freed African slaves were allowed to live. Apart from scarce mentions in historical documents, no signs remain of that neighbourhood once known for its Umbundu name Mocambo, which means village or haven.

🔒 Mercearia da Mila

Sourcing most supplies from local producers, Mercearia da Mila is a mix of grocery store, bakery and cafe that aims to make community-focused businesses trendy again. A reminder of the old *mercearias* (delis) that abounded in Lisbon in the past, here you can buy everything from fresh produce to fragrant coffee and a sandwich to go. *R Santos-O-Velho 38; www.merceariadamila.com; 8am-7pm.*

**Top: Museu da Marioneta
Below and below left: coffee and community at Mercearia da Mila**

Parnell Street & Around

Dublin

Rathmines

DUBLIN

One of the world's friendliest small cities, come for its rich history and literary heritage and stay for the pubs and the craic.

Travel less than 30 minutes from the vibrant centre and you can enjoy an ice cream on the beach or a mountain hike. Divided north and south by the River Liffey, Dublin is largely walkable or there are ample – if busy – public transport options (tram, bus, rail). Public bikes (www.dublinbikes.ie) are also available but, be warned, dedicated cycle lanes are shamefully lacking.

Just northeast of Dublin's main thoroughfare, O'Connell St, you'll hit Parnell St, home to Asian food and pop-up businesses. Leading off it is N Great George's St, as fine an example of Georgian architecture as you'll get in the city centre.

Strolling directly south from St Stephen's Green and crossing the Grand Canal, you'll come to the diverse cross-generational neighbourhood of Rathmines in about 20 minutes. You won't find too many high street chain stores here: it retains a modest, independent and friendly neighbourhood feel.

PARNELL STREET & AROUND

Parnell Street's hinterland has long been one of Dublin's most neglected neighbourhoods but a new luas (tram) stop has coincided with green shoots of new life. Something of a 'Little Asia' with its smattering of eastern eateries, phone shops and supermarkets, emerging young creatives following cheaper rents are helping evolve this exciting district. Coolest neighbourhood list? We said it first.

🎧 The Big Romance
If you remember the joy of listening to a favourite 45 record cover to cover, this atmospheric vinyl-only dive bar may just be your dream nightspot. Down a sublime toastie and pint of craft beer to the rich hi-fi sound of whole albums by Kate Bush, Prince or an eclectic DJ set. *98 Parnell St, Rotunda; http:// thebigromance.ie; from 4pm.*

🍴 Kimchi Hophouse
Dublin's oldest and best-loved Korean and Japanese joint is rightly famed for delicious *kimchi zigae* (stew with pork, tuna or tofu) and sashimi sets at affordable prices. Sip a soju cocktail in the garden. *160/161 Parnell St, Rotunda; http://hophouse.ie; 01-872-8313; noon-7pm.*

☕ Cobalt Café
An enormously atmospheric cafe, gallery and performance space, spread over four ramshackle floors. Catch university jazz, drag open-mic, amateur plays or string quartets in a candlelit upstairs drawing room overlooking one of Dublin's finest Georgian streets. *16 N Great George's St, Rotunda; 01-873-0313; 9.30am-4pm Mon-Fri.*

🏛 Darc Space Gallery
Located in the innovative award-winning 'cigar box' building, this not-for-profit gallery offers a cool space for exhibitions, debate and events related to contemporary architecture. *26 N Great George's St, Rotunda; http://darcspace.ie; 10am-5.30pm Mon-Fri, noon-3pm Sat.*

🍴 Mr Fox
Blustery Parnell Sq would be unlikely to feature if you asked a Dubliner for foodie tips. Yet secreted in a cosy basement lies Mr Fox, serving seasonal produce with a tongue-in-cheek twist. Try the house 'Walnut Whip'. *38 Parnell Sq W; www.mrfox. ie; 01-874-7778; lunch & dinner Tue-Sat.*

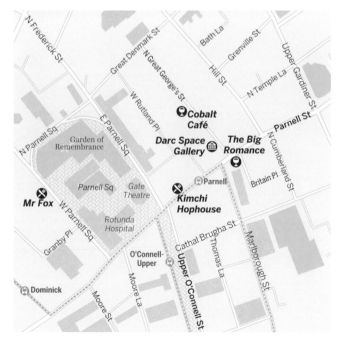

RATHMINES

A long established 'Flatland', Rathmines was always second home to country students and many immigrant workers, thanks to its centrality and abundance of Georgian townhouses converted into cheap bedsits. While rents have undoubtedly risen in recent years, its diversity has remained and with its second-hand shops, independent cafes and family-owned bookshop, the neighbourhood has largely avoided gentrification.

⭐ Stella Cinema
Kick off your evening with a whiskey sour in the beautiful upstairs cocktail bar before nestling in the bosom of this lavishly restored art deco cinema with sumptuous sofa seating, high ceilings and an ornate balcony area. Whether you catch a weekday blockbuster or a weekend brunch with a classic, it's a cinematic experience game-changer. You have been warned. *207-209 Rathmines Rd Lwr; http://stellatheatre.ie; from 5pm Mon-Thu, from 9am Sat & Sun.*

☕ Ernesto's
There's a glorious whiff of Cuba emanating from this super-friendly little cafe and that's without owner and fan of the island, Jonathan, even sparking up a cigar. Come for the Latin music, the welcome, the pink meringues and probably Dublin's best single-origin Central American coffee. Alternatively, catch one of the big-name charity gigs. *15 Rathgar Rd; 087 644 0451; 7am-6pm Mon-Fri, 9am-5pm Sat, 9.30am-5pm Sun.*

☕ Blackbird
A cheap and cheerful makeover has brought board games, tasseled standard lamps, odd vintage furniture and bearded bartenders to this formerly soulless super-pub. The outdoor (craft) beer garden area is thronged with drinkers in summer. *82-84 Rathmines Rd Lwr; 01-559-1940; from 4pm.*

🔒 The Hopsack
Arguably Dublin's, if not Ireland's, oldest and best-loved health food shop, regulars come not only for the natural supplements, raw juice, salad bar and eco-friendly products but for amiable advice from owner Finn and his staff. Look out for shop-based cookery demos and health-themed talks. *Unit 6A, The Swan Centre;*

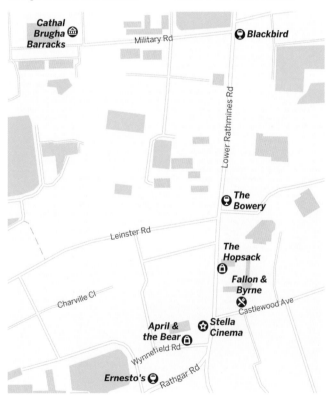

© 2020, Stella Cocktail Club

www.thehopsack.ie; 8.30am-8pm Mon-Wed, 8.30am-9pm Thu & Fri, 9am-7pm Sat, noon-6pm Sun.

✖ Fallon & Byrne

Locals welcomed the opening of this upmarket food hall – Dublin's answer to NYC's Dean & DeLuca – in one of Dublin's dingiest shopping centres, the Swan Centre. Come here for French and local cheeses, fine wines, wood-fired pizza and delicious, reasonably priced mains. Eat at the counter or in the suntrap outside. *39 Castlewood Ave; www.fallonandbyrne.com; 9am-8pm Mon-Thu, 9am-9pm Fri & Sat, 10am-8pm Sun.*

☻ The Bowery

Loosely themed around a pirate ship, this long dark den of fun has timber-decked walls and rum-barrel tables. It plays host to a surprising range of big-name music artists, comedy nights and the odd record fair. Friendly service includes delivery of hot

CATHAL BRUGHA BARRACKS

Tucked away off Rathmines' main drag, this still-working army barracks contains a little-known visitor centre and military archive. Mentioned by Joyce in *Ulysses*, this is where you can see the flag that draped murdered Irish independence leader Michael Collins' coffin, his pistols and other mysterious memorabilia. Reserve tours (10am to 12.30pm, Tuesday and Thursday) in advance at museumtours@defenceforces.ie.

wings (from adjacent restaurant Farmer Browns) to go with your cool beer. *196 Rathmines Rd Lwr; 01-541-4805; from 4pm.*

🔒 April & The Bear

A funky curated homewares and accessories shop on a Rathmines side street, this is the place to find gorgeous stuff you didn't know you needed (but soon fall in love with) like mouse-shaped lamps, art prints, perspex jewellery and cartoon wallpaper. *2 Wynnefield Rd; www.aprilandthebear.com; 10.30am-6pm Wed-Sat.*

Top: sultry Stella Cinema Bottom: Rathmines' swish food hall, Fallon & Byrne

© 2020, Fallon & Byrne

ARTS & CULTURE   **MUSIC & FILM**   **SPORTS & LEISURE**   **EATING**   **DRINKING** 🔒 **SHOPPING**

EDINBURGH

Simply the artiest place on earth during its August arts festival, the wonderfully theatrical city of Edinburgh rewards year-round exploration.

Edinburgh is broadly divided into two parts: a craggy medieval Old Town with skinny cobbled alleys and soaring stairways, and the magisterial Georgian New Town, featuring street after wide street of tall tenements and lofty town houses.

Within the New Town, though, are distinct village-like areas, of which gently bohemian Stockbridge, sitting walkably northwest of the city centre, is one of the most appealing.

North of Stockbridge, maritime Edinburgh comes into vivid focus at the salty suburb of Leith. The Royal Yacht Britannia is the biggest formal draw, as are the excellent seafood restaurants, their elegance a contrast with some grittier old-school pubs in this once sorely rundown area.

Edinburgh has a bike hire scheme, though its hills may test your muscles. Otherwise, hop on a bus to access Stockbridge or Leith, or just stretch your legs and walk your way round this most picturesque of cities.

EDINBURGH

LEITH

The setting for some of the more nefarious goings-on in the film *Trainspotting*, Leith hasn't always had the best reputation. But the area is on the up: you can eat superb seafood, as well as dipping into community events and classes. Take a bus from the centre of Edinburgh down wide Leith Walk, then wander the streets on foot.

🏛 Edinburgh Sculpture Workshop

Housed in a slender modern building tucked into a former railway cutting, the Sculpture Workshop is a hidden hub of artist activity in Leith, exhibiting members' work and running workshops on everything from concrete casting to smoke-fired ceramics. Their seasonal cafe, Milk, overlooks a cycle path and meadow. *21 Hawthornvale; https://edinburghsculpture.org; 9.30am-5pm.*

⭐ Leith Depot

Three musicians got together and created this fantastic community pub and music venue on a red sandstone Leith terrace. Downstairs, nurse a pint and enjoy mostly veggie and pescatarian food in the convivial bar. Upstairs there's live music nearly every night. *138-140 Leith Walk; http://leithdepot.com; noon-midnight.*

❌ Origano Café & Pizzeria

Leith is Edinburgh's version of Little Italy, with some delis and family restaurants dating back to the 1930s. Origano is a more recent iteration, located in a former India rubber mill converted with an eye to industrial chic. All the old standbys are on the menu: bruschetta, antipasti, great pizza and tiramisu. *236 Leith Walk; www.origano-leith.co.uk; 5-10pm Mon-Fri, noon-5pm Sat & Sun.*

🏛 Out of the Blue

To catch a real flavour of the Leith community, head to this beautifully restored 1901 drill hall where there's a fair-trade cafe, monthly flea market, ping-pong nights, dance, drama and acrobatics courses, art exhibitions and pop-up shopping opportunities. One hundred art studios boost the creative vibe. *36 Dalmeny St; www.outoftheblue.org.uk; 10am-5pm Mon-Sat.*

❌ Pitt Market

Street food comes to Leith: at this funky weekly yard market you can chow down on steak, shellfish, pho (noodle soup) and more, as well as listening to buskers and sampling local gins and beers. A vintage milk float dishes up coffees, ice cream and waffles. *125-137 Pitt St; www.thepitt.co.uk; noon-10pm Sat.*

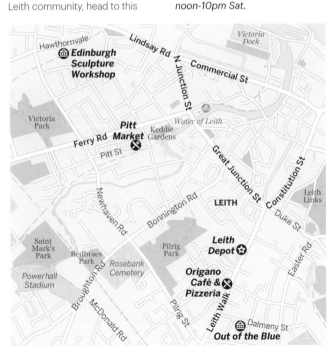

STOCKBRIDGE

To experience local Edinburgh life away from the tartan tat of the Old Town, head to leafy Stockbridge. The terraced 'colony' houses, built as model homes for the working poor, are fascinating for architecture fans, and the area excels in idiosyncratic independent businesses. Explore the streets and lanes on foot, or hop on a bike and cycle along the Water of Leith.

✖ Scran & Scallie

The name means 'food and scallywag', if you were wondering, and the menu uses the Scottish vernacular to introduce fusion concoctions such as Highland wagyu beef burger, and the traditional and slightly scary sheep's *heid* (head) Scotch broth. There's fish pie and fish 'n' chips on offer too, and tartan and tweed furnishings are combined with rustic Scandi decor. *1 Comely Bank; http://scranandscallie.com; noon-midnight Mon-Fri, from 8.30am Sat & Sun.*

✖ Sunday Food Market

Jaunty yellow-and-white awnings top the stalls at this tree-fringed local market, where you can buy artisan breads, local salmon and honey, crepes, Scotch eggs and coffee. There are also some good gifts on offer, such as handmade soaps and jewellery. *Saunders St; www.stockbridgemarket.com; 10am-5pm Sun.*

✪ Water of Leith

Edinburgh's main river is no shopping-trolley clogged horror, but rather a sylvan ribbon through the city, fringed by trees and with views of fine old mill buildings. Six bronze human figures by the artist Anthony Gormley dot the waterway between the Gallery of Modern Art and the sea, and the paths are ideal for walking, cycling and running.

⬢ Annie Smith Jewellery

This Ayrshire/Tel Aviv couple hand-make lovely jewellery in their teal-coloured shop each day. Specialisms include freshwater pearl pieces, small hammered heart pendants, and nature-inspired creations such as their coiled twig ring. *12 Raeburn Pl; www.anniesmith.co.uk; 10am-5pm Mon-Sat, from noon Sun.*

✪ Glenogle Swim Centre

A gorgeously restored Victorian swimming pool, with a galleried

Map of Stockbridge showing: Inverleith Park, Arboretum Pl, Botanic Gardens, Inverleith Tce, Water of Leith, Grange Cricket Ground, Hugh Miller Pl, Colville Pl, Collins Pl, Dunrobin Pl, Bell Pl, Glenogle Rd, Arboretum Ave, Portgower Pl, Glenogle Swim Centre, Edinburgh Academy, Saxe Coburg St, STOCKBRIDGE, Annie Smith Jewellery, St Bernard's Row, Water of Leith, Dean Bank La, Clarence St, Scran & Scallie, Raeburn Pl, Cheyne St, Bedford St, Dean St, Leslie Pl, Deanhaugh St, Smith & Gertrude, Miss Bizio Couture, Golden Hare Books, Kerr St, St Stephen St, St Bernard's Cres, Sunday Food Market

walkway supported by slender cast-iron pillars and light streaming from the partially glassed roof on even the dullest Edinburgh day. There's a sauna and steam room, plus a gym and fitness classes. *Glenogle Rd; www.edinburghleisure.co.uk; 7am-10pm Mon-Fri, 8am-4pm Sat & Sun.*

🔒 Golden Hare Books
An indigo blue shop-front painted with a golden hare announces this vibrant little book store, which sells literary fiction, poetry, a discerning collection of kids' stories and art and design titles. They run a 'low-commitment, high-reward' short-story reading club, as well as film nights, readings, talks and musical events. *68 St Stephen St; www.goldenharebooks.com; 10am-6pm.*

🔒 Miss Bizio Couture
Miss Bizio means business: this idiosyncratic and very personal collection of couture clothes puts the emphasis on quality rather than affordability. The owner has been collecting vintage fashion for 37 years, travelling everywhere from Paris to Tokyo for intriguing

shapes and fabrics. St Stephen St has several other second-hand stores, some geared to budget shoppers. *41 St Stephen St; www.instagram.com/missbiziocouture; 11am-6pm Thu-Tue.*

🎧 Smith & Gertrude
At this elegant little blue-painted place, try a flight, where three wines are paired with hunks of cheese. Vinyl is spun on the turntable, and the long central table makes for a communal feel. *26 Hamilton Pl; www.smithandgertrude.com; 4-11pm Tue-Thu, noon-late Sat & Sun.*

Top: Golden Hare Books
Left: charmingly rustic Scran & Scallie

BOTANIC GARDEN

Immediately north of Stockbridge sits the city's spacious, gracious botanic garden. It's a serious centre of research, hosting over a quarter of a million individual plants. The steamy Victorian glasshouses are well worth a look, plus there's a terrace cafe, skyline views and short courses where you can learn the arts of watercolour, pinhole photography or rustic flower arranging.

ARTS & CULTURE
 MUSIC & FILM
 SPORTS & LEISURE
 EATING
 DRINKING
 SHOPPING

Muswell Hill & Highgate

Stoke Newington

London

Bethnal Green to Mile End

Wapping & Rotherhithe

LONDON

Once ringed by independent villages, London was never content to be contained. Dig down to discover the small-town cores at the centre of the thriving capital.

This ever-expanding modern metropolis has swallowed hamlets whole, meaning the city doesn't have a single soul but several. Northerly Highgate and Muswell Hill are so leafy, their parks so vast and their urban cores so village-like that you might think you somehow ended up in the Cotswolds. Further east, Stoke Newington has seen a resurgence of interest, especially from property developers, but holds on tight to its community-first philosophy.

Towards the River Thames, the space between Bethnal Green and Mile End is still the heart of the old East End, where old school meets the next big thing. The maritime legacy of Wapping and Rotherhithe, straddling the Thames, is second to none in this once almighty seafaring city. The quiet cobbled streets today stand in stark contrast to the previously hectic docklands.

All of these neighbourhoods have stations on the Tube or train network, but internal explorations are most fruitful using your own two feet.

LONDON

MUSWELL HILL & HIGHGATE

The idyllic northern neighbourhoods of Muswell Hill and Highgate may well have tumbled out of a picturesque olde-worlde English storybook, reality given away only by the views of London's modern skyline rising like glassy exclamation points to the south. The heart of Highgate is still called 'the village', evidence enough of its independent attitude.

Parkland Walk

This 4km (2.5-mile) stroll rambles along an abandoned railway line before emerging into Victorian suburbia with views of the distant skyscrapered horizon, and then ducking back into an ancient woodland. The gloriously overgrown tunnels and train platforms are still in situ, now splashed with street art. Start at the top of Muswell Hill or in Highgate Wood. *www.parkland-walk.org.uk.*

Alexandra Palace

This grand Victorian-era 'People's Palace' is the de-facto cultural hub of north London, hosting big-name music gigs, exhibitions and an in-season ice rink and street food market. *Alexandra Palace Way; www.alexandrapalace.com.*

Highgate Cemetery

Stuffed with ivy-choked headstones, shroud-covered urns and solemn statues, this moody Gothic graveyard is the final resting place of Karl Marx, Douglas Adams and George Michael. *Swain's Ln; https://highgatecemetery.org; 10am-5pm Mar-Oct, to 4pm Nov-Feb; East Cemetery £4, West Cemetery (guided tour required, incl East Cemetery) £12.*

The Flask

If you haven't had enough with the otherworldly in Highgate Cemetery, this pub is supposedly haunted by the ghost of a barmaid who hanged herself in the cellar (where you can now sit and sip a pint). *77 Highgate West Hill; www.theflaskhighgate.com; 11.30am-11pm Mon-Sat, noon-10.30pm Sun.*

Hampstead Bathing Ponds

Rain or shine, devoted wild swimmers can be found bobbing in the murky waters of leafy Hampstead Heath's three ponds. Don't be put off by the water's tawny tone: it's routinely tested for quality. *Hampstead Heath; 020 7485 5757; from 7am, closing time varies by season; £2.*

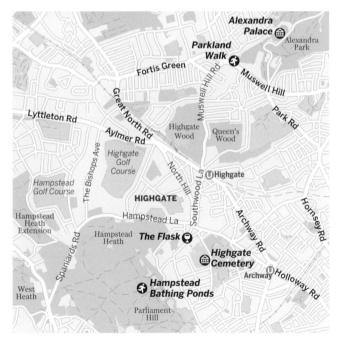

BETHNAL GREEN TO MILE END

Shoreditch gets all the name cred in the global atlas of boho cool, but its boundaries are as blurry as the night out you're sure to have. So it's worth a short saunter east to Bethnal Green and beyond to Mile End, where you can still get a world-class cocktail but it comes garnished with a more authentic slice of London life.

Redchurch Brewery
Housed in a railway arch down a narrow street lined with faceless blue rolldown shutters, Redchurch Brewery guarantees a convivial night out with punters milling amongst beer tanks and brewing equipment, or up on the mezzanine level playing darts or picking out the next vinyl for the record player. Beers are named after local micro-hoods: Bethnal Pale Ale, Old Ford Export, Hoxton Stout. *275-276 Poyser St; www. redchurch.beer; 5pm-midnight Thu & Fri, 2pm-midnight Sat.*

East London Liquor Company
This former glue factory turned distillery really sums up the essence of east London, and it's the first distillery to take up residence in the area – once an epicentre of booze production – in more than 100 years. Copper stills gleam from behind the bar, where cocktail shakers and their masters whip up concoctions from the menu or bespoke to your tastes. *Unit GF1, Bow Wharf; http://eastlondonliquorcompany. com; 5-11pm Tue-Thu, 5pm-midnight Fri, noon-12.30am Sat, noon-11pm Sun.*

Chiringuito
An unhurried Spanish beachside bar might seem like a false promise for distinctly urban and decidedly landlocked Bethnal Green, but that's the vibe that Chiringuito guarantees. In true east London fashion, the building is actually a repurposed public toilet, now with floor-to-ceiling windows to bear it all. Upstairs is a rooftop terrace, especially perfect in summer for watching life hurry on by. *Museum Gardens, Cambridge Heath Rd; www.chiringuito.co.uk; 9am-10pm Mon-Sat, 9am-8pm Sun.*

Map showing: London Fields, Mare St, Victoria Park Rd, Grove Rd, Regent's Canal, Victoria Park, BOW, Hackney Rd, Cambridge Heath, Redchurch Brewery, Old Ford Rd, East London Liquor Company, Satan's Whiskers, Roman Rd, Snap 500m (0.25 miles), Chiringuito, London Buddhist Centre, Bethnal Green Rd, Bethnal Green, E Pellicci, Renegade Winery, Cambridge Heath Rd, BETHNAL GREEN, Bethnal Green, Stepney Green, Mile End Rd

© 2020, East London Liquor Company

🍸 Satan's Whiskers

With its slatted blinds and darkened interior, Satan's Whiskers comes off as something of a mafia hangout from the outside. But enter below the neon sign and let your eyes adjust to the flickering tabletop candlelight, and feel welcomed by a daily-rotating cocktail menu, walls decked out in vintage French posters and fresh taxidermy, and a class hip-hop soundtrack. Give the devil his due. *343 Cambridge Heath Rd; 5pm-midnight.*

🌐 London Buddhist Centre

The real purpose of this ornate repurposed Victorian-era firehouse, on an otherwise nondescript stretch of Bethnal Green Rd, is given away only by the colourful fluttering prayer flags. The London Buddhist Centre brings an authentic side of the Far East to east London, and it's a tranquil space to meditate or set about realigning your chakras. *51 Roman Rd; www.lbc.org.uk; 10am-5pm Mon-Sat.*

KRAY TWINS IN THE EAST END

———————

Two of London's most notorious gangsters, Reggie and Ronnie Kray, ruled the streets of the East End in the 1950s and '60s, racking up a rap sheet like a bar tab – they were even the last prisoners held in the Tower of London. Many of their infamous haunts have been demolished, but one worth visiting for the history and the food is deliciously old-school caff E Pellicci. Opened in 1900, this beloved greasy spoon is still run by the same family.

🍷 Renegade Winery

Hidden behind a second-hand furniture store, Renegade Winery takes up residence on the lesser-known side of Bethnal Green Rd, calling itself east London's first urban winery. It gathers grapes from around Europe before then barreling and fermenting the wine right here in this railway arch. *Arch 12, Gales Gardens; https://renegadelondonwine. com; 5-11.30pm Wed-Fri, 2-11.30pm Sat, 2-11pm Sun.*

🔒 Snap

If you've fallen head over heels in love with east London, adorable Snap is a must-stop for a neighbourhood souvenir. E3, the local postcode, adorns everything from greeting cards to clothing. The ubiquitous silver nitrous oxide canisters usually found out on the street are used to decorate the window displays. *465 Roman Rd; https://snap-store.com; 10.30am-6pm Mon-Fri, 10am-5pm Sat.*

© 2020, Chiringuito

**Top: industrial chic at East London Liquor Company
Left: Spanish flair at Chiringuito**

STOKE NEWINGTON

Magnetic Stoke Newington clings on to its quirky charm, thanks in large part to the fact that most of the area is just slightly too far away from a Tube or train station, sparing it from most of the redevelopment of other nearby trendy east London neighbourhoods. Wonderful community-centric local shops, bars and restaurants crowd Stokey's high street and make this nook feel more like a village than part of the chaotic capital.

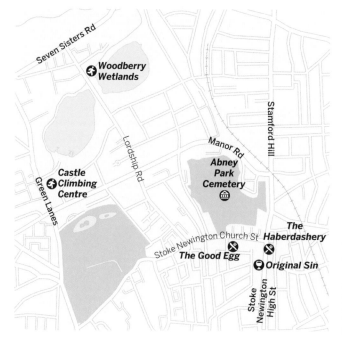

Castle Climbing Centre
Some 450 colour-marked rock climbing routes clamber up the walls inside this elegant former Victorian water pumping station, one of the largest climbing walls in London. Skill levels from total newbie to somewhere near free solo are catered for, and the routes, which can reach up to a vertigo-inducing 12.5m (41ft), are regularly reset. *Green Lanes; www.castle-climbing.co.uk; noon-10pm Mon-Fri, 9am-7pm Sat & Sun; £13.*

Woodberry Wetlands
Built in 1833 but closed to the public until just recently, the reed-lined Woodberry Wetlands were finally opened by celebrated naturalist and world's favourite grandpa David Attenborough. It's a serene habitat for birds, bats and plant life – a happy coexistence, considering the city of nearly 10 million on its doorstep. Walk the southerly path around the reservoir for a quintessentially contrasting London view of cat tails poking out of the reed beds with towering blocks of luxury flats in the background. *Lordship Rd; www.woodberrywetlands.org. uk; free.*

Abney Park Cemetery
A sister cemetery to Highgate, Abney Park is an enchanting urban ruin, where narrow paths meander among woodlands dotted with barely legible headstones. It was the burial ground for dissenters, including influential Presbyterians, Quakers and Baptists, such as Salvation Army founder William Booth. Don't miss the abandoned Gothic chapel; sign up for a guided tour if you want to poke around the interior. *215 Stoke Newington High St; https://abneypark.org; 8am-dusk; free.*

Original Sin
A cocktail den from the master mixologists at Happiness Forgets in Hoxton, named one of the top 50 bars in the world in 2017 and 2018, Original Sin is a brooding basement bar with unsurprisingly top-notch tipples. The drinks

are complex without being complicated and are presented with understated elegance to imbibers sunk deep in the plush booths. *129 Stoke Newington High St; http://originalsin. bar; 6-11pm Sun & Mon, 6pm-midnight Tue & Wed, 6pm-1.30am Thu-Sat.*

✖ The Haberdashery

A Stoke Newington brunch institution, The Haberdashery dishes out endless breakfasts and lunchtime cafe fare as if it were your nan's kitchen: food is infused with love and presented on mismatched vintage plates to hungry diners surrounded by walls covered in immaculate Victorian fireplace tiles. *170 Stoke Newington High St; www.the-haberdashery.com; 020 3643 7123; 9am-5.30pm.*

✖ The Good Egg

Working London's culinary trend

© 2020, The Haberdashery

of the moment – Levantine food meets modern European cuisine – the Good Egg, with its long opening hours, is many things to many people: a family-friendly cafe, a trendy restaurant and the best place in Stoke Newington for brunch. The trick

is that it consistently delivers. Expect queues, especially at the weekend. *93 Stoke Newington Church St; www.thegoodegg. co; 020 7682 2120; 10am-11pm Tue-Sun, 9am-4pm Mon.*

Clockwise from top: irresistible cakes at The Haberdashery; Abney Park Cemetery; Castle Climbing Centre

© DRG Photography / Shutterstock

© pxl.store / Shutterstock

WAPPING & ROTHERHITHE

It's easy to dredge up boatloads of maritime history in these two waterside neighbourhoods sandwiching the River Thames. Current residents are much tamer than the notorious slave traders and drunken sailors of yore: nearly every warehouse has been converted into modern living space after the industrial docks shipped out in the 1970s.

Mayflower

London's oldest Thameside pub, the 16th-century Mayflower is where the eponymous ship set sail for the New World. You can't get closer to the river without going in it: the tidal Thames laps at the shore just below the Mayflower's back terrace. The atmosphere is always cheerful, complemented by an open fire in winter. *117 Rotherhithe St; www. mayflowerpub.co.uk; 11am-11pm Mon-Sat, noon-10.30pm Sun.*

Brunel Museum

On this spot in 1843 was the world's most popular tourist attraction: the first underwater tunnel, brainchild of engineer Marc Isambard Brunel (father of famous engineer Isambard Kingdom Brunel) who suggested it as an alternative to a bridge crossing on the boat-choked Thames. In 2016, the former entrance shaft of the Thames Tunnel became accessible again and now regularly doubles as a live music venue and pop-up bar,

just as it did when it first opened. *Railway Ave; www.brunel-museum.org.uk; 10am-5pm; £6.*

Thames Path

The River Thames is only now recovering from years of pollution. This almost 300km (186 miles) path starts in the bucolic meadows and pristine rural villages of Oxfordshire before wiggling through the centre of London. The section through Wapping (or even better, a small detour through Shad Thames to Rotherhithe on the south side of the river) has the best urban aesthetic: traipse unhurried along cobbled streets, where small-scale old industrial cranes still dangle overhead. *https://tfl.gov.uk/modes/walking/thames-path.*

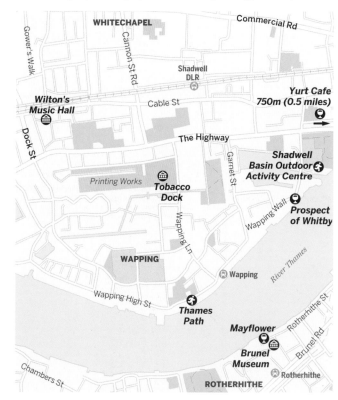

🏛 Tobacco Dock

This huge 19th-century brick vaulted warehouse was once used to store imported tobacco. It was abandoned by the 1980s, when developers tried in vain to transform this area into the 'Covent Garden of the East End' (apparently the ceiling level – equivalent to the height of two bales of tobacco – is too low to be of much use). Although Tobacco Dock still hasn't found another permanent job, it hosts pop-up street food festivals, live music, raves and film screenings. *Tobacco Quay, Wapping Ln; https://tobaccodocklondon.com.*

🏛 Wilton's Music Hall

One of the last surviving Victorian music halls in the world, shabby-chic Wilton's still hosts a wide programme of theatre, opera and comedy shows in a grand space with original cast-iron pillars, crumbling plasterwork, exposed brick and a beautiful carved balcony. The exterior was originally five separate Victorian-era houses. Even if you're not here for a show, get lost in the labyrinthine corridors in search of

GHOSTS OF EXECUTION DOCK

Wapping's foreshore is full of stairways leading directly into the Thames, which are eerily half-visible at high tide. Once busy transferring people and cargo to shore, they are now mostly abandoned, crumbling into the river. Wapping Old Stairs are thought to be the site of Execution Dock where pirates and smugglers received the 'Grace of Wapping' – being tied to a stake and left in the river until the rising tide washed over three times. Captain Kidd, a Scottish sailor turned pirate, met this grisly fate in 1701. A replica gallows can be seen in the river near the Prospect of Whitby pub.

a cocktail. *1 Graces Alley; www. wiltons.org.uk.*

🏊 Shadwell Basin Outdoor Activity Centre

Get down and dirty with this neighbourhood's defining characteristic in the historic Shadwell Basin, one of the few docks in the former Port of London that hasn't been landfilled. Kayaking and sailing are on offer, plus climbing and high ropes for landlubbers. *3-4 Shadwell Pierhead; www.shadwell-basin. co.uk.*

☕ Yurt Cafe

Run by a social enterprise, this welcoming tent has become a permanent neighbourhood fixture and a community staple. By day, freelancers lap up flat whites; evening events range from yoga and poetry readings to 'Philosophy on Tap'. Yurt Cafe has also started a trade school of sorts in which teachers lead classes on a bartering basis. *2 Butcher Row; https://precinct.rfsk.org/2-2/yurt-cafe; 9am-5pm.*

Top: faded grandeur inside storied Wilton's Music Hall Below: sign near Mayflower pub

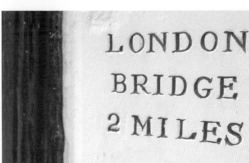

Gràcia

Barcelona

El Born

Barri Gòtic
El Raval

Montjuïc

BARCELONA

Barcelona has it all: modernist architecture, surrealist art, medieval lanes, hills, beaches and an unparalleled dining and bar scene.

BARCELONA

While Barcelona is vast, its key neighbourhoods are supremely walkable and many major attractions are found within an easy stroll of one another.

Barri Gòtic is ideal for those who enjoy getting lost in a medieval maze of streets, as well as a lively bar scene and browsing the city's oldest shops. Across the busy Via Laietana from Barri Gòtic, El Born is similarly good for shopping, wandering and dining, and is closer to Barcelona's most central beaches. Graffiti-decorated El Raval suits budget travellers into art, craft beer and diverse dining. El Raval has a grittier vibe than Barri Gòtic, though the two are separated only by the popular pedestrian boulevard of La Rambla. Family-friendly Gràcia is quieter and less spread out than chic Eixample further south, whereas Montjuïc is a big draw for fresh air fans and art lovers.

To get around, rent a bicycle or ride the efficient metro network.

EL RAVAL

The former red-light district of El Raval has morphed into a grungy, happening neighbourhood, synonymous with street art and skateboarding. MACBA (Museum of Modern Art) is located here, as is La Boqueria market; the narrow streets are dotted with restaurants, independent shops and venerable watering holes. Barri Gòtic, Eixample and El Born are within easy walking distance.

🏛 Reial Acadèmia de Medicina de Cataluña

If you have a passion for medicine or indeed neoclassical architecture, come to the Royal Academy of Medicine. Guided tours let you take in the anatomy lecture hall with its soaring ceiling, huge stained-glass windows, altar-like lectern and the marble table where cadavers used to be dissected. *C del Carme 47; www.ramc.cat; tours 10.30am, 11.30am & 12.30pm Wed & Sat; €8.*

🍷 Bar Marsella

The peeling ceilings, chandeliers and the dimly lit, wood-panelled interior give the impression that the decor hasn't changed since this absinthe bar opened in 1820. Place the lump of sugar on the fork, melt it into your absinthe glass using the water provided and enjoy the slow burn. *C de Sant Pau 65; 6pm-2am Mon-Thu, to 2.30am Fri & Sat.*

❌ Bar Pinotxo

This little counter bar inside La Boqueria market is a must-stop for foodies. It's been feeding locals since 1940 and the charming, bow-tied owner Juanito will point you to the day's specials. These might include *botifarra* (Catalan sausage), chickpeas with pine nuts, and *cap i pota* (veal stew). *Mercat de la Boqueria; https://pinotxobar.com; 6.30am-4pm Mon-Sat.*

✪ Filmoteca de Catalunya

The film archive of Catalonia doubles as Barcelona's best independent cinema. Catch a classic movie, a silent film with a live pianist providing the score, a Pedro Almodóvar flick or a Bollywood film festival. Films are screened in their original language, with Catalan or Spanish subtitles. *C de Savador Seguí 1; www.filmoteca.cat.*

🍷 Boadas Coctelería

Allegedly Barcelona's oldest cocktail bar, Boadas opened its doors in 1933 and past patrons include Hemingway and surrealist artist Joan Miró. The decor is still charmingly retro – all wood-panelled and mirrored – and bow-tied waiters still serve some of the best daiquiris in town. *C del Tallers 1; https://boadascocktails.com; noon-2am Mon-Thu, to 3am Fri & Sat.*

BARRI GÒTIC

The most atmospheric part of Barcelona is a palimpsest of Roman ruins, medieval churches, tiny plazas and contemporary architecture. It's a super-central location, separated from El Raval by the pedestrian boulevard of La Rambla, and an absolute joy to explore on foot. The maze of narrow lanes hides some of Barcelona's oldest shops, as well as bars and cafes.

✖ Can Culleretes

Down a tiny side street, parallel to La Rambla, Can Culleretes has had a long time to perfect its hearty Catalan dishes – after all, the restaurant's been around since 1786 and is Barcelona's oldest. Come here for goose slow-cooked with apples, grilled fresh fish, and pork with prunes and dates. *C d'en Quintana, 5; www.culleretes.com; 93 317 30*

22; 1.30-4pm & 8-10.45pm Tue-Sat, 1.30-4pm Sun.

🏛 Sinagoga Mayor

Discovered by accident in the 1990s, this is believed to be Barcelona's main medieval synagogue and the only one to have survived the late 14th-century pogroms. Of the two rooms, the first is a palimpsest of 13th-century walls, late Roman construction and 15th-century dyeing vats belonging to a family of crypto-Jews. The second chamber is the synagogue itself, its windows facing Jerusalem. *C de Marlet 5; www.sinagogamayor.com; 10.30am-6.30pm Mon-Fri, to 3pm Sun; adult/child €3/free.*

✖ Formatgeria La Seu

Run by a Scottish proprietress, this fragrant cheese shop smells like the feet of God and specialises entirely in rare farmhouse cheeses by small-scale producers from Catalonia and elsewhere in Spain. Come here for cheese and wine tastings, and to sample the cheese ice cream. *C de la Dagueria, 16; 93 412 65 48; www.formatgerialaseu.com; 10am-2pm & 5-8pm Tue-Sat.*

🔒 Herboristeria del Rei

Royalty – including Queen Isabella II – and nobles all shopped at this herb emporium in their time, and the 1857 decor feels like a time warp. Wares include medicinal herbs, perfumed soaps, plus Catalan

Map labels: BARRI GÒTIC · C dels Boters · C dels Capellans · Plaça de la Seu · C de Santa Llúcia · Plaça de Sant Iu · C dels Comtes · Plaça del Rei · Via Laietana · Cerería Subirà · C del Veguer · C de la Palla · C de la Llibreteria · C de Jaume I · CIUTAT VELLA · C del Pi · Plaça de Sant Felip Neri · C de Sant Sever · C del Bisbe · Carillón · Formatgeria La Seu · C de Sant Honorat · Sinagoga Mayor · Plaça de Sant Jaume · C de Marlet · C del Call · C de la Ciutat · C del Petritxol · C dels Banys Nous · Plaça de Sant Josep Oriol · C de la Boqueria · C dels Templers · La Manual Alpargatera · Can Culleretes · C de Ferran · C dels Palau · M Liceu · C d'en Quintana · C de n'Aroles · C de la Lleona · C d'Avinyó · C de Cervantes · Herboristeria del Rei · La Rambla · C del Vidre · C dels Escudellers · EL RAVAL · La Rambla dels Caputxins · Plaça Reial

marmalades and wines. Fun fact: scenes from *Perfume: The Story of a Murderer* were shot here in 2006. *C del Vidre 1; www.herboristeriadelrei.com; 2.30-8.30pm Tue-Thu, 10.30am-8.30pm Fri & Sat.*

© 2020, La Manual Alpargatera

🔒 La Manual Alpargatera

Espadrilles (rope-soled canvas shoes) have a long history, with the earliest prototypes found in the Catalan Pyrenees estimated to be around 4000 years old. This particular espadrille shop dates right back to the early 1940s, just after the Civil War; the shoes are ecologically made and past clients have included the likes of Salvador Dalí. *C d'Avinyó 7; www.lamanualalpargatera. es; 9.30am-1.30pm & 4.30-8pm Mon-Fri, from 10am Sat.*

🏛 Carillón

If you stand by the taxi stand on Plaça de Sant Jaume, you'll

EL CALL

Until the pogrom of 1391, a thriving Jewish community flourished in this corner of Barri Gòtic, among the tiny lanes of del Call, de Sant Honorat, dels Banys Nous and Baixada de Santa Eulàlia. It's still the most characterful part of the neighbourhood, with cafes, antique shops and candlelit bars all waiting to be discovered.

be able to see the 4898kg (771 stone), 49-bell carillon tower that tops the Palau de la Generalitat – the seat of Catalan government. Twice daily on weekdays the Palau's carillonist performs anything from traditional Catalan songs to tunes by the Beatles and U2. *Plaça de Sant Jaume 4; www.gencat.cat/presidencia/ carillo; performances noon & 6pm Mon-Fri.*

🔒 Cerería Subirà

Literally lighting up the lives of Barcelona's citizens for over 250 years, this candle emporium is the city's oldest surviving shop, founded in 1761. Beside the grand, free-standing staircase, framed by statues, holding candles aloft, you'll find dozens of their aromatic wares in all shapes and sizes. *Baixada de la Llibreteria 7; 93 315 26 06; www.cereriasubira.net; 9am-1.30pm & 4-7.30pm Mon-Fri, 9am-1.30pm Sat.*

© Nejron Photo / Shutterstock

Top: racks of shoes at La Manual Alpargatera
Left: exploring historic lanes in Barri Gòtic

MONTJUÏC

A vast hill dotted with many of Barcelona's parks, Montjuïc towers above the port. It's easily walkable to El Raval and Barri Gòtic, connected to Barceloneta via cable car that soars above the marina and is home to some of Barcelona's (and Spain's) best art museums. Accommodation and good dining options are found in Poble Sec, right by Montjuïc's slopes.

BARCELONA

✈ Jardines Mossèn Costa I Llobrera

Tucked away behind Hotel Miramar, this is the prickliest of the city's parks. Walking paths criss-cross this large desert plant garden, which features more than 800 varieties of cacti, including the majestic candelabra, and there are great views of the cruise ship port from here. *Ctra de Miramar; 10am-dusk.*

🏛 Refugi 307

Over 1000 air-raid shelters were constructed in Barcelona during the Spanish Civil War (1936–39). Where Montjuïc's lower slopes meet Poble Sec, the best-preserved of the surviving shelters provided safety to around 2000 people. There were no warning sirens; locals had to distinguish Franco's approaching bombers by sound. *C Nou de la Rambla 169; 93 256 21 22; tours by appointment Mon-Sat, 10.30am Sun (English), 11.30am Sun (Spanish); €3.50.*

🏛 MNAC Dome

Most visitors to MNAC don't know that they can view the striking dome interior for free. Head past the ticket desk and upstairs to the first floor, ease yourself into an armchair and gaze up at the ceiling frescoes by Lluís Plandiura, depicting the glorification of Spain. *Museu Nacional d'Art de Catalunya; www.mnac.es; 10am-8pm Tue-Sat, to 3pm Sun.*

🏛 Cementiri de Montjüic

Notable Barcelonans, including painter Joan Miró and architect Ildefons Cerdà, are seeing out eternity amidst cypress trees and hawthorn. Marble angels stretch their wings above elaborate mausoleums in this city of the dead. Most graves enjoy a sea view. *Mare de Deu de Port 56-58; www.cbsa.cat; 8am-6pm.*

✗ La Font del Gat

Its name taken from a *sardana* (traditional Catalan folk song), this garden restaurant is a favourite with ramblers. Order paella for two, the wallet-friendly *menú del día*, or mains like ravioli with black truffles. *Paseo de Santa Madrona 28; 93 289 04 04; 10am-6pm Tue-Fri, noon-6pm Sat & Sun.*

GRÀCIA

A former village that was eventually absorbed by the city, Gràcia retains a bit of a village feel. Known for Park Güell, Gaudí's outdoor masterpiece, it's a largely residential, walkable neighbourhood popular with young families and arty types, with some decent cafes, restaurants and independent boutiques dotted throughout. It's just north of Eixample and easily reachable by public transport.

🏛 El Turó de les Tres Creus

Visitors to Park Güell often miss one of its less obvious attractions. Head up the steps behind the viewing platform and follow signs to the Turó, a stone tower topped with three tau crosses (which appear elsewhere in Gaudí's work – like on La Sagrada Família) – a wonderful spot for panoramic views.

Park Güell; www.parkguelltickets. com; 10am-sunset.

🏛 Casa Vicens

Unlike the sinuous, flowing forms borrowed from nature that characterise Gaudí's later works, Casa Vicens is all sharp angles and corners, with the front of the building clad in Moorish-style mosaics and metalwork gracing the balconies and windows. *C de les Carolines 22; https://casavicens. org; 10am-8pm; €10.*

✖ Casa Pagès

This friendly neighbourhood institution has been run by Pedro and Albina since 1982 and serves up hearty breakfasts, classic tapas such as *patatas bravas, pimentos de padrón* (fried spicy little peppers), and *botifarra* (Catalan sausage), with a side of local gossip. *C de la Llibertat 19; 93 457 35 45; www.grupopages.es; 9.30am-12.30am Mon-Fri, 11am-1.30am Sat.*

🔒 Carme Trias Modart

An anomaly among Gràcia-based fashion designers who sell their own collections, Carme Trias specialises in custom-made wedding-wear alongside casual streetwear, and her creations are surprisingly affordable. Knee-length dresses are a speciality: check out the 'atlas dress' on display, printed with a globe map. *C d'Astúries 34; www.modart.es; 11am-2pm & 5-8.30pm Mon-Sat.*

🍷 Bodega Marín

Going strong since 1916, this family-run wine shop is packed to the rafters with barrels and bottles from all over Spain, many from Catalonia. Bring an empty wine bottle to fill, like in years past, or stop for a chat, a few *bocadillos* (little sandwiches) and homemade croquettes. *C de Milà i Fontanals, 72; 93 213 30 79; 7.30am-3pm & 5-11pm Mon-Fri, 8am-3pm Sat.*

EL BORN

Home to the Picasso Museum, minutes away from Barri Gòtic, and an easy walk from Barceloneta's beaches, El Born is another wonderfully central, walkable neighbourhood. The art and several offbeat museums aside, El Born's main draws are its multicultural dining scene, shopping and nightlife. Its narrow grid of streets is dotted with boutiques and patisseries, while Pg del Born is lined with bars.

🏛 Museu de Cultures del Món
Just around the corner from the celebrated and popular Museu Picasso, the well-curated Museum of World Cultures displays masks, carvings and artefacts that span the cultures of Oceania, Africa, Asia and the Americas. The shields and totem poles from Papua New Guinea are particularly impressive. *C de Montcada 12; https://* *museuculturesmon.bcn.cat; 10am-7pm Tue-Sat, to 8pm Sun; adult/under 16yr €5/3.50.*

🛍 Llibres i Papers Antics
Knowledgeable proprietor Ignais Solé I Sugranyes presides over this remarkable emporium of Catalunya's vintage posters, the oldest of which dates back to the 1920s. You'll also find ye olde bullfighting posters, and original art by the likes of Tàpies, Dalí and other Catalan surrealists. *C Assaonadors 10; www. llibresipapersantics.com; 4-7pm Mon-Fri.*

💧 Aire de Barcelona
If you come to Barcelona in the bleak midwinter, you'll greatly appreciate a visit to this restored hammam, left behind from eight centuries of Moorish legacy. There's a variety of treatments to choose from, the simplest being a 90-minute steam then soak in the ancient subterranean bath, followed by fresh mint tea. *Pg de Picasso 22; https://beaire.com; 9am-11pm, to midnight Fri & Sat; from €39.*

🏛 La Casa dels Entremesos
Papier-mâché *gegants* (giants) and *capgrossos* (giant heads) carried through the streets during certain feast days, dragons, Sardana dancers and other characters from Catalan mythology and festivals are found at this great repository of all things Catalan. Here you can learn all about the Porróllarg, Seguici de Sant Roc

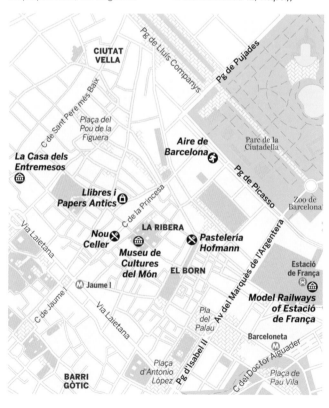

and other important Barcelona festivals; you may even catch some musicians practising for a procession of *gegants*. *Plaza de las Beates 2; www.lacasadelsentremesos.cat; 10am-1pm & 4-7pm Tue-Sat, 11am-2pm Sun; free.*

✖ Pastelería Hofmann

Cream-filled pastry horns, Catalan macarons, gooey brownies and slices of cheesecake topped with fresh berries lure passers-by into this superb Catalan bakery. This is one of several projects of self-taught Michelin-starred chef Mey Hofmann, whose sweet creations are lauded by Ferran Adrià, one of the most celebrated chefs of all time. *C dels Flassaders 44; 93 268 82 21; www.hofmann-bcn.com; 9am-2pm & 3.30-8pm Mon-Sat, 9am-2.30pm Sun.*

✖ Nou Celler

Decked out with antique maps and vintage posters, this heavy

© 2020, Nou Celler

FIRE DEVILS

Several nights a year, *diables de foc* (people dressed as devils) run through the streets of medieval Barcelona to the beat of drum groups, setting off fireworks as they go or carrying fireworks aloft on two-pronged pitchforks. Catch the spectacle of the *correfocs* (fire-runs) in late June in Revetlla Sant Joan and in La Mercè in September.

wooden-beamed restaurant specialises in classic Catalan cuisine with a twist. You'll find seasonal favourites here, such as *calçots* (chargrilled giant spring onions), as well as *botifarra* (Catalan-style sausage) with white beans, chicken with prunes, and a plethora of tapas to share. *C de la Princesa 16; 93 310 47 73; www.nouceller.com; 8am-11.30pm Mon-Fri, 10am-11.30pm Sat.*

🏛 Model Railways of Estació de França

Train aficionados make a beeline for the cellar rooms inside the Estació de França train station. A labour of love by the Associació d'Amics del Ferrocarril de Barcelona, this place lets you run the model locomotives around the tracks. There's also a wealth of vintage railway memorabilia to peruse and a library full of railway books and magazines. *C d'Ocata; www.aafcb.org; 6-9pm Tue, Thu & Fri, 5-9pm Sat.*

**Top: vintage-feel Nou Celler
Left: street life in El Born**

PARIS

Beyond Paris' landmark attractions, the city's history-layered streets are treasure chests of ancient monuments, curiosity-filled museums and ground-breaking creative spaces.

C entral Paris spans just 9.5km (6 miles) north to south and 11km (7 miles) east to west but as Europe's most densely populated city, it's packed with multifaceted neighbourhoods.

In the northern 18e *arrondissement* (city district), the areas north and east of Montmartre contain off-beat cultural centres, tucked-away bars and the vibrant 'Little Africa' quarter. Below here is South Pigalle, 9e, where enchanting mansions house museums, traditional food shops abound, and music scenes thrive. Northeastern, hilly Belleville, centred on the 20e, honours its working-class roots and artists. Bastille, spanning the inner east's 4e, 11e and 12e, has markets, bars and dining. Across the Seine, the Left Bank's Butte aux Cailles, 13e, retains village-like charm.

Easily walkable, it's also quick and cheap to zip around by metro, bus or the shared-bike scheme.

BASTILLE

Spiralling out into the 4e, 11e and 12e arrondissements from Pl de la Bastille (site of the former prison whose storming ignited the French Revolution), this lively neighbourhood has fantastic markets that continually spawn bistros, experimental new restaurants and wine bars in the surrounding streets. They're also perfect for picking up ingredients to picnic in local parks and squares.

❌ Marché d'Aligre
This street market, unusually for Paris, sets up six days a week. A flea market spreads over the neighbouring square. Its greatest asset is the adjacent covered market Marché Beauvau, where aromatic stands sell everything from spit-roasted chickens to shucked oysters and truffle oil. *R d'Aligre; street market 8am-1pm Tue-Sun, covered market 9am-2pm & 4-7.30pm Tue-Sat, 9am-2pm Sun.*

❌ Le Baron Rouge
Blackboards chalked with the day's offerings line the walls of this local institution. Pair its superb all-French wines – by the bottle, glass or carafe direct from the barrel – with cheese and charcuterie platters. *1 R Théophile Roussel; www.lebaronrouge.net; 01 43 43 14 32; 5-10pm Mon, 10am-2pm & 5-10pm Tue-Fri, 10am-10pm Sat, 10am-4pm Sun.*

➕ Jardin du Port de l'Arsenal
On the eastern side of Paris' 230-berth marina Port de l'Arsenal, this fragrant, terraced park has pergolas supporting climbing clematis, wisteria, roses and honeysuckle, garden beds planted with lavender and lawns to sprawl on while overlooking the bobbing boats. *Bd de la Bastille.*

🏛 Pavillon de l'Arsenal
A glorious art nouveau building with wrought-iron girders and a glass roof, where exhibitions span historic through to contemporary Parisian architectural projects (often incorporating scale models). *21 Bd Morland; www.pavillon-arsenal.com; 01 42 76 33 97; 11am-7pm Tue-Sun; free.*

❌ Le Grand Bréguet
An atypically Parisian ultra-contemporary building houses this multipurpose space with local art, furniture and light fittings for sale, an organic grocery and on-site cafe. Neighbouring establishments include organic bakery Ten Belles Bread and hip wine bar Louve. *17 R Bréguet; www.legrandbreguet.com; 09 70 75 54 59; kitchen 8am-9.30pm Mon-Sat, to 5pm Sun, bar to midnight Mon-Wed, to 2am Thu-Sat, to 8pm Sun.*

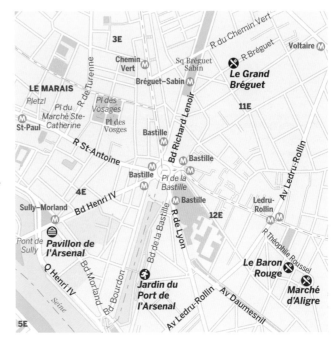

SOUTH PIGALLE

Immediately south of Paris' red windmill-topped cabaret Moulin Rouge in the 9e arrondissement, this gently sloping area was nicknamed 'La Nouvelle Athènes' in the 19th century for the Grecian-influenced townhouses developed on the site of orchards and *guinguettes* (open-air taverns). Vestiges from Pigalle's red light district have been repurposed in this increasingly happening neighbourhood, today often dubbed 'SoPi'.

🏛 Musée de la Vie Romantique

Hidden down a cobbled passageway, green-shuttered Nouvelle Athènes mansion Hôtel Scheffer-Renan was the home and studio of painter Ary Scheffer (1795–1858), hosting salons attended by Delacroix, George Sand, Chopin et al, evoked in the museum's exhibits. Its flowering garden has a delightful tea room. *16 R Chaptal; www. museevieromantique.paris.fr; 10am-6pm Tue-Sun; free.*

🏛 Musée National Gustave Moreau

It might be a national museum – symbolist painter Gustave Moreau bequeathed his home and studio to the French state on his death in 1898 – but this intimate place is an under-visited jewel. Moreau planned the museum to span his oeuvre; masterpieces include *Orpheus at the Tomb of Eurydice* and intricate *Jupiter and Semele*. *14 R de la Rochefoucauld; www. musee-moreau.fr; 10am-12.45pm & 2-5.15pm Mon, Wed & Thu, 10am-5.15pm Fri-Sun; adult/ child €7/free.*

🏛 Phono Museum

A niche museum even by Parisian standards, this wonderful place spans recorded-sound history from 1857 onwards. Crammed with vintage posters and 250 all-working phonographs including gramophones, record players and an art nouveau Pathé juke box playing original records, it also hosts concerts. *53 Bd de Rochechouart, 9e; www. phonomuseum.fr; 10am-6pm Fri & Sun, by appointment 9am-6pm Mon-Thu & Sat; adult/ child €10/5.*

🔒 Balades Sonores

Record store and more Balades Sonores ('Sound Walks') is a lynchpin of the local music scene. Set up by dedicated collectors

ingredients in the open kitchen. *24 R de la Tour d'Auvergne; www.aspic-restaurant.fr; 09 82 49 30 98; 7.30-10.30pm Tue-Sat.*

✈ Playground Duperré

Peering through the blue mesh fence between stately Haussmannian buildings reveals this hyper-coloured rubber basketball court in neon pink, yellow, blue and purple. It was designed by Paris company Ill-Studio for Nike and Stéphane Ashpool, the local basketball-playing founder of streetwear brand Pigalle, whose flagship boutique is at 7 R Henry Monnier. Directly opposite the court, at 17 R Duperré, supercool sportswear is sold at Pigalle Basketball Shop. *22 R Duperré; noon-7pm.*

who started out selling vinyl at the city's markets, it stocks everything from jazz, hip-hop, soul, funk, rap and psychedelia to obscure indie artists along with art and T-shirts. It also stages concerts and has its own micro label. *1-3 Av Trudaine; www.baladessonores.com; noon-8pm Mon-Sat.*

✖ Rue des Martyrs

Locals' favourite place for food shopping is the neighbourhood's north–south spine, R des Martyrs, lined with heady *fromageries* (cheese shops), prize-winning *boulangeries* (bakeries) and *pâtisseries* (pastry shops; some specialising in a single item such as madeleine cakes or choux pastry puffs), wine shops and specialisms like jams and teas.

✖ Aspic

Surprise is the byword at this pocket-sized bistro. Inspired chef Quentin Giroud produces gastronomic no-choice, seven-course menus from premium

COCKTAIL BARS

While red-light venues still exist around Pl Pigalle, many of South Pigalle's former hostess bars and bordellos now house cutting-edge cocktail bars. On R Frochot, 9e, try velvet-draped Lipstick (No 5), free-wheeling Glass (No 7), flaming scorpion bowls at tiki bar Dirty Dick (No 10) or absinthe concoctions at jazz bar Lulu White (No 12).

Clockwise from top left: Moulin Rouge; Rue des Martyrs; Balades Sonores

BUTTE AUX CAILLES

Quaint, car-free streets and charming architecture recall a rural French village, rather than the capital's 13e arrondissement. Lined with local restaurants and bars, the main strip, R de la Butte aux Cailles, comes alive at night. Nearby are enchanting parks, artesian springs and enticing food shops. The neighbourhood is on a little *butte* (hill) named for 16th-century landowner Pierre Caille, who had a vineyard here.

Puits Artésien de la Butte aux Cailles
Bring a bottle to fill with 28°C (82°F) water from the natural, 19th-century spring here, which is high in iron fluorine and low in calcium (its pure, refreshing taste is a vast improvement on Parisian tap water). *Pl Paul Verlaine.*

Piscine de la Butte aux Cailles
The artesian spring led to the 1924 construction of a spectacular vaulted indoor pool and outdoor pools, including a heated Nordic pool. *5 Pl Paul Verlaine adult/child €3.50/2.*

Square de la Montgolfière
This peaceful little square commemorates the world's first manned flight in a hot-air balloon designed by brothers Joseph-Michel and Jacques-Étienne Montgolfier. There are kids' play areas and ping-pong (bring bats and balls). *R du Moulinet.*

Marché Auguste-Blanqui
Stalls at this market, which sets up three times a week, overflow with fresh produce, flowers, kitchen gadgets, handbags, inexpensive clothes and more. To rest your feet, soak up the atmosphere from the terrace tables of retro bistro La Butte aux Piafs at 31 Bd Auguste-Blanqui. *Bd Auguste-Blanqui; 7am-2.30pm Tue-Fri, 7am-3pm Sun.*

Biérocratie
Craft beers from Paris, France and beyond fill this young, fun shop. Look out for cheese-and-beer pairing events with neighbouring *fromagerie* Quatrehomme. *32 R de l'Espérance, 13e; www.bierocratie. com; 11am-8pm Tue & Thu-Sat, 4-8pm Wed.*

Laurent Duchêne
This heavenly *pâtisserie* by Laurent Duchêne, who received the prestigious *Meilleur Ouvrier de France* ('Best Craftsperson of France') title, is lauded for its flaky, buttery croissants. *2 R Wurtz; www.laurentduchene.com; 01 45 65 00 77; 7.30am-8pm Mon-Sat.*

PARIS

AROUND MONTMARTRE

While Montmartre itself, crowned by hilltop basilica Sacré-Cœur and home to Pl du Tertre's portrait artists, is one of Paris' most famous neighbourhoods, there's plenty to explore in the 18e arrondissement away from the tourist crowds, particularly north on the back side of the *butte* (hill), and east in the beating heart of *petite Afrique à Paris* ('little Africa in Paris').

⊗ La REcyclerie
This cultural centre and urban farm occupies a former station of Petite Ceinture steam-train line. Eco workshops and a community garden supply its cafe. *83 Bd Ornano; www.larecyclerie.com; 01 42 57 58 49; 8am-10.30pm Mon-Sat, to 7pm Sun.*

✈ Piscine des Amiraux
This beauty of an art deco pool was built in 1930 by Henri Sauvage (designer of department store La Samaritaine), with original tiling in its changing cabins. *6 R Hermann-Lachapelle; www.paris.fr; adult/child €3.50/2.*

✪ Bab-Ilo
Backstreet bar Bab-Ilo puts on electrifying jazz and blues concerts in its tiny basement (capacity is only around 40 people). *9 R du Baigneur; www.babilo.lautre.net; 6pm-2am.*

☕ Café Lomi
Linger in this airy, bare-boards space, or take a three-hour coffee workshop on filter techniques or latte art. *3ter R Marcadet; www.lomi.paris; 8am-6pm Mon-Fri, 10am-7pm Sat & Sun.*

🔒 Maison Château Rouge
Browse colourful Afro-Parisian fashion by brothers Youssouf and Mamadou Fofana at their label's flagship store. *40 R Myrha; www.maison-chateaurouge.com; 11am-7pm Mon-Sat.*

🍺 Brasserie la Goutte d'Or
This brasserie has an industrial-style tap room and runs informal tours. *28 R de la Goutte d'Or, www.brasserielagouttedor.com; tap room 6pm-midnight Thu & Fri, 2-9pm Sat.*

⊗ Marché Barbès
Powdered *mbongo* (alligator pepper) and baobab pods are among the African specialities sold here. *Bd de la Chapelle; 8am-1pm Wed, 7am-3pm Sat.*

Map of Around Montmartre showing: Bd Ney, Porte de la Chapelle, La REcyclerie, Porte de Clignancourt, 18E, R Championnet, Piscine des Amiraux, R du Poteau, R Ordener, Simplon, Square de Clignancourt, Bd Ornano, R des Poissonniers, R de la Chapelle, Sq Léon Serpollet, Jules Joffrin, Marcadet-Poissonniers, Marx Dormoy, Lamarck-Caulaincourt, R Hermel, Bab-Ilo, Bd Barbès, Café Lomi, R Custine, Maison Château Rouge, R Stéphenson, R Marx Dormoy, Château Rouge, MONTMARTRE, LA GOUTTE D'OR, Sq Louise Michel, 9E, Brasserie la Goutte d'Or, R de la Goutte d'Or, Marché Barbès, Abbesses, Barbès Rochechouart, La Chapelle

BELLEVILLE

Historically an impoverished working class district, Belleville's inexpensive rents attracted artists, craftspeople and immigrants, especially from North Africa and Asia (Paris' second-largest Chinatown is here). Bars and restaurants continue to spring up in its eclectic streets, arrayed on a steep hill in the northeastern 20e arrondissement, extending into the 9e, 11e and 19e – but Belleville still retains its authenticity.

🏛 Ateliers d'Artistes de Belleville

Made up of 250-plus artists and some 130 studios, the Ateliers d'Artistes de Belleville (AAB) promotes both the neighbourhood of Belleville and its artists, mounting around 20 individual and collective exhibitions each year at its gallery (check the online agenda to make sure something's on), and organising the Portes Ouvertes des Ateliers d'Artistes de Belleville over four days in late May, when studios open their doors. *1 R Francis Picabia; www. ateliers-artistes-belleville.fr; approx 2-8pm Thu-Sun during exhibitions; free.*

🏛 Rue Dénoyez

Fans of street art should definitely seek out narrow little R Dénoyez, 20e. Vividly coloured graffiti covers the facades, bollards, planter boxes and more, with impromptu street-art events popping up in summer.

✪ Parc de Belleville

Stunning panoramas of Paris unfurl from the terrace at the top of precipitous Parc de Belleville, which shelters splashing fountains, playgrounds and sports equipment, and a vineyard, the Clos de Belleville, whose 140 vines produce wines sold in October. You'll often see locals practising tai chi on the park's lawns. *Main entrance on R des Couronnes.*

✪ Le Vieux Belleville

Step back into the Paris of yesteryear at this lovable local bar/bistro, where singers perform stirring *chansons* (heartfelt, lyric-driven French songs) by artists such as Édith Piaf – who was born in Belleville in 1915 – accompanied by accordions, typically four times a week. *12 R Envierges; www. le-vieux-belleville.com; bar/bistro 11am-3pm Mon & Wed, 11am-3pm & 8pm-2am Tue, Thu, Fri & Sat, concerts from 8.30pm.*

PARIS

19E

R Botzaris

Cheval D'Or ✪

R Lauzin

R des Dunes

R Pradier

R Clavel

Villa de l'Adour

R Mélingue

R Rébeval

Av Simon Bolivar

Pyrénées Ⓜ

R des Pyrénées

R Rampal

Le 50 – Belleville Brûlerie ✪

R de Belleville

BELLEVILLE

R Julien Lacroix

R Piat

R de Tourtille

R Lesage

Rue Dénoyez 🏛

R Ramponeau

Le Vieux Belleville ✪

R du Transvaal

R Dénoyez

20E

La Cantine de Belleville ✪

R Bisson

11E

Parc de Belleville ✪

R Vilin

R des Couronnes

Bd de Belleville

R de Pali

Ateliers d'Artistes de Belleville 🏛

R Julien Lacroix

Ⓜ Couronnes

R du Pressoir

⊗ La Cantine de Belleville

Head to this neighbourhood hangout at happy hour (5pm to 8.30pm) to catch it in full swing – it can feel like half of Belleville is here. Grunge-style furniture and posters plastering the walls are the backdrop for down-to-earth French classics like *confit de canard* (duck cooked slowly in its own fat) with sautéed potatoes and green salad. Concerts rock its vaulted cellar. *108 Bd de Belleville; www.lacantinebelleville.fr; 01 43 15 99 29; kitchen 10am-10pm, bar to 2am.*

☕ Le 50 – Belleville Brûlerie

Local coffee roaster Belleville Brûlerie supplies discerning cafes across Paris, and in 2019 opened its own cafe. With just 16 seats, 'Le 50' is decked out with timber-panelled walls, a zinc bar and classic round cobalt-blue bistro tables, and also sells bags of beans. *50 R de Belleville; www.cafesbelleville.com; 8am-7pm Wed-Fri, 9am-6pm Sat & Sun.*

INSIDER VISITS

Started as an initiative to provide young Belleville residents with work, utilising their insider knowledge to raise the little-visited district's profile, today Ça Se Visite (www.ca-se-visite.fr) operates in several Parisian neighbourhoods. It runs resident-led walking and *trottinette* (kick-scooter) expeditions. Visits introduce you to artists, shopkeepers and other locals while exploring Belleville's hidden corners.

⊗ Cheval D'Or

Belleville's dining scene received a shot in the arm in 2019 when acclaimed chef Taku Sekine took over a former Chinese dive joint. French-meets-Asian dishes include clams in lemongrass broth, beef and tamarind tartare, and steaming bao buns both savoury (with lacquered pork) or sweet (with *crème pâtissière*) served in a stylish stripped-back, bare-bones dining room. *21 R de la Villette; www.chevaldorparis.com; 7.30-11pm Wed-Sun.*

Top: accordion player
Below and left: Belleville Brûlerie's superb coffees

Noord

Amsterdam

Oost

AMSTERDAM

The tilted houses and glimmering canals from Rembrandt's day mesmerise, while freewheeling art and eating scenes stoke a modern buzz.

C entral Amsterdam looks like it popped out of a storybook: the gabled buildings, the spire-topped churches, the pretty ring of boat-dotted waterways, all from the 17th century. Many visitors stick to this core, which is also where you'll find Van Gogh's giddy paintings (at his eponymous museum) and Rembrandt's enormous *Night Watch* (at the treasure-packed Rijksmuseum) among the city's mega troves.

Venture beyond the centre and things get a bit more covert. Take the Oost (East) neighbourhood that lies, yes, east of downtown. It's prime for poking around multicultural markets and lush parks that are off the tourist grid. Meanwhile Noord (North), just across the river from downtown, rocks with avant-garde cultural centres and ultra-hip cafes. The compact core is easy to cover on foot, and trams hum efficiently to outlying neighbourhoods. Or do it the Dutch way and roll by bicycle; rentals are ubiquitous.

AMSTERDAM

OOST

One of Amsterdam's most culturally diverse neighbourhoods, Oost is gentrifying, but it still has plenty of streets where old Dutch fish shops sit adjacent to Moroccan and Turkish grocers. Gin distilleries tuck away in the woods, restaurants hide in living rooms, and the markets and parks brim with local life. It's about 3km (1.9 miles) from the city centre, accessible by several tram lines.

🅐 Dappermarkt

The 250 stalls of multi-ethnic wares make for a terrific browse. Colourful fabrics flap in the breeze and fragrant kebabs, dried fruit and fried fish beckon the hungry. *Dapperstraat, btwn Mauritskade & Wijttenbachstr; www.dappermarkt.nl; 9am-5pm Mon-Sat.*

🍸 Distilleerderij 't Nieuwe Diep

Housed in a former pumping station, this little distillery materialises amid the trees in Flevopark like something out of a fairytale. Grab a seat on the lakeside patio to sip house-made gins and fruit liqueurs. *Flevopark 13a; www.nwediep.nl; 3-8pm Tue-Sun Apr-Oct, to 6pm Nov-Mar.*

✕ Marits Eetkamer

Chef Marits' vegetarian restaurant nestles in her living room. She has since moved out, but she still uses the cosy space to whip up a set meal that changes monthly: lentil salad, grilled aubergine with candied tomatoes, and bean cassoulet. *Andreas Bonnstraat 34; www.maritseetkamer.nl; 020-776 38 64; 6pm-midnight Thu-Sat.*

🌳 Park Frankendael

Formerly the grounds of a 17th-century estate, Frankendael sports manicured gardens, winding pathways, nesting storks and a historic manor house. Bring a picnic and join the locals. An organic market takes place the last Sunday of each month. *Middenweg 72.*

✪ Studio/K

This staid brick building was once a school, but now it's a cool-cat arts centre. Indie movies, lectures, club nights and a popular terrace for drinks and vegetarian-friendly dishes draw neighbourhood types. *Timorplein 62; www.studio-k.nu; 020-692 04 22; 11am-1am Sun-Thu, to 3am Fri & Sat.*

✕ Roopram Roti

Follow the crowd into this Surinamese cafe and order a traditional roti. Locals swear the flaky flatbread plumped with curried chicken or lamb is the Netherlands' hot-spiced best. *1e Van Swindenstr 4; 2-9pm Tue-Sun.*

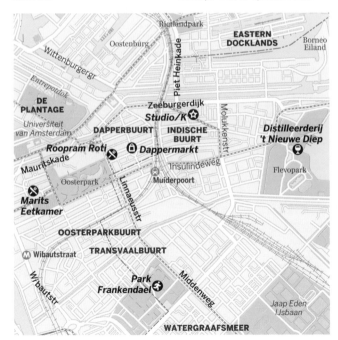

NOORD

A long-neglected industrial area, Noord has been reinvented as a counterculture hot spot full of street art, studios and out-there exhibition halls. It's also the gateway to the field-speckled countryside. Free 24-hour ferries make the quick trip between Central Station, Buiksloterweg, NDSM-werf and IJplein. Once in Noord it's easiest to roam around by bicycle.

🏛 NDSM-werf
Squatters took over NDSM, a former shipbuilding yard, after it fell into disuse, and they did a bang-up job turning it into an edgy arts haven. Today, the area has cool waterside restaurants, striking modernist architecture, a hangar full of art studios and an ex-USSR submarine in the harbour. When we passed through, the world's largest street-art museum

was set to join the action here in late 2019. *NDSM-plein; www.ndsm.nl.*

🏛 Sexyland
A different member takes over each day at this offbeat cultural centre and programs a public event, anything from a masked ball to a pancake party or knitting exhibition. A neon sign atop the graffitied former barracks marks the spot. *Ms van Riemsdijkweg 39; www.sexyland.amsterdam; monthly membership €2.50.*

🍴 Skatecafe
Inside a warehouse of peeling concrete walls, with schoolhouse tables under a disco ball, Skatecafe lets you hone your backside slash at the indoor skating bowl, listen to DJs on weekends or slurp oysters at the cafe. Skate lessons (€10 including board) held a few times per week. *Gedempt Hamerkanaal 42; www.skatecafe.nl; 3-11pm Wed, to 1am Thu, to 3am Fri & Sat.*

✪ Tolhuistuin
Anything goes at this bohemian venue on the banks of the IJ River: art shows in the exhibition hall, club nights in the music hall, live performances on the outdoor garden stage, and there are always drinks to be had on the sunny terrace with water views. *IJpromenade 2; www.tolhuistuin.nl; 11am-late.*

🔒 Neef Louis Design
The shop sprawls through a whopping warehouse where you

AMSTERDAM

can rummage for vintage and designer furniture. Mid-century bookcases, pendant lamps, old filing cabinets, neon signs and the odd horse statue turn up amid the stacks. *Papaverweg 46; www. neeflouis.nl; 10am-6pm.*

⊗ Landmarkt
This food market has an eatery stashed inside that makes a superb halt for a glass of beer or wine, a meaty sandwich on thick-cut bread, or fresh-smoked salmon and asparagus pasta. Greenery surrounds the outdoor patio. *Schellingwouderdijk 339; www.landmarkt.nl; 020-490 43 33; 9am-8pm Mon-Sat, 11am-7pm Sun.*

✈ Nieuwendammerdijk
Seek out this narrow street of wooden houses, some dating from the 16th century when shipbuilders and captains lived here, and time warps you to a bygone era. Nodding flowers and birdsong add to the fetching ambience, as do historic cafes serving bodacious apple tarts.

CYCLING IN NOORD

Noord is ideal for getting your bike on. Places are spread out, there isn't much traffic and there are lots of cycle routes. You can take bikes on the free ferries, or hire one on the Noord side, either through Orangebike (www.orange-bike.nl; Buiksloterweg 5c) or the Donkey Republic bikeshare app (www.donkey.bike).

⊗ Café de Ceuvel
Made entirely out of recycled materials, this kicky riverside hangout offers sustainably sourced snacks and drinks. Think fresh kombucha, elderflower soda and soups made with veggies from the rooftop greenhouse served alongside yoga classes, eco-themed film screenings and other events most evenings. *Korte Papaverweg 4; www.deceuvel. nl; 020-229 62 10; 11am-midnight Tue-Thu & Sun, to 2am Fri & Sat.*

⊗ Waargenoegen
You really have to look for this beatnik cafe. which hides behind a couple of furniture warehouses. Crazy-good toasted cheese sandwiches and milkshakes savoured on the makeshift patio reward all finders. *Papaverweg 46; 10am-4pm Mon-Fri, 9am-5pm Sat, noon-5pm Sun.*

Top: shipyard turned waterside hangout NDSM-werf
Below: herb-flecked cheeses

ROME

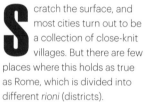

Regola   Monti

Trastevere   Pigneto

Rome

Rome is a city like no other, where modern Romans live in character-packed neighbourhoods amid the astounding remnants of their imperial history.

ROME

S cratch the surface, and most cities turn out to be a collection of close-knit villages. But there are few places where this holds as true as Rome, which is divided into different *rioni* (districts).

Take the bohemian yet chic area of Monti: it's ideal for well-heeled artsy types who like to glimpse the Colosseum at the end of the street. Meanwhile, the central district of Regola nestles next to beautiful Piazza Farnese, central yet under the radar.

Visitors looking to live the picture-perfect, ivy-hung dream should head to the cobbled streets of Trastevere. Locals in this neighbourhood consider themselves the most authentic original Romans. To experience a somewhat grittier atmosphere, head further out to the bohemian area of Pigneto.

Rome's historic centre is a surprisingly walkable destination. To cover longer distances, all you need to get around is the occasional hop on the bus, tram or metro.

MONTI

In ancient Rome, Monti ('mountains') was Suburra, full of brothels and sleaze. In the 19th century there were clashes between the *bulli trasteverini* (Trastevere geezers) and the *monticiani* (Monti dudes). Today, with boutiques, restaurants and bars all tucked into a few streets, artistic Monti is loved as much by tourists as it is by stylish local bohos, but there are still multiple hidden-away hangouts.

❌ Fatamorgana

Piazza Zingari ('of the Roma people') was named in tribute to the Roma killed by the Nazis during WWII. It's Monti's most tranquil spot, an ideal place to sit and eat an ice cream from Fatamorgana, one of the first of Rome's new guard of *gelaterie* (ice cream parlours), championing unusual flavours and the finest ingredients. *Piazza Zingari; www.facebook.com/ fatamorganamonti; 1.30-9.30pm Mon, to 10.30pm Tue-Thu, to 11pm Fri-Sun.*

✈ Piazza della Madonna dei Monti

At the base of one of the Monti's main drags, Via dei Serpenti, this *piazzetta* (little square) centres on a circular fountain, with a cafe to one side and boutiques around the edge. This is Monti's hub, and the perfect spot for coffee or to sit on the steps around the fountain. *Piazza della Madonna dei Monti.*

🏛 Blackmarket

Set slightly out of the way, high-ceilinged Blackmarket has a jumble of vintage leather sofas, and feels like you've wandered into a living room. Even better when there's a singer or live band crammed into an alcove. *Via Panisperna 101; www.blackmarketartgallery.it; 5.30pm-2am.*

🍷 Er Baretto

Although there are plenty of cool-for-cats cafe-bars around Monti, if you want a no-fuss neighbourhood place, go to Baretto. This is where Monti residents swing by for their morning cappuccino, mid-morning espresso shot, or molten hot chocolate (in winter). *Via del Boschetto 132; 7.30am-11pm Mon-Sat, from 8.30am Sun.*

❌ Pizzeria alle Carrette

This is an old-school Monti pizzeria, where the staff and menu have remained unchanged for decades. Start in the traditional way with *fritti* (fried snacks), such as deep-fried courgette flowers or *arancini* (rice balls) and then go on to charred-edge wood-fired pizzas with traditional toppings. *Via della Madonna dei Monti 95; noon-4pm & 6-11pm.*

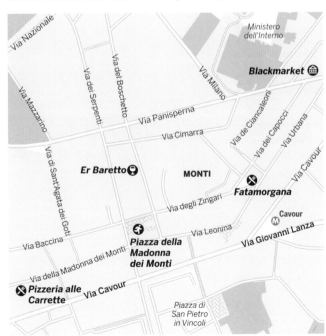

TRASTEVERE

Trastevere's very name is about its otherness, meaning 'across the Tiber (river)'. It's a romantic idyll of 17th-century houses with walls of tangerine, marigold and clay-red, nicely set off by cascades of tangled ivy and flapping washing lines. Such charm has not gone unnoticed, but there are still spots that feel thoroughly local, hidden away from the visiting hordes.

🏛 Gianicolo

Just behind Trastevere rises Janiculum (Gianicolo) Hill. A road winds up to the top, where Garibaldi once repelled an attack by French troops (there's a statue to him on the summit), but you can also cut through via stepped pathways. There's a kiosk on the top where you can have a drink overlooking the vast view, a sea of attractive orange-red rooftops, dotted by island-like domes. *Gianicolo.*

🔓 Porta Portese

As if Ebay spread out over the pavement every Sunday morning, this mish-mash market stretches for kilometres. It cuts a massive swathe from the riverside and the less touristy part of Trastevere, and is thronged with locals in search of a bargain. It originated as a black market after WWII, and still has some items of suspect provenance. *Via Portuense; 8am-2pm Sun.*

✖ Biscottificio Innocenti

Time stands still at this bakery in the Trastevere backstreets. Its white-tiled interior has signs in lettering from another age, the wall clock is from the 1950s, the cakes are weighed on a vintage scale, and the *brutti ma buoni* ('ugly but good') biscuits live up to the name. *Via della Luce 21a; 8am-8pm Mon-Sat, 9.30am-2pm Sun.*

🔓 San Cosimato Market

San Cosimato Market has been on this spot since the early 19th century, and some of its stallholders are descendants of the original vendors. On a large square, fruit and veg piles high, with globe artichokes in spring, and fat, round fennel in the winter. It's a great place to shop… and test your queuing mettle against the neighbourhood *nonni* (grandparents). *Piazza di San Cosimato; 6.30am-2.30pm Mon-Sat.*

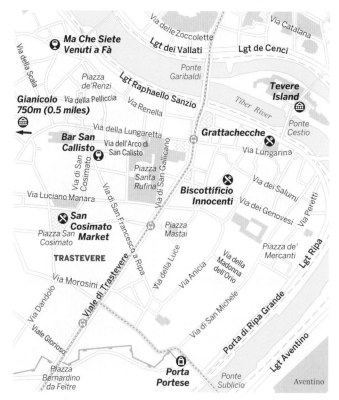

🍷 Bar San Callisto

This bar is forever old Trastevere, where tourists can come and go but the old-timers sipping their *caffè corretto* (with a shot of grappa) and impromptu gigs will endure, amid yellowed walls, metal chairs, tiled floors and piled-up boxes of Peroni. *Piazza di San Calisto 3; 6am-2am Mon-Sat.*

✖ Grattachecche

It gets hot in the Roman summer, and sometimes even a *gelato* won't do the job. To cool down, head riverside where the Ponte Cestio crosses to Tiberina Island. Here there are a few kiosks selling shaved ice topped with fruit and syrup. Best eaten perching on a riverside wall, to finish off an evening. *Lgt degli Anguillara; 9am-3am May-Sep.*

🍷 Ma Che Siete Venuti A Fà

A much-loved, almost pint-sized pub, here the bar is lined by polished pumps serving craft

© River Thompson / Lonely Planet

SACRED ISLAND

———

After an outbreak of plague in 291 BC, the Senate built a temple to Aesculapius, god of healing, on the Tevere River's lone island. During construction, a spring was discovered and the island was thereafter associated with healing. The building that occupies most of the island is still a hospital, Fatebenefratelli, founded by the 'do-good brothers' (a Catholic Order).

beers such as the American Hornet Invasion or English Wot Hop; ask for tastings before you choose. The long name is a Lazio supporters' chant: 'But what did you come here for?' sung to taunt opponents during matches when Lazio are on top. *Via Benedetta 25; www.football-pub.com; 11am-2am.*

Clockwise from top: San Cosimato Market; Ma Che Siete Venuti A Fà; sweeping views from Gianicolo

© duchy / Shutterstock

© JannHuizenga / Getty Images

PIGNETO

The traditional working-class neighbourhood of Pigneto feels like a small, self-contained town, with its low-rise, higgledy-piggledy apartment blocks, flapping with washing. Neo-realist 1960s filmmaker Pasolini set his film about post-war life here; *Accattone* captured its then lawless, outsider atmosphere. In the 2000s, artists and students began to move in and bars and restaurants opened, turning it into one of Rome's most popular nightlife districts, particularly amongst an artsy, guitar-toting crowd.

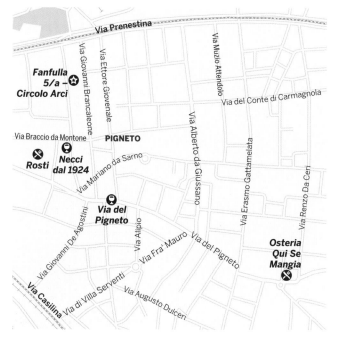

Necci dal 1924
Necci is a neighbourhood icon, having been here long before Pigneto became fashionable. It's tucked away in a residential street, off Via del Pigneto, and was director Pasolini's favourite hangout. Although it's undergone a few makeovers this neighbourhood cafe-bar still has atmosphere, with low-lit tables under mature trees. *Via Fanfulla da Lodi 68; www. necci1924.com; 8am-1am.*

Rosti
With Edison bulbs swaying gently in the trees overhead, Rosti is built in a former mechanics workshop. This leafy place has a 700-sq-m (7535 sq ft) garden, with a sand-gravel floor and spindly metal chairs. There's a popular brunch at weekends. *Via Bartolomeo D'Alviano 65; www.rostialpigneto. it; 5pm-1am.*

Via del Pigneto
Pigneto's pedestrianised thoroughfare is lined by pavement bars and cafes that spill across the street by night. Chairs and tables spread across the street turn it into a nightly party. *Via del Pigneto; market 6am-2pm Mon-Sat, bars around 5pm-1am.*

Fanfulla 5/a – Circolo Arci
A backstreet cultural centre, this classic Pigneto address has an underground feel, a barn-like space with bar, hodge-podge furniture, and a boho clientele sporting directional haircuts. Head here for electro DJs, on-the-up alternative bands and arty happenings: it'll always be interesting. *Via Fanfulla da Lodi 5a; www.fanfulla5a.it; 10am-2am, to 3am Sat & Sun.*

Osteria Qui Se Mangia
There are plenty of good restaurants in Pigneto, but this place has a local, tucked-away feel, a simple *osteria* that's as no-nonsense as its name: 'Here you eat', with classic Roman dishes such as *vignarola* (fried broad beans) and carbonara (pasta with bacon, egg and cheese). *Via del Pigneto, 307a; 1-3pm & 8-11pm Tue-Sat, 1-3pm Sun.*

ROME

REGOLA

Next to the tourist-filled area around Campo de' Fiori, Regola somehow remains quieter and off the beaten track. The district spreads southwest from Piazza Farnese to the bank of the Tiber River. It encompasses one of Rome's most beautiful streets, Via Giulia, laid out by famed Renaissance architect Bramante and adorned by Michelangelo, who built the bridge that frames the street.

❌ Supplizio

This gourmet street-food place proffers *suppli* (deep-fried rice balls) stuffed with mozzarella and traditional fillings; try *burro e acciughe* (butter and anchovies) and *cacio e pepe* (pecorino and black pepper). *Via dei Banchi Vecchi, 143; www.supplizioroma. it/en; 11.30am-10pm Mon-Sat.*

🏛 Oratorio Gonfalone

The 'Oratory of the Banner' was constructed for a local Catholic brotherhood, dating to the 13th century, and handed over to the state in 1890. It's nothing special from outside but step in to see the mind-bendingly ornate interior, decorated by a bevy of 16th-century Mannerist painters,

including Federico Zuccari. The Oratorio, just off lovely Via Giulia, also hosts regular free concerts. *Via del Gonfalone 32/A; www. oratoriogonfalone.eu; 10am-4pm Mon-Fri.*

🏛 Palazzo Farnese

Rome's finest Renaissance building is home to the French Embassy. It harbours frescoed ceilings second only to the Sistine Chapel, frenziedly fabulous artwork by Antonio Carracci. The building was designed by Michelangelo for Alessandro Farnese, of the powerful Farnese family, who later became Pope Paul III. There are regular guided tours; book at least a week ahead. *Piazza Farnese; http://inventerrome.com; tours 3pm, 4pm & 5pm Mon, Wed & Fri.*

🏛 Santa Maria dell'Orazione e Morta

This white-stone church, whose main doorway is topped by carved skulls and an hourglass, was the seat of the brotherhood who were historically responsible for burying Rome's abandoned dead; it's usually closed to visitors. *Via Giulia; closed for restoration.*

❌ Il Goccetto

Regola has become synonymous with Michelin-starred restaurants. However, for some neighbourhood vibe, quality antipasti to graze on, and an astounding range of wines, head to Il Goccetto, dimly lit and lined by wine bottles and local characters. *Piazza Madonna dei Monti; noon-2.30pm Tue-Sat & 6.30pm-midnight Tue-Sun.*

Nørrebro

Copenhagen

Vesterbro

COPENHAGEN

Serene design-maven Copenhagen is built along several waterfronts. Each neighbourhood has its own clearly defined character, be it ethnic enclave or hipsterville.

COPENHAGEN

Most new visitors are surprised to discover that Copenhagen has several central lakes. The district of Nørrebro (literally 'northern bridge') spreads northwest of these. Traditionally a left-wing, working-class area, this is today Copenhagen's most ethnically diverse district, as well as favoured by students and avant-garde businesses taking advantage of the cheaper rents. The plum places to stay are lakeside or in streets leading from the waterfront.

Stretching westwards from Copenhagen's central train station, Vesterbro (literally 'western bridge') is Copenhagen's bad boy made good. As the red-light district, it still has a few lap-dancing bars and sex shops at the station end, but increasingly it's home to Copenhagen's hippest residents, and property prices have rocketed. Its meatpacking district is an enclave of small independent restaurants and bars.

You can walk, bus and boat around Copenhagen, but by far the best way to get around is by bike.

NØRREBRO

Synonymous with left-wing leanings and militant squatters, multicultural Nørrebro began to gentrify in the last decade with an influx of vintage shops, creatives and students. The area has several Michelin-starred restaurants rubbing shoulders with shawarma take-aways. Nørrebro spreads northwest from Peblinge Sø lake, whose banks teem with joggers, cyclists and (in summer) locals sipping beer.

✪ Dronning Louises Bro (Queen Louise's Bridge)

The broad bridge across Peblinge Sø lake, built in 1887, has wide cycle lanes and pavements (so not too much motor traffic). Its benches fill up with impromptu parties on warmer evenings, when locals arrive with beers, wine and even a few sound systems. It's a beautiful spot – and when you look at Copenhagen bar prices, you can appreciate why locals decide to BYO. *Dronning Louises Bro.*

✪ GRØD

You know a neighbourhood is starting to change when a restaurant opens specialising solely in porridge. Locals swing by for vegan or non-vegan cockle-warming portions, with toppings including chestnut puree, apple and toasted almonds. *Jægersborggade 50; 7.30am-9pm Mon-Fri 9am-9pm Sat & Sun.*

✪ Ravnsborggade

Lined by antique dealers and second-hand shops, this street is great for window-shopping and a rummage. You're unlikely to find Danish 20th-century design, but older bargains and bric-à-brac, with paintings, toys and furniture as well as china, military badges and more. *Ravnsborggade; approx 11am-5pm Mon-Sat.*

✪ Nørrebrogade Flea Market

Nørrebro's Flea Market stretches along the mustard-yellow wall of Kierkegaard Cemetery, a narrow space where there's only room for one line of stalls. They're a magpie's fantasy of antiques, jewellery, ceramics, clothes and watches. The cemetery is the final resting place of Hans Christian Anderson as well as its namesake, philosopher Søren Kierkegaard. *Nørrebrogade 90; 7am-3pm Sat Apr-Oct.*

✪ Superkilen

A futuristic park, this piece of urban funk is divided into the Red Square, Black Market and Green Park. They're dotted by objects from all over the world, including a Moroccan fountain, Iraqi playground swings and Brazilian benches. *Mimersgade.*

VESTERBRO

What was once the meat-packing district is now one of the city's favourite evening hangouts. Vesterbro long had the questionable accolade of being Copenhagen's seediest neighbourhood, with residents crammed into 19th-century tenement blocks, and plenty of unsavoury transactions on the streets. A clean-up in the 1990s kick-started its transformation into the hipster 'hood of today, albeit still with rough edges.

Havnebadet Fisketorvet

There are several harbour baths all around Copenhagen, created by cordoning off pools from the waterways. The *havnebadet* (harbour bath) just outside the shopping centre of Fisketorvet is one of the most popular in the city, with separate diving, kids' and lap pools. On hot days they're all buzzing with locals cooling off. *Kalvebod Brygge 55; https:// svoemkbh.kk.dk/havnebade; 10am-6pm mid-May–mid-Sep.*

Bicycle Snake

In a city that lives on two wheels, cycle bridges are its arteries. This one opened in 2014, providing a way across from Dybbølsbro Bridge to Bryggebroen, another bike bridge crossing the harbour, connecting cyclists quickly and easily with Islands Brygge. *Bicycle Bridge; www.dw.dk/cykelslangen-bicycle-snake.*

Kalvebod Wave

The curvaceous Kalvebod Wave on the Vesterbro waterfront is typical of Copenhagen's outside-the-box approach to public spaces. It's populated by kayakers, with a fantastic kayak slide, runners, sunbathers and skaters. There's a Maritime Allotment mussel farm, helping to keep the water clean. Nonetheless, the water quality is variable so it's not a designated harbour bath. *Kalvebod Brygge; www.kobenhavnergron.dk.*

War Pigs Brewpub

Copenhagen's former meat market is the place to go if you want to eat out, with lots of excellent, casual restaurants with trestle tables outside. A local favourite is this metallers' brewpub where beers are craft, chefs are tattooed, and roasted meats are measured by weight and served direct onto the tray (Vikings don't need plates). *Flæsketorvet 25; www.warpigs.dk; 11.30am-midnight.*

Map of Vesterbro area showing: Oehlenschlægersgade, Vesterbros Torv, København Hovedbanegården (Central Station), TIVOLI, Skydebanehaven, Istedgade, Halmtorvet, København Hovedbanegården, Tietgensgade, FREDERIKSBERG, Absalonsgade, KØDBYEN, Bang & Jensen, Istedgade, Fermentoren, Kødbyen (Meatpacking District), War Pigs Brewpub, Sønder Blvd, VESTERBRO, Gødsbanegården, Skelbækgade, Kihoskh, Dybbølsgade, Kalvebod Wave, Ingerslevgade, Dybbølsbro, Vasbygade, Dybbølsbro, Bicycle Snake, Sydhavnen, Havnebadet Fisketorvet

⊗ Bang & Jensen

Once a pharmacy, this *hyggelig* (cosy) space is where you can go to experience the perfection of a Danish neighbourhood cafe-bar. It's a classic Vesterbro hangout, with vintage leather bar stools and chairs, and magazine-beautiful Danes tucking into open sandwiches and (later on) cocktails. *Istedgade 130; www. bangogjensen.dk; 7.30am-noon Mon & Tue, 7.30am-2am Wed-Fri, 10am-2am Sat, 10am-noon Sun.*

⊗ Fermentoren

An unassuming basement bar that you could blink and miss when passing, this is a perpetually busy craft beer haven, the kind of cosy, sitting-room bar where locals like to congregate. There are a few spindly wooden chairs and tables, or you can perch up at the bar to sup on beers such as Arcadian Orchard or Rock the Kezbek. *Halmtorvet; www.fermentoren. com; 3pm-midnight Mon-Wed, 2pm-1am Thu, 2pm-2am Fri & Sat, 2pm-midnight Sun.*

COPENHAGEN'S SHOOTING WALL

Just off Istedgade, there is an incongruous red-brick wall with spiked turrets and arches, looking like the facade of a castle. This is Skydebanehaven, built in 1787 for the Royal Copenhagen Shooting Gallery so that the people of Istedgade, the neighbouring street, would be protected from stray bullets from the shooting range that once existed beyond it.

⊗ Kihoskh

There are lots of 'kiosk' stores around Vesterbro, small grocery stores open late. This, however, is an upmarket version that's a neighbourhood hub, with organic food and some drinks in the most beautifully designed cans you're ever likely to see, with beers from favoured Copenhagen brewery Mikkeller and out-there choices like Pecan Psychosis, pecan and maple imperial stout. *Sønder Bd 53; www. kihoskh.dk; 7am-1am Sun-Thu, 7am-2am Fri & Sat.*

Top: Havnebadet Fisketorvet Below and left: Viking vibes at the War Pigs Brewpub

ARTS & CULTURE   MUSIC & FILM   SPORTS & LEISURE   EATING   DRINKING   SHOPPING

BERLIN

Grown-up yet surging with energy, Berlin is a potpourri of distinct districts riding high on creativity, palpable history and unbridled nightlife.

B erlin is a bon vivant, feasting on the smorgasbord of life, never taking things – or itself – too seriously. To truly connect with the spirit of the German capital, you need to have a poke around its neighbourhoods.

Using public transport, a bike or your own two feet, start your explorations in central Mitte, which is home to both the mother lode of blockbuster sights (Brandenburg Gate, TV Tower and more) and a playground of boho-chic creatives with boutiques, galleries, bars and restaurants to match. North of here, polished Prenzlauer Berg best reveals its charms on a leisurely daytime meander along leafy streets where cafe culture has been elevated to an art form.

South of Mitte, rags-to-riches Kreuzberg flaunts global-village pizzazz and delivers hot-stepping night-time action, although gritty-hip Neukölln across the Landwehr canal is hot on its heels. West of Kreuzberg, mellow Schöneberg hides plenty of offbeat surprises behind its genteel demeanour.

BERLIN

PRENZLAUER BERG

This pretty eastern district was the first to become gentrified after German reunification, quickly morphing from boho-grunge to boho-genteel. It's a delight to explore, especially from midday until the evening when its owner-operated cafes and boutiques are in full swing. Get off at Senefelderplatz, Eberswalder Str or Schönhauser Allee U-Bahn stations and start walking. On Sunday, a hugely popular flea market and karaoke show takes over Mauerpark.

⊕ Stadtbad Oderberger Strasse
Swim in a pool of nostalgia at one of Berlin's most beautifully restored bathing temples. Tucked within the eponymous hotel, it looks like a cathedral filled with water. Do laps while gazing up at the main hall's lofty ceiling, galleries and water-themed sculptures. *Oderberger Str 57; www.hotel-oderberger.berlin/bad; hours vary; pool €6, pool & sauna €15.*

✖ Alain Snack
With its rainbow-hued facade touting organic sausages, Alain Snack may look like your average contempo quick-feed

stop. In reality, though, it's a GDR-era institution famous for still serving *Ketwurst*, the East German equivalent of a hot dog: a ketchup-slathered sausage stuffed into a hollowed-out tubular bun. *Flevopark 13a; www.nwediep.nl; 3-8pm Tue-Sun Apr-Oct, to 6pm Nov-Mar.*

🏛 Platz des 9 November 1989
On 9 November 1989, the first breach of the Berlin Wall was at the humble Bösebrücke border crossing on Bornholmer Str. An outdoor exhibit on the original site documents that night's events next to a short section of the barrier. *Bornholmer Str 70, 24hr.*

✖ Hokey Pokey
The debate over Berlin's best ice cream may have local foodies in a headlock, but Hokey Pokey is a strong contender. People brave rock-star-worthy lines to get their fix of these creamy orbs of goodness in adventurous flavour combos. *Stargarder Str 73; www.hokey-pokey.de; 0176 8010 3080; 1-7pm.*

🔒 Yonkel Ork
Yonkel Ork is everything a gift store should be – fun, happy to see you and brimming with a cornucopia of hand-picked items from stamps to vases, toys to lamps and other knick-knacks sure to delight loved ones of all ages. *Pappelallee 63; www.yonkelork.de; 11am-7pm.*

MITTE

It may be tough to tear yourself away from the trophy sights punctuating Mitte, but those who do adopt a grass-roots approach to sightseeing will be richly rewarded. The labyrinthine lanes and clandestine courtyards of the old Jewish quarter around Hackescher Markt are especially fertile hunting grounds. Even the more buttoned-down Gendarmenmarkt area yields the occasional off-the-radar jewel.

🔒 Sawade

Cocoaphiles from kids to kaisers have kept this exquisite Berlin-founded chocolate emporium in business since 1880. Butter-rum truffles, pistachio-marzipan chocolates or melt-in-your-mouth nougat, each confection is an edible gem, handmade and beautifully displayed in their flagship store in the Hackesche Höfe courtyard ensemble. *Rosenthaler Str 39/40; https://sawade.berlin; 11am-7pm Mon-Sat.*

☕ Father Carpenter

If you've greeted the day with a fuzzy brain, blow away the cobwebs at this courtyard cafe favoured by Mitte creatives and clued-in shoppers. The high-octane java from their own roastery (served in pretty blue cups) and the scrumptious, energy-restoring baked goods and light meals might just do the trick. *Französische Str 33D; http://boulezsaal.de.*

🔒 Jünemann's Pantoffeleck

So old-fashioned they're hip again, Jünemann's grandpa-style house slippers have been keeping feet warm for well over a century. Ensconced in a wee basement on trendy Torstrasse, the family business handcrafts up to 80 pairs a day and hasn't changed designs in decades. The perennial bestseller is the orange-brown plaid model. *Torstr 39; www.pantoffeleck.de; 9am-6pm Mon-Fri.*

✕ Smart Deli

Authentic Japanese food in Berlin is as rare as snow in Tokyo, which is why Smart Deli is such a lucky find. Behind its cartoonish facade, the tiny joint serves up spot-on staples, including steamy noodle soups and brimming rice bowls. The unadon bowl, topped with grilled eel, is a top pick. *Novalisstr 2; www.smartdeli.org; 030-2068 7937; noon-10pm Mon-Fri, noon-6pm Sat.*

Map of Mitte showing streets and points of interest including Bernauer Str, Nordbahnhof, Brunnenstr, Veteranenstr, Wörtherstr, Senefelderplatz, Invalidenstr, Naturkundemuseum, Schokoladen, Smart Deli, Yarok, Torstr, Rosenthaler Platz, Jünemann's Pantoffeleck, Rosa-Luxemburg-Platz, Koppenplatz, Humboldt-Universität zu Berlin, Oranienburger Tor, Oranienburger Str, Weinmeisterstr, Tieranatomisches Theater, Friedrichstr, Oranienburger Str, Sawade, Father Carpenter, Monbijou Park, Spree River, Hackescher Markt, Bahnhof Alexanderplatz, Alexanderplatz, Bahnhof Friedrichstr, Friedrichstr, Grunerstr, Dorotheenstr, Humboldt Universität, Lustgarten, Klosterstr, MITTE, Unter den Linden, Pierre Boulez Saal, Brandenburger Tor, Auswärtiges Amt, Breite Str, Französische Str, Petriplatz, Hausvogteiplatz, MUSEUMSINSEL

BERLIN

© Eddy Galeotti / Shutterstock

⭐ Pierre Boulez Saal

Treat your ears to a concert at this next-gen performance space, conceived by Daniel Barenboim and designed by Frank Gehry. Programming is a mash-up of music from time-tested to experimental, which goes beautifully with the elliptical, modular space where you're never far from the musicians. *Rosenthaler Str 39/40; https://sawade.berlin; 11am-7pm Mon-Sat.*

❌ Yarok

There's no shortage of solid Middle Eastern kitchens in Berlin, but few cover the bandwidth of the region's most famous dishes with such panache as Yarok. It's the perfectly crispy falafel and zingy sauces that urge return visits, but newcomers might go for the generous mixed platter to sample all their tantalising bestsellers. Grab one of the tables on the pavement and tuck in. *Torstr 195; noon-midnight Mon, Tue, Thu & Sat, 2pm-midnight Wed, Fri & Sun.*

STUMBLING BLOCKS

Walking around Berlin, but especially the former Jewish quarter around Hackescher Markt, you'll come across *Stolpersteine* (stumbling blocks) – small brass plaques embedded in the sidewalks, each commemorating an individual persecuted or murdered by the Nazi regime. Part of an art project by Berlin-born artist Gunter Demnig, they are subtle but sombre reminders of this dark period in German history.

🏛 Schokoladen

In times of turbo-gentrification, Schokoladen is a true survivor. A rare vestige of the wild 1990s, the punk ethos culture club in a former chocolate factory still draws a cool and casual crowd with cheap beer, free foosball, charmingly chaotic decor and an eclectic line-up from readings and karaoke to concerts. *Ackerstr 169; www.schokoladen-mitte.de; 7pm-3am or later.*

🏛 Tieranatomisches Theater

Designed by Brandenburg Gate architect Carl Gotthard Langhans in 1790, the Veterinary Anatomy Theatre is a neoclassical masterpiece and the oldest academic building in town. The auditorium where horses and cows were once dissected now showcases exhibits that bridge science and art. Note the animal skulls adorning the sleek facade. *Phillippstr 13, Campus Nord, Haus 3; 2-6pm Tue-Sat.*

Top: street art in Mitte
Left: sleek roastery and cafe Father Carpenter

KREUZBERG

Though not the belle of the Berlin ball, gritty Kreuzberg has blossomed into one of the city's most happening and desirable districts, albeit with a split personality. While Kottbusser Tor and areas east radiate punky-funky party flair, the Bergmannkiez further west is more of a daytime destination with browsing and imbibing focused on Bergmannstr and its side streets.

Kirche might stir up your emotions. The bunker-like former church has been rebooted by the prestigious König Galerie, a prime purveyor of radical concept- and space-based art. *Alexandrinenstr 118-121; www. koeniggalerie.com; 10am-6pm Tue-Sat, noon-6pm Sun.*

✖ Heimweh

Heimweh is German for home sickness, and one bite of their yummy *kumpir* (Turkish-style stuffed potato) may indeed kindle longing for more. Help yourself to tea from the samovar and finish up with a divine tiramisu. *Skalitzer Str 100; www.facebook.com/ heimweh36; noon-10pm.*

🍷 Mampes Neue Heimat

Berlin's oldest liqueur brand (since 1831), Mampe all but disappeared in the 1990s but is now reconquering the capital from its base in an ex-brewery. At their HQ, you can learn about its bizarre David Bowie connection and sample the products, including their trademark Mampe Halb & Halb herb liqueur. *Am Tempelhofer Berg 6; http:// mampe.berlin; 10am-6pm.*

🔒 ManuTeeFaktur

Inspired by his planet-wide travels, charismatic tea alchemist Manu Kumar hand-mixes organic blends like the popular Indian masala chai. Drop by his workshop/store/ teahouse on the Landwehrkanal. *Paul-Lincke-Ufer 44a (2nd courtyard, entrance A); http:// manuteefaktur.com; approx 10am-2pm Mon & Fri, 2-6pm Wed & Thu, call to confirm.*

✖ Kreuzberger Himmel

In this sweet little restaurant, heaven (*Himmel*) smells like cardamom, cumin and chilli. In its kitchen, refugees from Syria, Afghanistan and Iraq bustle about to turn out soulful Syrian dishes – *fatoush* (salad) to *frikeh* (roasted durum wheat with lamb) and *kibbeh* (meatballs) to *kabse*

(a rice dish). *Yorckstr 89; www. kreuzberger-himmel.de; 5pm-midnight Tue-Fri, 10am-midnight Sat & Sun.*

🏛 König Galerie @ St Agnes Kirche

Brutalist architecture – essentially modernism on steroids – is hard to love, but a trip to the St Agnes

SCHÖNEBERG

Thin on touristic headliners, Schöneberg is a leafy, unhurried neighbourhood tailor-made for DIY daytime exploration on foot or bicycle. Potsdamer Str, Goltzstr and Akazienstr and their side streets offer especially rich pickings; it's a pleasure to poke around and soak up the local flavour in their many boutiques and cafes. The main U-Bahn stations are Nollendorfplatz and Lützowstr.

🏛 Museum der Unerhörten Dinge

Small, odd and utterly fascinating, this little private museum displays an incongruous collection of ordinary objects that come with amazing tales. Feel your mind bend at 'petrified ice', a snail that used to live in a dinosaur's stomach, or Goethe's stone rose. Enlightening or an elaborate hoax? You decide. *Crellestr 5-6; www. museumderunerhoertendinge.de; 3-7pm Wed-Fri.*

❌ Da Jia Lee

Don't let the ho-hum setting deter you – Da Jia Lee is tops among Chinese restaurants in town and the only one specialising in northeastern Dongbei cuisine. Drawing upon Russian, Korean and Mongolian influences, it's big on stews, including the Dongbei Pot starring spare ribs, beans and corn fritters. *Goebenstr 23; http:// dajiale-berlin.de; 030-2145 9745; noon-11pm.*

❌ Rocket & Basil

Rocket and Basil are the pets of Sophia and Xenia, German-Iranian sisters who grew up in Australia and now regale curious diners with their next-gen take on Persian cooking: made-with-love salads, soups and dishes like *tahdig* (jewelled rice) and *fesenjan* (pomegranate chicken). *Lützowstr 22; www.rocketandbasil.com; 0176 6176 7945; 9am-5pm Tue-Fri, 10am-4pm Sat & Sun.*

🍷 E & M Leydicke

Feel like you're on the set of neo-noir TV series *Babylon Berlin* at EM Leydicke. which has been pouring potables, including homemade schnapps, for over 150 years. *Mansteinstr 4; www.leydicke.com; 7.30-11pm or later.*

🏛 Pallasseum

If there were an award for Berlin's ugliest building, the Pallasseum would have a shot. Straddling a WWII bunker, the heritage-listed 1970s brutalist apartment building houses 2000 people with a penchant for creatively customised satellite dishes. It stands atop the demolished sports complex where Goebbels gave his 'total war' speech in 1943. *Pallasstr 3; http:// pallasseum-wohnbauten.de.*

NEUKÖLLN

No Berlin district has changed stripes so dramatically as Neukölln, whose northern part catapulted from ghetto-gritty to epicentre of cool in no time, in large part because of a small tsunami of expats and refugees. Zeitgeist-capturing stores, cafes, bars and restaurants now enliven many of its once-drab roads and squares, including Weserstr, Sonnenallee, Schillerplatz and Richardplatz. A cornucopia of discoveries awaits!

Hallmann & Klee

For an intensely satisfying breakfast experience, steer towards Hallmann & Klee in historic Rixdorf, a village in central Neukölln. Only organic ingredients, mostly by local producers, make it into the heavenly savoury or sweet spreads served amid vintage tables and mismatched chairs. Don't skip the fluffy quark with berries, walnuts and plums. *Böhmische Str 13; www.hallmann-klee.de; 030-2393 8186; 9.30am-3pm & 6-9.30pm Wed-Sat, 8.30am-6pm Sun.*

Zosse

Follow a cobbled alleyway to this cosy drinking den in a 19th-century blacksmith shop in historic Rixdorf. Whether cocktails by the wood-burning stove in winter or a cold beer in the summertime garden, Zosse is a chill place to transition from tourist-track frenzy to night-time relaxation. *Richardstr 37; www.facebook.com/ZosseBar; 6pm-midnight Tue-Fri, 4pm-3am Sat, 4-11.45pm Sun.*

Neuzwei

Hop on the slow-fashion train at Neuzwei, a stand-out among the Weserstr vintage boutiques. It's driven by Barbara Molnar, a stickler for quality who wants you looking fab in yesteryear's fashions. She's even designed the wooden furniture showcasing her timelessly beautiful clothes and accessories. *Weserstr 53; www.instagram.com/neuzwei; 1-7pm Tue-Sat.*

Körnerpark

Berliners are experts at upcycling public spaces. Case in point: the Körnerpark, a gravel pit turned enchanting baroque garden. Swing by to meditate by the cascades, sniff the roses, take selfies with cheeky statues, drop by the art gallery, or indulge in coffee and lemon cake in the cute cafe. *Schierker Str 8; www.körnerpark.de.*

BERLIN

✖ B.horn

This rustic-chic neighbourhood bar-restaurant combo feels as comfy as a well-worn glove. Gather your posse, stake out a hand-painted table and watch the kitchen wizards create shareable feasts from pulled mushroom burgers to tasty ribs and octopus. Stomachs sated, linger for out-of-this-world cocktails like the Agnostic Sour. *Flughafenstr 84; www.bhorn.berlin; 11am-2am Tue-Sun Mar-Oct, 5.30-2am Tue-Sat Nov-Feb.*

✪ Wolf Kino

The antidote to binge-streaming, crowdfunded Wolf is a two-screen bastion of international indie cinema in a former brothel. After immersing yourself in an under-the-radar flick, stick around after the credits to linger and philosophise with fellow cineasts in the cute cafe-bar, sometimes with the film-makers in attendance. *Weserstr 59; https://wolfberlin. org; cafe-bar 11am-late.*

HISTORIC RIXDORF

Asphalt road gives way to cobblestones, and turbo-urbanity fades to a quiet hum in Rixdorf, a village founded by protestant Bohemian refugees in 1737. Peel back its charms by kicking off an aimless wander at Richardplatz, the central square, with its old smithy and church, before moving on to the web of tranquil lanes lined by a growing number of cafes and restaurants.

✦ Stadtbad Neukölln

Public pools may not usually inspire a ticket stampede, but then Stadtbad Neukölln is not your average swimming hole. Built in 1914 when Germany was still ruled by a Kaiser, its architecture is indeed fit for royalty. Picture a colonnaded swimming hall guarded by water-spurting walruses, plus a Roman sauna straight out of Pompeii. *Ganghoferstr 3; www. berlinerbaeder.de/baeder/ stadtbad-neukoelln; approx 10am-10.30pm; €5.50.*

✦ Dschungel

In the wicked 'jungle' that is Neukölln, the Dschungel bar is a safe harbour for barflies. Its mixologists pour 'em strong amid fairytale decor of rainforest wallpaper, plants, vines and indoor trees. The dim lighting gives even pasty-faced scenesters a healthy glow. *Friedelstr 12; www.facebook. com/dschungel.berlin; 6pm-3am Sun-Thu, to 5am Fri & Sat.*

Top: leafy Körnerpark
Left: goodies at Hallman & Klee

© Peter Delius / Alamy Stock Photo

© 2020, Hallman & Klee

PRAGUE

Peering beyond Prague's charming Old Town reveals a city high on caffeine and unique cuisine, with amazing historic architecture at every turn.

Beyond majestic Prague Castle and the Old Town's astronomical clock lies the real Prague...and it's nearly devoid of tourists. Masterpieces can be found in Vršovice, Karlín and Vinohrady, spanning art nouveau, baroque and Gothic styles. Strolling is highly recommended in all three districts, allowing you to soak up the beautiful architecture.

Vršovice has become famous for Krymská street, where most of the neighbourhood's attractions can be found. Despite being quite hilly, the district is easily walkable and the tram line running through Vršovice makes it extra easy to get around.

If lazy weekend brunches are your cup of tea, laid-back Karlín is an excellent choice. Karlín's grid-like layout facilitates easy navigation between all its hot spots. Flat terrain also makes the neighbourhood extremely bike-friendly.

Vinohrady's attractions are scattered across the neighbourhood. Its convenient local transport, made up of a metro and several tramlines, means it's straightforward to explore.

VRŠOVICE

Vršovice beckons to football fans, cafe-goers and beer enthusiasts. Krymská, a street that recently received international acclaim for its lively atmosphere, became so popular that its inhabitants had to call on city officials to turn the volume down a notch, forcing bars and pubs to shush after 10pm. Nonetheless, the neighbourhood's character and bustling energy can still be felt.

Café v Lese

Inarguably the most original and alternative cafe on the legendary Krymská, 'Café in the Woods' serves as a local cultural centre. The underground 'cave' hosts concerts many days of the week, and the top floor acts as the cafe and bar area. *Krymská 12; www.cafevlese.cz; 4pm-2am Mon-Sat, to midnight Sun Sep-May, 6pm-2am Mon-Sat, 4pm-midnight Sun Jun-Aug.*

Jam and Co.

Fresh fusion bistro Jam and Co. contrasts with its rough and gritty Krymská surroundings. Relax in a breezy light interior with white exposed brick, enjoying the oft-changing menu of Asian dishes. *Krymská 152/1; www.jamandco.cz; 777 133 616; 11am-11pm.*

Plevel

Vegans, even those on the raw food diet, swear by Plevel. Meals are generously sized and feature vegetarian versions of beloved Czech classics. Their seasonally adjusted menu, including a fair share of gluten-free meals, can be enjoyed within the large-windowed retro venue, complete with grandma-style wallpaper. *Krymská 2; www.restauraceplevel.cz; 273 160 041; 11am-midnight Wed-Sat, to 10pm Sun.*

Xaoxax

Known as Xaoxax, Baobab, or simply Xao, this a unique little gallery-bookstore has a collection of rare finds for lovers of comics, graphics and illustrations in both book and art form. Ideal for anyone who loves the visual arts as much as the comforting feel and smell of books. *Krymská 29; www.xaoxax.cz; 2-7pm Tue-Fri, 11am-5pm Sat.*

Kino Pilotů

This reopened cinema follows in the footsteps of its historical predecessor, which was founded here in 1908. The two film halls, aptly named Luke and Han, are the perfect size for an intimate cinema experience. The ground-floor bar stays lively with cinema-goers stopping in for beer before or after screenings. *Donská 168/19; www.kinopilotu.cz; from 3pm Mon-Fri, from 9am Sat-Sun.*

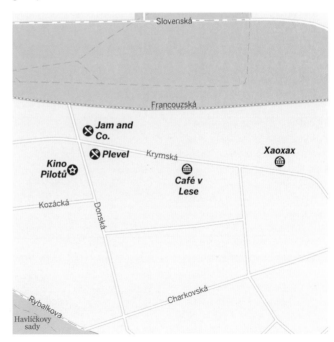

KARLÍN

This neighbourhood east of the Old Town was forced to completely reinvent itself after the damage caused by the 2012 floods, which left it in ruins. In a way, the restorations helped to establish an alternative side of Prague – rough around the edges but much more hip. It's impossible to find the same vibe in the occasionally artificial-feeling city centre; head instead to Karlín, which is liveliest at lunch hours and on weekends.

🏛 Kasárna Karlín

An exceptional space converted from former army barracks, Kasárna is host to concerts, a summer cinema, exhibitions and workshops. Since the space features a large sand pit, parents like to bring their children to play while they sip on cappuccinos. In summer, there's beach volleyball. *Prvního pluku 20/2; www. kasarnakarlin.cz; 1-11.30pm Mon-Fri, 10am-11.30pm Sat-Sun.*

✖ Lokál Hamburk

High-quality chain Lokál is a Czech classic in a modern coat. The Pilsner can be customised into a glass of half-beer half-foam (*šnyt*) or pure foam (*mlíko*). Any meal here is a safe bet but locals crave the fried cheese or beef sirloin (*svíčková*) and you'll have no regrets ordering a dessert like *větrník* (caramel-flavoured profiterole) or *rakvička* (crunchy, whipped cream-topped 'little coffin'). Take your beer to the park at Karlínské náměstí Square, everyone does it. *Sokolovská 55; www.lokal-hamburk.ambi.cz; 22 310 361; 11am-11.30pm Mon-Thu,*

11am-12.30am Fri, 11.30am-12.30pm Sat, 11.30am-11pm Sun.

🍺 Dva Kohouti

A microbrewery located right at the heart of Karlín, this recent addition to local drinking scene has quickly gained popularity. Hidden in a courtyard wedged between Lokál and Antonínovo pekařství, the outdoor space attracts food trucks, too. *Sokolovská 81/55; www. dvakohouti.cz; 4pm-2am Mon-Fri, noon-2am Sat, noon-10pm Sun.*

✖ Můj Šálek Kávy

The main coffee hub for any self-respecting hipster in Karlín. From coffee provided by the local Doubleshot roaster to scrumptious breakfast, 'My cup of coffee' never disappoints.

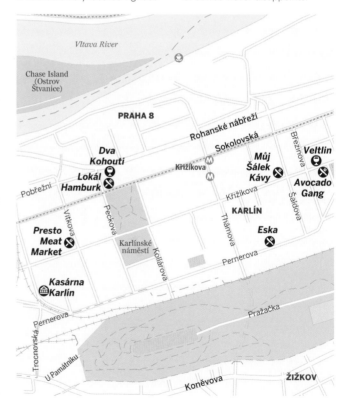

PRAGUE

© 2020, Dva Kohouti

In summer the whole area bustles with energy as people spontaneously form a lively crowd around the cafe. *Křižíkova 105; www.mujsalekkavy.cz; 725 556 944; 9am-10pm Mon-Sat, 10am-6pm Sun.*

⊗ Eska

Eska resurrects older methods of cooking, but it's one of Prague's most original restaurants. An ever-changing menu of inventive Czech cuisine is offered in this extraordinary space, where an open kitchen takes centre stage. The ground floor is an excellent place to watch the action and grab a quick bite. Alternatively, enjoy a full-blown meal in the spacious room upstairs. *Pernerova 49; www.eska.ambi.cz; 731 140 884; 8am-11.30pm Mon-Fri, 9am-11.30pm Sat-Sun.*

⊕ Veltlin

Veltlin specialises in authentic wines of the former Habsburg Empire. There is no wine list; instead, wine connoisseurs and amateurs alike are advised according to their current wine cravings. *Křižíkova 488/115; www.veltlin.cz; 5-11pm Mon-Sat.*

PRAGUE 7 FERRY 'HOL KA'

A small, wheelchair-friendly boat crosses the river over to the Holešovice district, stopping on the way at the Štvanice Island. The ferry operates from April to October, depending on weather conditions, and runs in 15-30 minute intervals. See schedules on www.paroplavba.cz/privozp7.

⊗ Presto Meat Market

Meat eaters swear by Presto, essentially a butcher's shop with a few tables. This place fills quickly at lunch – almost year-round the overflow of diners is squeezed into a tiny plastic tent outside Presto's door. *Vítkova 197/11; www.meat-market.cz; 732 326 666; 8-10.30am & 11am-3pm Mon-Fri.*

⊗ Avocado Gang

A rather new addition to the neighbourhood, Avocado Gang quickly gained locals' affection with their menu showcasing all things avocado. It's fun to share the long colourful table with everyone else, eat an 'avo-treat' and be merry. *Křižíkova 72; www.avocadogang.cz; 222 963 044; 8am-6pm Mon-Fri, 9am-8pm Sat.*

**Top: local brews at Dva Kohouti
Below: laid-back and convivial Avocado Gang**

© 2020, Avocado Gang

VINOHRADY

Stretching between lively Peace Sq (Náměstí míru) and George of Poděbrady Sq (Náměstí Jiřího z Poděbrad), the green district of Vinohrady offers Prague's richest array of flavours. Long beloved by Prague's early expats, Vinohrady prides itself on a wide range of cafes, international cuisine and stunning architecture covering styles from Gothic to art nouveau.

⊗ IF Café

Founded by one of Prague's most notable confectioners, this cafe offers everything a sweet-toothed patron could desire. Enjoy a long brunch, short coffee break or light meal while sitting elbow-to-elbow with other sugar-loving folks. *Tylovo Nám. 2; www.ifcafe.cz; 608 773 399; 8am-8pm.*

🔒 Moment

Shop for authentic, chic and affordable garments while helping others. Moment is a tiny chain of charitable second-hand shops with well-crafted collections. *Francouzská 592/7; www. moment-ops.cz; 10am-7pm Mon-Fri, 11am-5pm Sat.*

⊗ Cafefin

This first indicator of the rise of quality Vietnamese cafes in Prague, Cafefin often sees queues forming outside the door. *Bun bo nam bo* (noodles with beef), *banh mi* (baguette sandwiches) and more are served with immense visual appeal. *Nám Jiřího z Poděbrad 4; www.cafefinvpraze. com; 8am-9pm Mon-Sat, 10am-7.30pm Sun.*

⊗ Momoichi

A corner of Japan in the middle of Prague, complete with high-tech Japanese toilets, a bright interior with large windows and the Totoro mascot. The food is a hodge-podge of cuisines from hummus to dried salmon omelettes. Splurging on all things matcha, including cakes, comes highly recommended. *Římská 35; www. momoichi.cz; 721 364 002; 11am-10pm Tue-Fri, 10am-10pm Sat, 10am-6pm Sun.*

⊗ Bon Ramen

Locals and foreigners alike happily slurp *tonkotsu*, miso or *shoyu* ramen inside Bon, perhaps the most delicious and wallet-friendly spot brought about by Prague's recent ramen revolution. Those

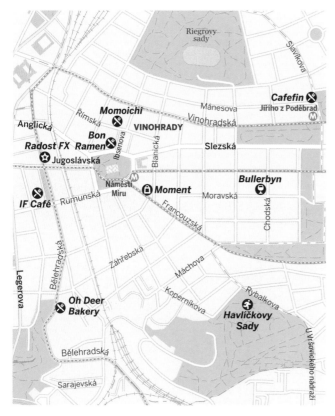

feeling adventurous can order a seemingly 'levitating' soba noodle dish. *Ibsenova 1234/1; www.bonprague.cz; 773 903 288; 11am-2.30pm & 5-9pm Tue-Sat, 11.30am-8.30pm Sun.*

🍺 Bullerbyn

A cafe and bistro by day, a bar by night. Serving bowls of fluffy popcorn is just one reason why Bullerbyn quickly acquired a loyal following. Details matter – shots are drunk from antique glasses, while the ladies' and gents' toilets are signposted with the names of characters created by Astrid Lindgren. *Chodská 1123/17; www.bullerbyn.cz; 11am-1am.*

❌ Oh Deer Bakery

This low-key bakery specialises in a Czech version of the 'cronut' (a hybrid croissant-donut), referred to by locals as a *crobliha*. These delicacies sell out every day, so it's best to arrive before noon. *Bělehradská 62; www.ohdeerbakery.cz; 731 224 898; 8am-5pm Mon-Fri, 9am-2pm Sat.*

© Fabiano Waewell / Shutterstock

PRAGUE'S PARK FOR WINE LOVERS

Havlíckovy Sady Park spreads from the upper slopes of Vinohrady down into Vršovice district. Start at the upper area's man-made grotto and Neptune fountain, continuing to the viewpoint at the Gröbe Villa. Next, stroll to the wooden gazebo lookout to enjoy some wine while gazing over the vineyards. It's open from 6am to 10pm, or to midnight from April to October.

✨ Radost FX

Vinohrady's most established music club sees a local crowd dance the night away to the rhythms of urban music (Thursday and Saturday) and EDM (Friday). Rihanna even filmed the video for 'Don't Stop the Music' right here in the club. *Bělehradská 234/120; www.radostfx.cz; 11pm-5am Thu-Sat.*

Clockwise from top: golden hour on Náměsti míru; Oh Deer Bakery; enjoying some Czech beer

© franticOO / Shutterstock

© 2020, Oh Deer Bakery

STOCKHOLM

Set on 14 islands, Stockholm has a close connection with nature and the sea, and intensely picturesque neighbourhoods that are always evolving.

The city of Stockholm began on the little island known as Gamla Stan (Old Town) way back in the 13th century. With its colourful gabled buildings and narrow alleyways, it is an inevitable visitor honeypot. But residents succeed in keeping the soul of the place intact: take your time and you can track down some of their favourite shops and spots.

Take a short walk south over a bridge and you'll arrive at to the much larger island of Södermalm, where Stockholm comes to play in summer: it's great for a picnic, a swim or a cycle round the lush parks. If you're in Stockholm to party, this is the spot: the bars, cafes and vintage stores are the coolest in the city.

When it comes to getting around, eco-minded travellers can make use of the city's very good bike scheme. Otherwise, efficient Stockholm also has the clean and speedy Tunnelbana, the city's art-bedecked underground network.

GAMLA STAN

This wonderfully attractive urban island is the historic heart of Stockholm, as well as the geographical centre of the city. Knock-out sights include the ancient cathedral, Storkyrkan, with its flamboyant statue of St George hacking the dragon, and the inspirational Nobel Museum. Stroll this compact and walkable district to discover some quirky shops and places to eat.

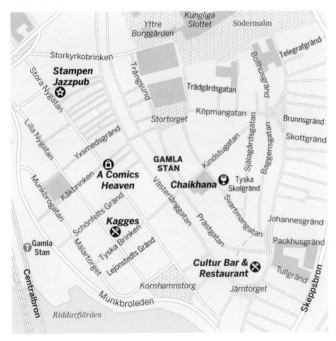

find manga, sci-fi and serial novels. *Stora Nygatan 23; www. comicsheaven.se; 11am-5pm.*

Chaikhana
Named for the teahouses dotted along the ancient Silk Road, Chaikhana serves teas from India, Africa and the Far East alongside scones and cakes. Purchase bags of your favourite brew or choose from their array of tea-making paraphernalia. Twice a month Chaikhana run tutored tea tastings. *Svartmangatan 23; www. chaikhana.se; 11am-6pm Tue-Sat.*

Stampen Jazzpub
Stampen Jazzpub has been trying to shake up Gamla Stan since 1968, when this old pawn shop was turned into a music venue. The antiques and oddments hanging from the ceiling are left over from its former incarnation. There's live jazz six nights a week – Dexter Gordon, Eartha Kitt and Dizzy Gillespie have all played at this legendary jazz hot spot. *Stora Nygatan 5; www.stampen.se; 5pm-late Tue-Sun, from 2pm Sat.*

Cultur Bar & Restaurant
With its Moroccan tiled floor, charcoal walls and long marble bar, Cultur favours an elegant contemporary feel. Scandi tapas is on the menu, and there's a good wine and cocktail list. On warmer days you can sit outside the terracotta-coloured building and watch passers-by on the cobbled street. *Österlånggatan 34; http:// culturbar.se; 11.30am-late Mon-Fri, from 1pm Sat.*

Kagges
This small but ambitious rustic restaurant was set up by two young chefs and serves New Nordic cuisine: small plates might consist of smoked cabbage with trout roe, or salmon with dill mayo. Order three to four dishes each to mix, match and share, and finish off with lingonberry dessert or whatever

other seasonal sweet they have concocted. *Lilla Nygatan 21; www. kagges.com; 5-11pm Wed-Sun.*

A Comics Heaven
An unexpected find in this sedate part of town, A Comics Heaven focuses mostly on modern American publications, though alongside Marvel you'll also

SÖDERMALM

If unshowy Stockholm has a hipster heart then this is it: Södermalm is known for its second-hand stores, cool cafes and bars, and for its complex of summer swimming pools. It is one of the larger of the city's 14 islands, and the nicest way to travel around its parks and attractions is by bike.

🔒 Hornstulls Marknad
Hornstulls Marknad is a waterfront flea market that makes a lovely weekend hangout from April to September, with stalls selling antiques, vintage clothes, gifts, fine foods and more. There are also some street food vendors. *Hornstulls strand 4; www. hornstullsmarknad.se; 11am-5pm Sat & Sun.*

🔒 Emmaus Stockholm
A large charity store supporting humanitarian work in the Western Sahara and Angola, Emmaus is also a great place to bag yourself a bit of Swedish chic. There are vintage clothes for men and women, plus a great array of crockery and bric-a-brac. *Peter Myndes backe 8; http:// emmausstockholm.se; 10.30am-7pm Mon, Tue, Thu & Fri, 1-4pm Sat & Sun.*

🔅 Eriksdalsbadet
This complex of indoor and outdoor pools (including two 50m pools) is a great hangout for Stockholmers. There's a learning pool, a diving tower and a water park for kids (under fours get into Eriksdalsbadet for free).

Bring a picnic or eat at their cafe. *Hammarby Slussväg 20; www. stockholm.se/eriksdalsbadet; 6am-9pm Mon-Fri, 8am-6pm Sat & Sun.*

🏛 Fotografiska
Fans of contemporary art photography should make a beeline for this new harbourfront exhibition space, which also houses an award-winning seasonal restaurant and a top-floor cafe with sweeping sea views. *Stadsgårdshamnen 22; www. fotografiska.com/sto; 9am-11pm Sun-Wed, 9am-11pm Thu-Sat.*

❌ Hermans
This bountiful veggie restaurant is a firm local favourite, with boho decor and a terraced garden with harbour views. Their buffet is an all-you-can-eat affair, showcasing tastes and recipes from all over the world: there are soups, curries, stews and more salad variations than you can believe. Hermans is also something of a community hub, with an events noticeboard and sociable communal tables. *Fjällgatan 23B; http://hermans.se/ en; 11am-10pm.*

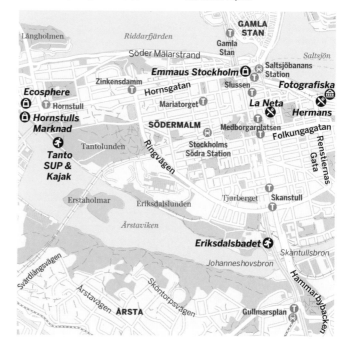

🔒 Ecosphere

Beautiful and ethical garb for men and women, made from sustainable materials and under good working conditions. Low-key elegance is the theme, from dainty jewellery to well-cut jumpsuits, shirts and Capri pants, and minimal but stylish accessories. *Bergsunds strand 32; http:// ecosphere.se; noon-6pm.*

🧭 Tanto SUP & Kajak

From June to August, rent a paddleboard or kayak and take to the calm waters around Södermalm. Visitors can embark on two-hour weekend kayaking tours with a guide, which take in the neighbouring island of Långholmen (which housed an infamous prison till 1974), as well as smaller Reimersholme. *Tantolunden; http://tantosok.se; 10am-6pm Fri-Sun.*

❌ La Neta

This is one of a small chain of funky and surprisingly authentic Mexican *taquerías* in Stockholm. The name roughly – and appropriately – translates to 'the real deal'. Seating is at long trestle tables and there's no waiter service: you pile your own plate with quesadillas and tacos. The decor is minimal with cool concrete, and bright coloured metal chairs add a dash of colour. The food is affordable, fresh and delicious. *Östgötagatan 12B; www. laneta.se; 11am-9pm Mon-Fri, noon-10pm Sat, noon-4pm Sun.*

MIDSUMMER MADNESS

Midsummer night in Sweden is celebrated with enthusiasm bordering on mania. Locals quit Stockholm en masse and head to the countryside, to wear flower garlands and do a curious jumping frog dance around a newly raised maypole. Pickled herring with new potatoes and sumptuous strawberry cake are knocked back with large quantities of cold beer and schnapps.

**Top: Ecosphere's ethical garb
Below: Södermalm's sparkling waterfront**

ARTS & CULTURE   MUSIC & FILM   SPORTS & LEISURE   EATING   DRINKING   SHOPPING

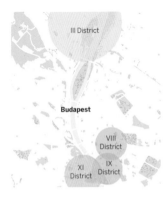

BUDAPEST

Some say Budapest is a city of pleasure, but plunge deeper and you'll discover artistic treasures and poignant stories threaded into the city's fabric.

BUDAPEST

It's easy to skim Budapest's surface with a visit to the Royal Palace, a dip in the Széchenyi Baths or a drink at Szimpla, but put your explorer shoes on and discover the city's lesser-known quarters.

Start by leaving the Jewish Quarter and take the crossing over Rákóczi út due west. Lose yourself in the shaded streets of the VIII District, lined with flaking palatial apartments and bohemian bars.

You can then continue over to the former industrial IX District perched on the river, and explore alternative cultural institutions and craft beer bars.

Take the bridge across the river to the XI District for literary cafes and private art galleries, or board the tram heading northwards to Óbuda (the III District), the city's oldest part.

Budapest is easily walkable, but you can venture into outlying neighbourhoods by tram, bus, metro or even boat.

IX DISTRICT

In the southern part of Pest, the IX is a former industrial area once busy with Danube-side warehouses, factories and docks. Its most famous landmark is the Central Market Hall, once part of this system as it used to have a canal where goods were delivered. Today, it's a rehabilitated area rich in cultural spaces, craft beer bars and parks.

🍷 Zwack Unicum Museum
Try the national bitters made from a guarded family recipe and a secret cocktail of 40 herbs and spices straight from the barrel. Descend into the cellars to learn all about Unicum, before exploring the museum charting the drink's history and the story of the Zwack family, as well as Europe's largest collection of miniature alcohol bottles. *Dandár u 1; http://unicum.hu/museum; 10am-5pm; 2400Ft.*

🍺 Élesztő
Grab a beer at this former glass factory, a ruin bar with 21 Hungarian craft beers on tap. Locals pack the tables inside and the benches in the industrial courtyard. Come Sunday morning for the farmers market. *Tűzoltó u 22; http://elesztohaz. hu; 3pm-3am.*

♨ Dandár Baths
If you're on a budget, take a dip at this forgotten thermal bath. Built in the 1930s, this small, no-frills bathhouse is popular with elderly locals and you won't hear English spoken. *Dandár u 7; http://dandarfurdo.hu; 6am-9pm* Mon-Fri, 8am-9pm Sat-Sun; 2000Ft.

🏛 Ziggurat
In the Millennial Cultural Quarter, this strange-looking complex is home to the Palace of Arts, the National Theatre and the Leopold Museum. The curiosity is named after the structures (ziggurats) built in ancient Mesopotamia, and functions as an art gallery that occasionally hosts temporary exhibitions. Stroll up the spiralling walkway to the top for fantastic views overlooking the river and the cultural complex's modern architecture. *Komor Marcell u 1.*

🏛 Trafó
Inside a former electric transformer building dating back to 1909, this avant-garde theatre stages productions ranging from modern dance to interpretative theatre, or new-wave circuses with a socio-political twist. Don't be surprised if you see naked people covered in glitter on stage, or if you come away with challenging ideas. *Liliom u 41; http://trafo.hu.*

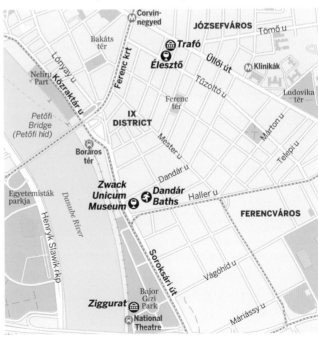

VIII DISTRICT

Many only dip into the VIII District for a visit to the Hungarian National Museum, but if you go further in, you'll find yourself among dilapidated palatial buildings, hidden parks, squares and quirky bars. Just across from the Jewish Quarter and Inner City, the VIII District is home to a large Roma community, artists, bohemians and social activists.

⭐ Urania Cinema

This gorgeous cinema is like an Indian palace fused with an opera house. Art-house films dominate the programme, with a diverse range of films screened in English or with subtitles. No time for a movie? Slip up to the first floor to the hidden cafe, resplendent with golden arches and turquoise silk wallpaper. *Rákóczi út 21; http:// urania-nf.hu; 10.30am-10pm.*

🌳 Füvészkert

This 18th-century botanical garden buried in the heart of the district belongs to a university but is open to the public. The walled garden transports you to the Far East when the cherry blossoms are in full bloom and to the tropics when you step inside its 19th-century palm house. *Illés u 25; www.fuveszkert.org; 9am-5pm; 1200Ft.*

🔒 Vintage Shop

If you're looking for a bronze belt shaped like a snake or a taffeta opera dress, head to this eclectic shop, which spills across two buildings. Find unique, vintage or second-hand items here – and at a low price, too. *Práter u 9; 10am-6pm Mon-Sat.*

🍸 Keret Klub

You won't spot this tiny bar with a mezzanine floor unless you know to look for it. You'll need to knock on the hidden door under the tiny lantern hanging above; if you can find it, someone will let you in. This late-night bohemian hangout transports you back in time with vintage frames, retro furniture and young people playing chess until 2am. Smoking is permitted inside. *Somogyi Béla u 16; www.facebook.com/pg/ Keretklub; 1pm-4am Mon-Fri, 3pm-4am Sat & Sun.*

🏛 Kerepesi Cemetery

It's worth escaping the crowds to visit monuments and mausoleums that remember Hungary's great dead. Explore

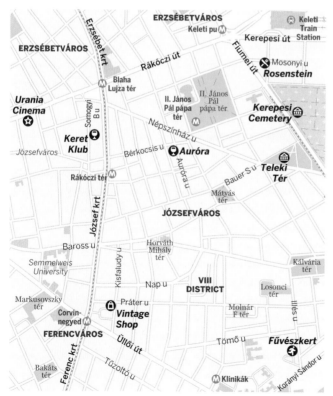

BUDAPEST

the graves and grand sepulchres erected for writers, politicians, and nobility in this walled 140-acre cemetery. Come after dark on 1 November when locals light candles in remembrance. *Fiumei út 16-18; http://fiumeiutisirkert. nori.gov.hu; 7am-6pm.*

🍸 Auróra

A ruin bar that doubles as a hub for NGOs and a community centre that also hosts concerts, refugee mixers and stand-up comedy. It's a liberal oasis – which is why its future is precarious – but hopefully this three-storey bar is here to stay. *Auróra u 11; http://auroraonline. hu; noon-11pm.*

BUDAPEST'S OTHER JEWISH QUARTER

A large Jewish community thrived in the VIII District from the late 19th century until the 1950s. Jews from Ukraine and Poland came to Teleki square to work as pedlars and artisans in the market. There were 50 *shuls* (prayer houses) in surrounding apartments; only one survives today on the ground floor at 22 Teleki Tér and still opens its doors each Sabbath.

✡ Rosenstein

This two-storey, six-room, family-run restaurant specialises in home-cooked Hungarian-Jewish food and has been running for 20 years. Try Jewish specialities like *cholent*, a slow-cooked bean-based stew. Rosenstein is one of the few traditional restaurants in Budapest not overrun by tour groups. *Mosonyi u 3, 1087; http://rosenstein.hu; noon-11pm Mon-Sat.*

Clockwise from top: Úrania Cinema; Vintage Shop; Kerepesi Cemetery

XI DISTRICT

The area clustered around Bartók Béla út is lined with art nouveau apartments, trendy cafes, restaurants and galleries. It's a hangout for creative Hungarians escaping the VII District's stag parties. Located in Buda, across from the IX District, it's a quieter area that stretches from Gellért Hill southwards along the Danube and to the west.

repurposed this abandoned section of the thermal baths, and now you can drink a few beers in one of these tile-clad former bathing pools. *Kemenes u 10; http://pagonykert.hu; 11am-10pm.*

🏛 A38
Grab a gig on board this former Ukrainian stone-carrying ship, permanently moored on the Danube. It's a popular venue for concerts, thanks to the large hall below deck, but there is also a bar and a cafe-restaurant area. *Petőfi híd Buda; http://a38.hu; 11am-11pm Mon-Sat.*

❌ Gdańsk
It's easy to miss this tiny, four-table Polish bookstore and bar on Bartók Béla út. You can grab a bottle of beer or a shot of vodka to wash down the homemade *pierogi* (dumplings) in a welcoming atmosphere. Gdańsk pulls in a local bohemian crowd and can get pretty packed in the evenings. During quieter times it's a cosy culinary refuge. *Bartók Béla út 46; www.facebook.com/gdansk.konyvesbolt; 11am-11pm Mon-Fri, 8-11pm Sat.*

🏛 Tranzit Art Cafe
Tranzit popped up in an old bus depot and became a cultural hub. It's a bar and restaurant but regularly hosts exhibitions and events, and screens films on the terrace in the summer. *Kosztolányi Dezső tér; http://tranzitcafe.com; 10am-10pm Mon-Sat.*

🌳 Kopaszi Gát
This needle-like 1km (0.6 miles) of land sticking out into the Danube was once a dam for the nearby art deco Kelenföld Powerstation. Today, it's been remodelled into a park populated by cafes, bars and restaurants. There are sandy areas around the dam for sunbathing and the bay

between the dam and the river bank is popular for sailing and watersports. *6am-10pm.*

🍺 Pagony Kert
The famous Gellért Baths used to be larger, but the children's section was closed down and cut off by a road. A seasonal bar and restaurant Pagony Kert

III DISTRICT

Óbuda, the III District, is Budapest's oldest neighbourhood and once an independent city. In 1873, Buda, Pest and Óbuda unified to become Budapest. Roman ruins, old factories and baroque houses lie scattered around the hilly district. Riverside bars and beaches are a popular hangout in summer, especially when the Sziget Festival arrives.

🏛 Hercules Villa

Hidden under concrete high-rises, the Hercules Villa is an unexpected archaeological site. This preserved Roman villa gets its name from a stunning mosaic featuring the hero. Stop over if you're visiting the nearby Aquincum archaeological site on a Sunday. *Meggyfa u 21; 11am-1pm Sun Apr-Oct; free.*

🏛 Kiscelli Museum

A monastery turned military barracks sets the scene for this quirky museum, which features old shop signs, a vintage pharmacy, and arts and crafts from past centuries. Do visit the old stone church attached to the complex, it's used for temporary exhibitions. *Kiscelli u 108; http://kiscellimuzeum.hu; 10am-4pm Tue-Sun Nov-Mar, to 6pm Apr-Oct; 1600Ft.*

🍷 Fellini Római Kultúrbisztró

Grab a colourful deckchair on this secluded beach and relax with a rosé. Fellini is more than just a bar, it's a cultural hub with concerts and beach-side movie screenings. Get away from the tourists in the downtown ruin bars in the summer and watch the Danube flow past. *Kossuth Lajos üdülőpart 5; http://felliniromai.hu; 2-10pm.*

🍷 Két Rombusz

Nearby Két Rombusz is a bar run out of two vintage double-decker buses. You can also book in advance to use their campfire or grill facilities for free. *Római part 43; www.facebook.com/ketrombusz; 4-11pm.*

🚢 Óbuda Island

This 267-acre island becomes the 'Island of Freedom' during the Sziget Festival in August, but typically it's a park popular with locals that's a less touristy alternative to Margaret Island. The southern end is interesting with its former shipyard featuring old industrial buildings.

🏛 Thermae Maiores

Beneath a flyover lie the ruins of a Roman bath. This complex was used by Roman soldiers from the 1st to 4th centuries; look for the entrance in the underpass leading to the number 1 tram. *Szőlő u 72; 10am-5pm Tue-Sun; free.*

Bosphorus
Shore

Fener &
Balat

Istanbul

Kadıköy

ISTANBUL

In a city of storied streets at the meeting of east and west, these neighbourhoods show Istanbul's European and Asian, ancient and contemporary faces.

T he former capital of the Ottoman and Byzantine Empires is one of the world's largest cities and the only major city on two continents, with Europe and Asia separated by the Bosphorus strait. If this sprawling urban jumble of mosques, bazaars and over 15 million souls starts to feel overwhelming, focus on its neighbourhoods.

The Fener and Balat area, a tapestry of tumbledown Ottoman houses, stately mosques, murals and chador-clad shoppers alongside the Golden Horn waterway, is recognised by Unesco for its historical significance but receives a fraction of the visitors seen in the Old City to the southeast. It's a similar story in Kadıköy, a 30-minute ferry trip from the Old City and fashionable Beyoğlu, and a culinary destination for its produce market and restaurants. Back on the European side of the Bosphorus, the moneyed waterfront suburbs northeast of Beyoğlu are where Istanbullus come to relax. You can cover all three areas on foot.

ISTANBUL

KADIKÖY

Cosmopolitan residents of Istanbul's European side once dismissed the Asian side as the gateway to conservative Anatolian Turkey, but skyrocketing property prices have caused a Manhattan-to-Brooklyn-style charge across the Bosphorus. Kadıköy is leading the evolution of the Asian shore, with vibey bars and graffiti murals complementing the traditional charms of its produce market and coffee houses. Getting there by ferry is half the fun.

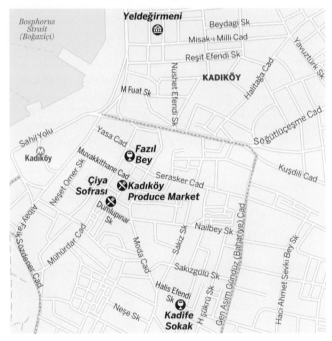

explore the area. *Güneşlibahçe Sokak; Mon-Sat.*

🚇 Kadife Sokak
The Asian side of Istanbul's answer to the Bar Streets of Bodrum, Marmaris and Kuşadaşı, Kadife is the local choice to finish the afternoon over beer and backgammon. There are some great bars on the street, including arty Arkaoda and punky Karga Bar, and it's always especially lively before local soccer team Fenerbahçe's home games.

☕ Fazıl Bey
On the *kahvehane* (coffeehouse) strip in the produce market, Istanbul's favourite branch of its small, century-old *Türk kahve* (Turkish coffee) chain roasts, grinds and brews beans on site, serving the sludgy drink with a cube of Turkish delight. *Serasker Cad 1; www.fazilbey.com.tr; 8am-11pm.*

🏛 Yeldeğirmeni
Since the Mural Istanbul festival began in 2012, the Yeldeğirmeni area, running north from the produce market to the Haydarpaşa train tracks, has become a street gallery of epic murals. *http://muralistanbul.org.*

❌ Kadıköy Produce Market
Kadıköy Pazarı (Market) is the foodie version of the Grand Bazaar, with rack upon rack of fresh local produce from fruit and veg to roasted nuts and olive oil. It's home to some excellent cafes and speciality shops, including seafood stall and restaurant Kadı

Nimet Balıkçılık, honey purveyor Honeyci, and Ali Muhiddin Hacı Bekir, part of a 240-year-old *lokum* (Turkish delight) chain. Culinary tour operator Turkish Flavours (www.turkishflavours.com) visits on its walking tours of two or three food markets on two continents. Mornings are the liveliest time to

❌ Çiya Sofrası
In the produce market, this *lokanta* (eatery serving ready-made food) and kebab restaurant serves classic and obscure dishes from meze plates and hearty *çorbalar* (soups) to *köfte* (meatballs) and rice dishes. *Pappelallee 63; www.yonkelork. de; 11am-7pm.*

FENER & BALAT

On the western shore of the Golden Horn (Haliç), easily reached by ferry or bus, these Unesco-protected neighbourhoods mix rickety late-Ottoman houses, hip cafes and some the city's most important Byzantine, Greek and Jewish sites. Climbing the hills to the grand Ottoman mosques, you'll find that the locals are an equally diverse crowd ranging from artists to Anatolian immigrants.

🏛 Patriarchal Church of St George

This 19th-century Greek Orthodox church houses treasures including Byzantine mosaics, a contemporaneous wood-and-inlay patriarchal throne, an ornate wooden iconostasis (screen of icons) and the Column of Christ's Flagellation. It is part of the Ecumenical Patriarchate compound, the symbolic headquarters of the Greek Orthodox Church. *Sadrazam Ali Paşa Cad, Fener; www.ec-patr.org; 8.30am-4.30pm.*

🏛 Mihrimah Sultan Mosque

The great Ottoman architect, Mimar Sinan, was in love with Süleyman the Magnificent's favourite daughter, Mihrimah, who commissioned him to design this 16th-century mosque at Istanbul's highest point. The frustrated Sinan symbolised his unrequited love for Mihrimah ('sun and moon' in Farsi) through the symmetry between the landmark mosque and its namesake in Üsküdar: as the sun sets behind this mosque, the moon rises behind the other. *Ali Kuşçu Sokak, Edirnekapı; dawn-dusk.*

☀ Mihrimah Sultan Hamamı

Part of the Mihrimah Sultan *külliye* (mosque complex), this plain but clean restored hamam has a friendly neighbourhood atmosphere and separate sections for men and women. *Fevzi Paşa Cad 333, Edirnekapı; www. mihrimahsultanhamami.com; 9am-8pm.*

🏛 Yavuz Sultan Selim Mosque

Istanbullus love visiting this hilltop 16th-century mosque, the last resting place of Selim I (aka Selim the Grim), for a picnic on the terrace with its sweeping views over the Golden Horn. It's next to a Roman cistern turned park in the conservative Çarşamba district, home to women in black chadors and men with beards. *Yavuz Selim Cad, Çarşamba; dawn-dusk.*

Map labels: Eyüp 1.5km (1 mile); BALIKHANE; AVCI BEY; BALAT; KASIM GÜNANI; Golden Horn (Haliç); Savaklar Cad; Ayvansaray Cad; Mürselpaşa Cad; Coffee Department; DRAMAN; Vodina Caddesi; EDİRNEKAPI; KATIP MUSLIHITTIN; HIZIR ÇAVUŞ; FENER; Mihrimah Sultan Mosque; Salma Tomruk Cad; Fethiye Cad; Forno; Phanar Greek Orthodox College; Patriarchal Church of St George; Mihrimah Sultan Hamamı; Karagümrük Stadium; KARAGÜMRÜK; BEYCEĞİZ; ÇARŞAMBA; Yavuz Sultan Selim Mosque; SULUKULE; Fevzi Paşa Cad; Darüşşafaka Cad; Tabakyunus Sk

🏛 Phanar Greek Orthodox College

Fener's own Hogwarts, known as *kırmızlı kale* (the red castle), is a landmark towering above jumbled rooftops. Incredibly, the 19th-century Ottoman Greek pile houses Turkey's oldest educational body, which predates the Ottomans' arrival in Constantinople. It still has a handful of students. *Sancaktar Cad, Fener; closed to public.*

☕ Coffee Department

Recharge at this temple to the bean, with its sacks of coffee and wood-and-metal seating. Sample the baristas' handiwork and grab a bag from the global selection of beans roasted on site. *Kürçü Çeşmesi Sokak 5a, Balat; www. coffeedepartment.co; 9am-6pm.*

✖ Forno

With its colourful tiles and long table, cheerful Forno feels like your foodie friend's kitchen, but only a pro could turn out pide, pizza, *lahmacun* (Arabic-style pizza), desserts and buffet breakfasts this good. Ingredients include meat from the family butcher and spices

EYÜP

─────────

Hop on a bus or ferry along the Golden Horn to this nearby pilgrimage site, where stalls sell religious souvenirs, tourist tat and street snacks around the tombs of Sokullu Mehmet Paşa, a Bosnian-born Ottoman grand vizier, and Ebu Eyüp el-Ensari, a friend of the Prophet. From the latter, Istanbul's foremost Islamic shrine, catch the cable car or walk uphill through the cemetery to Pierre Loti Café for Golden Horn views.

from the market. *Fener Kireçhane Sokak 13, Balat; www.fornobalat. com; 10am-9pm Tue-Sun.*

🔒 Vodina Caddesi

Wander along this thoroughfare to enjoy the contrasts between antique shops and groceries, crumbling Ottoman houses and graffiti murals, local hipsters and more conservative Muslims, chic cafes and marketeers selling veg from vans. It's busiest during the day from Monday to Saturday.

**Top: Balat's colourful houses
Below and left: well poured brews at Coffee Department**

BOSPHORUS SHORE

On the European shore of the continent-dividing Bosphorus strait, this affluent strip has the city's highest concentration of late-Ottoman palaces, pavilions and *yalıs* (waterfront mansions). Accessed by ferry, tram, funicular, metro and bus, it's known for Dolmabahçe Palace and the 'Golden Mile' of nightclubs. Locals prefer a stroll in pretty Ortaköy.

Palace Collections Museum

Duck round the corner from the crowded Dolmabahçe Palace to this museum in the warehouse-like palace kitchens, which exhibits royal items used during the late Ottoman Empire and early Turkish Republic. With several thousand exhibits from portraits and photos to tea sets and prayer rugs, it's like poking through the sultan's apartments. *Beşiktaş Cad, Beşiktaş; www.millisaraylar.gov.tr; 9am-5pm Tue-Sun.*

Yıldız Park

Frolicking and picnicking in this hillside park is an Istanbul ritual, especially when tulips bloom in spring. It's home to the 19th-century Yıldız Chalet, Sultan Abdül Hamit II's hunting lodge, and the Malta Kiosk, where Abdül Hamit imprisoned his brother Murat V after deposing him. The showroom at the gate of the Yıldız Porselen Fabrikası sells the factory's porcelain whirling dervishes and mugs depicting Ottoman sultans. *Çırağan Cad, Yıldız; www.millisaraylar.gov.tr.*

Istanbul Naval Museum

This museum of Turkish naval history houses an impressive collection of 19th-century imperial caïques, ornately decorated wooden rowboats used by the royal household. In the square opposite is the tomb designed by Mimar Sinan for Barbarossa ('Red Beard'), the admiral of Süleyman the Magnificent's all-conquering fleet. *Beşiktaş Cad 6, Beşiktaş; www.dzkk.tsk.tr; 10am-5pm Tue-Sun.*

Ortaköy Mosque

Dwarfed by the Bosphorus Bridge, this bijou baroque-style mosque in the former fishing village of Ortaköy was designed for Sultan Abdül Mecit I by Nikoğos Balyan, one of the Dolmabahçe Palace architects. Dating to 1855, the pretty white waterfront building contains some

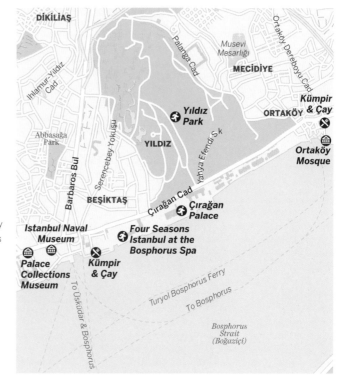

ISTANBUL

excellent Arabic calligraphic panels, executed by Abdül Mecit himself, beneath its ornate ceiling. *İskele Meydanı, Ortaköy; dawn-dusk.*

⊕ Çırağan Palace

Sultan Abdül Aziz attempted to outdo the Dolmabahçe Palace, built by his older brother and predecessor Abdül Mecit, by commissioning Nikoğos Balyan to design this fusion of European neoclassical, Ottoman and Moorish styles. At the luxurious Kempinski hotel inside, with its lobby boutiques, five restaurants and bars, well-heeled local clientele and photos of celebrity guests, non-guests can wander the gardens around the Bosphorus-side pool or just put their Ottoman slippers up. *Çırağan Cad 32, Beşiktaş; www. kempinski.com.*

✖ Kümpir & Çay

Strolling along the Bosphorus takes you to the soul of the city,

especially when accompanied by a tulip-shaped glass of *çay* (tea) and a snack. Two of the best areas for waterside refreshments are the cafes and bars on pedestrianised promenade İskele Yolu, where you

can watch the ferries heading in and out of Beşiktaş Ferry Dock, and the *kümpir* (stuffed baked potato) and sweet waffle stands behind Ortaköy Mosque. *2 İskele Yolu, Beşiktaş & Mecidiye Köprüsü Sokak, Ortaköy.*

⊕ Four Seasons Istanbul at the Bosphorus Spa

Istanbul's ladies who lunch are more likely to be seen in this exquisite spa than the Old City's aged hamams. Float beneath skylights in the pillared indoor pool and enjoy treatments from hamam experiences to massages. *Çırağan Cad 28, Beşiktaş; www. fourseasons.com/bosphorus; 9am-9pm.*

Top: Ortaköy Mosque
Left: glasses of çay

MOSCOW

Russia's mindbogglingly eclectic capital has a place for it all: medieval architecture, Soviet gigantism and cutting-edge modernity.

MOSCOW

Thoroughly renovated in recent years, Moscow comes as a pleasant surprise to first-timers and those who haven't been around in a while. Surreal, eclectic and always steeped in geopolitical intrigue, it has made a giant leap forward in liveability and visual appeal. There is much more to Moscow than the magnificent Kremlin and vestiges of the Soviet period.

With its vast historical centre refurbished to give pedestrians prevalence over cars and many parks nicely spruced up, Moscow has become ideal for long walks through diverse neighbourhoods. Each reveals the cultural layers that form the delicate texture of this unusual city. The flavour of old Russia preserved in Zamoskvorechye, the Parisian elegance of Chistye Prudy and spooky shadows of Bulgakov's characters populating Patriarshy Ponds are complemented by a fascinating restaurant scene, as well as top-notch cafes and bars.

CHISTYE PRUDY

The Chistye Prudy area combines one of Moscow's most romantic spots with the best of its restaurant rows, along ul Maroseyka, not to mention a cluster of excellent bars and cafes at the junction of Chistoprudny and Pokrovsky boulevards. Traverse the shady boulevard and marvel at the beautiful pond before treating yourself to exotic teas or craft beer.

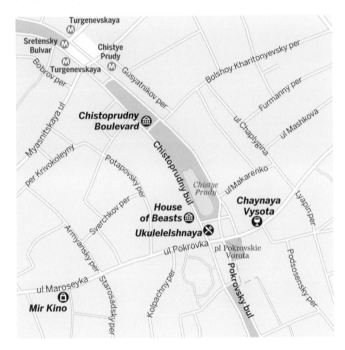

🏛 Chistoprudny Boulevard

This romantic stretch of green, complete with a placid pond that turns into a skating rink in winter, is a highlight of the Boulevard Ring. In its middle, the monument to Kazakh poet Abay Kunanbayev has turned into a Russian protest icon after briefly serving as a venue of anti-government protests in 2012. *Chistoprudny bul.*

🏛 House of Beasts

There is a whole bestiary of mythical animals adorning a seven-storey art nouveau residential building that graces Chistoprudny boulevard. Terracotta bas-reliefs, which cover the entire facade, are inspired by the stone carvings on a famous medieval cathedral in the city of Vladimir. *Chistoprudny bul 14.*

🔒 Mir Kino

You'll instantly realise how retro the 1990s are already looking when you enter this cramped shop selling what used to be underground Soviet music, from Aquarium and Viktor Tsoy to obscure bands few experts ever heard of...all recorded on, well, CDs and DVDs. A tiny cafe in the premises serves Korean *pyanse* (also known as *mandu*) dumplings. *Ul Maroseyka 8; https://vk.com/mirkinomsk; 10am-9pm.*

🍵 Chaynaya Vysota

Combined with a Christian bookstore, this tea room and ice cream parlour brings together exotic flavours from Russia's many climatic zones – from Siberian fir tree cones to feijoa fruit grown in the Caucasus. *Ul Pokrovka 27 str 1; http://cha108.ru; 495-225 5996; 11am-midnight.*

✖ Ukuleleshnaya

This small bar grew out of a shop selling ukuleles, some of which still adorn the walls. It's a good place to try local craft beer or grab a gourmet burger in a pleasant setting more conducive to conversations than wild partying. *Ul Pokrovka 17; http://uku-uku.ru; 495-642 5726; noon-2am.*

ZAMOSKVORECHYE

Imperial grandeur or Soviet brutalism – you won't find any of that in the quaint lanes of Zamoskvorechye, a vast area across the Moscow river from the Kremlin. Built by merchants who lived separately from aristocracy, it is the most distinctly Russian part of the city, with low-rise mansion houses and a plenitude of onion-domed churches.

🏛 Novokuznetskaya Metro Station

Opened at the height of World War II, the marble-clad station is graced with striking ceiling mosaics dedicated to people of different professions, from steel workers to gardeners, who contributed to the war effort. Walls are adorned with bronze shields dedicated to the defenders of key Soviet cities. *Novokuznetskaya Metro; http://mosmetro.ru; 5.30am-1am.*

🏛 SS Martha & Mary Convent of Mercy

A massive whitewashed brick wall on ul Bolshaya Ordynka conceals an art nouveau masterpiece that fuses femininity with traditional Russian spirituality. German-born Grand Duchess Elizabeth sold her possessions to build it in honour of her husband, who was killed by terrorists. Her idea was to create a temporary safe haven for suffering women from all social strata. She was executed by the Bolsheviks in 1918, having served the rest of her life as a nun here. *Ul Bolshaya Ordynka 34; www.mmom.ru; 7am-7pm.*

🏛 Church of St Nicholas at Pyzhy

With five onion domes and an exquisite belfry, this dazzlingly white 17th-century church is a glittering example of what old Russia looked like on the eve of Peter the Great's forceful westernisation campaign. *Ul Bolshaya Ordynka 27A/8; http://moral.ru; 7am-7pm.*

🍺 Parka

'Parka' is a *banya* (bathhouse) term, hence the sauna-like decor. And just like a proper *banya*, this is a very relaxing place. The friendly bartenders let you try any beer before you commit to buying a pint. Many of the brews (most of them local) have crazy 'Runglish' names, that is, in an endearing hybrid of Russian and English words. *Pyatnitskaya ul 22 str 1; www.facebook.com/parkacraft; noon-6am.*

🍸 Mitzva Bar

An inconspicuous door leads into a vaulted cellar decorated with Judaic and Masonic symbols. An excellent cocktail bar with friendly service, it also serves modern Middle Eastern food, including creative takes on gefilte fish (stuffed carp) and tajine (North African stew). *Pyatnitskaya ul 3/4 str 1; https://mitzva.bar; 495-532 4224; 3pm-3am.*

✖ Vay Me

Georgian fast food sounds like sacrilege, but this little canteen is a great place to grab a quick *khachapuri* (cheese pastry), *kharcho* (spicy soup) or *khinkali* (large Georgian dumplings), accompanied with an assortment of *kompots* (sweet drinks with pieces of fruit). *Pyatnitsky per 8 str 1; https://vaimecafe.com; 495-646 0220; 10am-11pm.*

✖ Björn

A neat cluster of fir trees on a busy

© Gubin Yury / Shutterstock

street hides a Nordic gem that deserves a saga to glorify its many virtues. Björn presents futuristic Scandinavian cuisine straight out of a science fiction movie. From salads to desserts, every dish looks deceptively simple, visually perfect and 23rd-century. *Pyatnitskaya ul 3; http://bjorn.rest; 495-953 9059; noon-midnight.*

Clockwise from top: street in Zamoskvorechye; Mitzva Bar; Church of St Nicholas at Pyzhy

© 2020, Mitzva Bar

© Elena Lar / Shutterstock

PATRIARSHY PONDS

It feels like a pleasant residential neighbourhood. But dark magic reigns in Patriarshy Ponds and things happen that you'd only expect at Halloween...a Russian sort of Halloween. Patriki, as locals call it, owes its spooky reputation to Mikhail Bulgakov, who populated it with a giant talking cat, Satan disguised as a Western tourist, and other characters.

⊕ Patriarshy Pond

Although the area's name renders the word 'pond' in plural, two of the three historical ponds were drained back in the 19th century. The one that remains is a magnet for locals who picnic on banks and benches on summer nights or skate the ice in winter.

⌂ Bulgakov Museum

Unloved but spared by the Soviet authorities, writer Mikhail Bulgakov occupied a flat here in the early 1920s and settled it with the dodgy characters from his best-known novel *Master & Margarita*, a scathingly subversive anti-Soviet satire. The block now houses an arts centre, theatre and a small museum. *Bolshaya Sadovaya ul 10; www.dombulgakova.ru; noon-7pm Tue, Wed & Fri-Sun, 2-9pm Thu; adult/child R150/50.*

⌂ Ryabushinsky Mansion

Also known as the Gorky House-Museum, this fascinating 1906 art nouveau mansion was designed by architect Fyodor Shekhtel and

gifted to author Maxim Gorky in 1931. The house is a visual fantasy with sculpted doorways, ceiling murals, stained glass, a carved staircase and tilework. *Malaya Nikitskaya ul 6/2; 11am-5.30pm Wed-Sun; adult/student R400/150.*

✖ Jerusalem

You don't normally come to a prayer house for earthly pleasures, but the rooftop restaurant at Moscow's main Hasidic synagogue serves Middle Eastern fare and offers a heavenly view. *Bolshaya Bronnaya ul 6; www.facebook. com/jerusaleminmoscow; 495-690 6266.*

✖ Moscow-Delhi

Strange and fantastic things happen in the Patriarshy, like instant teleportation to a north Indian kitchen where people consume delicious *thali* set menus while listening to the sweet chitchat of Kashmiri cooks. *Yermolayevsky per 7; www.facebook.com/ MoscowDelhi; 925-193 1916; 10am-11pm Tue-Sun.*

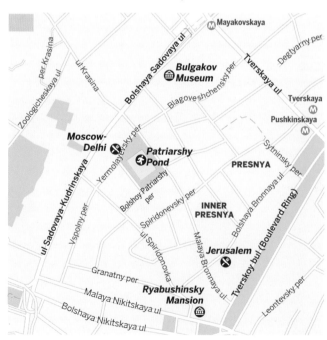

VDNKH

There is a lot to ponder here regarding the nature of totalitarianism. But the architecture of this town-sized area, designed to showcase Soviet achievements, is unquestionably stunning. Palatial pavilions representing Soviet republics and industries line a wide promenade reminiscent of the National Mall in DC, while the syringe-shaped Ostankino TV tower looms in the distance.

🏛 People's Friendship Fountain
In the second square from the main gate, this fountain is surrounded by 16 gilded female figures wearing ethnic costumes that represent Soviet republics. The mysterious 16th figure stands for the Karelo-Finnish republic disbanded in 1956.

🏛 Space Pavilion
With an elegant glass cupola, this enormous building is packed with rockets, landing capsules and entire space stations, some of which you can walk through. A life-sized replica of the Voskhod rocket was installed at the main entrance in 1967. *http://cosmos.vdnh.ru; 11am-8pm Tue-Sun; adult/student R500/250.*

🏛 Worker & Kolkhoz Woman
Probably the holiest of Soviet icons, this brutally powerful monument depicts a fierce-looking couple of giants raising the hammer and sickle, which symbolise the union of peasants and the working class. *http://moscowmanege.ru; exhibition hall 10am-10pm Mon-Thu, to 11pm Fri-Sun; adult/child R1000/500.*

🏛 Ostankino Tower
At 540m (1770ft) this is the world's fourth-tallest tower, which comes with a 337m-high (1105ft) observation deck open for visitors. From the top, there are 360-degree views and – horror! – a glass floor. *Ul Koroleva 15 k2; https://tvtower.ru; 10am-10pm Mon-Thu, to 11pm Fri-Sun; adult/child R1000/500.*

🏛 Cosmonautics Museum
The soaring 100m (328ft) titanium obelisk outside VDNKh is a monument 'To the Conquerors of Space', built in 1964 to commemorate the launch of Sputnik. In its base at the Cosmonautics Museum, find the first Soviet rocket engine and moon rover Lunokhod. *Pr Mira 111; www.kosmo-museum.ru; 1am-7pm Tue, Wed & Fri-Sun, to 9pm Thu; R250.*

✖ Moskovskoye Nebo
Like VDNKh itself, the menu represents the USSR's republics, most notably Ukraine. However, the quality of borsch and chicken kiev is notably better than in Soviet times. *Pr Mira 119 str 422; 499-650 0031; noon-11pm.*

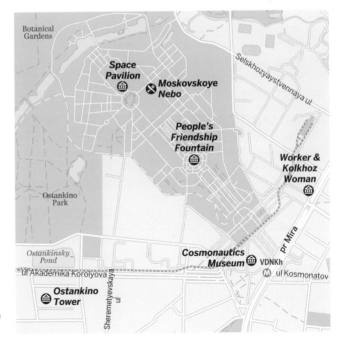

SECRET CITY · 171

NORTH AMERICA

ARTS & CULTURE   MUSIC & FILM   SPORTS & LEISURE   EATING   DRINKING   SHOPPING

Downtown
Oakland &
Lake Merritt

San Francisco

Inner Richmond &
Inner Sunset
The Haight & Dogpatch &
Cole Valley Potrero Hill

SAN FRANCISCO

From Alcatraz to the Golden Gate Bridge, San Francisco's icons can fill days of sightseeing – but the city's heart beats loudest in its eccentric neighbourhoods.

Everyone has a vision of San Francisco: the wide blue bay, beatnik pubs piled between art deco skyscrapers, *that* bridge... Beyond seedy pockets of the downtown area, this is a jubilant, 'anything goes' kind of city filled with tireless night owls, music lovers and voracious gourmands fed by chefs setting the latest food trends.

Well-touristed neighbourhoods in SF – never 'San Fran' – deserve their popularity. There's the Mission District with its murals, and the 'Painted Ladies', peacock-like houses in Alamo Square. But to live like a Bay Area local, shout out your martini order in a darkly glamorous dive bar in The Haight, twirl a fork at a chic restaurant in Inner Sunset, or ponder art

in post-industrial Dogpatch. Neighbouring Oakland, across the bay, dances to a different beat – usually after midnight in a sticky-floored live music bar.

Public transport in SF can seem like a jigsaw with a few missing pieces. Plot a course using buses, metro, BART (rail) across the bay, and the ride-share apps designed in nearby Silicon Valley.

THE HAIGHT & COLE VALLEY

Counter-culture enclave Haight-Ashbury (aka The Haight) was hippie ground zero in the 1960s. From the giant fishnet-stockinged legs (a popular photo-op) to the house where Janis Joplin lived, it's a riveting place to stroll, get pierced or buy anarchist poetry books. A few blocks south is well-heeled Cole Valley, replete with places to drink and dine.

🍸 Zam Zam

Observe the dark arts of mixology from a bar stool at Zam Zam. Persian-style murals and back-lit bottles create the smouldering setting of this Haight institution, founded in 1941. Long-time drinkers fondly reminisce about Zam Zam's scowling former owner; fortunately the bar has lost none of its slightly sordid charm since changing hands, and the martinis remain outstanding. Cash only. *1633 Haight St; 3pm-2am.*

📚 Bound Together Books

All fired up to overthrow capitalism but in need of a little written guidance? This anarchist bookstore has the toolkit for when the revolution comes, from thought-provoking 'zines to well-known treatises on racial equality and LGBT+ rights. *1369 Haight St; https://boundtogetherbooks. wordpress.com; 11.30am-7.30pm.*

🍽 Zazie

American tipping protocol (usually 20% of a restaurant bill) can inspire furtive calculator use in travellers. Take a night off at gratuity-free Zazie, whose ethical working culture puts a smile on the faces of staff and punters. Brunch classics like eggs Benedict and croque monsieur give way to French-inflected dishes by evening. *941 Cole St; www.zaziesf.com; 415-564-5332; 9am-2pm & 5-9.30pm.*

☕ Cafe Reverie

Though it looks like an ordinary cafe as you enter, Reverie has a few aces up its sleeve. There's excellent, Antipodean-style coffee, a lovely green back patio, and reasonably priced pinot noir to sip outside. *848 Cole St; http://cafe-reverie.cafes-city.com; 6.30am-9pm Mon-Fri, 7.30am-7.30pm Sat & Sun.*

🏛 Charles Manson House

Understandably, local residents would rather forget that murderous cult leader Charles Manson lived here during the summer of 1967. Take a discreet photo, and pretend you got lost en route to the Janis Joplin house. *636 Cole St.*

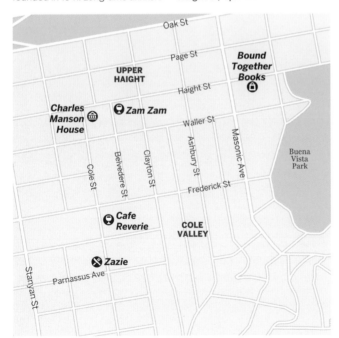

DOGPATCH & POTRERO HILL

Lofty Potrero Hill basks in sunshine and sparkling views of SF. In the mid-20th century, artists and LGBT+ residents set the neighbourhood's spirited tone. These days Potrero Hill's coveted brunch spots conspire with raucous bars to keep things interesting. Bayside Dogpatch, just east, is grittier, with saloons and restaurants hiding in converted warehouses. Arrive by Muni along 3rd St or by Caltrain (22nd St).

🎵 Bottom of the Hill

Even hard-to-please music lovers will be in awe of the genre-defying acts that grace this bar at the foot of Potrero Hill. Whether you need old-school punk, Mongolian folk metal, tropical Afro-Latin or southern gothic blues, there's something new to delight or torment your ear drums every night of the week. Some gigs include free barbecue in the ticket price (yes, really) and drinks are good value and generously poured. *1233 17th St; www.bottomofthehill.com.*

🍷 Ruby Wine

European wines are a speciality at Ruby, a pocket-sized bar and bottle shop. Potrero Hill locals love this place so much that they're willing to spill out from the snug, woodsy bar and stand in the street, conversing with friends over several glasses of grüner veltliner. Join the throng for Friday wine tastings (5pm to 9pm) or buy a bottle to go.

1419 18th St; https://rubywinesf. com; noon-10pm Sun-Thu, to midnight Fri & Sat.

❌ Goat Hill Pizza

The name of this long-standing sourdough pizzeria is a nod to the days that followed the 1906 earthquake, when goats could be seen wandering among rubble in these steep streets. The welcome's as warm as a pizza oven; order in to eat at no-frills, wipe-clean tables or take a box of goodness home. Our pick is the rich, creamy Hilda's Favorite, slathered in pesto and (appropriately) goat's cheese. Go early for Monday evening's all-you-can-eat. *300 Connecticut St; www.goathillpizza.com; 415-641-1440; 11am-11pm.*

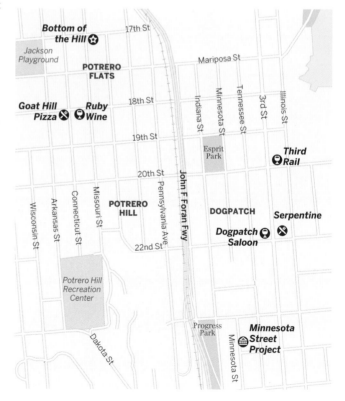

SAN FRANCISCO

Minnesota Street Project

These three warehouses are quintessential Dogpatch: monochrome exteriors that give nothing away, but breathtaking displays within. Nonprofits and art galleries share this airy space. Contemporary artists showcase their work for sale, but there's no hard sell – Minnesota Street Project is also a no-strings-attached art hub for the neighbourhood. Come to be wowed by avant-garde sculptures, stick around for cocktail-fuelled Indian fusion cuisine at adjoining restaurant Besharam. *1275 Minnesota St; http://minnesotastreetproject. com; approx 11am-6pm; free.*

Serpentine

Dogpatch's austere buildings conceal countless places to eat and drink, and Serpentine, with its post-industrial design and Californian comfort food, is one of the best. Serpentine excels at boozy brunches: Bloody Marys come ornamented with a rainbow bouquet of pickled veggies, and the enormous *chilaquiles* (tortilla chips laden with cheese, pork and egg) can ease even persistent hangovers. Reserve ahead. *2495 3rd St; www.serpentinesf.com; 415-252-2000; 10am-2.30pm Thu-Sun & 5-10pm Mon-Sat.*

Third Rail

In keeping with the excellent cocktails, beers and abundant whiskies, Third Rail has also raised the game with its signature bar snack, jerky. Morsels of dried meat are paired with beers and spirits and receive gourmet presentation. We keep coming back for Cajun-style jerky but the 'Red Eye', seasoned with coffee and chilli, has the most kick. Veggies, you aren't forgotten: there's also shiitake mushroom jerky to chew on. *628 20th St; http://thirdrailbarsf. com; 3pm-late.*

Dogpatch Saloon

If all these converted warehouse bars and queue-for-it brunches feel a little, well, hipster, then the unpretentious Dogpatch Saloon will bring you back down to earth with a cold beer. This cosy joint dates to 1912, still with its original bar plus an antique-effect tiled floor and working fireplace. The decor evokes old times, the punters bellow good times. *2496 3rd St; http://dogpatchsaloon. com; 2pm-2am Mon-Thu, noon-2am Fri & Sat, 10am-late Sun.*

Top: bar snacks at Third Rail
Left: Potrero Hill views of the city and bay

INNER RICHMOND & INNER SUNSET

West of the seamy, storied Haight area, Inner Richmond and Inner Sunset sandwich the east side of Golden Gate Park. Residential Inner Richmond is overlooked by visitors but alive with globe-spanning restaurants and wine bars; board a bus from Embarcadero. South of the park, sliced by Muni line N, is infamously foggy Inner Sunset, tinged with the cultures of 20th-century Chinese and Irish migrants.

✖ Osteria Bella

Just occasionally, an Italian eatery beyond the bounds of the *bel paese* (beautiful country) knocks it out of the park. Osteria Bella is one such place, with effusive service, avowedly authentic Italian cooking (three-ingredient carbonara, squid-ink spaghetti) and a judiciously chosen wine list. You'll be talking about their truffled gnocchi – firm, yielding, swirled in the most buttery of sauces – for days. *3848 Geary Blvd; https://osteriabella.com; 415-221-0305; 11am-10pm Wed & Thu, 11am-11pm Fri, noon-10pm Sat, 11am-9pm Sun.*

⊖ High Treason

Unadorned oenophile den High Treason pours mostly European and Californian wines by the glass, accompanying a menu that roams somewhere between tapas (charcuterie plates, cider-lavished sprouts) and junk food for gastronomes (like duck fat fries or popcorn in porcini brown butter). *443 Clement St; www.facebook. com/hightreasonsf; 4.30-10pm Mon-Wed, noon-11pm Thu-Sat, 2-10pm Sun.*

⊖ InnerFog

A joke at the expense of Inner Sunset's mist-laden microclimate, InnerFog is an appealing bar that excels at good-value happy hours (4pm to 6pm) and quality vintages. Wines are mostly local, European and South American, and delicious enough to deserve pairing with a cheese or charcuterie board. *545 Irving St; http://innerfog.com; 4-9pm Sun-Tue, 4-11pm Wed & Thu, 4pm-midnight Sat & Sun.*

✖ Marnee Thai

Not just another neighbourhood

Map labels: Clement St · High Treason · Osteria Bella · Geary Blvd · Anza St · Balboa St · THE RICHMOND · Cabrillo St · Fulton St · 15th Ave · Park Presidio Blvd · 10th Ave · 6th Ave · 3rd Ave · Parker Ave · Rossi Playground · Turk St · University of San Francisco · Golden Gate Park · Lily Pond · Stow Lake · Shakespeare Garden · National AIDS Memorial Grove · Kezar Dr · Stanyan St · Little Shamrock · San Francisco's Hometown Creamery · Lincoln Way · Green Apple Books · Marnee Thai · InnerFog · THE SUNSET · 9th Ave · 7th Ave · Irving St · Frederick St · COLE VALLEY · University of California, San Francisco

Thai restaurant, this outstanding place reels you in with jewel-like decor and delivers a menu that roves far beyond the pad Thai and green curry standards. Seasonal menu variations bring *khanom khrok* (rice flour and coconut milk griddle cakes); plantain and duck curry; and pork belly with Thai basil. Consider reserving even on a weeknight (you're in SF, after all) or there's space for a few diners on stools by the counter. *1243 9th Ave; www.marneethaisf.com; 415-731-9999; 11.30am-9.30pm Sun-Thu, to 10pm Fri & Sat.*

🔒 Green Apple Books

SF does late-opening bookstores very well, and Green Apple is a fine place to rummage shelves between drinks and dinner. In a turn-of-the-20th-century building, this beguilingly old-school bookstore comes complete with creaky stairs and gas lamps on the upper floor. Love letters to California, firebrand feminist literature, history and travel writing... it's all here, attended to by suitably book-crazy staff. *1231 9th Ave; www.greenapplebooks. com; 10am-10pm.*

MYSTERIES OF GOLDEN GATE PARK

Signature sights are the Japanese Tea Garden, Conservatory of Flowers and Botanical Gardens. But for Golden Gate Park's alternative intrigues, pose by the early 20th-century carousel and seek out the National AIDS Memorial Grove. Locals will ask if you know about the bison (yes, west side of the park). They may also say there's a ghost or Loch Ness-style monster in Stow Lake (we won't confirm or deny).

🍺 Little Shamrock

A real-deal Irish pub with pedigree, the 1890s-founded Little Shamrock is ancient by SF standards. It poured sodas to survive the Prohibition era (or so bar staff swore at the time); today it draws students and young professionals to its living-room setting. Order a beer, sink into an armchair and stare up at antique mirrors, old photographs and clocks – one of them hasn't

ticked since the earthquake of 1906. *807 Lincoln Way; 3pm-late Mon-Thu, from 2pm Fri, from 1pm Sat & Sun.*

❌ San Francisco's Hometown Creamery

So-called 'artisan' ice creams are churned out at countless parlours across the city, but the desserts at the Hometown Creamery genuinely taste like well-guarded home recipes. Local ingredients are blended into small-batch ice creams – as they describe it, a 'farm-to-cone' experience – and rotating flavours range from bananas foster (real banana and a splash of bourbon) to sweet red bean with sake-soaked cherries. Don't deny yourself a double scoop, the flavours might be gone by tomorrow. *1290 9th Ave; www. sfhometowncreamery.com; noon-10pm.*

**Top: Green Apple Books
Below: Golden Gate Park's
Japanese Tea Garden**

DOWNTOWN OAKLAND & LAKE MERRITT

SF's cooler sister across the bay, Oakland is where creative types fled when the Silicon Valley boom sent rents sky-rocketing. While the East Bay is less of a secret than it once was, the downtown area is rife with intriguing bars and shops, and Lake Merritt's close by for a glimpse of city-side nature. It's a short trip by BART from Embarcadero.

🍸 Cafe Van Kleef

Little-known fact: vodka cocktails taste better with a backdrop of taxidermy. So hop onto a bar stool at Cafe Van Kleef and order a Greyhound, vodka with fresh grapefruit juice and a whopping wedge of grapefruit balanced on top. We also like the salt-rimmed version and the naughty Bluehound, with tequila switched in. Chat up your neighbours, make eye contact with some creepy antique dolls, and realise you've still got plenty of change for a tip because these are Oakland prices and it's happy hour. *1621 Telegraph Ave; https://cafevankleef.net; noon-2am Tue-Fri, 6pm-2am Sat & Sun, 4pm-2am Mon.*

✖ The Fat Lady

Rumour has it that this 19th-century building was previously a brothel – there's your conversation-starter over a romantic dinner at The Fat Lady. The Victorian interior is bejewelled with Bay Area history, like original lead-lined stained-glass windows, old signs and Tiffany lamps. The menu leans longingly towards Europe with French onion soup, ribeye steak and Greek-style lamb with a feta garnish. *201 Washington St; www.thefatladyrestaurant.com; 510-465-4996; 11.30am-10pm Mon-Fri, 9am-11pm Sat, 9am-3pm Sun.*

🏛 Oakland Museum of California

Progressive and family-friendly, the Oakland Museum of California is reason alone to visit the East Bay. Learn California's history while crouching in a concrete pipe or sitting in a four-engine Douglas DC-8 plane. Sidle through gardens, and just try to resist the Oakland merch in the gift shop. Visit on a Friday, when food trucks and drinks kick off a party atmosphere from 5pm. *1000 Oak St; http://museumca.org; 11am-5pm Wed & Thu, 11am-10pm Fri, 11am-6pm Sat & Sun; adult/child $16/free.*

SAN FRANCISCO

Map labels

Mountain View Cemetery 3km (2 miles)
Telegraph Ave
20th St
19th St Oakland
Cafe Van Kleef
Brush St
Martin Luther King Jr Way
14th St
12th St
11th St
Snow Park
Bellevue Ave
Oaktown Spice Shop 300m (0.2 miles)
Lakeside Dr
Lake Merritt Trail
Wolfman Books
12th St Oakland City Center
Luckyduck Bicycle Cafe
8th St
7th St
Broadway
Franklin St
Webster St
Harrison St
OAKLAND
Madison St
Oak St
Lake Merritt
Oakland Metro Operahouse
The Fat Lady
Webster St Tube
Harrison St
Madison Park
Oakland Museum of California
Lake Merritt
Channel Park
Laney College
Jack London Square
Amtrak Station
San Francisco Bay
Evergreen Cemetery 7km (4.5 miles)
Alameda Island
Alice St Mini Park
Estuary Park

🔒 Wolfman Books

Oakland has a bevy of worthwhile bookstores, with 1973-founded Walden Pond Books deservedly hogging bookworms' attention. Wolfman is the wild-card choice: it's a small press and a simmering cauldron of literary events, championing writers from marginalised groups. *410 13th St; http://wolfmanhomerepair. com; noon-6pm Sun-Wed, to 9pm Thu-Sat.*

🧭 Lake Merritt Trail

Spanning 4.9km (3.1 miles) around Lake Merritt, this mixed-use walking and cycling trail takes a leisurely circuit around the USA's oldest designated wildlife refuge, home to dozens of bird species like herons, pelicans and rare ducks. Rent a boat, tour the volunteer-run bonsai garden or take a detour for a photo op outside cute but creepy Children's Fairyland, a 1950s theme park. *www.lakemerritt.org.*

✖ Luckyduck Bicycle Cafe

Bicycle shop and espresso joint Luckyduck is just one venue that proves which Bay Area

UNSETTLING CEMETERIES

Dark histories are revealed in Oakland's cemeteries. Evergreen Cemetery has a mass grave in which are buried more than 400 bodies from the Jonestown cult's mass murder-suicide in Guyana, which claimed many Californians among its 918 lives. Meanwhile Mountain View Cemetery is the final resting place of Elizabeth Short, victim of the so-called 'Black Dahlia Murder', an unsolved case that has gripped the popular imagination since it was reported in 1947.

neighbourhood really wears the hipster crown. Their menu includes vegan options like jackfruit and avocado on focaccia. *302 12th St; www.luckyduckoakland.com; 510-891-1830; 8am-7pm Tue-Sat.*

⭐ Oakland Metro Operahouse

Craving prog rock, guitar-abusing thrash or tormented heavy metal? This black-box theatre will have you screaming 'hell yeah' with your fists in the air. Great acoustics and a messy, all-in crowd. *522 2nd St; https://oaklandmetro.org.*

🔒 Oaktown Spice Shop

Flare your nostrils at this spice boutique, where the correct treatment of cinnamon sticks is passionately debated and quality ras el hanout, a Moroccan spice mix, is more treasured than gold. Buy individual spices or blends of their own devising, like Persian Lime Curry Rub. *546 Grand Ave; https://oaktownspiceshop.com; 10am-7pm Mon-Fri, 10am-5pm Sat & Sun.*

Top: inhale deeply at the fragrant Oaktown Spice Shop Left: Mountain View Cemetery

ARTS & CULTURE MUSIC & FILM SPORTS & LEISURE EATING DRINKING SHOPPING

PORTLAND

Creative, friendly and overflowing with quirk, Portland, Oregon, lives up to its hipster reputation while simultaneously being full of surprises.

Portland is famously hip and you'll find its coolest enclaves spread across the city, particularly in and around downtown and on the east side. The Hawthorne neighbourhood has had the longest run of attracting the weird and wonderful while Alberta Arts has taken it slower, with a chilled-out hippie vibe. Mississippi has historically been pretty grungy but newer generations attracted to its edgy music scene have incited gentrification. The Pearl, west-side Portland's most arty urban centre, has seen so many new buildings go up in recent years that entire blocks can change within a few months. Downtown has gone more upscale too, but has retained its historical edifices and grittier corners, never ceasing to surprise with its creative activities, food and everything in between.

Each of these neighbourhoods is very walkable. Rent an orange Biketown city bike or hop onto public transit to travel between them all.

HAWTHORNE

Hawthorne is where Portland is its most Portland-y. Some of the city's best restaurants and quirky shopping are here, all frequented by 20-somethings with green hair, couples casually dressed in matching unicorn onesies, grey-haired hippies, you name it. It's an easy place to navigate as it runs east along SE Hawthorne Street up to around SE 52nd Ave.

⊗ Harlow

Gluten-free? Vegan? Just want something tasty that will make you feel good? This delightfully bright space with refurbished farmhouse tables and crystal chandeliers offers everything from creative bowls and soups to guilt-free biscuits and gravy, green juices and not-so-healthy, boozed-up cocktails. *3632 SE Hawthorne St; www.harlowpdx.com; 8am-9pm Mon-Sat, 8am-3pm Sun.*

⊕ White Owl Social Club

Mingle with the hippest of hipsters on the gorgeous patio (great fire pit), in the bar or out on the lively dance floor. Check the schedule for everything from EDM to comedy nights. The after-party for the World Naked Bike Ride in June sometimes ends up here, if that tells you anything. *1305 SE 8th Ave; www.whiteowlsocialclub.com; 3pm-2am.*

🔒 House of Vintage

Hawthorne is vintage shopping heaven and House of Vintage may be its pinnacle. The 1200 sq metres (13,000 sq ft) here house 55 dealers selling mostly clothing, plus furniture and art. It's not dirt cheap, but chances are you'll find something you love. *3315 SE Hawthorne; www.houseofvintagenw.com; 11am-7pm, to 9pm Fri & Sat.*

🏛 National Hat Museum

The largest hat museum in the USA has nearly 2000 hats arranged throughout a heritage mansion. Reserve a 90-minute tour to learn more about *chapeaux* than you thought possible, and historical snippets of this intriguing 'hood. *1928 SE Ladd St; www.thehatmuseum.com; three daily tours Thu-Sat.*

✪ Bagdad Theater & Pub

People come here to watch blockbusters, but even if the film is terrible, no one leaves this fabulously ornate, circa 1927 theatre disappointed. Grab a beer and order a burger to be served to your plush seat. Afterwards, make use of the pub and restaurant to revel a bit longer in that Golden Age of film feeling. *3702 SE Hawthorne St; www.mcmenamins.com; 11am-midnight.*

BUCKMAN
KERNS
Laurelhurst Park
LAURELHURST
SE Stark St
Lone Fir Cemetery
SE Belmont St
SUNNYSIDE
White Owl Social Club
500m (0.25 miles)
SE Salmon St
House of Vintage
Bagdad Theater & Pub
Harlow
SE Hawthorne Blvd
National Hat Museum
SE 34th Ave
SE 37th Ave
Seawallcrest Park
SE Harrison St
RICHMOND
LADD'S ADDITION
HOSFORD-ABERNETHY
SE Division St

THE PEARL & DOWNTOWN

The city's heart, where you'll find many of Portland's famous sights and entertainment, plus business people and bicycle commuters going to and fro. The Pearl is the arty, up-and-coming quarter while downtown spreads past city-block sized Powell's Books and the Alphabet Shopping District to Pioneer Sq and Portland State University.

Smith Teamaker

Portland legend Steven Smith started Stash and Tazo tea companies, but Smith Tea is his swan song, the culmination of his tea-making knowledge. Stop by the headquarters in a historic blacksmith shop for tea flights, mocktails and lattes, or sign up for a workshop or tea-paired meal. Factory tours ($10) are on Fridays at 2pm. *1626 NW Thurman St; www.smithtea.com; 10am-6pm.*

Darcelle XV

This outrageously camp and ever-popular Las Vegas–style cabaret bar has been entertaining Portlanders for over 50 years. Now in her 80s, Darcelle XV is the world's oldest drag queen performer. Programming beyond the nightly female impersonator performances include glamour pageants (as opposed to beauty) and male strippers. *208 NW 3rd Ave; www.darcellexv.com; approx 8pm-midnight Tue-Sat.*

Ground Kontrol

Pinball wizards, Donkey Kong dorks and Tetris titans should load up on quarters and head directly to this temple of video games from the 1970s, '80s and '90s. DJs spin music some nights and there's food and drinks to help fuel your high-score aspirations. *115 NW 5th Ave; www.groundkontrol.com; noon-late.*

Lan Su Chinese Garden

For mid-city tranquillity, head to this lily pond surrounded by flower gardens, ornate traditional Chinese buildings and two-storey tea house serving light meals. Tours are held throughout the day or reserve for dance or music performances, tai chi classes, calligraphy lessons and more. *239 NW Everett St;*

www.lansugarden.org; 10am-7pm
(to 4pm in winter).

⚡ Glowing Greens

You came to Portland to play
pirate-themed, indoor, glow-in-
the-dark mini golf, right? OK even
if you didn't, this is a suitably weird
place to pop into on a rainy day
or if you're travelling with kids.
Mini golf too soft? Try out axe-
throwing and set free your inner
ninja. *509 SW Taylor St; www.
glowinggreens.com; noon-9pm,
to 11pm Fri & Sat.*

✖ Pine Street Market

Everyone knows about Portland's
outdoor food truck pods, but this
place brings vendors indoors,
shines them up a bit and gives you
a comfortable (but often crowded)
place to enjoy it all. The selection
includes Olympia Provisions
(sausages and beer). Kim Jong
Smokehouse (Korean street food)
and Wizbangbar, ever-popular
Salt & Straw ice cream's soft-serve
outlet. *126 SW 2nd St; www.
pinestreetpdx.com; 11am-9pm*

© Jess Kraft / Shutterstock

SPRINGFIELD IN PORTLAND

What do Flanders, Lovejoy
and Quimby have in
common? They're Portland
streets and names from *The
Simpsons!* Matt Groening
grew up on Evergreen
Terrace (the same street
the Simpsons live on) in
Portland and graduated
from Lincoln High School
(go there to look for 'Bart
Simpson' scrawled by
Groening in wet cement).
Look for more parallels
around town.

Mon-Thu, 8am-11pm Sat, 8am-
10pm Sun.

🏛 Freakybuttrue Peculiarium

Here's a museum as weird as
Portland aims to be: get an
interactive coffin experience, a
selfie as you undergo an alien
autopsy and much more. It's tiny,
cluttered and kind of dirty but
that's all part of the fun. *2234 NW
Thurman St; www.peculiarium.
com; 11am-6pm Fri-Mon.*

**Top: neon sign in Portland
Below and below left: Pine
Street Market, a magnet for
discerning food-lovers**

© 2020, Pine Street Market

© 2020, Pine Street Market

ALBERTA ARTS

This is Portland's arty, hippie neighbourhood; it's become one of the most sought-after places to live on the east side. While the bars and restaurants fill up, especially on weekends, it's pretty mellow around here most days and it's a relaxing place for an urban wander. Check out the many beautiful murals from NE 15th to NE 30th Aves.

Great Notion Brewing

Creamy, hoppy beers here avoid the bitterness of many West Coast IPAs, which makes this brewery stand out in beer-competitive Portland. Also try fruity varieties and sours. It's always 'hopping' at the pub and there's internationally inspired food. *2204 NE Alberta; www.greatnotionpdx.com; noon-10pm, to 11pm Fri & Sat.*

StuStuStudio

This tiny shop is a co-op retail space for Portland craft artists, selling jewellery, greetings cards, ceramics and more. You might find postcards featuring stylised paintings of Portland bridges, dagger-shaped earrings, the perfect coffee mug for your mom, or who knows? You'll have to go in to see. Very reasonable prices. *1627 NE Alberta St; www.stustustudio.net; noon-6pm Wed-Mon.*

Grilled Cheese Grill

Relive your childhood with a gourmet twist at this food truck with seating in an old school bus. The sandwiches range from cheddar on white bread to melted brie, olive tapenade and even a burger patty. Table tops are decorated with 1970s-era school photos. And yes, you can ask for the crusts to be cut off. *1027 NE Alberta St; www.grilledcheesegrill.com; 11.30am-8pm, to 2.30am Fri & Sat.*

Alberta Street Gallery

This gallery holds works from 30 local artists. Events are on the calendar such as art talks, or more unusual options like drinking and painting workshops. It's the hub of the neighbourhood's art community. *1829 NE Alberta St; www.albertastreetgallery.com; 11am-7pm Mon-Thu, 11am-9pm Fri, 9am-9pm Sat & 9am-5pm Sun.*

Last Thursday

Celebrate the last Thursday of every month at this wild art and music fair. Expect circus performers, Native American musical groups, art stalls, food and (especially during the warmer months) throngs of people. It starts out family-friendly then degenerates as the night wears on. *NE Alberta St (btwn 15th & 30th Aves); http://lastthurspdx.org; 6-9pm.*

PORTLAND

MISSISSIPPI

Here's a mix of gentrification – slick new buildings housing shiny cocktail bars and upscale restaurants – with cool-kid grunge, like indie music, weird shops and cheap food trucks. The blend makes Mississippi a haven for lovers of art, music, beer and food, and gives the impression that you've stumbled a little off the tourist radar.

Mississippi Records

Dig through the stacks at this record store (with an eponymous recording label) for limited releases, international finds or just music you love, on vinyl for a great price. Sip coffee at the cafe then don't miss the basement, to peruse The Portland Museum of Modern Art. Cash only. *5202 N Albina St; noon-7pm.*

Paxton Gate

Ethically sourced taxidermy and bugs are just a few of the things you'll find in this science-oriented shop. There's a design aspect too, which may inspire home decoration urges involving framed, felted human hearts, a map of the solar system or a giant, fossilised snail. We've warned you. *4205 N Mississippi Ave; www.paxtongate.com; 11am-7pm.*

Mississippi Studios

A music venue designed and owned by musicians – so it's not only a cut above the competition sound-wise, it's just plain cooler. The attached Bar Bar serves good burgers and beer indoors or on a heated patio. Check out the schedule to see which bands are playing, and get tickets in advance as shows can sell out early. *3939 N Mississippi Ave; www.mississippistudios.com; 11am-2am.*

Spin Laundry Lounge

Stuff your clothes into an energy-efficient washing machine, order a beer, coffee and/or snacks (smoothie bowl, avocado toast etc) and chill. There's wi-fi for those who need to work and also sports on TV. You can also leave, wander the neighbourhood and get a text message when your load is done. *750 N Freemont St; www.spinlaundrylounge.com; 8am-11pm.*

Ruby Jewel

Take handcrafted ice cream then squish it in between two freshly baked cookies, is there a better formula? Choose ice cream flavours from salted caramel to Oregon Strawberry then match them with a cookie like brown sugar or chocolate chip. The ingredients are sourced from around the Pacific Northwest. *3713 N Mississippi Ave; www. rubyjewel.com; noon-10pm.*

🏛 ARTS & CULTURE   ⭐ MUSIC & FILM   🏃 SPORTS & LEISURE   🍴 EATING   🍷 DRINKING   🔒 SHOPPING

Lower Lonsdale

Vancouver

Kitsilano   Commercial Drive

Main Street

VANCOUVER

In urban, outdoor-oriented Vancouver, set between the mountains and the sea, the city's neighbourhoods offer a mix of cultural and active experiences.

R adiating out from downtown Vancouver, which sits on a peninsula surrounded by water, the city's neighbourhoods have different styles but are close to the urban core.

The west side, where hip Kitsilano is located, was historically wealthy and is full of restored heritage bungalows and upscale restaurants. More recently, craft brewers, artists and young families have brought new vibrancy to Vancouver's east side, particularly around Main St and Commercial Dr.

Across the Burrard Inlet from downtown, linked by two bridges and a ferry, North Vancouver has both suburban and industrial districts, rising into the North Shore Mountains. In waterside Lower Lonsdale, condo towers and a contemporary art museum share the streets with cafes. Nearby, you can ski, snowshoe or hike, and still be back at the waterfront in time for happy hour.

Vancouver's neighbourhoods are walkable and bicycle-friendly, and with the city's broad-ranging transit system, you don't need a car to get around with ease.

KITSILANO

Environmental organisation Greenpeace started in Kitsilano, once a hippie enclave on Vancouver's affluent west side. 'Kits' is now an upscale residential and commercial district, where restaurants, yoga studios and coffeehouses line West 4th Ave, and sun seekers and runners play along always-busy Kits Beach. Buses connect downtown and Kits; you can also walk or cycle across the Burrard Bridge.

⊕ Kitsilano Pool

Not only does Kitsilano have one of the city's most popular beaches, it's also home to North America's longest saltwater pool. Extending 137m (450ft), it overlooks the beach and boasts views of the downtown skyline, drawing summer lap-swimmers and families who flock to its kid-friendly waterslides. *2305 Cornwall Ave; 604-731-0011; mid-May–mid-Sep; adult/child $6.10/$3.05.*

✕ Mak 'n' Ming

Mak 'n' Ming aims high, serving imaginative, Asian-influenced, multi-course dinners in a tiny storefront. Try sashimi with watercress or halibut with white asparagus and nori. Reserve ahead. *1629 Yew Street; www.maknming. com; 604-737-1155; tasting menu $83; from 5pm Tue-Sun.*

⊕ The Running Room

Runners: do you want to explore Kitsilano but don't know where to go? This athletic-wear store hosts a free year-round run club, open to runners from newbies to marathoners. There's no need to register, just show up at the store and join the scheduled runs. *2112 W 4th Ave; www.runningroom.com; 6pm Wed & 8.30am Sun; free.*

🔒 Middle Sister

This compact West 4th boutique carries fashionable women's clothing and accessories from Canadian and Korean designers, stocking items you're unlikely to find elsewhere. The shop's owner, Linda Sin, a 'middle sister' in her own family, has said that middle children often have to shout louder to be heard over their siblings; she's opted to express herself though the distinctive items she carries in her store. *2137 W 4th Ave; www. middlesister.ca; 11am-6pm.*

✕ Beaucoup Bakery

It's worth seeking out tiny Beaucoup Bakery for freshly baked croissants, fruit tarts and salted chocolate rosemary cookies. This petite French-style cafe also makes a small selection of sandwiches and seasonal savoury items. *2150 Fir Street; www.beaucoupbakery. com; 604-732-4222; 7am-5pm Tue-Fri, 8am-5pm Sat-Sun.*

English Bay / Hadden Park / False Creek Ferry / Vanier Park / Kitsilano Pool / Kitsilano Beach Park / Cornwall Ave / Burrard St / Broker's Bay / York Ave / Mak 'n' Ming / KITSILANO / Middle Sister / The Running Room / W 4th Ave / W 5th Ave / Burrard St / Fir St / Beaucoup Bakery / Granville St / Yew St / Arbutus St

COMMERCIAL DRIVE

The east side Grandview-Woodlands neighbourhood, centered around eclectic Commercial Dr, was once the heart of Vancouver's Italian and Portuguese communities. Vestiges of this heritage remain, even as natural foods markets, cafes and microbreweries replace the pasta makers and traditional bakeries. From downtown Vancouver, the SkyTrain's Expo line takes you to Commercial-Broadway Station, at the south end of the commercial strip of 'The Drive'.

⊕ Rio Theatre
Built in 1938, the restored Rio Theatre, just off Commercial Dr, programmes quirky films and festivals, hosts concerts and organises offbeat special events. At their Friday late-night movie showings, you get a discount if you arrive in costume. *1660 E Broadway; www.riotheatre.ca.*

⊖ Spade Coffee & Spirits
A hip, locally popular hangout, white-walled Spade Coffee & Spirits starts the day with coffee, Italian-style pastries and freshly made breakfast bowls, moving on to salads, sandwiches and cocktails later in the day. *1858 Commercial Dr; www.spadecoffee.ca; 8am-7pm Mon-Fri, 8am-6pm Sat & Sun.*

⊗ La Grotta del Formaggio
This Italian deli is the place to buy cured meats, cheeses and other imported Italian food. They also prepare hearty sandwiches to go, layering prosciutto, salami, cheese, olives and more on fresh focaccia. *1791 Commercial Dr; www.lgdf.ca; 604-255-3911; 9am-6pm Mon-Sat, 10am-6pm Sun.*

⌂ Havana Vancouver
Though this friendly joint does serve Latin-influenced food, come for drinks (especially on the sunny patio) or for the regular performances in its 60-seat backroom theatre, a varied line-up of stage, music and comedy events. Leave time for a mojito or local craft beer before or after the show. *1212 Commercial Dr; www. havanavancouver.com.*

⊗ Portuguese Club of Vancouver
Founded as a social club, the Portuguese Club of Vancouver operates an old-school restaurant that's open to the public, serving dishes like grilled sardines, pork and clams, or piri-piri prawns. The best time to go? When Portugal's soccer team is playing, and loyal fans come to cheer the televised

VANCOUVER

matches. *1144 Commercial Dr; www.facebook.com/PCOVCLUB; 604-251-2042; 8.30am-4pm Tue, 8.30am-11pm Wed-Sun.*

© 2020, Havana Vancouver

Vancouver East Cultural Centre

Nicknamed 'The Cultch', this venue offers a diverse, multicultural mix of theatre and music events – many featuring LGBT+, indigenous or other under-represented themes or artists – in its historic building off Commercial Dr and in the nearby York Theatre. *1895 Venables St; www.thecultch.com.*

Odd Society Spirits

While breweries line the streets around Commercial Dr, spirits lovers should head to this small-batch distillery and tasting lounge, where you can sample East Van Vodka, Wallflower Gin and other products. They also make an unusual, and excellent, bittersweet vermouth. *1725 Powell St; www. oddsocietyspirits.com; 1-11pm Thu-Sat, 1-7pm Sun.*

CRAFT BEER IN 'YEAST VAN'

East Van, as East Vancouver is known, has had such a recent boom in craft breweries that the neighbourhood has been nicknamed 'Yeast Van'. Many of these microbreweries are within walking distance of Commercial Dr. Plan a tasting tour with stops at Strange Fellows Brewing, Parallel 49 Brewing, Bomber Brewing, and many more. Check out www. bcaletrail.ca.

The Pie Shoppe

Every pie-lover's destination for a slice or a whole box of homemade deliciousness. Look for year-round varieties like chocolate-pecan or apple-cinnamon, as well as seasonal fruit pies, from peach to blueberry to rhubarb. They shut down early if the pie is gone. *1875 Powell St; www.thepieshoppe.ca; 604-338-6646; 11am-6pm Wed-Sat, 11am-5pm Sun.*

Clockwise from top: rustic-chic Havana Vancouver; quality tipples at Odd Society Spirits; baked goodies at The Pie Shoppe

© 2020, The Pie Shoppe

© Cause and Affect / 2020, Odd Society Spirits

MAIN STREET

Beginning in Chinatown and the gritty Downtown Eastside, Main St passes the Olympic Village, a condo community that housed athletes during the 2010 Winter Games. As the street rises uphill from downtown, the neighbourhood gets funkier, with street art and microbreweries. The Main St/Science World SkyTrain station borders Chinatown and False Creek, and buses run regularly along Main St.

🏊 Creekside Kayaks

Rent a kayak or stand-up paddleboard at Creekside Kayaks to explore the city by water. You don't need paddling experience, although the company also offers three-hour introductory workshops for kayak novices who'd like some guidance. Tip: take your skyline photos from this side of the False Creek waterfront. *1 Athletes Way; www.creeksidekayaks.ca; 11am-sunset Mon-Fri, 9am-5pm Sat & Sun May–mid-Oct; from $20/hour.*

🍺 33 Brewing Experiment

While 33 Acres Brewing Company offers beer samples and weekend waffle brunches in its main tasting room, next door at 33 Brewing Experiment you can sip new brews, like Fluffy Cloud IPA or lemongrass-scented Vietnamese lager, before they're officially released. *25 West 8th Ave; http://33brewingexp. com; 11am-11pm.*

🌲 Dude Chilling Park

It started as a prank. An artist replaced the city-installed sign at Guelph Park, purporting to rename the green space 'Dude Chilling Park'. After the city threatened to remove the fake signage, so many people protested that the humorous signpost, which the artist donated, was installed permanently. *Brunswick St at East 8th Ave.*

🍽 Burdock & Co

This locavore bistro uses ingredients from around the region in dishes like rosemary-smoked mussels, heirloom carrot salad, or their signature fried chicken. On Mondays, Burdock & Co changes its tune when a DJ runs 'Disco Dumpling Night', an evening of music and potstickers. *2702 Main St; www.burdockandco.com; 604-879-0077; from 5pm Mon-Fri, 10am-2pm & from 5pm Sat & Sun.*

🛍 Vancouver Special

Named for a style of two-storey home built in Vancouver during the 1960s and '70s, Vancouver Special stocks design-conscious kitchenware, household objects and art books, some from local creators and others from around the globe. *3612 Main St; www. vanspecial.com; 11am-6pm Mon-Sat, noon-5pm Sun.*

Map showing: Thornton Park, Creekside Kayaks, Main St, Terminal Ave, MOUNT PLEASANT, W 2nd Ave, Great Northern Way, China Creek Park, W 7th Ave, Jonathan Rogers Park, 33 Brewing Experiment, W Broadway, Dude Chilling Park, E Broadway, Burdock & Co, E 11th Ave, Main St, Kingsway, Fraser St, SOUTH MAIN (SOMA), Vancouver Special, E 20th Ave

LOWER LONSDALE

In less than 15 minutes, the SeaBus ferry cruises from downtown to North Vancouver's Lower Lonsdale district, with great views of the Vancouver skyline and the industrial waterfront along the way. Condo towers, museums and commercial developments have sprung up shoreside in this urban suburb, where the Shipyards Building hosts a summer night market with food trucks and live entertainment.

🍺 Green Leaf Brewing Company

Amid the food stalls and touristy shops at Lonsdale Quay Market, next to the ferry docks, Green Leaf Brewing Company crafts beers like Lloyd's Lager or Les Saisonniers Saison, which you can sample in the waterview tasting room. *123 Carrie Cates Ct; www. greenleafbrew.com; 11am-10pm Mon-Thu, 11am-11pm Fri & Sat, 11am-9pm Sun.*

🏛 Polygon Gallery

This metal and glass gallery exhibits contemporary Canadian art, particularly photography. Check out the skyline views from the second-floor terrace of this reflective-clad building, which locally based Patkau Architects designed to feel both modern and industrial. *101 Carrie Cates Ct; www.thepolygon.ca; 10am-5pm Tue-Sun; by donation.*

🔒 Mo's General Store

Inspired by the old-fashioned general store, Mo's carries an eclectic mix of kitchenware, locally made sauces and spice mixes, cards and souvenirs. *51 Lonsdale Ave; www.mosgeneralstore.com; 8am-6pm Mon, 8am-8pm Tue-Sat, 9am-6pm Sun.*

❌ Coconama

East of Lonsdale Ave, the yoga studios and sushi bars give way to engine repair shops and furniture finishing workshops. That's where you'll find Coconama, a chocolatier incorporating Japanese flavours like *hojicha* (roasted green tea), black sesame or yuzu into their delicate bonbons. *264 E 1st St; www. coconama.com; 604-770-1200; 10am-6pm Wed-Mon.*

🏃 North Shore Spirit Trail

Follow the waterfront walkway west from Lonsdale Quay onto a 6.5km (4-mile) walking and cycling route that takes you past a community of floating homes, through Squamish First Nation land, and along the shoreline. *www.cnv.org/spirittrail.*

❌ Lift Production Bakery

Detour off the Spirit Trail to Lift Production Bakery for pastries to go, like chocolate brownies or giant cookies. *700 Copping St; www. liftproductionbakery.com; 8am-4pm Mon-Fri, 9am-4pm Sat & Sun.*

Lift Production Bakery 500m (0.25 miles)

NORTH VANCOUVER

North Shore Spirit Trail

Chesterfield Ave

W 2nd St

W 1st St

Lonsdale Ave

W Esplanade

Mo's General Store

E 2nd St

Polygon Gallery

E 1st St

SeaBus to North Vancouver

Green Leaf Brewing Company

E Esplanade

Coconama

Vancouver Harbour

SEATTLE

Yes, it's rainy. But that's why Seattle has such awesome indoor culture: coffee shops, microbreweries, galleries. And when the sun does shine – glory!

SEATTLE

S eattle is a city of water and mountains – Puget Sound and the Olympics to the west, Lake Washington and the Cascades to the east and Mt Rainier looming in the south. Its geography has shaped its boom-and-bust history: first a timber outpost, then a gold rush boom town, then a shipbuilding centre, now a tech hub, with a much-imitated culture of outstanding music, food, coffee and beer.

Today, Seattle's a patchwork of neighbourhoods so distinct they could practically be their own cities. North of the Lake Washington Ship Canal, Ballard was once a working-class Scandinavian community. It's morphed into a hip walkable district of local bars and boutiques, but still wears its history proudly. Southwest of downtown is beachy, residential West Seattle, with a strip of groovy seafront cafes and bars. Near the city's southern border is Beacon Hill, one of the city's most multi-cultural neighbourhoods, with food to match.

BEACON HILL

You'll know Beacon Hill by the enormous art deco building – a 1930s-era former Marine hospital – crowning its northern ridge like a castle. From here, the low-key, mostly residential neighbourhood spreads south in a column along the west side of I-5, connected to downtown by light rail. In mostly white Seattle, it's known for its multicultural make-up and large immigrant population.

🏛 The Station

More than just a coffee shop, this neighbourhood gathering place is committed to social justice, hosting open-mic sessions, youth writing workshops, and an annual block party. The coffee's excellent, and the cinnamony Mexican hot chocolate is a treat. *1600 S Roberto Maestas Festival St; www.* thestationbh.com; 6am-8pm Mon-Fri, 8am-6pm Sat & Sun.

❌ Despi Delite

On Saturday mornings locals line up for oven-warm *pan de ube* (bread stuffed with purple yam), *ensaymada* (a sweet, cheesy bun) and other Filipino treats at this friendly bakery, open since 1988. Old-fashioned donuts are a hit. *2701 15th Ave S; http://despidelitebakery.com; 206-325-2114; 7.15am-6.30pm Mon-Fri, to 6pm Sat.*

✈ Jefferson Park

Communities come together at this grassy green space, with a golf course, bowling green, cricket pitch (hang around on weekends to see the local Samoan team play), skate park and playground. On its western edge is the Beacon Food Forest, an edible landscape of fruit trees and vegetable gardens that serves as a community food pantry. *3801 Beacon Ave S; 4am-11.30pm.*

🍺 Perihelion Brewery

Locals sip creative ales and nibble house-made soft pretzels and brisket sandwiches at this friendly microbrewery, whose twinkly lights make grey Seattle Februaries feel cosy. Try a smoky-sweet Johnny Tacoma Scottish ale or a Lost in Space blackberry mead, made with honey and blackberry puree. *2800 16th Ave S; www.perihelion.beer; 4-10pm Tue-Thu, to 11pm Fri, noon-11pm Sat, noon-9pm Sun.*

❌ Bar del Corso

Bar del Corso used to be a secret shared only between locals or those in the know, but word of the restaurant's wood-fired pizzas and Italian-inspired small plates has spread. Expect a wait, especially on weekend evenings. Order a (pleasingly potent) negroni to pass the time... *3057 Beacon Ave S; www.bardelcorso.com; 206-395-2069; 5-10pm Tue-Sat.*

Despi Delite ❌ 🏛 The Station   S Waite St   S Lander St
Perihelion Brewery 🍺   🚇 Beacon Hill
S Stevens St
Bar del Corso ❌   S Hanford St   Beacon Ave S   21st Ave S   23rd Ave S   S Mc Clellan St
15th Ave S
S Hinds St   S Hinds St
S Spokane St
BEACON HILL   ✈ Jefferson Park

BALLARD

Bounded by water on two sides – the canal to the south and Shilshole Bay to the west – laid-back Ballard still bears traces of the fishing village it once was. There are few major 'sights', just block after block of sweet wooden bungalows and a walkable commercial district stuffed with indie boutiques, craft beer bars, restaurants and art spaces.

❌ Larsen's Bakery
One of Ballard's few remaining Scandinavian businesses, Larsen's has been a neighbourhood institution for 45 years. Pastries like flaky, almond-stuffed kringles and braided cardamom bread are hot out of the oven at 5.30am. *8000 24th Ave NW; www.larsensbakery. com; 206-782-8285; 5.30am-7.30pm Mon-Sat, to 6pm Sun.*

❌ San Fermo
In Seattle's oldest house, a pair of connected white cottages from the 1850s, is this Platonic ideal of a neighbourhood trattoria, with cushioned banquettes and a patio for summer cocktails. Pasta's the thing here: try the house Bolognese or ravioli stuffed with Dungeness crab. *5341 Ballard Ave NW; www.sanfermoseattle.com; 206-342-1530; 5-10pm, brunch Sat & Sun.*

🔒 Scandinavian Specialties
Locals stock up on cloudberry preserves, salty Finnish liquorice, marinated herring and other Nordic staples at this cute little gourmet store, then grab a smørrebrød (open-faced sandwich) for lunch at the cafe. *6719 15th Ave NW; www.scanspecialties.com; 10am-5.30pm Mon-Sat, 11am-4pm Sun.*

✈ Golden Gardens Park
On warm days, half of Ballard winds up in this sound-side public park to lounge on the sandy beach, birdwatch in the wetlands and hike through the maritime forest. After-dark beachfront bonfires at the barbecue pits are a local summer tradition. *8498 Seaview Pl NW; 4am-11.30pm.*

☕ Slate Coffee Roasters
This teensy minimalist spot takes coffee verrrry seriously, serving its espresso in glasses so you can see the colour and banning granulated sugar (you can have syrup, if you wish). Its showpiece is a 'deconstructed latte' – a three-glass flight with espresso, then fresh milk, then the two combined into a latte. *5413 6th Ave NW; 206-235-6564;*

Golden Gardens Park • Loyal Way NW • Larsen's Bakery • NW 80th St • NW 80th St • 24th Ave NW • 15th Ave NW • 8th Ave NW • 32nd Ave NW • Salmon Bay Park • Scandinavian Specialties • BALLARD • NW 65th St • NW 65th St • Slate Coffee Roasters • Tides and Pines • NW Market St • Hiram M Chittenden Locks • Nordic Museum • Push/Pull • San Fermo • Leary Ave NW • Peddler • FREMONT • MAGNOLIA • Salmon Bay • INTERBAY • Gilman Ave W • Ballard Bridge

© 2020, Peddler Brewing Company

7am-5pm Mon-Wed & Fri, 8am-
5pm Sat & Sun.

🏛 Nordic Museum

In a stunning contemporary
building, this well-curated
museum tells the story of Seattle's
Scandinavian immigrants through
artefacts and interactive exhibits.
Special exhibit subjects have
ranged from the prints of Finnish
design house Marimekko to the
art of the Swedish crime novel.
Locals love the cafe, Freya, for
juniper-smoked salmon and
aquavit cocktails. *2655 NW Market
St; www.nordicmuseum.org;
10am-5pm Tue & Wed, Fri-Sun; to
8pm Thu.*

🍺 Peddler

What could be more Seattle than
a bike-themed microbrewery? At
Peddler you can cycle up, park
your bike inside, pump up your
tyres, then settle in the kid- and
dog-friendly beer garden with
a Seattle Haze IPA with a vegan
hot dog from the on-site food
truck. *1514 NW Leary Way; www.*

HIRAM M CHITTENDEN LOCKS

Ballard's most popular
attraction is this century-
old engineering feat (3015
NW 54th St, 7am-9pm), a
series of ship locks allowing
boats to travel between
Lake Washington, 20ft
above sea level, and the
Puget Sound. Alongside,
a fish ladder lets salmon
complete their seasonal
migration; watch through
a series of underground
windows then visit the
adjacent botanical gardens.

*peddlerbrewing.com; 4-10pm
Wed, to 11pm Thu & Fri, 11am-
11pm Sat, noon-8pm Sun.*

🏛 Push/Pull

In an industrial space near the
water, this underground art and
comics collective is part gallery,
part workspace, part community
centre. Sign up for a sketching or
bookmaking workshop, or stop by
to pick up a print and take a turn
on the vintage pinball machine.
*5484 Shilshole Ave NW; http://
pushpullseattle.weebly.com; 11am-
7pm Mon-Wed, to 9pm Thu-Sat,
10am-7pm Sun.*

🔒 Tides and Pines

Billing itself as a 'Pacific Northwest
Lifestyle Shop', this trendy spot
is the place for pine-smelling
handmade soap, chunky knitted
sweaters and reusable market
bags printed with 'Ballard'. *5410
22nd Ave NW; 206-420-8119;
http://tidesandpinesshop.com;
11am-7pm.*

Top: microbrews at Peddler
**Left: waterfront houses
in the picturesque former
fishing village of Ballard**

© cdrin / Shutterstock

WEST SEATTLE

Seattle was founded on this thumb-like peninsula, when the Denny Party of pioneers landed here in 1851. It has a breezy, beach town vibe, especially around Alki, with its chowder houses and sand volleyball courts. Local businesses cluster along California Ave, which runs north-south. Avoid annoying bridge traffic by taking the water taxi from downtown. Sunset views over the Olympics are dreamy.

Schmitz Preserve Park

This 53-acre park has one of the only old-growth forests left in Seattle, whose mammoth conifers, dripping ferns and carpets of moss make hikers feel like they've gone back in time 100 – or 1000 – years. There's no signage inside, but it's only got 2.7km (1.7 miles) of trail so it's hard to get too lost. *5551 SW Admiral Way; 6am-10pm.*

Alki Spud Fish & Chips

Top Pot Doughnuts

Schmitz Preserve Park

SW Admiral Way

Hiawatha Park

ALKI

SW Hanford St

SW Charlestown St

Duwamish Longhouse and Cultural Center 3km (2 miles)

Beach Dr SW

Me-Kwa-Mooks Park

WEST SEATTLE

Easy Street Records

SW Alaska St

Origins Cannabis

Puget Sound

49th Ave SW

California Ave SW

Fauntleroy Way SW

35th Ave SW

New Luck Toy

Beveridge Place

Colman Pool 2km (1.5 miles)

SW Morgan St

Colman Pool

On a point of land sticking out into Puget Sound, this outdoor saltwater pool is immensely popular with locals, who swim in view of the Olympics and the occasional pod of orcas. You can't drive in; getting here is an agreeable 20-minute walk or bike ride through Lincoln Park. *8011 Fauntleroy Way SW; noon-7pm late Jun-early Sep.*

New Luck Toy

West Seattle cool kids dig into American Chinese classics to the sounds of old-school hip-hop at this kitschy-cool restaurant and karaoke bar, all glossy black walls, red paper lanterns and lucky cat figurines. The back bar slings slushy tiki drinks into the wee hours. *5905 California Ave SW; http://newlucktoy.bar; 4pm-2am.*

Easy Street Records

It's hard enough to find a decent indie record store left in America, but one with in-store concerts, staff with three decades' experience, and a cafe serving music-themed brunch dishes (the Johnny Cash Special is steak and eggs, the Green Day is a spinach salad)? That's practically a miracle. *559 California Ave SW; http://easystreetonline.com; 9am-9pm Mon-Sat, to 7pm Sun.*

Alki Spud Fish & Chips

Locals take a break from swimming or stand-up paddleboarding to order the cod-and-fries meal at the walk-up window of this 1935 Alki Beach

SEATTLE

institution. *2666 Alki Ave SW; www.alkispud.com; 206-938-0606; 11am-9pm.*

🏛 Duwamish Longhouse and Cultural Center

The Duwamish people were the original inhabitants of this land, and they're still fighting for federal recognition of their tribal status, which comes with benefits like healthcare and education grants. This traditional wooden building hosts opportunities to learn about the tribe's culture, from basket-weaving workshops to storytelling nights. *4705 W Marginal Way SW; www.duwamishtribe.org; 10am-5pm Tue-Sat.*

🔒 Origins Cannabis

Washington was the first state to legalise recreational marijuana, and Seattle's got some of the classiest, more comprehensive dispensaries in the country. This chic, wood-panelled shop has encyclopaedic 'budtenders' to steer customers to the right products, from vapes to edibles like sea salt caramels. *4800 40th Ave SW; www. originscannabis.com; 8am-11.30pm Mon-Sat, 9am-9pm Sun.*

LOG HOUSE MUSEUM

A historical curiosity in Seattle's oldest neighbourhood, this museum (3003 61st Ave SW, noon-4pm Thu-Sun) was built in 1903 from Douglas fir trees as a carriage house. When all around it was moved or demolished to lay out West Seattle, the house miraculously survived and now sits amid a dense urban grid rather than dense forest.

🍺 Beveridge Place

On foggy nights there's nowhere cosier than this wood-panelled pub, with worn-in couches, stacks of board games, and dozens of beers on tap, plus 150 different bottles. Patrons can bring their own food – or their own dog. *6413 California Ave SW; www.beveridgeplacepub. com; 2pm-2am Mon-Fri, from noon Sat & Sun.*

❌ Top Pot Doughnuts

A small local chain, Top Pot's Alki location is the perfect destination for an early morning beach walk. Their craggy, dense 'old-fashioneds,' with glaze seeping into every crack, are legendary. Coffee ain't bad either. *2758 Alki Ave SW; www.toppotdoughnuts. com; 206-466-6839; 6am-6pm Mon-Fri, from 7am Sat & Sun.*

**Top: West Seattle
Below: flick through vinyl
at Easy Street Records**

LOS ANGELES

LA is known for sprawl but the word doesn't do justice to its vast expanse. Think of it more as a series of small cities, scattered from the Pacific Ocean to the mountains.

Surfers, car-clogged freeways, long streets lined by palm trees and bungalows, taco trucks and celebrity-studded hot spots... everyone has a vision of Los Angeles, but the real one is more surprising than the standard Walk of Fame and Venice canals (though we've nothing against them).

To experience the many sides of this sunny, surprising metropolis within America's most populous county, try out these four neighbourhoods for size. The shifting colossus that is LA includes the artsy retreat of Topanga Canyon in the Santa Monica Mountains and the foodie delights of centrally located historic Koreatown. Find art galleries and bike trails along the LA River in Atwater Village/Frogtown, and the Chicano history and delicious dining scene of Highland Park to the northeast. Beat the traffic by taking cabs or ride-shares when you can, or go full-SoCal with a convertible rental to cruise along the canyon roads. We promise your efforts will be rewarded.

LOS ANGELES

TOPANGA CANYON

It's no wonder laid-back and secluded Topanga, nestled between Malibu and Pacific Palisades, has harboured generations of artists. The area is virtually unchanged since its hippie heyday; population 8000, this small, bohemian village feels like a genuine retreat, an oasis from the schmoozing and smog, reached by climbing scenic roads. It's an ideal place for those looking to recharge and find inspiration.

✖ Inn of the Seventh Ray

Organic dining in an idyllic courtyard draws celebrities and respite-seekers to this rustic woodland setting, an LA classic that's far removed from the urban bustle. The romantic and calm location explains its enduring popularity. Drop into the nearby Spiral Staircase afterwards to pick out some crystals and New Age books. *128 Old Topanga Canyon Rd; www.innoftheseventhray.com; 310-455-1311; 9.30am-3pm & 5.30-9.30pm.*

🔒 Hidden Treasures

If you need a new look for that lunch at the Inn of the Seventh Ray, this is your spot: overflowing with vintage clothing and costume wear, they have unique, effortlessly bohemian outfits to suit the most discerning eye. *154 S Topanga Canyon Blvd; www. hiddentreasurestopanga.com; approx 10.30am-6.30pm.*

✦ Topanga State Park

Though populous, Los Angeles County also boasts rugged, remote beauty in the canyons and faults of the country's largest park within city limits. The hike to Eagle Rock is popular, accessible from the main trailhead at Trippet Ranch. The park can be reached from the Pacific Coast Hwy or the 101/Ventura Fwy. *20828 Entrada Rd; www.parks. ca.gov; 8am-6.30pm.*

✦ Topanga Creek Outpost

This nationally top-ranked, award-winning bike shop offers rentals as well as equipment for bike touring, and the shop experts can provide the gear and info for an awesome time exploring Topanga State Park. *1273 Topanga Canyon Blvd; www.topangacreekoutpost. com; closed Sun & Wed, approx 9.30am-4.30pm.*

✦ Topanga Beach

Surfers flock here at the base of Topanga Canyon on Malibu's most southern beach. Less well-suited for swimmers, it has a long right-hand break that's good for both longboards and shortboards, and attracts plenty of wave fanatics when the swell is good. Limited parking. *18700 Pacific Coast Hwy; https://beaches.lacounty.gov/topanga-beach.*

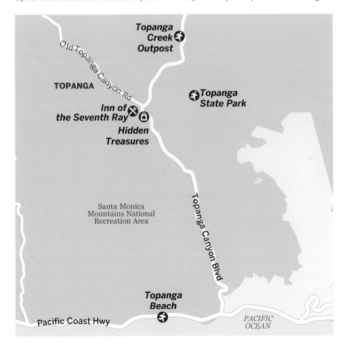

HIGHLAND PARK

This northeastern LA district filled with Craftsman-style houses was originally one of LA's first subdivisions, and later became a tight-knit Hispanic community. While nearby Eagle Rock has been a quirky charmer for years, Highland Park is finally getting some of the attention for itself. Best of all, the Metro Gold Line now speeds visitors straight to Highland Park's heart...and its iconic chicken boy statue.

✘ Joy on York

This is LA, so there's never just one food culture in the mix. Joy on York makes inventive Taiwanese dishes that pay homage to the food at Taipei's night markets and the food of the owners' grandparents, all while being thoughtful about building a community in this growing 'hood. Angelenos wouldn't have it any other way. *5100 York Blvd; www.*

joyonyork.com; 323-999-7642; noon-10pm.

✘ Donut Friend

Ever wondered where to find a fully customised vegan donut? Look no further. Giant donuts, miniature donuts, cakes made of donuts...if someone can dream it, they can (probably) make it. Try the decadent flavours at the original location in Highland Park, and marvel at how utterly fabulous vegan baking can taste. *5107 York Blvd; http://donutfriend.com/wp3; 7am-10pm, closed Mon.*

🥤 Galco's Soda Pop Shop

Based in the area for over 100 years, this small shop turned from an Italian deli to an incredibly entertaining emporium of sodas from the world over, with plenty of craft beer on hand, too. If there's a drink they don't sell, it probably can't be had anywhere. The nostalgic charm of the shop itself is a big part of the appeal. *5702 York Blvd; https://sodapopstop.com; 9am-6.30pm Mon-Sat, to 4pm Sun.*

✘ El Huarache Azteca

Authentic *huaraches* (the word means 'sandal' in Spanish) are made of masa corn flour and are generously topped at this small family restaurant. In a city that worships the almighty taco, it might cause some partisans to switch their allegiance. Wash down your meal with cold *agua fresca*, refreshing blends of fresh fruit with water. *5225 York Blvd;*

Bob Baker's Marionette Theater

Joy on York ✘
Donut Friend ✘
El Huarache Azteca ✘

Meridian St

York Blvd

Galco's Soda Pop Shop 🥤

N Ave 54

N Avenue 50

N Figueroa St

Highland Park Bowl 🎳

🏛 **Avenue 50**

© Danielle Bernabe / 2020, Highland Bowl

https://elhuaracheazteca
live.com; 323-224-0429;
8am-9.30pm.

🏛 Bob Baker's Marionette Theater

Over 2000 handmade puppets of impressive artistry are used in more than 300 performances annually here, continuing the life's work of founder and Disney puppeteer Baker. Relocated to a home in Highland Park as of 2019, this is an institution that has helped to form the memories of untold numbers of children in Southern California and is still going strong. *4949 York Blvd; www.bobbakermarionette theater.com.*

🏛 Avenue 50

Exhibits by Chicano/a and Latinx artists, alongside community events, classes and more, have been the focus of this gallery for 20 years. As the neighbourhood changes, Avenue 50 continues to provide a space for homegrown

TRANSIT BOOM

With the 2028 LA Olympics drawing closer, the city is making major transit investments. The Gold Line isn't the only one expanding: a Westside subway is planned, along with new connections to LAX, downtown and the Valley, and improved bus service all over. Visitors can already start getting around using some of these expansions.

talent. Dropping in for a visit is a great way to tap into the vibrant culture that has sustained the area for decades. *131 N Ave 50; http://avenue50studio.org; 10am-4pm, except Mon & Fri.*

⊕ Highland Park Bowl

Once a Prohibition-era combined pharmacy and bowling area where 'patients' obtained and filled their alcohol prescriptions, Highland Park Bowl has been refurbished to vintage glory. It attracts a buzzing crowd both for its events and the attractive bowling lanes in which to throw a strike. An attached music room keeps alive the memory of the building's second iteration as Mr T's Music Room. *5621 N Figueroa St; www.highlandparkbowl.com; 5pm-2am Mon-Fri, 11am-2am Sat & Sun.*

**Top: Highland Park Bowl
Left: aerial views of
Highland Park's ruggedly
beautiful backdrop**

KOREATOWN

A glamorous destination in the '20s, '30s and '40s, centrally located Koreatown suffered during the Rodney King riots but it's now as vibrant a place as any. LA is home to the country's biggest population of Koreans, with great Korean food, Korean spas and karaoke joints abounding as a result. But the population is diverse, as the excellent Mexican restaurants and cutting-edge new eateries attest.

Chunju Han-il Kwan

Korean BBQ, bibimbap, tofu, kimchi, dumplings...they all have their moments here in Koreatown, but Chunju Han-il Kwan is a temple to hot pot, and specifically to *budae jjigae*, or 'army stew'. This type of hearty traditional stew is their speciality, and it's as filling and flavourful as can be. It's tucked into an unassuming shopping mall, as all great food in LA tends to be. *3450 W 6th St; www.facebook. com/chunjuhanilkwan; 8am-11pm Mon-Sat, 10am-10pm Sun.*

Here's Looking At You

The creative minds behind Here's Looking At You have a seasonally changing menu fusing eclectic influences with ingredients sourced from local providers, all served in a stylish setting. It's not what most people picture when they envision Koreatown, but this neighbourhood lives to surprise all comers. The weekend brunch is immensely popular. *3901 W 6th St; www. hereslookingatyoula.com; 213-568-3573; 6-9pm daily & 10.30am-2.30pm Sat & Sun.*

Beer Belly

True to the name, Beer Belly has a wide variety of frequently changing craft beers on tap to wet your whistle. Fried chicken sandwiches, duck fat fries and other rich bar foods with a twist complement the considerable beer list. You might want a salad the next day while you rebound. *532 S Western Ave; www.beerbellyla.com; approx 5pm-1am.*

Guelaguet-za

There is just as much, or more, Spanish spoken on the streets here as there is Korean, and the location of this much-lauded Mexican restaurant is testimony to the area's deep Latinx roots. Oaxacan-inspired and colourfully decorated, the centrepiece of

Map

Vermont/Beverly ⓜ

Beverly Blvd

Beverly Blvd

N Normandie Ave

HANCOCK PARK

W 3rd St

S Normandie Ave

S Virgil Ave

Beer Belly WILSHIRE CENTER

Chunju Han-il Kwan

Here's Looking At You

W 6th St

Wilshire/Vermont ⓜ

Wilshire/Western

Lafayette Park

ⓜ Wilshire/Normandie

Wilshire Blvd

The Wiltern

Pharaoh Karaoke Lounge

W 7th St

Wi Spa

S Western Ave

Irolo St

W 8th St

S Vermont Ave

S Hoover St

KOREATOWN

Ardmore Park

Guelaguet-za

W Olympic Blvd

the excellent menu is the rich *mole* sauce, which is even used to flavour the *chilaquiles* (a saucy tortilla dish worth trying). *3014 W Olympic Blvd; www.ilovemole. com; 213-427-0608; approx 9am-10pm.*

⭐ Pharaoh Karaoke Lounge
Karaoke offerings are as plentiful as one might expect for a place called Koreatown, some with an upscale vibe, others in the more Western, belt-it-out-in-public style. Here at Pharaoh Karaoke Lounge in the Wilshire Center there are numerous private rooms in which to select songs with your closest friends. Reservations recommended. *3680 Wilshire Blvd, Ste B-02; www.pharaoh.us; 6pm-2am.*

🏛 The Wiltern
Apart from the regular music, comedy events and movie screenings that happen here, it's the glory of the art deco space that really warrants checking out The Wiltern, built in 1931

by the important (and prolific) local architectural firm Morgan, Walls & Clements. This is one of the city's largest theatres and it stands out for its unmatched tile work, murals and an entrancing sunburst ceiling. *3790 Wilshire Blvd; www.wiltern.com.*

✈ Wi Spa
Hot and cold baths, saunas, massages and spa treatments, separate men's and women's areas, and even a zone for kids – everything you need for total relaxation can be found at Wi Spa. You could easily spend a day here hopping between rooms, pools and treatments. Oh, and it's open 24 hours a day. Newbies to Korean spas will be converted, while veterans come as often as they can. *2700 Wilshire Blvd; www.wispausa.com; 24hr.*

Top: refreshing cocktails at Here's Looking At You
Left: welcome to Koreatown

ATWATER VILLAGE

Adjacent to hipster Silver Lake, artist haven Frogtown and Griffith Park, diverse Atwater Village on LA's east side has an impressive cluster of cool boutiques and shops, plus some of the most innovative and well-executed food you can find in LA. Its location on the LA River links it to other parts of the city, and makes exploring by bike a possibility.

Proof Bakery

LA has drool-worthy bakeries run by talented pastry chefs, and this one from Korean-American Glendale native and baker Na Young Ma can compete with the best of them. As the name indicates, technique is everything and it shows in the cakes and croissants. The cappuccinos are excellent as well. *3156 Glendale Blvd; http://proofbakery.com; 8am-4pm.*

Wanderlust Creamery

We're probably biased in favour of the concept at Wanderlust Creamery, where ice creams are based on places across the world. The Japanese neopolitan is particularly inspired and they've carried a Chinese White Rabbit milk candy flavour in the past. It makes for a wildly different type of ice cream parlour and might even inspire customers to go travelling themselves. *3134 Glendale Blvd; www.wanderlustcreamery.com; approx noon-11pm.*

Tacos Villa Corona

Although Atwater now boasts a great falafel shop in Dune and a host of more upscale dining joints, neighbourhood OG Tacos Villa Corona can't be beat for speed, price and authenticity. Breakfast burritos and tacos are fast, cheap, filling and as tasty as they could possibly be. They're closed in the evening. *3185 Glendale Blvd; 8am-2pm Tue-Fri & Sun, 6am-noon Sat.*

The Juice

If you haven't had any engineered juice on your trip to LA, did you really even visit? The smoothies and juices don't come cheap here, but in health-obsessed LA, you're paying for custom blends of fresh organic fruit and vegetables, put raw through the cold press. *3145 Glendale Blvd; https://thejuicela.com; 8am-7pm.*

🔒 Alias Books

Bibliophiles will want to bookmark this one. Used and rare books line the shelves of this store, with robust holdings in film, photography, art and philosophy. An offshoot of Alias Books in West LA, the original location closed in 2017 after 58 years in business, but the Atwater Village outlet is still going strong. *3163 Glendale Blvd; www.aliasbookseast.com; 11am-8pm Mon-Thu, to 9pm Fri, 10am-7pm Sun.*

✪ LA River Trail

Prepare to have your perception of LA as bumper-to-bumper car traffic blown wide open. Running through northeast LA's Glendale Narrows from Griffith Park all the way to Dodger Stadium Elysium in the south, passing Los Feliz and Silver Lake as well as Atwater Village, this bike path along the river makes this area surprisingly navigable without a car. *http://lariver.org.*

© Max Mills / 2020, Wanderlust Creamery

LA RIVER

—————

Frequent floods of the LA River in the '30s wrought havoc on the communities along the 82km (51-mile) path, leading to it being paved over to control the flow. Most people picture it as an eyesore, but the times are changing. The river's neglect is being rehabilitated under a master plan from the city and renowned designer (and LA resident) Frank Gehry.

🔒 Individual Medley

Window-shopping here is a dangerous pastime: it has every kind of tempting item on display, all carefully selected and crafted by artisans from near and far. After perusing this well-designed store and its achingly cool goods, check out the neighbouring boutiques on Glendale Blvd for home decor and clothing. *3176 Glendale Blvd; https://individualmedleystore. com; 10am-7pm.*

Top: global flavours at Wanderlust Creamery Below: home decor at Individual Medley

© Marielle V Chua / 2020, Individual Medley

MEXICO CITY

It's not hard to find a good taco in Mexico City's historic centre. But many of the city's coolest attractions are tucked away in the southern neighbourhoods...

Many of Mexico City's key points of interest – including the Aztec ruins at Templo Mayor, the Catedral Metropolitana (Metropolitan Cathedral), and Zócalo plaza, the largest square in Latin America – are located in the Centro Histórico, or historic centre. A half-hour stroll or 15-minute bike ride west from the busy centre, the architecturally fascinating neighbourhood of Colonia Juárez awaits with quaint cafes, galleries and indie theatres.

Further from the historic centre but easily accessible by metro, the twin neighbourhoods of Roma and Condesa are home to independent bookshops, stylish boutiques and some of the best restaurants in town. Much further south, an hour-long journey from downtown that involves both a metro ride and a 15-minute stroll, Coyoacán attracts waves of visitors to Frida Kahlo's one-time home. But its lesser-known highlights, including quirky museums, an artisan marketplace and some of the city's best street food, are worth the trip, too.

JUÁREZ

Juárez was once Mexico City's grandest neighbourhood. But its many Parisian-inspired mansions, built in the early 20th century, were badly damaged in the massive earthquake of 1985. The neighbourhood has been revitalised and its proximity to downtown – easily reached on foot, by bike or on the Metrobus – make it especially appealing to visitors who want to go off the beaten path.

📖 Bucardón

Sleek bookstore and cafe by day, laid-back bar and live music venue by night, this eclectic cultural centre wears many hats...and they're all stylish. Browse through poetry and photography books or check out the latest artist exhibitions over a *café con leche*, then stick around for mezcal specials, readings, and DJ-spun tunes after dark. *Donato Guerra 1; www.bucardon.com; cafe & bookshop 7.30am-6.30pm Mon-Sat, bar 6.30pm-2am Tue-Sat.*

❌ Pixza

The house speciality at this gourmet Mexican-style pizzeria is *pizza azul* (blue pizza), named for the blue corn in the dough, with Oaxaca cheese and locally produced toppings from squash blossoms to dark and spicy pasilla chiles. For every five pizzas ordered, Pixca donates one to a Mexican community in need. *Liverpool 162; www.pixza.mx; 1-8pm Tue-Thu, 2-9pm Fri-Sat, 2-8pm Sun.*

🏛 MUCHO Museo de Chocolate

In Mexico, chocolate is as old as the hills. This charming museum in an antique house celebrates the tradition with interesting exhibits and hands-on activities explaining the legacy of chocolate-making in Mexico. There's an on-site cafe (devoted to chocolate, of course) and a gift shop selling edible souvenirs. *Milan 45; www.mucho.org.mx; 11am-5pm.*

🚲 Distrito Fijo Club de Ciclismo

What started out as a small club for urban cycling enthusiasts is now a cafe and bicycle workshop where you can grab a coffee, meet like-minded travellers, and plan your journey (try free bike-share Ecobici or rent downtown). *Liverpool 61; www.dfcc.mx; 7am-9pm Fri & Mon-Wed, 8am-4pm Sat-Sun.*

🔒 Vintrend

Hunting for a vintage poncho or a perfect pair of Mexican aviators? Look no further than this thrift shop. The eco-minded owners don't just sell second-hand blazers and sunglasses: they also showcase work by up-and-coming designers. *Venecia 19; www.vintrend.com.mx; 1-7pm Mon-Tue & Thu-Fri, noon-7pm Sat, noon-5pm Sun.*

Map labels:
SAN RAFAEL
Antonio Caso
Av Parque Via
Jardín del Arte
Plaza de la República
Av de la República
Puerto 1808
Bucardón
Bucareli (Eje 1 Poniente)
Jardín Luis Pasteur
Paseo de la Reforma
Plaza Reforma
Plaza José María Morelos
MUCHO Museo de Chocolate
Distrito Fijo Club de Ciclismo
Balderas Ⓜ
JUÁREZ
Mercado Cuauhtémoc
Dr Río de la Loza
Mercado Insurgentes
Vintrend
Av Chapultepec
Cuauhtémoc Ⓜ
Av Cuauhtémoc
❌ Pixza Ⓜ Insurgentes
ROMA
Jardín Dr Chávez
Av Oaxaca
Plaza Río de Janeiro

ROMA & CONDESA

It's no secret that the twin neighbourhoods of Roma and Condesa, an easy metro ride south from the Centro Histórico, form Mexico City's unofficial capital of cool. But there are plenty of treasures to discover, from vintage shops to taco joints, while wandering these colourful streets – or pedalling along them on one of the city's complimentary Ecobici bicycles.

Patio Aurora

Hidden away in one of Roma Norte's elegant townhouses (the building dates from 1903), Patio Aurora is well known to local cocktail enthusiasts. The bar specialises in gin (a nice break from mezcal) and the moody candlelit interiors and beautiful terrace, with trees growing up through the middle of it, are the perfect venues to linger over a drink. *Álvaro Obregón 126, Roma Norte; www.auroraroma.mx; 5pm-2am Mon-Sat.*

Mercado Roma

This stylish three-storey marketplace is different from many of its counterparts in the city: it's not a traditional market that's been open for decades, but an upscale food and drink emporium that's only a few years old. Stop in to sample gourmet snacks, relax over a cold beer, or pick up supplies for a picnic. *Querétaro 225, Roma Norte; www.mercadoroma.com; 9am-8pm Sun-Wed, 9am-1am Thu-Sat.*

Mama Rumba

Standing in refreshing contrast to the neighbourhood's many trendy hangouts, this lively salsa club and bar offers dance lessons several nights a week, set to a soundtrack of live Cuban music and DJ-spun beats, before the late-night crowd rolls in and the place gets packed. *Querétaro 230, Roma Norte; www.facebook.com/mamarumba.rl; 9pm-3am Wed-Thu.*

Centro Cultural Bella Época

Located inside one of Condesa's glamorous art deco buildings, the Centro Cultural Bella Época (Belle Époque Cultural Center) is an architectural landmark that houses an excellent bookstore, the Librería Rosario Castellanos. There's also a coffee shop and a children's activity area. *Tamaulipas 202, Condesa; www.facebook.com/CentroCulturalBellaEpoca; 10am-8pm.*

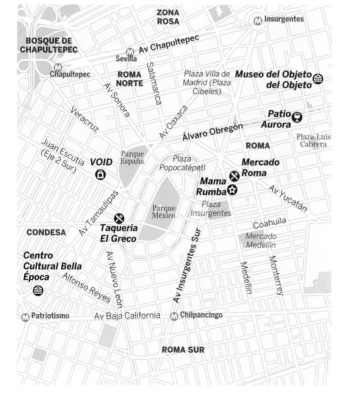

❌ Taquería El Greco

You can get a great taco anywhere in Mexico City. But the best *tacos arabes* (literally 'Arabic tacos'), made with pork that's seasoned and grilled on a spit, shawarma-style, are at this hole-in-the-wall taco shop in Condesa. *Michoacán 54, Condesa; 2-10.30pm Mon-Wed, 2pm-4am Thu-Sat.*

🔒 VOID

Step inside a showcase of mid-century Mexican fashion, Hermès handbags, and vintage English scarves at this high-end vintage boutique located inside a 1930s-era art deco house in Condesa. There's an adorable cafe inside, too. *Parral 5; www.voidmx. com; 11am-8pm Mon-Sat, 11am-7pm Sun.*

🏛 Museo del Objeto del Objeto

The Spanish name of this unusual museum is a play on words, setting the tone for the light-hearted but fascinating exhibits you'll see on display

ROMA ON THE BIG SCREEN

Released in 2019, Alfonso Cuarón's Oscar-nominated film *Roma* was shot in the Mexico City neighbourhood of the same name, which is where Cuarón grew up. Set in the early 1970s, the black-and-white film offers a look at daily life in Roma, nicknamed the Barrio Mágico (Magical Neighbourhood), before its relatively recent gentrification.

here. The 'Museum of the Purpose of the Object' focuses on the relationship between communication and design as expressed through pop culture artefacts from cookbooks to Coca-Cola bottles. *Colima 145, Roma; www.elmodo.mx; 10am-6pm Tue-Sun.*

Clockwise from top: tables at Patio Aurora; ice cream from Mercado Roma; explore the city on an Ecobici bicycle

COYOACÁN

Once a village near Mexico City, Coyoacán is well known as the stomping grounds of celebrated Mexican artist Frida Kahlo, and travellers still flock here to tour Casa Azul (Blue House), her former home and studio. It's a commitment to get here – allow yourself at least an hour in transit time from downtown – but the neighbourhood's lively marketplaces and offbeat museums are worth the detour.

❌ Mercado de Coyoacán

Come for the deep-fried quesadillas, stay for the colourful photo ops, exotic birds and people-watching opportunities. Bustling Mercado de Coyoacán (Coyoacán Market) has been an iconic symbol of the neighbourhood since 1921, with two storeys of food stands, fruit and vegetable stands, butchers and artisan crafts. Grab an *agua de jamaica* (hibiscus water) and make the rounds before choosing a venue for breakfast, lunch or a snack. *Ignacio Allende s/n; 8.30am-6.30pm.*

☕ Café Negro

Stylish coffee shops have been popping up right and left in Coyoacán to accommodate the constant stream of visitors who make the Frida Kahlo–themed pilgrimage here. Café Negro is one of the best, roasting beans sourced from the southwestern Mexican state of Guerrero. Come for breakfast or an afternoon pick-me-up, and try the artisanal hot chocolate made from Oaxacan chocolate; unlike many cafes in town, it's also open late. *Centenario 16; www.facebook.com/ CafeNegroMX; 8am-11pm.*

⚙ Fonoteca Nacional

This one-of-a-kind cultural centre, known as the 'House of Sounds of Mexico', celebrates the nation's audio heritage: music, of course, but also opera, podcasts and the spoken word. The sound library, which is free to enter, has permanent exhibitions and hosts a rotating schedule of orchestral concerts, poetry readings, lectures and festivals. The gardens are a wonderful place to take a break from sightseeing. *Francisco Sosa 383; www.fonotecanacional.gob. mx; 10am-7pm Mon-Fri, 10am-6pm Sat.*

🍸 La Bipo

This bar and restaurant has multiple personalities: the peaceful ground level is the perfect place to sip a

Cineteca Nacional

Ⓜ Coyoacán

Plaza Coyoacán

Panteón Xoco

Av Cuauhtémoc

Av Río Churubusco (Circuito Interior)

Casa Azul

Av México

La Rosa

Ⓜ Viveros

Viveros de Coyoacán

Jardín del Centenario

Parque Allende

Mercado de Coyoacán

La Bipo

COYOACÁN

Plaza Santa Catarina

Café Negro

Jardín Centenario

Plaza Hidalgo

Centro Cultural Elena Garro

Fonoteca Nacional

Cantina La Coyoacana

Plaza de la Conchita

Jardín Frida Kahlo

Av Miguel Ángel de Quevedo

Parque Dos Conejos

© E Rojas / Shutterstock

coffee and plan your adventure through Coyoacán, while upstairs, a festive bar awaits, specialising in craft cocktails made with indigenous Mexican ingredients. Gourmet snacks offer a twist on traditional local dishes, and live music brings in a crowd on weekend evenings. *Malintzin 155; www.labipo.com.mx; noon-2am Wed-Sat, noon-midnight Sun-Tue.*

🏛 Centro Cultural Elena Garro

Literary travellers won't want to miss the modernist Elena Garro Cultural Center, where walls are lined with books about Mexican history, architecture and art, and a busy calendar of cultural events, from acoustic guitar concerts to children's activities (particularly on weekends) brings in a steady stream of locals. Named for the prize-winning writer Elena Garro, it's a hub of activity. *Fernández Leal 43; www.educal.com.mx/ elenagarro; 10am-9pm.*

⭐ Cineteca Nacional

If your idea of a great evening involves sitting under the stars, enjoying an artisanal ice cream cone or sipping a cold *cerveza*

FRIDA KAHLO'S BLUE HOUSE

Fans of Frida Kahlo make the trip to Coyoacán to visit the Casa Azul (Blue House), the artist's one-time home and studio, now a museum. The house is littered with personal belongings that evoke Kahlo's long, often tempestuous relationship with husband Diego Rivera and the leftist intellectual circle they entertained here. Casa Azul is no secret: arrive early to avoid the crowds.

(beer) while watching a film projected on a huge screen, the National Film Archives is the place to go. The architecturally striking space also features concerts and lectures, and there's an excellent cafe. *México Coyoacán 389; www. cinetecanacional.net.*

✖ Cantina La Coyoacana

Cue up the mariachi band and pop a tortilla chip into your mouth: La Coyoacana delivers the experience you were dreaming of when you planned a trip to Mexico. This cheerful *cantina* has leafy patio seating, a full bar and a large dining room where musicians perform and waiters take orders for tacos and tequila. Try the *tlacoyo*, a tortilla-like corn patty topped with cheese and beans. *Higuera 14; www.lacoyoacana.com; 1pm-1am Tue-Sat, noon-10pm Sun, noon-midnight Mon.*

Top: Casa Azul, the home of legendary artist Frida Kahlo Below: stylish Café Negro

North Loop

Clarksville

Austin   East Side

AUSTIN

Sunny days, balmy, music-filled nights and a vibe that defines laid-back, the capital of Texas is unmissable and deserves all its hype.

Legendary music venues, pretension-free bars where you can while away the hours on a starlit patio, food trucks serving memorable treats for just a few dollars, world-class cultural festivals like Austin City Limits and South by Southwest (SXSW), and an over-riding laid-back vibe that is practised here like no place else – all of this and much more are what make Austin, well, Austin.

These pleasures come thicker than a bowl of local chilli in and around Austin's centre, from downtown through UT (University of Texas) and everywhere in between. Fabled 6th St and nearby Red River St hum from night until day. But linger in these popular areas and you might just rub elbows with more visitors than locals.

Lose the crowds by venturing into nearby neighbourhoods to soak up the local vibe. See for yourself how the city of Austin has redefined what's mellow and hip, even as it blends various other cultures into its own intoxicating brew.

CLARKSVILLE

All you need is your feet to reach leafy Clarksville, just west of downtown. Follow the public trails along Shoal Creek, then wander streets lined with beautiful old homes, where little commercial strips offer the kinds of shops and restaurants you wish were in *your* neighbourhood. Austin's buzz seems far from these bucolic blocks, rather than just around the corner.

✖ Jeffrey's

Texans love their beef, and the dry-aged steaks at this neighbourhood bistro are among the best in the city. But you might want to wear a beret with your boots as the menu has a distinct French accent; picture a rich pat of foie gras butter atop your T-bone. The bar is a refined haven for martinis and other adult drinks. *1204 W Lynn St; www.jeffreysofaustin.com; 512-477-5584; 5.30-10pm.*

✈ Pease Park

From a George Custer campsite to a focus of failed gold-rush dreams, this rocky, naturalistic park on Shoal Creek has a history as colourful as Austin. Even today it draws attention for its annual Eeyore Birthday Party, held in honour of the long-faced donkey from the Winnie the Pooh stories. *1100 Kingsbury St.*

✈ Shoal Creek Trail

From Lady Bird Lake in the south to 38th St in the north, this winding trail stretches almost four beautifully natural miles (6km) right through the heart of the city. The namesake creek ebbs and flows beside you along the length as you walk or pedal past limestone cliffs and trees that offer welcome shade. *Pease Park; https://shoalcreekconservancy.org.*

🍷 Wink Wine Bar

Slip into this pocket-sized wine bar where you can enjoy a fine glass of vino along with creative light bites. It's a classy neighbourhood hangout where the hellos are hearty and the back slaps bracing. *1014 N Lamar Blvd; www.winkrestaurant.com; 512-482-8868; 5-11pm.*

✖ Nau's Enfield Drug

Who needs retro style when you can go authentic? If the windows at Nau's were topaz it would complete the frozen-in-amber vibe at this veteran soda fountain and drug store in Clarksville. Feast on a burger and a thick shake, then get your prescription refilled. *1115 W Lynn St; http://nausdrug.com; 512-476-3663; 7.30am-4pm Mon-Sat, 10.30am-3.30pm Sun.*

Map showing Clarksville area with Tarrytown, Old West Austin, Central Austin, Judge's Hill, Charles Forest, House Park, Clarksville, Downtown. Streets include Mopac Expwy, Enfield Rd, Windsor Rd, Pease Rd, Niles Rd, N Lamar Blvd, Leon St, W 24th St, W 22nd St, Woodlawn Blvd, Waterson Ave, W 10th St, W 9th St, W 6th St, Patterson Ave, Campbell St, Pressler St, Blanco St, Kingsbury St, Shoal Creek, Palm Plaza Pocket Park, West Austin Neighborhood Park, Shoal Creek Greenbelt, Duncan Park. Points of interest: Jeffrey's, Nau's Enfield Drug, Pease Park, Shoal Creek Trail, Wink Wine Bar.

EAST SIDE

Somewhat amorphous but easily found on the compass, East Austin fans out, yes, east of I-35 and encompasses a number of sub-neighbourhoods like the trendy and close-in East Cesar Chavez. But don't stop there, press on for the kinds of dives and off-beat hangouts that have long defined the city. Frequent buses rumble along Rosewood Ave plus E 7th and E 12 Sts.

⊗ Saigon Le Vendeur

This food truck is really a food container, which is good as the lack of wheels means it's not going anywhere soon. People queue up for splendidly fresh Vietnamese classics like the loaded grilled chicken *bahn mi* (baguette sandwich) and spicy pork vermicelli. *2404 E 7th St; http:// saigon7th.com; 512-351-6916; 11am-9pm Mon-Fri, to 5pm Sat.*

⊗ Marcelino's

Just east of the East Side's Hispanic soul, Marcelino's is proof that it's never too early for a taco. This tiny hole-in-the-wall makes tacos so good, you'll swear they're powering the sun's rise into the sky. Tell them what you want inside and the cheery staff will knock them out right in front of you. *901 Tillery St; www. marcelinosfoods.com; 512-926-1709; 6am-1pm Mon-Sat.*

🍺 Zilker Brewing Co

As stylish as it is tasty, Zilker's brewery is a mash-up of styles. The drinking area's furnishings and bar are made with custom wood, as well as gleaming stainless-steel brewing vats. You can't get closer to the beer, unless you drink it – which you'll want to do as it's flat out tasty. Don't miss the orange-hued Marco IPA. *1701 E 6th St; www. zilkerbeer.com; 4-10pm Tue-Wed, noon-midnight Thu-Sat, to 8pm Sun.*

🍺 King Bee Lounge

Though at first glance it looks like a neighbourhood dive, King Bee Lounge reveals layers of surprises that defy the stereotype. King Bee specialises in frozen cocktails that some might call frou-frou. The house special, the Bee's Knees, is rich with honey and loaded with alcohol. The inside is dark with an air of mystery, the outside terrace is chill with plenty of air. *1906 E 12th St; 512-600-6956; 5pm-2am.*

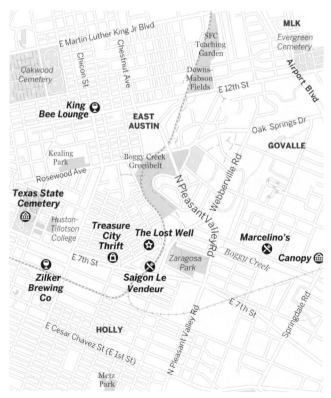

✪ The Lost Well

At this perfectly grungy dark and dirty temple-cave to hard rock and metal, there would be a hipster- and bro-proof fence outside, if they could just invent one. Instead, they use attitude to keep 'em out, even if under it all, The Lost Well is about as friendly as they come. Bands with big regional followings headline and it gets packed inside and out on weekends. *2421 Webberville Rd; www.thelostwell.com; 4pm-2am Mon-Fri, 2pm-2am Sat & Sun.*

🏛 Canopy

An only-in-Austin special: a vast Goodwill warehouse was beautifully transformed into almost four dozen artist spaces and galleries. There are works in every medium imaginable. Many of the artists already have international acclaim while others are on their way. *916 Springdale Rd; http://canopy.bigmedium. org; hours vary.*

© VSCO / 2020, Marcelino's

CEMETERY FOR TEXAS LUMINARIES

Amidst pockets of redevelopment, the East Side feels old yet vibrant. Easily the least lively place here is the Texas State Cemetery. Almost anyone who was once anyone in the Lone Star state is buried here, starting with Stephen F Austin, a Texas founding father. Look for other luminaries plus hundreds of Civil War dead.

🔒 Treasure City Thrift

In a city where debates over the best thrift store have fuelled many a PBR session, this smallish place is a strong contender. It could easily be called the Treasure Chest – you'll dig deep for bargains on surprisingly fine finds. Prices are extra low because Treasure City Thrift is run by a non-profit collective dedicated to environmental and economic justice. *2142 E 7th St; http://treasurecitythrift.org; 10am-7pm Mon-Fri, noon-6pm Sat & Sun.*

© 2020, Zilker Brewing Co.

© 2020, Zilker Brewing Co.

Clockwise from top: taco temple Marcelino's; beers and beckoning signs at Zilker Brewing Co

NORTH LOOP

North Loop is shady, thanks to all the trees; colourful, thanks to local proclivities for brightly painted buildings; and ultra-chill, thanks to its continuing affordability. The spine is the eponymous North Loop Blvd, which morphs into E 53rd St. Look for purely Austin funk in shops and on the walls of the many bar-turned-cafes. Buses aplenty speed up N Lamar Blvd.

🏛 Elisabet Ney Museum

In a city where being 'different' is almost a self-defeating cliché, this museum is truly different. First, it's in a crenellated castle; second, its namesake was something of an 1880s German renaissance woman. Ney was a famous sculptor who did busts of folks with names like Bismarck in the old country; re-established in Texas, her subjects had names like Houston and Austin.

See her works here. *304 E 44th St; www.austintexas.gov/Elisabetney; noon-5pm Wed-Sun.*

❌ Bistro Vonish

The star of a food truck pod, this vegan outlet will make any carnivore forget their preferences while putting a smug smile on the faces of devotees. The menu has global influences, top picks include sweet potato *arepas* (filled cornmeal buns) and black garlic bruschetta. Added flavour comes from spunky seasonings such as habanero jam. *701 E 53rd St; www. bistrovonish.com; 512-579-9854; noon-9pm Tue-Fri, 10am-9pm Sat & Sun.*

🍷 Tigress Pub

Affable, creative, offbeat. Known for its home-crafted cocktails, this tiny bar is Austin in a nutshell. Consider the Native Tongue, a literally intoxicating genre-busting concoction of saffron gin, pineapple syrup, dry vermouth and cardamom bitters. Cosy up on a stool inside or outside on the small, flower-lined terrace; a merry band of locals welcome newcomers. *100 W N Loop Blvd; https://thetigresspub.com; 4-11pm Tue-Sun.*

🔒 Guzu Gallery

On a little strip devoted to pop culture, Guzu mixes a gallery with shows devoted to pop art with a shop where you can buy old vinyl, vintage fanzines, offbeat toys and oddities sourced worldwide. That goth cartoon you thought no one else knew about? They have the

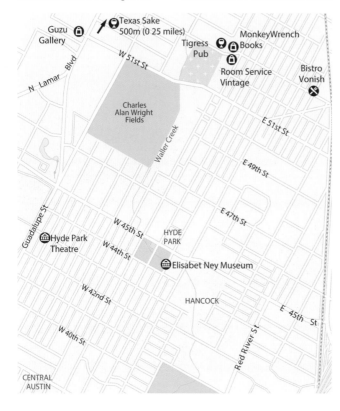

AUSTIN

merch here. *5000 N Lamar Blvd; http://guzugallery.storenvy. com; 11am-7pm Mon-Sat, noon-6pm Sun.*

🔒 Monkeywrench Books

Aiming right at the capitalist machine, this volunteer-run anarchist bookstore lives up to its name. In between rows of books devoted to progressive topics and subjects far beyond the mainstream, discover real finds like anarchist colouring books. Watch for events like readings that are more screed than poetry. Experiences vary depending on the vols on duty when you show up. *110 North Loop Blvd E; www. monkeywrenchbooks.org; noon-6pm Mon-Thu, to 8pm Fri-Sun.*

🔒 Room Service Vintage

That floral sofa you saw last week abandoned on the kerb has a future! Mid-century furniture at its finest is showcased in this crammed-to-the-rafters store.

© 2020, Hyde Park Theatre

In between the Formica, look for vintage clothes and more. *107 E North Loop Blvd; www. roomservicevintage.com; 11am-7pm.*

🏛 Hyde Park Theatre

A gritty theatre producing gritty plays (no, that's not thunder, it's the air-conditioner). The troupe here stages new works renowned for their dramatic power plus award-winning shows that are literally just off Broadway. Time your visit for FronteraFest, a five-week winter festival of theatre produced by HPT and featuring over 800 performers. *511 W 43rd St; www. hydeparktheatre.org.*

Top: performance at Hyde Park Theatre
Below and below left: vegan flair at fabled food truck Bistro Vonish

© 2020, Bistro Vonish

© 2020, Bistro Vonish

ARTS & CULTURE   MUSIC & FILM   SPORTS & LEISURE   EATING   DRINKING   SHOPPING

New Orleans

French Quarter

Bywater & the Marigny

CBD & Lower Garden

Garden District, Uptown & Carrollton

NEW ORLEANS

A grande dame who loves to party, New Orleans has fiery jazz dens, independent shops and a dazzling dining scene, as well as a strong and close-knit community spirit.

Spread along the meandering Mississippi, New Orleans' diverse districts showcase colourful architecture and burgeoning creativity. The city's birthplace is the French Quarter, with historic streets hiding top restaurants, vintage theatres and creative art spaces. East of the Quarter, the Marigny and Bywater are fertile ground for taking in the city's indie cred, with record shops, backyard wine bars and eclectic music halls scattered among Creole cottages. West of the Quarter, the CBD and Lower Garden District are favourite haunts for art lovers, with the city's best galleries – as well as plenty of culinary temptations.

Keep rolling on the St Charles Ave streetcar to Uptown, and Carrollton beyond. The mansion-lined 'hood has plenty of secrets, like brassy music joints, a green oasis and the city's oldest cinema.

New Orleans' bike share (Blue Bikes) is useful for getting around this pancake-flat town. There's also bus and streetcar service.

FRENCH QUARTER

Home to cobblestone streets, colonial architecture and legendary watering holes, the French Quarter is both the oldest district in New Orleans and its most famous destination. Plenty of shops and bars cater to tourists (check out Bourbon St), but 'the Quarter' has its share of boutiques, restaurants and cultural venues favoured by locals. It's delightfully walkable and easily reached by streetcars from Uptown and Mid-City.

✖ Longway Tavern

A short stroll from St Louis Cathedral, this charming spot has a courtyard in back where you can linger over well-made cocktails and sharing plates (white anchovies, fried calamari, home fries with pork belly...). Join the after-work crowd at happy hour (4pm to 7pm) for $5 Moscow Mules and $20 bottles of wine. *719 Toulouse St; www. longwaytavern.com; 504-962-9696; 4pm-midnight Mon-Thu, from 11.30am Fri-Sun.*

🏛 Le Petit Théâtre du Vieux Carré

One of America's longest-running community theatres hosts cutting-edge drama, musical theatre and classical productions (Shakespeare included), along with the odd burlesque show and jazz concert. It's set in a 1790s building, and with just 323 seats, you're guaranteed an intimate performance. *616 St Peter St; www.lepetittheatre.com.*

🔒 Queork

When it comes to sustainability, few products can compete with cork, which is made from bark (trees are not cut down). Cork is also durable, stain resistant, waterproof, antimicrobial and – at least in this elegant shop – stylish when used to create handbags, wallets, sandals, jewellery, iPhone covers and even yoga mats. *838 Chartres St; www.queork.com; 10am-6pm.*

🍸 Jewel of the South

In a Creole cottage on the Quarter's northern fringes, this handsome tavern opened to acclaim in early 2019. Blended drinks, an enticing courtyard and nattily attired bartenders add a dash of class to a neighbourhood better known for booze bars. *1026 St Louis St; www.jewelnola.com; 4pm-midnight.*

🏛 The Starlight

Catching a concert here feels like being invited to a private soirée by that bohemian jazz-loving New Orleanian uncle you never knew you had. The place is all class with glittering chandeliers and antique mirrors, with live music filling the double parlour most nights. *817 St Louis St; www.starlightloungenola.com; 2pm-2am.*

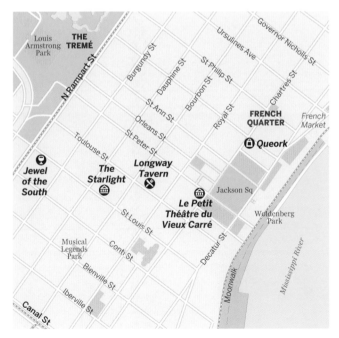

BYWATER & THE MARIGNY

Spreading east of the French Quarter, the Marigny and Bywater are gateways to bars, live music gardens, bohemian cafes and record shops. Behind the train tracks, the fine waterfront park offers a breezy escape, with uncommon views of the Mississippi. Go by bike from the Quarter; for the Marigny, hop on the Rampart-St Claude Ave streetcar.

🍷 Elysian Bar

Set in the former rectory of an 1875 Catholic convent and school, the Elysian Bar has loads of style, with an artfully designed parlour and a photogenic bar that would make Gaudí proud. Stop in for bespoke cocktails and creative small plates. The former church next door is part of the same property (the award-winning Hotel Peter & Paul) and hosts occasional performances, concerts and community events. *2317 Burgundy St; www. theelysianbar.com; 10.30am-midnight.*

✪ Siberia Lounge

A well-worn mainstay of the Marigny, Siberia stages comedy and drag shows, indie rock and the odd avant-garde brass band. Thursday night is better known as the Eastern Bloc Party, where you can catch bohemian bands belting out Bulgarian gypsy jazz, klezmer jams, Balkan hip-hop and other wondrous combinations. *2227 St Claude Ave; www. siberialounge.com; 4pm-2am.*

🔒 Euclid Records

Vinyl lovers unite at this beloved, two-storey record shop in the Bywater. There are many treasures to be unearthed amid seemingly endless bins of new and used records. Euclid hosts occasional concerts and outdoor film screenings, and the location is great for a ramble. *3301 Chartres St; http://euclidnola. com; 11am-7pm.*

✪ Bacchanal

Listening to live music on a moonlit night in a ramshackle backyard is one of the great Bywater experiences. Order wine and cheese from the shop up front, grab a table in back (go early!) and let the night unfold. There's also food (creative sharing plates), and a tiny upstairs retreat when the weather sours. *600 Poland Ave; www.bacchanalwine.com; 11am-midnight.*

⊗ N7

Secreted behind a wooden fence, the barely signed N7, with its hidden plant-framed courtyard and old-fashioned dining room feels like something right out of a film set. The thoughtfully curated selection of French and Italian wines pairs brilliantly with the imaginative decor – not to mention the creative French-Japanese fusion cuisine. *1117 Montegut St; www.n7nola.com; 6-10pm Mon-Thu, to 11pm Fri & Sat.*

✦ Crescent Park

This 2.3km (1.4-mile) greenway along the riverfront provides a fine respite from the city streets. Lined with native flower beds,

© Sasha Weleber / Getty Images

MUSIC BOX VILLAGE

Equal parts dreamscape, sculpture garden and sonic playground, the Music Box Village houses a wondrous assortment of cottage-sized installations. Levers and pulleys activate celestial horns and haunting wind chimes, and marimba-like keyboards invite wandering hands. By night, Music Box also stages hometown icons and artists from abroad.

bike paths and abandoned piers with fine views over the muddy Mississippi, Crescent Park is a great place for a run or a stroll. You can also join in one of the free fitness dance classes, like 'Move Ya Brass' from 10am to 11am on Saturdays. *Off N Peters St; www.crescentparknola.org; 6am-7.30pm.*

⊗ The Franklin

A stylish redesign of a former corner grocery store, The Franklin is one of the Marigny's most creative gastrobars. It's the perfect place to start off the night, with imaginative cocktails and delectable sharing plates like grilled octopus or beef tartare with smoked egg yolk. Stop in for happy hour (5pm to 7pm) specials, including $6 margaritas and $5 *pommes frites* (French fries). *2600 Dauphine St; www.thefranklinnola.com; 504-267-0640; 5-10pm Sun-Thu, to 11pm Fri & Sat.*

**Top: the Marigny's waterside walking paths
Left: classic drinks at chic watering hole The Franklin**

© 2020, The Franklin

CBD & LOWER GARDEN

An easy walk or streetcar ride from the Quarter, the CBD (Central Business District) is a hub of the arts scene, home to the densest concentration of galleries in New Orleans. A locavore food market, obscure boutiques and a classy dinner club add to its appeal. Further out, the Lower Garden District is another easy-to-reach neighbourhood with craft cocktail bars and one of Nola's best microbreweries.

🚋 Barrel Proof

There's an artful jauntiness to Barrel Proof, with its corrugated iron walls, plank ceiling and long dark wood bar, and the tables out front make the perfect setting for people-watching. The menu has an astonishing variety of bourbon, whiskey and scotch, and cocktails blend fine spirits with creative touches; the 'Alright Alright Alright' is both lush and smoky with its blend of Longbranch bourbon, amaro and artisanal 'tobacco bitters'. *1201 Magazine St; www. barrelproofnola.com; 4pm-1am Sun-Thu, to 2am Fri & Sat.*

❌ Auction House

Part of a wave of food markets that have arrived in the city in recent years, Auction House has a tempting assortment of bites you can eat in a hurry, including delicious Argentine-style empanadas, crispy Indian dosas and plump oysters – plus a full bar at the centre of the culinary action. Great spot before hitting the nearby galleries. *801 Magazine St; www.auctionhousemarket. com; 504-372-4321; 7am-10pm Sun-Thu, to 11pm Fri & Sat.*

🏛 Contemporary Arts Center

A pillar of the arts scene, the CAC hosts a stellar line-up of temporary exhibitions oriented toward themes of social justice, ecology and human rights. The small theatre within stages dance, musical groups and multidisciplinary shows. *900 Camp St; www.cacno.org; 9am-5pm Mon-Fri, 11am-5pm Sat; $10.*

🔒 Freda

Inside the Ace Hotel, Freda is a tiny boutique that stocks one-of-a-kind apparel (eye-catching smocks, two-tone jeans, twirly

NEW ORLEANS

skirts) as well as colourful vases, perfume oils and locally made jewellery. Owner Susannah Lipsey's store channels a bit of the desert-like, art-loving design of her other store in Marfa, Texas. *600 Carondelet St; www.shop-freda. com; 10am-8pm Mon-Sat, 11am-7pm Sun.*

✪ Little Gem Saloon

This elegant jazz den lets listeners enjoy first-rate performances in a dinner-like setting that's a far cry from the grittiness of Frenchmen St. The food is upscale Creole comfort fare: gulf seafood *bouillabaisse*, white bean ragout with roasted potatoes, leek and cheddar biscuits. Book a table online to avoid missing out. Cover charges range from $20 to $30. *445 S Rampart St; www. littlegemsaloon.com; 5-10pm Tue-Fri, 6-11pm Sat, 11.30am-2.30pm & 5-10pm Sun.*

♘ Urban South

Microbreweries are in no short

FIRST SATURDAYS!

On the first Saturday of every month, the galleries, museums and creative spaces of the Arts District (on and around Julia St) premier new exhibitions from 6pm to 9pm. It's festive, with free wine and snacks as New Orleanians go gallery-hopping. Nearby cafes, bars and restaurants also host special events. Check out www. artsdistrictneworleans.com for a list of galleries.

supply in New Orleans, but Urban South warrants the praise from beer connoisseurs for its fine IPAs, farmhouse ales and creative seasonal brews (like CàPhê, a Vietnamese-style coffee stout). The spacious taproom is a fun, family-friendly space, and a fine place to watch the Saints game if you have kids in tow. *1645 Tchoupitoulas St; www. urbansouthbrewery.com; noon-9pm Sun-Thu, to 10pm Fri & Sat.*

🏛 Octavia Art Gallery

The gallery scene is a fairly dispersed affair in New Orleans. Julia St, however, is a major thoroughfare for art lovers, with Octavia a great first stop when exploring the city's creative side. You'll find impressive exhibitions here, with works by up-and-coming artists from both the USA and abroad. Cuban and Cuban-American artists are particularly well represented. *440 Julia St; www.octaviaartgallery.com; 10am-6pm Tue-Sat.*

Top: Auction House
Left: rising artists on display inside Octavia Art Gallery

GARDEN DISTRICT, UPTOWN & CARROLLTON

Oak-lined avenues, verdant parks and gardens fronting antebellum mansions set the stage for one of the city's most photogenic districts. Architecture aside, this is the place for extraordinary dining, only-in-New Orleans stores and surprising night spots. Use the St Charles Ave streetcar to reach Uptown and Carrollton from the CBD and the French Quarter. Bikes and buses are handy for the Garden District.

✖ Pascal's Manale

Opened back in 1913, Pascal's Manale is an old-school classic, with a front-room bar that looks like it hasn't changed since Woodrow Wilson was in office.

Present most evenings, Thomas 'the Uptown T' Stewart stands at the helm of the tiny oyster counter shucking perfect oysters. The front oyster bar is purely a stand (and slurp) affair. Those looking for comfort head to the white-tablecloth dining room in the back for Pascal's legendary barbecue shrimp (jumbo-sized, cooked in butter with the perfect amount of Creole spices). *1838 Napoleon Ave; http://pascalsmanale.com; 504-895-4877; 11.30am-9pm Mon-Fri, 5-10pm Sat.*

✪ Maple Leaf Bar

There's never a bad night to catch a live show at this Uptown classic, but when Rebirth plays on Tuesday nights, visitors from all across the city flock to Maple St. Musicians crowd the tiny stage, creating an incredible wall of fiery brass that fills the entire place – from the ramshackle bar at stage left to the open-air terrace in the back. Founded back in Treme in 1983, the Rebirth Brass Band has vaulted to stardom, even winning a Grammy in 2012. *8316 Oak St; www.mapleleafbar.com; 3pm-5am.*

✪ Prytania Theatre

Going strong since 1914, the

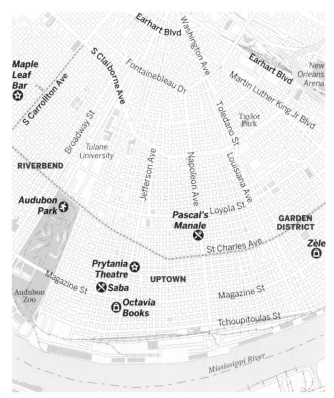

NEW ORLEANS

© 2020, Octavia Books

aubergine and Moroccan carrot salad. Piping hot pitta bread comes straight from the wood-burning oven...no need to order, it keeps arriving until you can eat no more! Don't neglect the cocktails. *5757 Magazine St; www. eatwithsaba.com; 504-324-7770; 11am-10pm Wed-Fri, 10am-10pm Sat & Sun.*

🔒 Zèle

When strolling the shops along Magazine St, make sure you plot your itinerary around Zèle. This colourful emporium represents the works over 100 vendors. You'll find locally made jewellery, crafts, skincare products and artwork. It's a great one-stop shop for unique gift ideas. *2841 Magazine St; www.facebook.com/ZeleNOLA; 10.30am-6pm Tue-Sat, noon-5pm Sun.*

Top: Octavia Books
Below: jumbo barbecue
shrimp at Pascal's Manale

red brick Prytania is the oldest continuously operated cinema in America's South. The iconic single-screen theatre shows a mix of first-run Hollywood releases as well as classics from the past – including Monty Python, Alfred Hitchcock and the occasional midnight screening of *The Rocky Horror Picture Show*. *5339 Prytania St; www.theprytania.com.*

🔒 Octavia Books

One of New Orleans' best-loved indie bookshops, Octavia is an inviting place to browse for new fiction. Well-read staff can provide tips. There are sections dedicated to local and regional authors, and you can catch readings. *513 Octavia St; www. octaviabooks.com; 10am-6pm Mon-Sat, to 5pm Sun.*

✈ Audubon Park

Uptown's lush park, with its duck-filled lakes and towering live oaks, makes a fine spot for a picnic, stroll or a serious run. A 2.9km (1.8 miles) path loops around the park, and there's a golf course, two playgrounds and a

little-known clubhouse cafe with weekend brunches. The St Charles Ave streetcar rolls right past the northern entrance of the park. *St Charles Ave (nr Calhoun St); https://audubonnatureinstitute. org/audubon-park.*

✗ Saba

An award-winner that hits all the right notes, Saba serves outstanding Mediterranean small plates, like wood-roasted asparagus, creamy hummus topped with blue crab, charred

© 2020, Pascal's Manale

CHICAGO

Cloud-scraping architecture and world-class museums give the city heft, while dive bars, cultural centres and neighbourhood eateries give it heart.

CHICAGO

You could spend all of your time in Chicago's steely core and never run out of Instagram fodder, from the city's sky-high buildings to its star art collections and top-chef food scene.

But it's in the farther-flung districts where a true view of city life reveals itself. You'll see it to the north in Edgewater, a hub for cafe hoppers and artsy shoppers. It emerges in Logan Square, a buzzy haven to the northwest, which serves as a prime stomping ground for chowhounds and has a bar on practically every corner. It pops up to the southwest in Pilsen, which lures with Mexican culture and bohemian nightlife, and in neighbouring Bridgeport, which offers bars and galleries aplenty in grittier environs.

The city spreads far and wide, though it's easy enough to make your way around Chicago on public transport – mainly the rackety L trains, with buses picking up the slack.

EDGEWATER

Edgewater is hyper local, almost like its own village within the city. Timeworn bars mix with modern foodie restaurants, funky shops, storefront theatres and laid-back gay and lesbian venues. It's a haul from downtown, though the Red Line L train and bus 22 along Clark St take you right to it. Edgewater's core along Clark St is walkable.

🏛 Leather Archives & Museum

Seek out this little venue camouflaged on a residential block and bondage gear, steel chastity appliances and erotic art displays are your reward, all focused on educating about S&M and fetish cultures. *6418 N Greenview Ave; www.leatherarchives.org; 773-761-9200; 11am-7pm Thu & Fri, to 5pm Sat & Sun; $10.*

🔒 Woolly Mammoth Antiques & Oddities

Satisfy your morbid leanings at this antiques shop, where cases are stuffed with all manner of the macabre: freaky dolls' heads, taxidermied animals and more. *1513 W Foster Ave; www.woollymammothchicago.com; noon-7pm Wed-Sun, from 1pm Mon, from 3pm Tue.*

🔒 Alleycat Comics

Alleycat hides in a narrow lane between two shops on busy Clark St, with just a wee sign pointing the way. Cool comic books, manga and zines await those who find it. *5304 N Clark St; www.alleycatcomics.com; 773-907-3404; 11am-8pm Mon-Sat, to 6pm Sun.*

🍺 Simon's Tavern

A neighbourhood stalwart for nearly a century, Simon's draws rock-and-roll types who hang out in the dingy light feeding the jukebox and sinking a pint or three. Cash only. *5210 N Clark St; 773-878-0894; 11am-2am Sun-Fri, to 3am Sat.*

✖ Lost Larson

At this design-forward bakery, be tempted by Scandinavian-style cardamom buns, breads made from house-milled wheat, and chocolate croissants that'll knock your socks off. *5318 N Clark St; www.lostlarson.com; 773-944-0587; 7am-7pm Wed-Sun.*

🏛 Neo-Futurist Theater

The offbeat auditorium presents 30 plays in 60 minutes. Members of the troupe write and perform their own mini shows, which range from brazen to sad to foulmouthed and funny. The clock starts, and the actors race to get through the repertoire, which becomes ever more manic as the deadline approaches. A dice throw determines your admission cost. *5153 N Ashland Ave; www.neofuturists.org; 11.30pm Fri & Sat, 7pm Sun.*

Map labels:
ANDERSONVILLE
🏛 Leather Archives & Museum 2.5km (1.5 miles)
W Balmoral Ave
W Summerdale Ave
Lost Larson ✖
Alleycat Comics 🔒
W Berwyn Ave
N Paulina St
N Ashland Ave
N Clark St
N Glenwood Ave
W Farragut Ave
W Farragut Ave
Simon's Tavern 🍺
Woolly Mammoth Antiques & Oddities 🔒
W Foster Ave
Neo-Futurist Theater 🏛
W Winona St
UPTOWN

LOGAN SQUARE

Street-art-swashed Logan Square retains an outsider's edge, even while gentrification is taking root. It's chock-a-block with gastronome eateries tucked in modest storefronts, thrifty cocktail lounges, dive bars and artsy music clubs. And its button museum is one of a kind. The neighbourhood is relatively close to downtown; the Blue Line L train swings smack through its middle.

🏛 Busy Beaver Button Museum

Who knew? Busy Beaver Button Company stashes a museum inside its office building. Peruse thousands of oddball badges on display, hawking everything from Duran Duran to 'Betty Ford for First Lady' to Bat Woman. There's even one from George Washington's campaign. *3407 W Armitage Ave; www.buttonmuseum.org; 10am-4pm Mon-Fri; free.*

🍫 Katherine Anne Confections

Chocoholics get weak-kneed in this shop. Truffles are the star, available in caramel latte, mocha walnut, Manhattan cocktail and 170 other flavours. The bijou cafe pours drinking chocolates bobbing with enormous marshmallows. Order a flight if you can't decide between the 10 luscious types. *2745 W Armitage Ave; www.katherine-anne.com; 11am-7pm Tue & Wed, to 9pm Thu & Fri, 10am-9pm Sat, 11am-5pm Sun.*

🍸 Cole's

Who can resist a neon-bathed dive bar with free entertainment? Not the neighbourhood's young and thrifty. They pile in to Cole's to swig microbrews in the front room, and see bands and comedians on the back-room stage. *2338 N Milwaukee Ave; www.coleschicago.com; 5pm-2am Mon-Fri, 4pm-3am Sat, 4pm-2am Sun.*

✝ The 606

An elevated train track converted into a smart trail 4.3km (2.7 miles) long, the 606 unfolds inconspicuously overhead. It runs not only through Logan Square, but also the adjoining districts of Wicker Park and Humboldt Park. There are frequent access points and it's easy to sidle off to kicky bars and eateries for a break. California Ave is a popular place to ascend. *www.the606.org; 6am-11pm.*

🛍 Wolfbait & B-girls

Funky womenswear and accessories by local designers.

Weren't you looking for a hand-dyed mini dress made from repurposed boxer shorts, or some edible chocolate candles? It's all here, and then some. *3131 W Logan Blvd; www.wolfbaitchicago.com; 10am-7pm Mon-Sat, to 4pm Sun.*

✪ Whistler
Its sign is unobtrusive, but the art in the window is not. The nifty space is part gallery, part cocktail lounge and part venue for local indie bands, jazz combos and DJs. There's never a cover charge, but it's your job to buy a snazzy drink to fund the performances. *2421 N Milwaukee Ave; www. whistlerchicago.com; 6pm-2am Mon-Thu, 5pm-2am Fri-Sun.*

✪ Ground Control
It doesn't make much fuss, sitting quietly amid storefronts, but Ground Control's gravy-sauced fried tofu, beer-braised greens and other Southern-tinged vegetarian dishes deserve big-time renown.

© 2020, Busy Beaver Button Museum

3315 W Armitage Ave; www. groundcontrolchicago.com; 773-772-9446; 5-10pm Tue-Thu, 5-11pm Fri, 11am-11pm Sat, 11am-9pm Sun.

🏛 Galerie F
A low-key spot immersed in the street-art scene, Galerie F puts on fresh exhibitions and sells rad prints, stickers and band posters. The basement offers a chill place to hang out and play chess. *2415 N Milwaukee Ave; www. galeriefchicago.com; 11am-6pm Mon & Thu-Sun.*

✪ Rosa's Lounge
Chicago's musical claim to fame is the electric blues, and Rosa's is an authentic club to hear a fret-bending set. The humble joint is well off the beaten path, with an arm's-length-away stage and top local players wailing on it. *3420 W Armitage Ave; www.rosaslounge. com; 8pm-2am Tue-Sat.*

Clockwise from top: Busy Beaver Button Museum; a housefront in Logan Square; truffles and treats at Katherine Anne Confections

© Nathalia Segato Tomaz / Shutterstock

BRIDGEPORT

A working-class district whose factories point to its industrial past, Bridgeport might just be Chicago's most underrated neighbourhood. It's morphing into a pocket of cool, sprinkled with art studios, gastropubs and community taprooms. Alas, the L train isn't convenient here. Bus 8 along Halsted St is handy, but a car is your best bet to get around.

A Place by Damao
It's still a bit of a secret that Chinatown has spilled over to next-door Bridgeport, though foodies are making the trek. Damao's chicken gizzards, pork dumplings, thick-cut noodles and other hot-spiced Chengdu street food are several reasons why. *2621 S Halsted St; www.bydamao.com; 312-929-2088; noon-10pm Mon-Thu, 11am-10pm Fri-Sun.*

Marz Community Brewing
Set in an industrial corridor amid scads of factories, Marz is the place to come for churro-flavoured stouts and ginger-tinged saisons sipped alongside hardcore home brewers and artists. *3630 S Iron St; www.marzbrewing.com; noon-11pm Tue-Thu, to midnight Fri & Sat, to 10pm Sun.*

Bernice's Tavern
Steve runs this trinket-laden bar, which he inherited from his mom Bernice. It has been in the family for 50-plus years, a neighbourhood favourite known for its wild Wednesday night bingo games and Lithuanian liqueur shots. Cash only. *3238 S Halsted St; 312-961-5516; 3pm-midnight Mon, 3pm-2am Wed-Fri, 11am-3am Sat, noon-midnight Sun.*

Co-Prosperity Sphere
Anything goes at this experimental cultural centre, where you might encounter an evening of '90s no-wave bands, a Dungeons & Dragons gaming night or a DJ-fuelled dance party among the far-out programmes. *3219 S Morgan St; www. coprosperity.org.*

Palmisano Park
See startling views of the downtown skyline while standing on this bucolic patch of prairie that's been carved from an old quarry. Walking paths criss-cross the area, a fishing pond beckons, and you'll likely have them all to yourself. *2700 S Halsted St; 6am-11pm.*

CHICAGO

Duck Inn

Concealed between industrial plants and tidy homes at Bridgeport's edge is this cosy gastropub, where the house speciality is a wooden cutting board laid out with a shareable rotisserie duck and fat-crisped potatoes. It's a true neighbourhood spot; the chef's family even lives down the block from the Inn. *2701 S Eleanor St; www.theduckinnchicago.com; 312-724-8811; 5-11pm Tue-Thu, 5pm-midnight Fri & Sat, 10am-midnight Sun.*

Zhou B Art Center

The Zhou brothers bought their huge old warehouse years ago and invited artists to set up shop. Now it houses galleries and studios for more than 50 painters and sculptors. Groovy exhibitions take place on the first and second floors. The open studios night on the third Friday of every month (from 7pm to 10pm) allows for further exploration. *1029 W 35th St; www.zhoubartcenter.com; 10am-5pm Mon-Sat.*

BUBBLY CREEK

Bubbly Creek is the nickname for the waterway at Bridgeport's southwestern fringe. It's a legacy of Chicago's role as hog butcher for the world, when the stockyards operated here in the early 1900s. Slaughterhouses fed their waste into the water, where it rotted and emitted bubbles that rose continuously from its depths. Locals don't tend to linger for long, on account of the stench; clean-up is still ongoing.

Kimski

You won't spy many restaurants like Kimski, a Korean-Polish mash-up that cooks in a style the owners pretty much invented. Polish sausages with soju mustard and *pierogi* (dumplings) with tamari-spiked sour cream are among the creations that hit the tables. Attached to a hip beer bar. *954 W 31st St; www.kimskichicago.com; 773-823-7336; 5-11pm Tue-Sat, noon-9pm Sun.*

Bridgeport Art Center

Dozens of art studios burrow into the former Spiegel Catalog Warehouse, and many offer classes to learn woodworking and mosaic making. The obscure Maritime Museum also hides inside, with its collection of Native American birchbark canoes, vintage sextants and models of early schooners that sailed around Chicago's shores. *1200 W 35th St; www.bridgeportart.com; 8am-6pm Mon-Sat, to noon Sun.*

Top: Chengdu street food at A Place by Damao
Left: hop-head favourite Marz Community Brewing

PILSEN

Pilsen is the center of Chicago's Mexican community, with the bakeries, taquerias, murals and impressive art museum to prove it. It's also home to Chicago's hipster underground, so eclectic bars and restaurants merge into the scene. It's not far from downtown, most easily reached by the Pink Line L train to 18th St, with most sites walkable from there.

✖ Don Pedro Carnitas

Here's how it goes at Chicago's best taco joint: a guy with a jumbo knife chops juicy pork pieces onto your plate, his colleague adds minced onions, coriander, pickled jalapeños and warm tortillas, and you inhale it all at the bare-bones tables in back. The pithy menu at Don Pedro Carnitas also includes brain tacos and spicy goat stew. Cash only. *1113 W 18th St; 312-829-4757; 6am-6pm Mon-Thu, 5am-5pm Fri-Sun.*

🏛 National Museum of Mexican Art

It's a special institution that has docents roaming the galleries ready and willing to explain the semen-acrylic style of painting (that's bodily fluids mixed with pigments). Colourful folk art and politically charged works likewise grace the walls. *1852 W 19th St; www.nationalmuseumofmexicanart.org; 10am-5pm Tue-Sun; free.*

🍺 Skylark

Pilsen's bohemian crowd slouches over tater tots and craft beers inside this vaguely signposted dive bar, where a vintage photo booth and pinball machine lurk in the dim neon glow. Cash only. *2149 S Halsted St; www.skylarkchicago.com; 4pm-2am Sun-Fri, to 3am Sat.*

✪ Thalia Hall

Built in 1892 and modelled on Prague's opera house, the concert hall today hosts buzzy rock bands, with the occasional Mexican dance troupe, comedian and hard-grooving sax player thrown in for spice. A gastropub and raucous piano bar also sneak on-site. *1807 S Allport St; www.thaliahallchicago.com.*

🍺 Alulu Brewery & Pub

Alulu is easy to miss, with the discreet entrance tucked down a little alleyway, but find it and you'll hunker down in an inviting

CHICAGO

Map labels

W Roosevelt Rd
University of Illinois at Chicago
S Ashland Ave
Addams Park
LITTLE ITALY
S Halsted St
16th Street Murals
Halsted St (Metra)
18th St
La Michoacana Premium
Pilsen Community Books
Harrison Park
Pilsen Outpost
La Catrina Cafe
National Museum of Mexican Art
Thalia Hall
Don Pedro Carnitas
Alulu Brewery & Pub
Dvorak Park
PILSEN
Skylark
S Ashland Ave
W Cermak Rd
S Halsted St
S Blue Island Ave
Halsted
BRIDGEPORT
Adlai Stevenson Expwy

© 2020, Alulu Brewery

🍴 La Catrina Cafe

A brightly painted, mom-and-pop spot beloved in the community, La Catrina is full of artists and activists hobnobbing over coffee drinks like the Dirty Abuelita (Mexican hot chocolate with a shot of espresso). *1011 W 18th St; www.facebook.com/ lacatrinacafeon18; 7am-9pm Mon-Thu, 7am-6pm Fri, 8am-6pm Sat & Sun.*

space that pours imperial stouts, farmhouse ales and watermelon sours among its line-up. Beer cheese curds and other creative pub grub helps soak it up. *2011 S Laflin St; www.alulubrew.com; 5pm-2am Mon-Thu, 3pm-2am Fri & Sun, 3pm-3am Sat.*

🔒 Pilsen Outpost

One-of-a-kind T-shirts, zines, paintings and posters stock shelves at this artist-run gallery and shop. Quirky exhibitions change monthly. *1637 W 18th St; www.pilsenoutpost.com; noon-8pm Wed-Fri, 11am-7pm Sat, 11am-5pm Sun.*

❌ La Michoacana Premium

You can't miss this ice cream shop. Really: the shop's exterior is a glowing neon pink likely visible from space. Gorgeous, fruit-studded *paletas* (popsicles) are the treat to beat, though enormous scoops in rum raisin and pineapple coconut have their merits, too. *1855 S Blue Island Ave; www. lamichoacanapremiumpilsen. com; 312-226-9600; 7am-11pm Mon-Thu, to midnight Fri-Sun.*

16th STREET MURALS

———

Pilsen is famous for its murals. The 16th Street railroad embankment unfurls a particularly rich vein, with 50 works adorning a 2.4km (1.5 miles) stretch between Wood and Halsted Sts. The Pink Line L station at 18th Street is near the strip's western end. It's walkable, or rent wheels at the Divvy bike-share (www.divvybikes. com) outside the station.

🔒 Pilsen Community Books

Enter the small shop and walls of books stacked floor-to-ceiling greet you. Climb the ladder to reach for a hard-boiled detective novel, or maybe that glossy book on ferns. *1102 W 18th St; www. pilsencommunitybooks.org; 11am-6pm Sun & Mon, to 9pm Tue-Sat.*

Top and top left: pub grub and beers at Alulu Brewery Below: historic storefronts in Pilsen

© Conchi Martinez / Shutterstock

Atlanta · Decatur · East Atlanta

ATLANTA

If Atlanta were a person, they would have a loud laugh, a pie in the oven, a million ideas, and a welcoming hug for everyone.

ATLANTA

Big, booming, sprawling Atlanta is the energetic capital of the New South. Friendly and multicultural, its residents are eager to boost their home city. They're starting businesses and schools, opening galleries, cooking in cutting-edge restaurants, creating innovative music scenes, and promoting sustainable culture. Anyone imagining quaint Southern charm will be surprised – Atlanta's more about high rises than antebellum mansions, which were burned down in the Civil War.

The city's enormous size means each neighbourhood feels more like an independent village. It also means cars are the transport of choice, though the bus and rail systems are improving. A 15-minute drive southeast from downtown, walkable East Atlanta is full of low-rise pubs, coffee shops, and tattoo parlours attracting a young, diverse, arty crowd. Further east, the once-bland suburb of Decatur has bloomed into one of Atlanta's most liveable neighbourhoods, with some of the best food.

DECATUR

East of downtown lies the progressive little city of Decatur. It's a popular spot for young professionals and families, who like its historic downtown, green spaces and independent local businesses. In recent years its food scene has boomed, with hip New Southern restaurants, global eateries and microbreweries. The MARTA train station makes it possible to visit as a car-free day trip from central Atlanta.

✗ Leon's Full Service

In an old gas station, funky Leon's serves innovative New American cuisine with a global twist – veggie *banh mi* sandwiches, strip steak with sesame-nori butter, Moroccan-spiced fried chickpeas. *131 E Ponce de Leon Ave; 404-687-0500; www.leonsfullservice. com; 5am-midnight Mon, from* 11.30am-midnight Tue-Thu & Sun, to 2am Fri & Sat.

🔒 Dekalb Farmers Market

Just outside town in a warehouse the size of a plane hangar, this mind-boggling supermarket carries food from across the earth. Pyramids of papayas! Towers of spices! Aquariums of catfish! The cafeteria has it all, from samosas to oxtail stew. *3000 E Ponce de Leon Ave; www.dekalbfarmersmarket. com; 9am-9pm.*

🏛 Decatur Square

Small-town charm abounds in the square by Decatur's historic courthouse, lined with restaurants, boutiques and galleries. In warm weather the bandstand hosts free Saturday concerts. *101 E Court Sq.*

✪ Eddie's Attic

Insiders consider this intimate 'listening room' one of Atlanta's best live music spots. Acts from rockabilly bands to cello ensembles play on a small stage while guests sip wine and chow on tacos. *515-B N McDonough St; http:// eddiesattic.com.*

🔒 HomeGrown Decatur

This sassy boutique specialises in crafts and art from local makers: honeybee-shaped earrings, 'Smash the Patriarchy' stickers and prints of Dolly Parton. There's a graffiti-covered vintage fridge in the front (sign your name), and a shrine to '80s icon Mr T in the back. *412 Church St; www. homegrowndecatur.com; 10am-9pm Mon-Sat, noon-8pm Sun.*

✗ Chai Pani

This trendy space draws crowds with its twists on Indian street snacks – think kale pakoras and grilled paneer salads. *406 W Ponce de Leon Ave; 404-378-4030; www. chaipanidecatur.com; 11.30am-3pm & 5.30-9.30pm Sun-Thu, to 10pm Fri & Sat.*

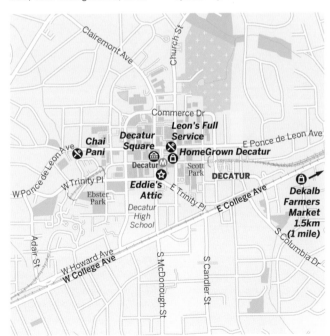

EAST ATLANTA

Just south of I-20, East Atlanta is the opposite of the tony high-rise neighbourhoods north of downtown. It's funky and budget-friendly, a place where dreadlocked and tattooed graphic designer types work on laptops in cafes by day and go to punk shows at night. The walkable East Atlanta Village (EAV) commercial district is all about vintage shops, hookah lounges and indie music clubs.

⭐ Starlight Drive-In

Open since 1949, this beloved drive-in theatre – one of the country's last – is a slice of pure vintage Americana. Double features of Hollywood blockbusters are $9 for adults, $1 for kids, leaving you plenty of cash for popcorn and a Coke (another home-grown Atlanta favourite). *2000 Moreland Ave SE; www. starlightdrivein.com.*

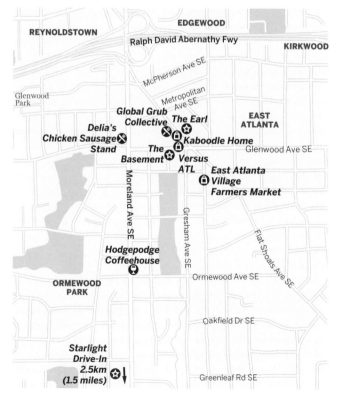

⭐ The Earl

This legendary rock 'n' roll bar has been the place to catch indie acts for 20 years. With walls shellacked with peeling posters, cheap cans of Pabst Blue Ribbon and a gorgeously greasy bar burger, it has just the right dose of dive bar character. *488 Flat Shoals Ave SE; www.badearl.com; 11.30am-3am Mon-Fri, to midnight Sat & Sun.*

✖ Global Grub Collective

The picnic tables at this small community food hall are packed at lunchtime, as locals dig into dishes from various vendors – *banh mi*, ramen, poke bowls, all washed down with tall icy cups of bubble tea. Different restaurants have different hours; something's always open between 11.30am and 9pm between Tuesday and Saturday. *479-B Flat Shoals Ave; http://wesukisuki.com.*

☕ Hodgepodge Coffeehouse

This raw industrial space with mismatched seating, local art, gender-neutral bathrooms and vegan alterna-milks is a hit with EAV's arty laptop-toting crowd. There's even a 'zine library full of quirky handmade little publications from local writers and illustrators. *720 Moreland Ave SE; http:// hodgepodgecoffee.com; 7am-7pm Mon-Sat, from 8am Sun.*

🔒 Kaboodle Home

Anyone looking for a vintage typewriter, a mid-century modern lounge chair or a portrait of Elvis embossed on a cookie tray is in the right place at this treasure cave of retro, antique and upcycled furniture and homeware. *485 Flat Shoals Ave SE; www.kaboodleatlanta.com; noon-8pm Wed-Fri, 11am-9pm Sat, noon-6pm Sun.*

✪ The Basement
The sweaty dance parties in this frill-free subterranean spot are some of the most fun to be had in the 404 area code. Disco, '80s and '90s nights draw the biggest crowds. *1245 Glenwood Ave SE; http://basementatl.com; 5pm-2am Mon-Thu, 10pm-3am Fri & Sat.*

🔒 East Atlanta Village Farmers Market
EAV's arty, earthy vibe shines in full force at this seasonal market, with organic veggies, artisan stalls, delightfully stinky cheeses, homemade kombucha vendors and more. It's a chatty place, perfect for picking up local tips. *572 Stokeswood Ave; 4-8pm Thu Apr-Nov.*

EAST ATLANTA STRUT

On a Saturday in September all of East Atlanta comes out to parade, play goofy carnival games, compete in a beard contest, eat, drink and generally make merry. There's face-painting and bouncy castles for the kids, stages for local bands, and a street market of craft vendors. The one-day festival raises money for local charities. Check out http://eastatlantastrut.com.

🔒 Versus ATL
Street fashion devotees go nuts for the retro '80s and '90s sportswear at this curated boutique. Vintage Chicago Bulls warm-up jacket? 1996 Atlanta Olympics tee? Original Air Jordans? Simpsons 'Don't Have a Cow, Man' trucker cap? Yes, yes, yes and yes. Expect to pay top dollar for anything rare. *493 Flat Shoals Ave SE; www.vsatl.com; 1-6pm.*

✖ Delia's Chicken Sausage Stand
Unbelievably moreish chicken sausages with a wild array of toppings are served from a walk-up stand. Try 'Da Bomb', with eggs and cheese on a Krispy Kreme donut bun, if you dare. And don't leave without a red velvet 'cake shake'. Oh, and it's open all night on weekends. *489 Moreland Ave SE; www.thesausagestand.com; 404-474-9651; 7am-10pm Mon-Thu, 24hr from 7am Fri-10pm Sun.*

Above: Atlanta skyline
Left: Delia's Chicken Sausage Stand

© ronaldashleylaneir / 500px

© 2020, Delia's Chicken Sausage

ARTS & CULTURE MUSIC & FILM SPORTS & LEISURE EATING DRINKING SHOPPING

TORONTO

Toronto's honed a reputation for food and drink, but growing like a teenager, it is also secretive and full of surprises.

Among the neighbourhoods of old Toronto, Little Portugal, a residential ethnic enclave on the city's west side, has long been known for its well-tended flower beds, magnolia trees and Portuguese food. Then the beard and sneaker set arrived, giving exponential rise – and international attention – to a more diverse collection of independent coffee stops, bars and restos, particularly along 'west Queen West' and around Trinity Bellwoods Park.

As babies were born and rents skyrocketed, the 30-plus crowd began cycling across the Don Valley Parkway to the grittier 'east side', buying fixer-uppers in Leslieville, where they've been quietly enjoying unobstructed skyline views, easy lake access, brunch venues and micro-breweries. Some of the most satisfying spots are in and around the neighbourhood's northern boundary, Gerrard St, attracting urban explorers ready to stumble upon the next big thing. Both neighbourhoods are navigable by bicycle or on foot; streetcars along west-east axes offer streamlined travel to downtown.

LESLIEVILLE

Amid the whitewashed brick, tiled flooring and Scandinavian-inspired interiors, gentrifying Leslieville harbours less-polished gems behind unassuming storefronts, tucked around street corners or in former factories, or plopped in stretches of commercial wilderness. Queen East pedestrian traffic thickens on weekends; head north to the nexus with Little India for the latest discoveries. Take the Queen or Carlton streetcar from downtown.

❌ Eulalie's Corner Store

Kitschy, colourful garage sale decor (think flamingos and random portraiture) with a down-to-earthiness reminiscent of small-town bars. Locals love the tart cocktails, burgers and one-of-a-kind mac and cheese and brussels sprouts. *1438 Gerrard St E; www.eulaliescornerstore.com; 647-350-6263; 4pm-2am.*

🍷 Vatican Gift Shop

Concealed behind a tiny mock storefront, imbibing cocktails, scarfing Neopolitan pizzas, and rocking out to live music at this speakeasy with churchy Romanesque touches may induce guilt. *1047 Gerrard St E; Wed-Sat 7pm-late.*

🍷 WAYLA Bar

The name (What Are You Looking At) is ironic, as you'll miss it if you blink. Facilitated fun with dance parties, comedy nights and karaoke, it's got a rep for inclusivity and 'zero tolerance for intolerance'. *996 Queen Street E; www.waylabar.ca; Mon-Sun 8pm-2am.*

🛍 In the Groove

Collectors of vintage records are kids in a candy store after stepping into this minty-coloured place. The cataloguing of 50,000 titles seems honourary PhD-worthy – don't miss the Soul Shack, an additional space packed with groovy tunes out back. *1174 Queen St E, www.inthegrooverecords.com; noon-6pm Tue, noon-6pm Thu-Sun.*

☕ Dundas and Carlaw

Housed in a nondescript former textile factory, this place is a prize for morning coffee or local microbrews, charcuterie and music on hot summer nights. *1173 Dundas St E; www.dundasandcarlaw.com; 7am-midnight Mon-Fri, 9am-2am Sat, 9am-noon Sun.*

🚲 Leslie Street Spit

Keep cycling south on Leslie St to a nature reserve and hub for migrating birds – expect Hitchcock-esque moments along with spectacular sunsets and skyline views. *www.tommythompsonpark.ca; free.*

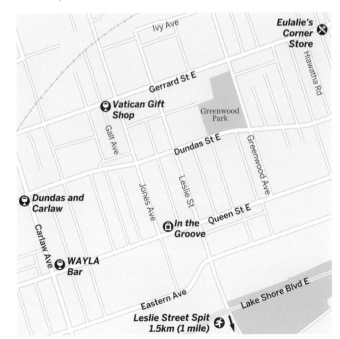

LITTLE PORTUGAL

Perfect for the cashed-up or lazy traveller, Little Portugal is easy on the eyes and a cinch to navigate. Its main arteries are quickly filling with food, drink and galleries, all of them best explored on foot. With Queen West getting saturated, entrepreneurs now push west along Dundas St, where tiny coffee shops, tropical plant shops and vintage clothing are a 'thing'.

✖ Wallflower

So named for its location at the very fringes of a hip strip, this dark, French-inspired bar/bistro is dressed up with floral fabric and wallpaper; tall bouquets adorn a beautifully cluttered bar. Locals in tees and sweats and couples on date nights tuck into the signature devilled eggs, steak and hearty vegetarian options. *1665 Dundas St W; www.facebook.com/WallflowerTO; 647-352-5605; 5pm-2am.*

🔒 The Fountain

Inconspicuous, intimate local bar and art gallery with a folksy – even witchy – vibe (think skeletons and taxidermy), neighbours stop in for classic cocktails and inventive potions. *1261 Dundas St W; 416-262-4986; 7pm-2am.*

✖ Major Treat

Fronting a barber shop (The Town Barber), this take-away spot offers a short menu of first-rate coffee classics and amps the 'coffee and ...' trend with a shortlist of the city's most scrumptious pastries and baked goods. Locals are beginning to bypass the (perfectly fine) bakery next door. *1158 Queen St W; 416-507-9920; 7am-6pm.*

⊕ Fix Coffee and Bikes

Tucked on a residential street in a former corner Portuguese grocery, this local hangout combines an airy coffee bar and brunchery with a repair and bicycle shop, plus bike gallery with rotating exhibits and events. *80 Gladstone Ave; www.fixcb.ca; coffee 7.30am-5.30pm Mon-Fri, shop 8am-6pm Mon-Fri, 9am-5pm Sat & Sun.*

🔒 Mahjong

Located by the pink glow in its bodega storefront, you'll pass security, push through a heavy curtain and soon emerge through a keyhole to arrive at the best party in town. Tropical murals and hues of Singapore Sling complement playful, herbaceous cocktails.

LITTLE ITALY

College St

Black Dice Cafe

✖ Wallflower

Dundas St W

🔒 Mahjong
🔒 The Fountain

Ossington Ave

Dufferin St

Venezia Bakery

✖ Gift Shop

⊕ Fix Coffee and Bikes

WEST QUEEN WEST

Lansdowne Ave

✖ Major Treat

Queen St W

Vog Vault 750m (0.5 miles)

King St W

Pulsating tunes and Chinese small plates round out the sensory experience. *1276 Dundas St W; www.mahjongbar.com; 6pm-2am.*

🏛 Vog Vault

Canadian designer John Fluevog's shoes are internationally known, but many a Torontonian has passed this shop not knowing it houses a gravity-defying photo experience in the former bank's vault. *686 Queen St W; www.fluevog.com; 11am-7pm Mon-Wed, 10am-8pm Thu-Sat, 11am-6pm Sun.*

🍸 Gift Shop

Accessed through an easy-going barber shop (Barber & Co.) occupying a former art studio, this cocktail lounge ministered by 'Bartender H' is a cool chemical lab delivering pure alchemy. *89B Ossington Ave; www. donnellygroup.ca/giftshop; 8pm-2am Tue-Sun.*

🚇 Black Dice Cafe

Off-hours bartenders drink at this eye-popping 'Japanese rockabilly' bar with 1950s American

PORTUGUESE PASTRIES

———

All this cycling (or drinking) will leave you with a hearty appetite. Residents nurse their hangovers and pay homage to the culture that started it all by frequenting the area's longtime Portuguese bakeries on Dundas or Ossington for breads and home-cooked Portuguese food. Toronto residents will visit the neighbourhood for the *pastel del nata* custard tarts (*natas*) alone: Venezia Bakery is a good place to start.

paraphernalia and elements of a deconstructed bowling alley. Sake cocktails and whiskies feature prominently. *1574 Dundas St W; http://blackdicecafe.com; 7.30pm-2am.*

Top: nibbles at Mahjong Below and below left: Fix Coffee and Bikes

Upper Northwest DC

Adams Morgan, Dupont & U Street

Georgetown

Washington, DC

WASHINGTON, DC

Famed for grand architecture and the marble-lined corridors of power, America's capital also harbours scenic, tree-lined neighbourhoods crackling with energy.

The modern beating heart of Washington lies about 2km (1.2 miles) due north of the National Mall. Dupont Circle is a whirl of artfully designed restaurants and cultural spaces, while nearby Adams Morgan draws party people with its burgeoning bar scene. Northeast, the U Street Corridor is the soul of a historic African American neighbourhood, with candle-lit gastropubs, mural-lined alleys and buzzing clubs.

Some 2km (1.2 miles) southwest of Dupont Circle, villagey Georgetown has old brick townhouses lined with upscale shops and eateries. The location by the Potomac also offers riverfront dining and aquatic adventures.

North of Georgetown, peaceful neighbourhoods skirt the western edge of vast Rock Creek Park, forming Upper Northwest DC, one of Washington's most charming, overlooked districts, dotted with indie theatres and shops, cultural centres and serene cafes.

A metro moves between neighbourhoods and there's a bike sharing system (Capital BikeShare).

WASHINGTON, DC

GEORGETOWN

Older than Washington, Georgetown is a neighbourhood of Federal-style architecture, cobbled streets and an inviting stretch of waterfront. The leafy lanes hide some intriguing hangouts, including a charming tea house, a boutique-filled alley and one of the loveliest gardens in the city. Georgetown isn't on a metro line, though it's a pleasant bike ride from the mall along the Potomac.

🌳 Dumbarton Oaks Garden

In the warmer months, the Dumbarton Oaks Garden is a dazzling blaze of colour, with flower-lined walkways, trickling fountains, rose gardens and wisteria-covered arbours. Come in spring for dazzling cherry blossoms or in autumn for the fiery colours of changing elm, oak and beech leaves. *Cnr R & 31st Sts NW; www.doaks.org/visit/garden; 2-6pm Tue-Sun mid-Mar-Oct; $10.*

☕ Ching Ching Cha

This delightful tea room feels like a world removed from the bustling city beyond. The simple, Zen-like space provides a suitable sanctuary for lingering over beautifully prepared cups of tea, with dozens of varieties on offer. You'll also find dumplings, veg-centric lunch specials and sweets like *mochi* (rice cakes). *1063 Wisconsin Ave NW; www.chingchingcha.com; 11am-8pm Thu-Mon.*

⛵ Thompson Boat Center

See DC's captivating landscape from out on the calm waters of the Potomac River. The Thompson Boat Center can get you outfitted with a kayak, canoe or stand-up paddleboard in a hurry. You can also sign up for lessons if you need a refresher (or an intro) to sculling. *2900 Virginia Ave NW; www.boatingindc.com; 8am-7pm.*

🍴 Fiola Mare

Overlooking the Potomac, Fiola Mare serves some of the best seafood in the city, like mouth-watering oysters from east and west, Maine lobster and tender sea urchin. Vaunted Italian chef Fabio Trabocchi helms this beautifully designed dining room. It feels a bit like dining inside a luxury yacht. *3050 K St NW; www.fiolamaredc.com; 202-525-1402; 11.30am-2pm & 5-10pm Tue-Sun.*

🛍 Cady's Alley

A slew of glittering boutiques sprinkled along a cobblestone lane. You'll find runway-ready apparel, stylish accessories and home design shops, plus an appealing Austrian-style cafe (Leopold's Kafe Konditorei) around the corner from M street. *Off 3rd St NW; www.cadysalley.com; approx 10am-6pm Mon-Sat, noon-5pm Sun.*

KALORAMA

Reservoir Rd NW

Dumbarton Oaks Garden

Oak Hill Cemetery

Rock Creek

GEORGETOWN

Georgetown University

Q St NW

Wisconsin Ave NW

Rock Creek

M St NW

Cady's Alley

Ching Ching Cha

Pennsylvania Ave NW

Whitehurst Fwy

Francis Scott Key Bridge

Georgetown Waterfront Park

Washington Harbour Complex

Rock Creek Park

K St NW

Potomac River

Fiola Mare

Thompson Boat Center

UPPER NORTHWEST DC

These leafy lanes and meandering boulevards are home to atmospheric hangouts, including a cafe nestled near an iconic cathedral and Washington's best bookshop. It's also the gateway to DC's semi-wilderness escape, Rock Creek Park. A car's useful to get around this spread-out area; you can also find ride-sharing services.

✈ Rock Creek Park

Though within easy reach of downtown DC, Rockwood Park provides an easy escape into the wilderness. Encompassing over 800 hectares with 52km (32 miles) of trails, this leafy oasis is home to forest-lined streams, flower-strewn fields and the moss-covered remnants of old grist mills and Civil War forts. Pick up a trail map and park info from the helpful rangers at the Nature Centre, off Glover Rd. *5200 Glover Rd NW; www.nps.gov/rocr.*

❌ Open City Cafe

One of DC's best-kept secrets is the charming cafe and lunch spot set in a historic building a few steps from Washington National Cathedral. The octagonal building was a former baptistry, and its tall ceilings and stained-glass windows make a fine setting for lattes and buttery pastries, avocado toast or portobello sandwiches. Afterwards, take a stroll in the fragrant Bishops Garden right outside. *3101 Wisconsin Ave NW; www.opencitycathedraldc.com; 202-965-7670; 7am-6pm.*

🔒 Politics & Prose

For a front-row perspective on the major events shaping society today, pay a visit to this long-running indie bookshop. Politics & Prose has one of the best author reading series on the planet, with a mix of novelists, biographers, historians, poets and politicians appearing on the nightly docket. There's also a proper coffeehouse and wine bar (with full menu) on the lower level. *5015 Connecticut Ave NW; www.politics-prose.com; 9am-10pm Mon-Sat, 10am-8pm Sun.*

🏛 Maison Française

The Maison Française hosts a

Map labels:
Somerset Park · Avalon Theatre · Macon Bistro & Larder · Newlands Park · Rock Creek Golf Course · Friendship Heights · CHEVY CHASE · Military Rd NW · River Rd NW · Western Ave · Comet Ping Pong · Fort Reno Park · Politics & Prose · Rock Creek Park · Massachusetts Ave NW · Nebraska Ave NW · Reno Rd NW · TENLEYTOWN · Tenleytown-AU · FOREST HILLS · Wesley Circle · Soapstone Valley Park · Van Ness-UDC · CLEVELAND PARK · Melvin C Hazen Park · Piney Creek Park · Battery Kemble Park · Glover Archbold Park · Open City Cafe · Cleveland Park · 34th St NW · National Zoological Park · Foxhall Rd NW · Wesley Heights Park · Wisconsin Ave NW · Woodley Park · WOODLEY PARK · FOXHALL · Foundry Branch · Normanstone Park · ADAMS MORGAN · Whitehaven Park · Dumbarton Oaks Park · KALORAMA · Maison Française · GEORGETOWN

packed calendar of events for lovers of the arts, including film screenings, classical concerts, food festivals and more. Not surprisingly, many events have a Gallic focus – this is the headquarters of the French Embassy, after all. Some events are free but online registration is usually required. *4101 Reservoir Rd NW; www.franceintheus.org.*

⭐ Avalon Theatre

This two-screen movie house is a big source of local pride. It's DC's oldest cinema (opened 1922) and a nonprofit community-run affair, showing foreign films and indie features you won't find elsewhere. The cafe serves wine, beer, pastries and other snacks, so you can enjoy a film with a drink. *5612 Connecticut Ave NW; www. theavalon.org.*

❌ Macon Bistro & Larder

Homespun southern cooking meets French refinery in this imaginative restaurant and provisions shop set in a landmark 1920s building. The seasonal menu showcases combinations like lobster and grits (a cornmeal dish) and Maryland rockfish with spring ramps and red onion marmalade – best finished with a flourless chocolate cake. The top spot is the dining room, with its vintage fixtures and garrulous vibe. *5520 Connecticut Ave NW; www. maconbistro.com; 202-248-7807; 11am-2pm & 4-10pm.*

❌ Comet Ping Pong

There's craft beer and a fun all-ages crowd at Comet, which serves up the neighbourhood's best wood-fired pizzas. Play a round of table tennis while you wait for your pie. Most nights you can hear live bands – indie, punk rock, electro-pop and other sounds. *5037 Connecticut Ave NW; www.cometpingpong. com; 202-364-0404; 5-9.30pm Mon-Thu, 11.30am-11pm Fri & Sat, 11.30am-9.30pm Sun.*

© Orhan Cam / Shutterstock

**Top: Rock Creek Park
Left: firebrand books at
Politics & Prose**

ADAMS MORGAN, DUPONT & U STREET

This trio of lively 'hoods offers some of the best dining, drinking and culturally minded pontificating in town. Setting the scene are vintage cocktail dens, African stores and places to eat, and an underground arts space. Dupont Circle and U St are linked to other parts of DC by separate metro lines. Adams Morgan is a 1km (0.6 miles) walk or bike ride north of Dupont Circle.

🍴 Roofers Union

In the midst of the buzzing eateries and drinking dens of 18th St, the Roofers Union is a standout for creatively configured spaces across three floors. Stop in the cosy first-floor bar for an easy-going wine-centric menu. The airy second floor, with its floor-to-ceiling windows, is the go-to spot for craft beer, while the third-level rooftop offers fabulous views over the neighbourhood. Feast on American comfort food with global accents; reserve ahead on weekends, especially for RU's popular brunch. *2446 18th St NW; www.roofersuniondc.com; 202-232-7663; 5pm-2am Mon-Fri, from 11am Sat & Sun.*

🏛 Dupont Underground

Hidden beneath the city streets a few steps from one of DC's busiest traffic circles lies this former trolley car station transformed into a creative arts hub. Beside the old rail tracks, you can catch immersive theatre performances, avant-garde gallery installations and multimedia shows. Check the website to see what's on and to reserve tickets. The entrance is near a Starbucks; look for the stairs leading beneath a red Dupont Underground sign. *19 Dupont Circle NW; www.dupontunderground.org.*

⭐ Eighteenth Street Lounge

Set in a mansion off busy Connecticut Ave, the Eighteenth Street Lounge has a warren of rooms with vintage sofas, glittering chandeliers and flickering candles – creating the impression of an exclusive house party rather than a nightclub. It's a memorable setting for Latin jazz, reggae, funk and other bands that hold court all week long. Go on a weeknight to beat the crowds. *1212 18th St; www.18thstlounge.com; 5pm-2am Sun & Tue-Fri, 9pm-3am Sat.*

Map labels: Songbyrd Record Cafe & Music House; Roofers Union; COLUMBIA HEIGHTS; MERIDIAN HILL; Kalorama Park; Meridian Hill Park; Florida Ave NW; ADAMS MORGAN; Green Zone; W St NW; Florida Ave NW; Busboys and Poets; Columbia Rd NW; Zawadi; U Street-Cardozo/African American Civil War Memorial; KALORAMA; New Hampshire Ave NW; 16th St NW; 13th St NW; Connecticut Ave NW; DUPONT CIRCLE; R St NW; Dupont Underground; Q St NW; LOGAN CIRCLE; Dupont Circle; Stead Recreation Center; Logan Circle; Massachusetts Ave NW; DOWNTOWN; Dupont Circle; New Hampshire Ave NW; Rhode Island Ave NW; Vermont Ave NW; 13th St NW; Scott Circle; Thomas Circle; M St NW; Eighteenth Street Lounge

🏛 Busboys and Poets

Equal parts bookstore, cafe, restaurant and events space, Busboys and Poets hosts a progressive line-up of author readings, film screenings, poetry nights and open discussions on hot social topics. The eclectic menu features comfort fare with vegan options. B&P has other locations around DC, though the original 14st St location has the best vibe and events line-up. *2021 14th St NW; www.busboysandpoets.com; 7am-midnight Mon-Fri, from 8am Sat & Sun.*

🍸 Green Zone

This 2018 newcomer to Adams Morgan quickly garnered a loyal neighbourhood following for its combination of brilliant craft cocktails, rare beers and delicious Middle Eastern street food. Iraqi-German founder Chris Hassaan Francke spent years honing his recipes, and creativity shines through in drinks like the 'Saz'iraq', made with rye, dates and Arabian and Peychaud's Bitters. *2226 18th St NW; www.facebook.com/thegreenzonedc; 5pm-2am Tue-Sun.*

PASSPORT DC: A GLOBAL CELEBRATION

During the month of May, Washington hosts more than 100 globally themed cultural events, including street festivals, art exhibitions and live performances, with groups from every corner of the globe. Numerous embassies hold open houses, making it a great time to explore some of the grand architectural treasure located near Dupont Circle. Check Passport DC (www.passportdc.oncell.com) for maps and schedules.

🔒 Zawadi

On buzzing U Street, Zawadi stocks an extraordinary array of crafts and artwork from across Africa. You'll find a thoughtfully curated selection of jewellery, textiles, baskets, colourfully bound journals, wood carvings, masks, clothing, paintings and other great gift ideas (in fact, *zawadi* means 'gift' in Swahili). *1524 U Street NW; www.zawadiarts.com; noon-7pm Mon & Thu-Sat, 1-6pm Sun.*

⭐ Songbyrd Record Cafe & Music House

Live bands and DJs take the stage most nights in the funky downstairs den of this retro cafe and record shop. Songbyrd is also a laid-back daytime spot, with fair-trade organic coffee and tasty sandwiches. There are new and used albums for sale, and weekday drink specials (from 5pm to 7pm). *2477 18th St NW; www.songbyrddc.com; 8am-10pm.*

Top: Busboys and Poets Below: Dupont Circle's turreted townhouses

ARTS & CULTURE   MUSIC & FILM   SPORTS & LEISURE   EATING   DRINKING   SHOPPING

Kensington
Fishtown

Northern
Liberties

Philadelphia

South
Philly

PHILADELPHIA

Once you've seen the Liberty Bell and the Rocky statue, go off the beaten path to check out Philadelphia's best distilleries and indie bookshops.

PHILADELPHIA

L ike most visitors to Philly, you're here for the cheesesteak, a peek inside Independence Hall, and the chance to run up the steps of the Philadelphia Art Museum, Rocky-style. But in several of the city's quickly revitalising neighbourhoods, lesser-known pleasures await curious travellers.

A few miles north of historic Old City, find a trio of neighbouring districts: stylish Fishtown, with its cocktail bars, boutiques and coffee shops; down-to-earth Kensington, known for its classic distilleries and warehouse spaces transformed into modern lofts and cafes; and waterfront Northern Liberties, with its retro diners and theatres. All are accessible by SEPTA (the subway line), trolley or a quick Uber ride.

On the other end of town, South Philly – a pleasant stroll, bus ride, or car from the historic centre – is steeped in immigrant traditions. It's a place where Cambodian immigrants make fantastic French baguettes, and you can try a Lebanese-Italian sandwich.

SOUTH PHILLY

Stretching south from Philadelphia's historic centre, South Philly is a large area that's nonetheless wonderful to wander around on foot. The Italian Market, which occupies 10 city blocks, is one of the oldest open-air marketplaces in the USA, and it's a perfect base for exploring this culturally diverse neighbourhood.

🏛 History of Italian Immigration Museum

Italian immigrant culture is key to Philadelphia's identity. This little-known museum traces the path of Italian explorers in the Americas, the waves of Italian vendors, shoemakers, tailors and labourers who found a new home in Philadelphia, and the legacy of Italian-Americans in sports, art and politics. *1834 E Passyunk Ave; www.filitaliainternational.com; 9.30am-2.30pm Mon-Fri, 11am-7pm Sat, 11am-5pm Sun.*

❌ Bitar's

South Philly is often associated with the Italian immigrant community. But historically, the area around 10th & Federal has also been a major centre of Lebanese culture, and Bitar's is one of the best places to sample traditional dishes. For a uniquely Philadelphian delicacy, try the Angelo Cataladi sandwich, a Lebanese-Italian mash-up with roasted pepper spread and cheese. *947 Federal St; www.bitars.com; 10am-8pm Mon-Sat.*

🚇 RIM Café

At this offbeat cafe in Philly's Italian Market, an eccentric French chocolatier (René, with the help of his wife, Belle) grinds and processes artisanal beans to make decadent drinks like 'The Volcano', which he tops off with fresh shavings from an enormous block of chocolate. *1172 S 9th St; www.rimcafe.net; 6-11pm Wed-Fri, noon-midnight Sat, noon-10pm Sun.*

🏛 Philadelphia's Magic Gardens

You might walk right past the entrance to Philadelphia's Magic Gardens, not realising that a whimsical wonderland is just inside. The passion project of eccentric local artist Isaiah Zagar, the 'gardens' include one-of-a-kind galleries and an open-air maze colourful mosaics and quirky treasures. *1020 South St; www.phillymagicgardens.org; 11am-6pm Wed-Mon; $10.*

❌ Artisan Boulangerie Patissier

Owned and operated by Cambodian immigrants, Artisan Boulangerie Patissier does exquisite baguettes, Vietnamese coffee and sandwiches with a French twist. *1218 Mifflin St; www.facebook.com/artisanboulangeriephl; 7am-5pm Tue-Sat, 8am-4pm Sun.*

FISHTOWN

Ask a local: they'll tell you Fishtown is one of the most fashionable neighbourhoods to live in...or to go for coffee, drinks, lunch or shopping. It's hard to find a parking spot on these streets lined with elegant townhouses, cocktail bars and boutiques; it's best to cycle here (or to get dropped off). Luckily, you won't need wheels to explore this relatively walkable neighbourhood.

Jinxed

You could get lost for ages in this little shop of curiosities. Whether you're in the market for antique hand-drawn maps, a vintage Polaroid camera, an art deco tea set, or French comic books – or if you're just killing time between lattes and cocktails on Fishtown's busy Frankford Ave – a stop at Jinxed is a must. *1331 Frankford Ave; www.jinxedphiladelphia. com; 11am-7pm Mon-Sat, 11am-8pm Sun.*

Bottle Bar East

Though it looks like a typical bottle shop from outside, climb the staircase to find the relaxed bar and art gallery upstairs. Especially in contrast with Fishtown's high-end cocktail bars, Bottle Bar East is a laid-back place to linger over a craft beer or two: there are 16 options on tap, plus a short menu of charcuterie and boutique wines by the glass. *1308 Frankford Ave; www.bottlebareast.com; 11.30am-2am.*

The Art Dept

With a gallery, vintage store, and a busy calendar of cultural workshops, The Art Dept is a non-profit arts organisation at the heart of Fishtown's creative community. Stop into the Colored Vintage shop to peruse '60s-era sundresses and pieces handmade by local designers, then check out pop-up installations by Philadelphia artists in the adjacent gallery space. *1638 E Berks St; www. artdeptphilly.com; noon-8pm Tue-Sat.*

Ulises

A relatively new addition to Fishtown, this indie arts bookstore and gallery revolves around 'curatorial seasons'. Every few months, the owners select a theme, then invite artists and writers to contribute their work. On weekends it's a great place to browse through artists' books or attend a lecture on topics ranging from education to migration to

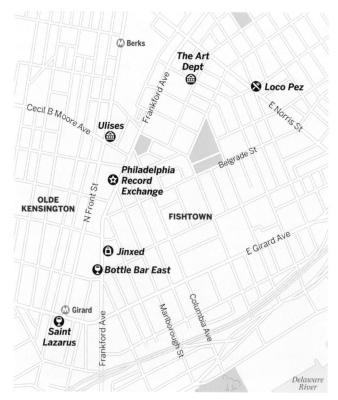

intimacy. Many events are free. *31 E Columbia Ave; www.ulises.us; noon-6pm Sat-Sun.*

✖ Loco Pez
Fittingly for a neighbourhood named Fishtown, Loco Pez ('Crazy Fish' in Spanish) is locally famous for its delicious tacos. This cool cash-only spot specialises in Los Angeles–style street food from quesadillas to burritos; there's a generous happy hour every day with signature cocktails, as well as a very long list of craft beer and tequila to choose from. Ask about the secret menu. *2401 E Norris St; www.locopez.com; 11am-1am.*

🍸 Saint Lazarus
In a neighbourhood that's quickly gentrified in recent years, this down-to-earth bar and nightclub remains true to Fishtown's indie roots, featuring local DJs, comedy sets, $5 drink specials, not to

© f11photo / Shutterstock

ONE FISH, TWO FISH
Fishtown's name derives from the neighbourhood's history. Located on the banks of the Delaware River, the area was a hub of the German American-dominated fishing industry in the 18th and early 19th centuries. Today, you'll spot whimsical fish symbols left and right, from fish-themed street art to fish mosaics to fish-shaped garbage cans.

mention the lively Tuesday night 'hangouts'. The light-hearted and inclusive atmosphere at Saint Lazarus (locally referred to as 'the Saint') is a huge part of the bar's enduring appeal among locals. *102 W Girard Ave; www. facebook.com/saintlazarusbar; 1pm-2am.*

⭐ Philadelphia Record Exchange
Go analogue at this old-school record shop where locals buy and sell used vinyls and cassette tapes. More than a store, it's a cultural hub for the neighbourhood's music enthusiasts and a great place to find out about under-the-radar concerts and events happening around Fishtown. (When in doubt, just ask one of the knowledgeable staff members for their recs.) *1524 Frankford Ave; http://philarecx.com; 11am-8pm.*

© 2020, The Art Dept

Top: the city skyline from Ben Franklin Bridge
Left: rummage-worthy vintage at The Art Dept

KENSINGTON

Quickly gentrifying Kensington, Fishtown's rough-and-tumble neighbour, offers a number of hidden gems, from a BYOB mini-golf course to renovated distilleries. Though the area is much safer than it used to be, it's still best to use caution when coming and going, especially at night: ride-share services are particularly useful if you're coming from Center City.

Evil Genius Beer Company
The unusual names of the beers – one light lager is called 'The Painting Was a Gift, Todd' while an Irish-style ale is named 'Help! I Accidentally Built a Shelf' – let you know you're not in a typical bar. This quirky brewpub, complete with a tasting room and a dog-friendly beer garden, is a gem. *1727 N Front St; www.evilgeniusbeer.com; 4-10pm Wed, 4pm-midnight Thu, 2pm-midnight Fri, noon-midnight Sat, noon-9pm Sun.*

Keystone Mini Golf
Billed as the city's first 18-hole indoor outdoor BYOB mini-golf course, Keystone Mini Golf offers an active alternative to the cafe and bar circuit. There's an arcade and a snack bar on-site; it's kid-friendly until 9pm. Check online before going. *161 Cecil B Moore Ave; www.keystoneminigolf.com; 5-11pm Thu-Fri, 1pm-midnight Sat, 1-8pm Sun; adult/child $12/7.*

Gryphon Coffee Co.
This indie coffee roaster tends to be a little calmer than the area's most popular coffee shops (La Colombe in Fishtown, we're looking at you). Come for excellent flat whites, gourmet egg sandwiches, pop-up art exhibitions, and a little peace and quiet. *100 W Oxford Street; www.gryphoncoffee.com; 7am-3pm Mon-Fri, 8am-3pm Sat.*

Que Chula Es Puebla
Homemade corn tortillas, complimentary snacks while you wait, huge portions...this low-key BYOB is neighbourhood Mexican at its best. Try the chorizo tacos (or for something lighter, the house ceviche). If the weather's nice, take an order to the park two blocks east. *1356 N 2nd St; www.chulaespuebla.com; 10am-9pm Sun-Thu, 10am-10pm Sat-Sun.*

Stateside Distillery
If you think that a cold-filtered, GMO-free, single-grain, corn-based vodka sounds like a spirit invented in *Portlandia*, you're not far off the vibe of industrial-chic Stateside Distillery. Tip: distillery tours, usually $10, are free on Thursdays. *1700 N Hancock Street; www.statesidevodka.com; 5-10pm Thu, 5pm-midnight Fri, noon-midnight Sat, noon-7pm Sun.*

NORTHERN LIBERTIES

Directly north of Philadelphia's historic Old City, Northern Liberties was a popular artists' enclave in the '90s. The neighbourhood sits on the shore of the Delaware River, and arriving here along the waterfront (walking and biking are both good options) is a particularly lovely way to approach these streets lined with tea shops and vintage theatres.

The Random Tea Room & Curiosity Shop

The name says it all. There's plenty of tea to drink at this cultural space and cafe, from Chinese greens to South American yerba mate, plus an antique shop, photography exhibits, monthly concerts, tarot card readings, even a miniature spa where you can book a Swedish massage or acupuncture. *713 N 4th St; www.therandomtearoom.com; 10am-8pm.*

One Shot Coffee

Forgot to bring a book? No problem: One Shot Coffee has a great cafe downstairs, while upstairs is a beautiful library. It's a cosy place to take a break from technology and enjoy reading over a latte. *217 W George St; www.1shotcoffee.com; 7am-5pm.*

Ruba Club

This retro-glam social club and concert hall has been around for over a century. Today, Ruba Club's original vaudeville-style theatre hosts live music and cabaret, while the Prohibition-style cocktail bar on the lower level is a stylish venue for drinks. *416 Green St; www.rubaclub.org; 10pm-3am Thu-Fri, 11pm-3am Sat-Sun.*

Philadelphia Distilling

Raise a glass at the state's first craft distillery to open since Prohibition. Philadelphia Distilling is more than a place to sip perfectly mixed cocktails like a Vesper or The Bee's Knees: it's a living museum with hand-hammered copper stills and wooden fermentation vessels. *25 E Allen St; www.philadelphiadistilling.com; 4-11pm Thu-Fri, 1-11pm Sat-Sun.*

Silk City

At this hipster-friendly diner, you'll eat your scrambled eggs and coffee inside a diner car built in 1952 in Paterson, New Jersey that was moved to Philly two years later. The name 'Silk City' is a nod to Paterson's silk manufacturing history. *435 Spring Garden St; www.silkcityphilly.com; 10am-2am.*

ARTS & CULTURE   MUSIC & FILM   SPORTS & LEISURE   EATING   DRINKING   SHOPPING

Harlem

Astoria

New York

Williamsburg & Bushwick

Sunset Park & Red Hook

North Shore, Staten Island

NEW YORK CITY

Secret places in a city of 8.6 million people? They won't be empty, but NYC's lesser-visited venues are full of unanticipated character.

Nothing stays secret in NYC. With so many people perpetually seeking 'hidden' experiences, NYC feels forever found. But that doesn't mean all places see the same crush of crowds. Generally, the further from celebrated centres an establishment (or whole neighbourhood) is, the more true to community character it's likely to be. And secret it might feel.

More visitors are steering clear of Manhattan's overtouristed crossroads and exploring other boroughs, often facilitated by NYC Ferry's water connections. These neighbourhoods are complex outer-borough districts just one water-transit hop from Manhattan or, for culturally rich Harlem, one step beyond most visitors' Manhattan journeys. In Queens, Astoria delivers food-rich diversity; Staten Island, an unexpected sense of place; and in Brooklyn's Williamsburg, Bushwick, Sunset Park and Red Hook, entrepreneurial spirit in surprising places.

SUNSET PARK & RED HOOK

Once mainly European, Sunset Park's population is now predominantly Chinese, Mexican and Dominican. Red Hook is changing too, but from tradesmen to modern makers like foodies and artists. Both of these Brooklyn neighbourhoods are conveniently reached via ferry from Manhattan to once-industrial waterfronts abuzz with entrepreneurial activity, especially in places like Sunset Park's Industry City.

❌ Ricos Tacos

Modest but welcoming, Ricos has been dishing up some of Sunset Park's best taquitos, tostadas, tacos and other Mexican specialities for longer than most. *505 51st St; 718-633-4816; 11am-2am.*

🍸 Barrow's Intense Tasting Room

The ginger liqueur is distilled on site, but the other 150-plus spirits for sale are crafted throughout New York state. The tasting room is located in Industry City, a repurposed warehouse district now home to approximately 400 makers fabricating everything from food to fashion. *86 34th St; http://barrowsintense.com; noon-evening.*

❌ Fei Long Market Food Court

In Brooklyn Chinatown, inside the right-out-of-Asia Fei Long Market, a bustling food court's stalls stew up dumplings, hot pots, stir-fries and more, but with limited English signage. Be adventurous! *6301 8th Ave; 718-680-0118; 7.30am-8pm.*

🏛 Waterfront Museum

Moored to Pier 44, the Lehigh Valley wooden cargo barge is a museum devoted to expanding public access to NYC's waterfront by teaching about history and life along NY's rivers. *290 Conover St; http://waterfrontmuseum.org; free; 4-8pm Thu, 1-5pm Sat.*

🍸 Sunny's Bar

This dive bar looks and feels like it did when longshoremen worked the old Red Hook docks. The difference? Today's clientele, live music and art. *253 Conover St; http://sunnysredhook.com; 5pm-late Mon-Fri, 11am-late Sat & Sun.*

🍸 Red Hook Winery

Wines are produced here, from grape to bottle, using fruit grown in New York state. It's surprisingly unknown, despite the quality nectars, tastings, tours and harbour views. *175 Van Dyke St; http://redhookwinery.com; noon-6pm.*

Red Hook Winery — Pier 41
Sunny's Bar — Coffey Park
CARROLL GARDENS
Waterfront Museum
RED HOOK
Smith-9th Sts
Upper New York Bay
Beard Street Warehouses
Beard St
Red Hook Recreational Area
GOWANUS
Erie Basin
Red Hook Channel
Gowanus Canal
Gowanus Bay
Prospect Ave
PARK SLOPE
Gowanus Expwy
Bay Ridge Channel
Barrow's Intense Tasting Room
25th St
GREENWOOD HEIGHTS
Bush Terminal Piers Park
4th Ave
36th St
39th St
Green-Wood Cemetery
45th St
Sunset Park
SUNSET PARK
53rd St
Fei Long Market Food Court
1.5km (1 mile)
9th Ave
❌ Ricos Tacos

WILLIAMSBURG & BUSHWICK

These may now be Brooklyn's most famous neighbourhoods. However, along with notoriety have come increased visitor traffic and loss of concealment, especially in western Williamsburg. For hidden corners, the rehabilitated industrial and deeply residential areas have the most to offer. Any finds here can sometimes feel like secrets uncovered, whether cafes, bars, restaurants or small cultural centres.

⭐ Freehold

A self-declared 'hotel without hotel rooms', Freehold is a large venue with multiple spaces for food and drink, live music and comedy, artist showcases and plenty of party. *45 S 3rd St; http://freeholdbrooklyn.com; 7am-late.*

🏛 City Reliquary

This non-profit community museum's permanent exhibit is a single room packed with eclectic kitsch from NYC's past: photos, artefacts, old landmark souvenirs. *370 Metropolitan Ave; http://cityreliquary.org; noon-6pm Thu-Sun; adults/children $7/free.*

🍺 Spuyten Duyvil

A classic beer bar hides in plain sight behind an unassuming facade. But the chalkboard list of 100-plus brews (especially Belgian), meat and cheese plates, and a large backyard make it exceptional. *359 Metropolitan Ave; http://spuytenduyvilnyc.com; 5pm-late Mon-Fri, noon-late Sat-Sun.*

❌ The Meat Hook

More than just a butcher! Regenerative agriculture and animal welfare underpin the meat counter in this whole-animal shop that also arranges classes on sausage making and knife skills. *397 Graham Ave; http://the-meathook.com; 10am-8pm Mon-Sat, 11am-7pm Sun.*

❌ Carthage Must Be Destroyed

There's no street sign, so yes, walk down that driveway to the brick warehouse out back. That's where this vegetarian-friendly, pink-themed, photogenic-but-no-photos-allowed, Australian restaurant dishes

up excellent, healthy, organic fare. *222 Bogart St; http://carthagemustbedestroyed.com; 9am-4pm.*

✖ Ichiran NY Brooklyn

Perhaps NYC's best *tonkotsu* ramen is all that's served in this industrial backstreet location: fresh noodles in natural pork-bone soup with a spicy red sauce. Get intimate with the ramen in solo dining booths. *374 Johnson Ave; http://ichiranusa.com; 11am-11pm Sun-Thu, 11am-midnight Fri-Sat.*

✖ Queen of Falafel

It's a hipster hole-in-the-wall in a hipster 'hood, but it's also absolutely delicious – generations-old Moroccan and Middle Eastern recipes prepared in a family-run falafel cafe. *2 Wyckoff Ave; http://queenfalafel.com; 11am-11pm Mon-Sat, 11am-10pm Sun.*

✪ House of Yes

In search of a funky performance,

BROOKLYN STREET ART FANTASIA

'Visit the Bushwick Collective, started in 2011 by Bushwick native Joe Ficalora,' says Jessica Festa of NYC Photo Journeys. 'Surrounding the Jefferson Street L station are 15-plus blocks of floor-to-roof murals by world-renowned artists. Nearby, east of the Montrose Avenue L station in E Williamsburg, large-scale pieces also abound alongside wheatpaste, yarnbombing and more.'

dance and art space where the unexpected is the usual? Say yes to Yes, an innovative circus and cabaret with DJs after hours. *2 Wyckoff Ave; http://houseofyes.org.*

🏛 Molasses Books

Refreshingly local and unpretentious, Molasses is a combo used bookstore and cafe-bar with a full event calendar including readings, karaoke nights and chess meet-ups. Books can be bartered for food or drink. *770 Hart St; 11am-midnight Mon-Fri, 10am-midnight Sat-Sun.*

☕ Variety Coffee

In Brooklyn's high-stakes coffee scene, this under-sung local roaster serves excellent espresso in bright and comfy digs, here and in four other NYC locations. *146 Wyckoff Ave; http://varietycoffeeroasters.com; 7am-9pm.*

Top: Williamsburg Bridge's steely silhouette Left: open-air art at the Bushwick Collective

© Ryan DeBerardinis / Shutterstock

© Christian Mueller / Shutterstock

NORTH SHORE, STATEN ISLAND

Staten Island recently declared itself the 'Unexpected Borough', and full of surprises it is! Unfortunately, most visitors get little further than St George, the North Shore terminus of the free, 25-minute ferry from Manhattan. There's plenty more to the island, of course, but also lots of hidden culture and gastronomy no more than a 30-minute walk or 15-minute bus ride away.

🏛 Snug Harbor Cultural Center & Botanical Garden
A 15-minute bus (the S40) from Borough Hall, this amazing, historical, 83-acre arts and culture centre boasts the Staten Island Museum, Staten Island Children's Museum, 14 botanical gardens, a working farm and much more. *1000 Richmond Tce; http://snugharbor.org; dawn-dusk; free.*

✖ New Asha
Small, simple and fantastically affordable, New Asha sits in a small cluster of Sri Lankan restaurants and has outspoken fans devoted to its authentic seasoning. *322 Victory Blvd; http://places.singleplatform.com/new-asha; 9am-9.30pm Wed-Mon.*

🏛 Sri Lankan Art & Cultural Museum NY
Inaugurated in the nearby Lakruwana restaurant, this first Sri Lankan museum outside Sri Lanka moved to its own location to display Sri Lankan art, artefacts, Buddha statues, ceremonial gear and more. *61 Canal St; http://srilankanmuseny.org; 11am-5pm Fri-Sun; adults/students $8/7.*

🍺 Craft House Gastropub
While many beer-lovers patronise the close-at-hand Flagship Brewery, savvy locals prefer the broader local beer selection by Kills Boro (brewed in the back) and gastropub food here. *60 Van Duzer St; http://crafthousesi.com; 5pm-late Mon & Wed-Fri, noon-late Sat & Sun.*

🔒 Every Thing Goes Book Cafe
A pillar of the Staten Island community for used books, art, workshops, local music and theatre. *208 Bay St; http://etgstores.com/bookcafe; noon-late Tue-Sat.*

🏛 National Lighthouse Museum
This small, self-guided museum tells the fascinating story of lighthouses throughout the world. *200 The Promenade at Lighthouse Point; http://lighthousemuseum.org; 11am-5pm Tue-Sun; adults/students/children $7/4/free.*

Map showing: Snug Harbor Cultural Center & Botanical Garden, Richmond Tce, Upper New York Bay, New York Ave, National Lighthouse Museum, The Flagship Brewing Company, STATEN ISLAND, Craft House Gastropub, Every Thing Goes Book Cafe, New Asha, Forest Ave, New York Ave, Sri Lankan Art & Cultural Museum NY, Lakruwana.

ASTORIA

Queens claims top billing as the most diverse county in the USA, and wonderfully walkable Astoria – located along the East River, 15 subway minutes from midtown Manhattan – is arguably its most multicultural neighbourhood. This is reflected in Astoria's many cultural anchors, especially places to eat, representing its Greek, Middle Eastern, Eastern European, South American and other residents.

✖ Gregory's Corner Taverna

Astoria hosts many souvlaki-centric tavernas, but rustic, out-of-the-way and easily-overlooked Gregory's is a local favourite, beloved for fresh, flavourful and seriously authentic Greek cuisine (or rather, *kouzína*). *26-02 23rd Ave; http:// gregoryscornertaverna.net; noon-10pm Mon-Fri, to 6pm Sat & Sun.*

✖ Kabab Cafe

Don't let the unassuming storefront throw you; step in to Chef Ali's old-school Egyptian culinary wonderland. The best approach: order what's fresh or recommended, even if it surprises you. *25-12 Steinway St; http:// kebabcafe.food74.com; 1-5pm & 6-10pm Tue-Sun.*

✖ AbuQir Seafood

Unremarkable decor veils superb seafood. Select from the iced daily selection of fresh, whole fish, molluscs and crustaceans. Choose from fried, grilled or baked. Add sides. Delight! *24-19 Steinway St; http://abuqirseafoodqueens.com; 1-10pm.*

✖ Istria Sport Club

Ring the buzzer and politely ask to dine at this discreet, quasi-private social club serving excellent Croatian cooking to local expats. *28-09 Astoria Blvd; http:// istriasportclub.com; afternoon-10pm Wed-Sun.*

🍺 ICONYC Brewing Company

The beers of this intimate, bright tap room are notable for their unique flavours. It's BYO food and has a vinyl-record DJ station. *45-13 34th Ave; http://iconycbrewing. com; 4pm-late Wed-Fri, noon-late Sat & Sun.*

✖ Arepas Cafe

Here it's all about authentic Venezuelan cuisine: *pabellóns* (shredded meat platters), *parrillas* (sautéed meat) and *arepas* (grilled cornmeal patties stuffed with mixed ingredients). *33-07 36th Ave; 718-937-3835; 11am-10pm.*

⚘ Socrates Sculpture Park

Until 1986 an abandoned dump site, this waterfront park now doubles as an open-air public art space. It's kitty-corner from The Noguchi Museum. *32-01 Vernon Blvd; http://socratessculpturepark. org; 9am-sunset; free.*

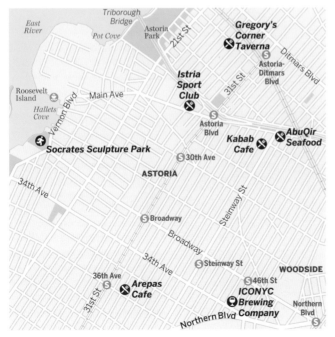

HARLEM

Harlem is big and hardly homogeneous. While Greater Harlem spans upper Manhattan, West Harlem, with its dramatic river views, is largely Hispanic, the centre is where black culture finds full expression, and East Harlem's busy streets have long been known as El Barrio (Spanish Harlem). This diversity gives Harlem its celebrated depth of character, expressed through food, art, music and community institutions.

Amy Ruth's

Today there are far fewer true, old-school soul food places in Harlem. Of those that have survived, Amy Ruth's is a local favourite. Try the chicken and waffles – a classic! – or other southern fare such as glazed ham, fried catfish, barbecued ribs and shrimp 'n' grits. *113 W 116th St; http://amyruths.com; 8.30am-11pm Sun-Thu, 8.30am-5.30am Fri-Sat.*

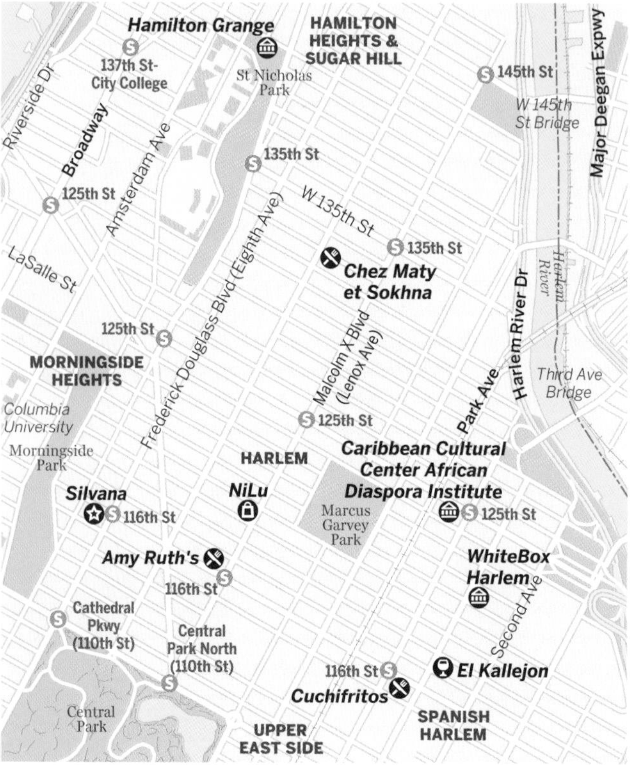

Hamilton Grange

With *Hamilton*-mania in full swing, Harlem's only national memorial has been rediscovered. Not the original location of the only house Hamilton ever owned, it's still the original structure, with a visitor centre and historically furnished rooms. *428 W 141st St; http://nps.gov/hagr; 9am-5pm Wed-Sun; free.*

Chez Maty et Sokhna

West African food is the highlight at this casual Senegalese restaurant, previously called Keur Sokhna. Large portions of meaty *dibi* and spicy *yassa* hit the spot, alongside American dishes, if desired. *2249 Adam Clayton Powell Jr Blvd; 212-368-5005; 9am-2am.*

Silvana

Silvana is a dynamic social hub with a street-level, art-filled cafe-restaurant (with a Middle Eastern menu) and intimate downstairs bar featuring a wide-ranging mix of live music performances, good cocktails and an easygoing crowd. *330 W 116th St; http://silvana-nyc.com; cafe 8am-10pm; bar 4pm-4am.*

NiLu

For touristy West African crafts and goods, people go to the Malcolm Shabazz Harlem Market (52 W 116th St); for contemporary, Harlem-themed art and souvenirs, however, little NiLu is a must. *191 Lenox Ave; http://shopnilu.com; 11am-8pm Tue-Fri, 9am-8pm Sat-Sun.*

WhiteBox Harlem

Set in a different old firehouse, this reincarnation of a formerly downtown non-profit art space is committed to bringing site-specific art and cultural exhibits and programmes to East Harlem. *213 E 121st St; http://whiteboxny.org; hours vary; free.*

Caribbean Cultural Center African Diaspora Institute

Located in a refurbished firehouse, the CCCADI presents pioneering exhibitions, workshops, performances and educational programming about communities in the African diaspora. *120 E 125th St; http://cccadi.org; 1-6pm Tue-Fri; adults/children $5/free.*

El Kallejon

On a quiet side street (in keeping with its name), this Mexican gem brings to Spanish Harlem a true and toothsome taste of south of the border, a wine and sangria bar, and (sometimes music-filled) backyard grill included. *209 E 117th St; http://elkallejonlounge.com; 3pm-late Tue-Sat, 2-9.30pm Sun.*

Cuchifritos

Cuchifritos are the fried staples of Puerto Rican cooking. They come in all shapes, sizes and ingredients. And on busy E 116th Street, this bustling counter-service place is *cuchifritos* central. Ask for help or just point and say *por favor!* *168 E 116th St; 212-876-4846; 10am-1am.*

HARLEM'S CHANGING IDENTITY

'A sense of community that Harlem has long been known for still prevails amidst gentrification,' said Teri Johnson of Harlem Candle Co. 'But a new Harlem Renaissance is happening, and long-term and new residents (of all ethnicities) are helping define this multicultural neighbourhood so revered for its impact and significance in art and culture.'

© age fotostock / Alamy Stock Photo

© Guillaume Gaudet / Lonely Planet

Top: murals in central Harlem
Above: hanging out in Harlem
Left: elegant brownstones

Harvard
Square

Beacon
Hill

Boston

South
End

BOSTON

Celebrated for its revolutionary history and cultural institutions, Boston is nonetheless a city of vibrant neighbourhoods and local curiosities.

Historic events, cultural institutions, immigrant influxes and good old urban planning have created the dynamic city that is Boston. And its neighbourhoods reflect all of these influences, in their celebrated landmarks and in their local haunts.

In central Boston, Beacon Hill is one of the city's most elegant and historic neighbourhoods, where well-heeled residents stroll and shop and sip cappuccino amid early 19th-century red-brick row houses. By contrast, the South End is a modern hot spot for trendy dining and

contemporary art, thanks to its ethnic diversity and thriving gay and artistic communities. West of the city (and across the river), Harvard Square is the vibrant neighbourhood surrounding the esteemed university, its streets overflowing with cafes, theatres, book stores and buskers.

BEACON HILL

Famed for its narrow cobblestoned streets and stately townhouses, Beacon Hill evokes the grace and grandeur of 19th-century Boston. Explore the neighbourhood's history amid age-old institutions, green spaces and hidden spots for eating, drinking and shopping. These elegant streets are supremely walkable, although its mostly grid pattern has some unexpected oddities, so consult your map.

🏛 Boston Athenæum

Reserve ahead to tour this esteemed private library, established in 1807. Aside from the handsome building and half a million volumes, the Athenæum also claims an impressive art collection with an emphasis on New England artists. If you can't make the tour, visit the first floor for fascinating temporary exhibits in the Calderwood Gallery and evocative cemetery views from the Long Room. *10½ Beacon St; www. bostonathenaeum.org; noon-8pm Tue & 10am-4pm Wed-Sat; admission/tour $10/2.*

➎ Charles River Esplanade

The annual 4th of July fireworks on the Esplanade are no secret. But many visitors don't realise that there's no better place to spend any sunny day, whether paddling around the Charles River Basin or cycling the winding paths of this riverside park. Graced with abundant shade trees and cooling waterways, the Esplanade stretches for almost 5km (3.1 miles) along the south bank of the Charles River. *www.esplanadeassociation.org.*

❌ Grotto

A romantic subterranean hideaway where the lighting is dim, the atmosphere is intimate and the Italian fare is delectable. You can order *à la carte* but the three-course *prix-fixe* menu is hard to beat. *37 Bowdoin St; www. grottorestaurant.com; 617-227-3434; 11.30am-10pm Mon-Fri, 5-10pm Sat & Sun.*

❌ Beacon Hill Hotel & Bistro

This convivial, sunlit French bistro is a local favourite. For brunch, vanilla pancakes are a sure-fire win and the eggs Benedict is perfection on a muffin. *25 Charles St; https:// beaconhillhotel.com; 800-640-3935; 11.30am-9pm Mon-Fri, 9am-10pm Sat & 9am-9pm Sun.*

🔒 Eugene Galleries

Bustling Charles St is a charmer, its red-brick sidewalks lit by wrought-iron street lamps and lined with cafes and intriguing antique shops. Don't miss this tiny gallery, crammed with old prints and maps, especially focusing on Boston and New England. *76 Charles St; 11am-6pm Tue-Sat, noon-6pm Sun.*

Map showing Beacon Hill area including: Longfellow Bridge, Massachusetts General Hospital, WEST END, New Chardon St Courthouse, Bowdoin, Charles River, Cambridge St, Charles/MGH, Saltonstall Building, Grotto, Storrow Dr, Charles River Esplanade, BEACON HILL, Louisburg Square, Ashburton Park, Massachusetts State House, Eugene Galleries, Beacon Hill Hotel & Bistro, Boston Athenæum, Suffolk University, Park St, DOWNTOWN, Beacon St, Boston Common, Cathedral Church of St Paul, Public Garden, Charles St, Tremont St, BACK BAY, The Lagoon, THEATER DISTRICT

HARVARD SQUARE

The streets around Harvard University were once known for being offbeat, edgy and blissfully bohemian. Nowadays, Harvard Square can feel like an outdoor shopping mall, with many upscale restaurants and national chains. But you can still find vestiges of old Harvard Square. Parking is a challenge, so take the T (subway) and explore on foot.

Mt Auburn Cemetery
Head 2km (1.2 miles) west from Harvard Square to reach this tranquil oasis, replete with lovely landscaping, artistic monuments and notable gravesites. The diversity of trees and flowering plants makes the garden cemetery an excellent place to spot migrating birds in April and May. *580 Mt Auburn St; www.mountauburn.org; 8am-7pm.*

Collection of Historical Scientific Instruments
On the ground floor of the Harvard Science Center, the university exhibits (some of) its collection of 20,000 scientific instruments. Some dating back hundreds of years, the pieces inspire rumination about the history of astronomy, geography, medicine, and even time-telling. Also impressive: the various elements from the Cyclotron Laboratory, circa 1984. *Science Center 136, 1 Oxford St; 11am-4pm Sun-Fri.*

Club Passim
Club Passim is not a secret – it's a legend. But, tucked into a basement in a Harvard Square alleyway, it still has the intimate atmosphere of an underground music club. And even after 60 years, it's still Boston's best venue for folk, blues, bluegrass and other acoustic music. *47 Palmer St; www.passim.org.*

Brattle Theatre
Dating to 1890, the Brattle Theatre is an old-timey movie house (with a balcony!) showing contemporary independent and foreign films, as well as classic fare from decades past. Popular screenings include *Casablanca* on Valentine's Day, cartoons on some Saturday mornings, lots of double features,

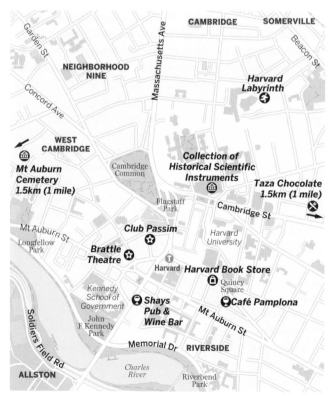

and various oddball film festivals. *40 Brattle St; www.brattlefilm.org.*

✈ Harvard Labyrinth

Tucked into a quiet corner of the Harvard Divinity School campus, this small labyrinth is modelled on a 13th-century design from the Notre-Dame de Chartres Cathedral. The unicursal route offers a walking path for spiritual seeking – or just a respite from the hustle and bustle of Harvard Square. *2-86 Museum St.*

☕ Café Pamplona

Low ceilings and yellow walls are the hallmarks of this tiny European cafe, a beloved Harvard Square institution since 1958. It's still a gathering place for poets, playwrights and philosophers who come to discuss, debate, doodle and drink espresso. The patio is a delight when weather permits. *12 Bow St; www.cafepamplona. weebly.com; 11am-9pm.*

🍷 Shays Pub & Wine Bar

Most of Harvard Square has gone upscale but Shays remains casual and convivial, welcoming all comers. Graduate students and university admin congregate here, propping themselves up at the bar or jostling for a place on the patio. Definitely more pub than wine bar. *58 John F Kennedy St; www.shayspubwinebar.com; 11am-1am.*

🔒 Harvard Book Store

In a world where independent book stores are becoming more rare, the Harvard Book Store (not affiliated with the university) is a standout. In addition to the standard offerings, there are unexpected and excellent staff recommendations, a basement crammed with bargains and a full schedule of author talks. *1256 Massachusetts Ave; www.harvard. com; 9am-11pm Mon-Sat, 10am-10pm Sun.*

❌ Taza Chocolate

You don't need a golden ticket to tour the Taza Chocolate Factory, located 2km (1.2 miles) east of Harvard Square. A pioneer in direct trade and proponent of traditional production techniques, Taza makes delicious, decadent, unrefined, stone-ground chocolate from bean to bar – and they're proud to show you how it's done. Reserve in advance for the 45-minute tour. *www. tazachocolate.com; $8.*

Clockwise from top left: Mt Auburn Cemetery; treats at Taza Chocolate; distinguished tomes at Harvard Book Store

SOUTH END

Boston's innovators have transformed the landscape in South End, a former industrial area. What once was a warehouse is now an art studio; what looks like a parking lot is actually a playground. Stroll around this sprawling neighbourhood, now the city's most coveted address, and search deep beneath the surface to discover its creative spirit.

⊕ Underground at Ink Block

With cars whizzing by on the interstate above, the desolate space at the end of Traveler St was an unlikely place for anything good. And yet, here is Boston's newest urban playground and outdoor art gallery, featuring bike trails, fitness classes, food trucks and – best of all – vast displays of bold and beautiful street art. *Traveler St; www.undergroundinkblock.com.*

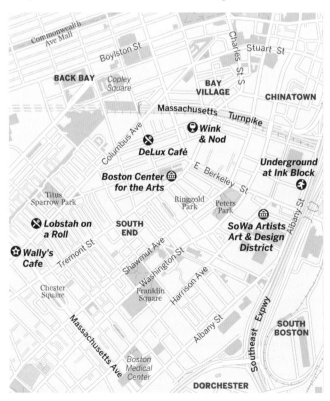

⌂ Boston Center for the Arts

Go to the Theatre District to see the mainstream musicals that are playing across the country. But come to the BCA to see cutting-edge, contemporary performances by independent companies. The BCA is home to a dozen local theatre and dance groups, many of which explore themes like cultural diversity, gender nonconformity and social justice. *539 Tremont St; www. bcaonline.org.*

✪ Wally's Cafe

Wally's is all about the music – jazz, blues and funk, every night of the week, often created by students from the nearby Berklee College of Music. No cover charge. No fancy cocktails. Just grit, grooves and good vibes. *427 Massachusetts Ave; www. wallyscafe.com; 6pm-2am.*

⍟ Wink & Nod

Only a small brass sign marks the entrance to this South End speakeasy, which serves expensive but exquisite craft cocktails in its fancy-pants interior. The 'rotating kitchen' changes hands twice a year, inviting chefs to design the menu and do their thing. *3 Appleton St; www.winkandnod. com; 5pm-2am Mon-Sat.*

✖ Lobstah on a Roll

There are a dozen sandwiches on the menu, but the joint's name (however regrettable) tells you what you need to order. Arguably one of the best lobster rolls in the city, this baby is 185g (6½ oz) of

chunky lobster meat, served on a fresh challah roll with mayo or butter. There's counter seating and a handful of tables, but be prepared to take away.
537 Columbus Ave; www. lobstahonaroll.com; 617-903-4005; 10.30am-8pm.

✖ DeLux Café

Defying the gentrification that has swept the South End, Delux is keeping it real. Album covers adorn the walls and Christmas lights hang above the bar. The menu revolves around super-satisfying comfort food, such as burgers, grilled cheese and roast chicken. You can get a Schlitz Tall Boy (a retro, 16-oz can of beer) for $4 – but don't worry, there's also a selection of craft beers on tap.
100 Chandler St; 617-338-5258; 5pm-1am.

FIRST FRIDAYS

The SoWa Artists Art & Design District (www. sowaboston.com) is the epicentre of the South End art scene, bursting with art galleries, summertime markets and special events. Come on the first Friday of the month to sneak a peek inside the studios and hobnob with artists. You might even go home with something arty.

Clockwise from top left: lobster roll; handsome streets of the South End; Boston Center for the Arts

OCEANIA

Leederville

Northbridge
Central Perth

Perth

Fremantle

PERTH

One of the planet's most isolated cities, Perth is a patchwork of vibrant neighbourhoods imbued with worldliness and creative soul.

PERTH

L ife in Perth, a city of 2.14 million Western Australians, unfolds beneath a near-permanent canopy of blue sky. Kissed by the Indian Ocean breeze, Perth is a progressive place with global eats and a booming small-bar scene. Yes, it's the most isolated city of its size on the planet, but this remoteness fosters an outward-looking world view. Instead of heading to Sydney on holiday, locals jet to Bali, the Maldives, Singapore, Sri Lanka...while direct flights to London deliver Europe's virtues in 17 hours.

Outside of walkable Central Perth and adjoining Northbridge (north, over a bridge!), getting around by train is easy: the boho port of Fremantle is to the south; arty and foodie Leederville is a couple of stops northwest. Central Perth is all business, but harbours secretive bars and multicultural places to eat. Northbridge is Perth's party-prone zone, but also hosts the city's top museums and galleries. Forget about isolation: Perth is going places.

CENTRAL PERTH

At first glance, Perth's CBD (central business district) can seem a little soulless – a grid of glass towers and unsmiling corporate types. But dig deeper: the laneway bar scene here is kickin', and this is where Perth gets its farmers-market groove on. Add a few good live-music venues to the mix and Central Perth suddenly looks very appealing.

🍸 Halford

If you can find it, secreted away in a city basement, Halford is one of Perth's best cocktail bars. Sidle up to the bartender, order a whisky sour and scan the crowd of glam downtowners. It's a moody, theatrically lit space with vintage charm to burn. Don't dare dress down. *State Bldgs, cnr Hay St & Cathedral Ave;*
www.halfordbar.com.au; 4pm-2am Sat-Wed.

🔒 Perth City Farm

The plains around Perth and the Perth Hills are fertile terrain: here's where you can squirrel out the best local, organic produce – eggs, fruit, veg and baked goods – every Saturday morning. Chase off your hangover at the cafe,
tour the veggie patch...or both! *1 City Farm Pl; www.perthcityfarm. org.au; 8am-noon Sat.*

❌ Le Vietnam

Hungry? Central Perth has a dizzying array of international eateries, including this blink-and-you'll-miss-it Vietnamese joint, serving the best *banh mi* (Vietnamese baguettes) in the West. Order the pulled-pork version and a heart-starting Vietnamese coffee and see what the afternoon delivers. *1/80 Barrack St; www.facebook.com/ levietnamcafe; 08-6114 8038; 7.30am-3pm Mon-Fri.*

⭐ Amplifier

Perth has produced some awesome bands over the years: Jebediah, The Triffids, The Sleepy Jackson, Tame Impala... Most of them have played at innocent-looking Amplifier at one stage or another (usually the early stage: it ain't a massive room). The nightclub Capitol is here too, if you're more DJ-aligned. *Rear 383 Murray St; www.amplifiercapitol. com.au.*

🍸 Whipper Snapper Distillery

Hey look, a whisky distillery nooked onto the edge of downtown Perth! Take a tour of this mural-spangled, out-of-the-way moonshiner and sample their 'Upstart' Australian whisky, made from 100% WA ingredients. *139 Kensington St; www. whippersnapperdistillery.com; 7am-5pm Mon-Fri, 8am-4pm Sat, from 11am Sun.*

FREMANTLE

On the southern end of Perth's train network, 30 minutes from the city, Fremantle is a charismatic harbour 'hood with a cache of Victorian buildings. Like any port, the world washes in on the tide and washes out again, leaving the locals buzzing with global zeitgeist. 'Freo' thrums with live music, craft-beer bars, bookshops and seafood shacks.

🚆 Norfolk Hotel
Craft beer and Fremantle – it's a symbiotic relationship. Little Creatures brewery on the waterfront gets all the press, but a little bit away from the fray, the old Norfolk pumps a diverse array of ales. Excellent pizzas and a shady warm-night courtyard are equally hard to resist. *47 South Tce; www. norfolkhotel.com.au; 11am-midnight Mon-Sat, to 10pm Sun.*

🏛 Fremantle Arts Centre
Built by convicts, this amazing old limestone structure in the back blocks was once a lunatic asylum. The cafe here is one of Freo's best, while exhibitions, summer courtyard concerts and kids' activities are pure magic. *1 Finnerty St; www.fac.org.au; 10am-5pm.*

⭐ Mojos
The Fremantle live music scene is at once accessible (buskers aplenty) and deliciously underground (grungy left-field music rooms). Long-running Mojos falls squarely into the latter category, with weekly open-mic nights, local bands and touring minstrels of the indie rock persuasion. *237 Queen Victoria St; www.mojosbar.com. au; 5.30pm-midnight Mon-Tue, from 5pm Wed, to 1am Thu-Sat, 4-10pm Sun.*

✖ Propeller
A typically inventive Freo business, Propeller features a blue shipping container doubling as a coffee-window and bar, inside a sunny cafe-bistro. Sip a Bloody Mary to go along with your Middle Eastern breakfast. *222 Queen Victoria St; www. propellernorthfreo.com.au; 08-9335 9366; 8am-late.*

🏛 Bon Scott Statue
Legendary hellraiser and frontman of Australian hard-rock band AC/DC, Ronald Belford Scott (1946–80), aka 'Bon', moved from Scotland

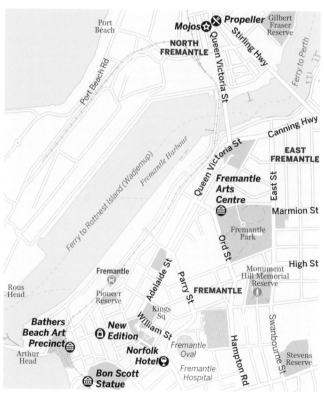

to Fremantle with his family in 1956 – the old town still adores him. Check out his statue down by Fishing Boat Harbour or pay your rockin' respects at Fremantle Cemetery: enter near the High and Carrington St corner – Bon's plaque is 15m (49ft) along the path on the left. *2026 Mews Rd; www.gregjamessculpture.com.*

🏛 Bathers Beach Art Precinct

A long-neglected Fremantle pocket, Bathers Beach has been reborn as a vibrant arts precinct. Galleries and studios occupy the heritage cottages and warehouses behind the beach (which happens to be the only beach in WA with a liquor licence). The Walyalup Aboriginal Cultural Centre is here too, hosting exhibitions of local Aboriginal language and arts. *Captains Ln; www.facebook. com/bathersbeachartsprecinct.*

🔒 New Edition

Perth's best bookshop occupies a sunny little corner in Fremantle, to which it's been luring the local literati for three decades.

THE FREMANTLE DOCTOR

This local medic is actually Perth's famous summer sea breeze, which cools the city and provides sweet relief to the sun-stroked locals. The breeze peaks between noon and 3pm, reaching wind speeds of up to 37km/h (23mph). Hot tip: hit the beach in the morning, before the Doctor flattens the surf and blows sand in your face.

On the shelves, the main focus is Australian fiction and nonfiction: pick up a copy of Tim Winton's *Eyrie*, which paints Freo in a loving, rough-edged light. Readings, poetry slams and book launches happen with pleasing frequency. *Cnr High & Henry Sts; www. newedition.com.au; 9am-9pm.*

Clockwise from top left: creative cafe fare and cocktails at Propeller; Fremantle's Leighton Beach

LEEDERVILLE

Leederville is what every big city needs: a neighbourhood enclave of cafes, restaurants, bars and shops with a distinctly boho, offbeat vibe. Perth's urban culture can lean towards the mainstream at times, but Leederville offers sweet relief for anyone arty, subversive or just a little bit different. Hang out at local haunts and catch the vibe.

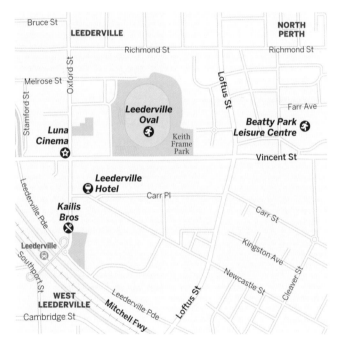

Kailis Bros
'I'm on a seafood diet: I see food, then I eat it.' Jokes aside, for some of WA's best seafood, duck into Kailis Bros. Established in 1926 (here on Oxford St since 2000), Kailis is the place for some fresh red emperor, flame snapper or blue swimmer crabs to go. There's a cafe, too. *101 Oxford St; www.kailisbrosleederville. com.au; shop 8am-6pm, cafe 7am-late.*

Luna Cinema
Like all Australian cities, Perth has lost most of its charming old neighbourhood cinemas to a tide of multiscreen megaplexes... but not the Luna. This art deco art-house cinema has been here since 1927, when movies were still silent. Check out the awesome mural on Vincent St. *155 Oxford St; www.lunapalace.com.au.*

Leederville Hotel
If you're thinking, 'You know, all these cafes are great, but where's the pub?', wander down Newcastle St. The lovely old redbrick Leederville Hotel has been beering it up since 1897 and has recently morphed into several venues under one roof. Hit the bar at Bill's, the main room here. *www.leedervillehotel.com; 742 Newcastle St; 08-9202 8282; 11am-late.*

Leederville Oval
This lush ground hosts the East Perth Royals football team, who compete in the West Australian Football League (WAFL) in winter. The Royals haven't been playing particularly regally of late, but continue to inspire deep passions in Leederville locals. Catch a game if you can. *244 Vincent St; www.wafl.com.au.*

Beatty Park Leisure Centre
Built for the Commonwealth Games, hosted by Perth in 1962 (who knew?), this excellent swim centre has indoor and outdoor pools, water slides and a vast gym. If Leederville's eats and drinks have been weighing you down, here's where to lighten up. *220 Vincent St; www.beattypark. com.au; 5.30am-9pm Mon-Fri, 6.30am-7pm Sat & Sun; swimming adult/child $7/5.*

NORTHBRIDGE

Hankering for a drink? Of course you are! Northbridge is a prime spot for a little quenching. Many of the bars along William St are big, brawly beer barns without much style or substance, but there's a new breed of quirky local secrets. Northbridge is also home to the estimable galleries, museums and theatres of the Perth Cultural Centre.

candlelit and woody, with barkeeps who know their stuff. It's arguably Perth's best bar (oh how they argue). *Nicks La; www.facebook. com/sneakytonys; 4pm-midnight.*

✖ The Standard

This bar is as good for a few adventurous Mod Oz share plates as it is for a late-night negroni or a Western Australian Eagle Bay Black IPA. Order some caramelised kangaroo with sesame soy, pineapple and lime and see where the conversation takes you. *28 Roe St; www.thestandardperth.com. au; 08-9228 1331; 4pm-midnight Mon-Thu, from noon Fri & Sat, to 10pm Sun.*

✪ Rooftop Movies

For a dose of art-house, classic and edgy new-release film, truck up to the sixth floor of this Northbridge car park. Comfy beanbags, wood-fired pizzas and craft beers await (and the views of the city skyline aren't bad either). *68 Roe St; www.rooftopmovies. com.au; Tue-Sun late Oct–late Mar; tickets from $16.*

🏛 Perth Institute of Contemporary Arts

The vast New Museum for WA and Art Gallery of Western Australia are obvious Perth highlights, but 'PICA' (pee-kah) is much more discreet and experimental: unconventional installations, performances, sculpture and video...plus the PICA Bar for coffee, cocktails and occasional live tunes. *Perth Cultural Centre; www.pica.org.au; 10am-5pm Tue-Sun.*

🍷 Alabama Song

Kick-start your Northbridge bar crawl with a dose of the Deep South at one of Northbridge's best back-alley bars. Sequestered, bespoke and offbeat, Alabama Song is festooned with Americana, bar staff pouring a dizzying array of whiskeys and bourbons. Rye paradise! *Lvl 1, behind 232*

William St; www.facebook.com/ alabamasongbar; 6pm-2am Wed-Sat, from 8pm Sun.*

🍷 Sneaky Tony's

To sneak into Sneaky Tony's, a secretive little bar off Nicks La in Chinatown, you'll need the password (try 'Open Sesame'... or check Facebook). The vibe is

ARTS & CULTURE   MUSIC & FILM   SPORTS & LEISURE   EATING   DRINKING   SHOPPING

MELBOURNE

Fall down Melbourne's rabbit hole to be richly rewarded with an edgy fusion of grit and glamour. Its diverse 'hoods each have a different tale to tell.

Melbourne draws its cosmopolitanism and quirk from a patchwork of village-like neighbourhoods. Subcultures are rife, with inner-north suburbs like Brunswick and Fitzroy rocking a hipster-grunge vibe, while nearby Northcote sits orderly and relaxed. To the east, Collingwood is an up-and-comer that flaunts a hardened industrial image, and to the south, Windsor hangs between the yuppie Yarra-side suburbs and the beach, content as a locals-only secret. The common thread across all neighbourhoods is their buzzing high streets, lined with bars, shops, restaurants, cafes and venues.

Melbourne's hub-and-spoke tram network makes these inner suburbs a mere clack away from the CBD (Central Business District). Windsor, Northcote and Brunswick are also connected by a train line. Explore on foot to up the odds of stumbling upon Melbourne's lauded street art. Nip down side streets, too – the city's allure is in the covert.

MELBOURNE

COLLINGWOOD

Collingwood is a former industrial precinct that has dealt with its surplus of warehouses by turning them into breweries and giant street art canvases. The colour and booze is intermingled with cafes, music venues and outlet stores along busy Smith Street, with the odd surprise tucked down a back street. Hip yet unpolished, Collingwood suits the inquisitive ambler.

🏛 Backwoods Gallery
Stroll down Easey St to find one of the core drivers behind Melbourne's renowned street art scene. This small, unsuspecting gallery has been operating for a decade and is responsible for the lion's share of commissioned street art around the city. Backwoods hosts exhibitions in a space shared with warehouse bar Paradise Alley. *25 Easey St; www.backwoods. gallery; noon-6pm Tue-Sun.*

🍺 The Mill Brewery
On a quiet street off Collingwood's main drag, a roller door retracts to reveal a chilled-out brewery unafraid of creativity. The two on-site brewers experiment with flavours depending on the season and their mood, meaning ingredients such as habanero chilli or grapefruit zest could lace a batch. *40 Sackville St; www. themillbrewery.com.au; 4-10pm Wed & Thu, to 11pm Fri, 1-11pm Sat, to 9pm Sun.*

✖ Trang Bakery and Café
The hands-down local favourite at this no-frills cafe is the crispy pork *banh mì*. A tray of crackle-topped roast sits ready to wedge into a super-fresh bread roll with coleslaw, peanut sauce and sliced green chilli. Seating is limited, so befriend a stranger at one of the footpath tables. *382 Smith St; 8.30am-5pm.*

✖ Chotto Motto
This Japanese-inspired diner has lolly-pink fluoro lights, a carp kite strung across the ceiling and a beer vending machine by the door. *Gyoza* (dumplings) are served in quantities of 10 or 20 as a crispy, pan-fried wheel; crunchy fried *karaage* can be done chicken, rockling or cauliflower style. Dunk it all in flavourful house-made chilli oil. *287 Wellington St; www. chottomotto.com.au; 5-10.30pm Mon-Thu, to 11pm Fri, 3-11pm Sun.*

🍸 Above Board
With no signage, Above Board is the exclusive lair of in-the-know cocktail aficionados. The bar seats just 12 people and is designed to promote interaction between mixologists and guests. A classic cocktail list mirrors the air of simple elegance. *Chopper Ln; www. aboveboardbar.com; 5pm-1am.*

Map of Collingwood showing: Mater St, Leicester St, Rose St, Emma St, Blanche St, Budd St, Hotham St, Wellington St, Gold St, Keele St, Kerr St, Gore St, Smith St, Chotto Motto, Trang Bakery and Café, Easey St, Backwoods Gallery, Argyle St, Sackville St, The Mill Brewery, Easey St, COLLINGWOOD, Budd St, Sackville St, Johnston St, Bedford St, Wellington St, Dight St, Campbell St, Perry St, Above Board, Greeves St, Perry St

FITZROY

Embracing the wacky and wonderful, Fitzroy has scooped up some of the finest exemplars of Melbourne culture. Graffitied streets intersect rows of Victorian-era buildings; shop-owners and restaurateurs wear their social consciousness proudly; and the resident spectrum goes from highbrow to hippie, with miscellany not just accepted but encouraged. The night economy thrives and music never stops.

✕ Smith & Daughters

Golden chicken schnitzel, braised beef ragu, prosciutto panzanella...it reads like a mainstream menu. The unwritten subtext is that animals contribute zilch to S&D's dishes. Rather, soy protein, 'shrooms and rice paper stand in as sly substitutes. This place is not only perfect for full-blown vegans and transitioning omnivores, but solo diners too, given many meals can be made as half-serves. *175 Brunswick St; www.smithanddaughters.com; 6pm-late Mon-Fri, 10am-late Sat and 10am-3pm Sun.*

⊗ Elysian Whisky Bar

The Elysian's appeal is in its obscure selection of 350-odd whiskies sourced from independent producers around the world, lined up neatly behind a long, Californian redwood bar. Diehards can sample precious top-shelf potions, the curious and casual can be steered towards a spirit line fit for beginners, and non-whisky drinkers can order a wine or cocktail. *113 Brunswick St; www.theelysianwhiskybar.com.au; 4.30pm-1am Tue-Sat.*

✕ The Rochester Hotel

The Rochey puts a fresh spin on pub food with a sophisticated Southern Indian menu. All ingredients are locally sourced and ethically produced, and the signature fiery fish curry is regularly tweaked to suit the day's catch. While the hotel is worth a visit for the cuisine alone, fancy G&Ts and craft beers make it a prime landing pad for a big night out. *202 Johnston St; www.rochey.com.au; 2-11pm Mon-Wed, to 1am Thu, noon-3am Fri-Sat, to 11pm Sun.*

🔒 Rose Street Artists' Market

Every weekend, Melbourne's creatives congregate in a graffitied Fitzroy backstreet to lay out their handcrafted goods. Browse stalls showcasing jewellery, ceramics, art and clothes and chat to the talent behind them. You can even buy an exotic pot plant if your baggage allows. When you get peckish, the Young Bloods Diner serves food next door. *60 Rose St; www. rosestmarket.com.au; 10am-4pm Sat & Sun.*

🔒 Vegan Style

In a bid to prove that fashion and animals can be mutually exclusive, everything in this store is 100% vegan and fits the Fitz to a tee. The range focuses on sneakers, boots and dress shoes for the lads and lasses, but also includes handbags, belts and wallets. The fact that all materials are also environmentally sustainable means purchases are completely guilt-free. *345 Brunswick St; www.veganstyle. com.au; 11am-6pm Mon-Wed, to 7pm Thu-Fri, 10am-7pm Sat, 11am-5pm Sun.*

❌ Cutler & Co

Fitzroy's epitome of sophistication lies in an old metalwork factory, since converted into an elegant

© 2020, Rose Street Artists' Market

© Elize Strydom / 2020, Rose Street Artists' Market

LOCAL VOICE

'It's a quirky suburb – nothing ever surprises you around here – plus it has some of the best restaurants and bars in the country. If you went on a bar or food crawl in Fitzroy, you could do it in a 500m radius. Just the square bordered by Brunswick, Gertrude, Smith and Johnston Streets has everything you could ask for.'
– Yao Wong, co-owner of the Elysian Whisky Bar

---

restaurant with leather booth seating and swish green granite walls. Sunday lunches are a weekly highlight, with a generous degustation menu seasonally tailored to showcase local produce. The accompanying wine list goes for days. *55-57 Gertrude St; www.cutlerandco.com.au; 03-9419 4888; from 6pm Tue-Sun & from noon Sun.*

✪ The Workers Club

A Monday is as good as a Friday when travelling, so The Workers Club abides by a fancy-free schedule and puts gigs on loop every night of the week. Mondays are attractive for cash-strapped, music-loving punters, when drinks whittle down to student prices and DJs spin into the night. Free music and $4 pints? Hella yeah. *51 Brunswick St; www. theworkersclub.com.au; noon-late Tue-Sun, from 4pm Mon.*

Top and top left: handcrafted bargains at Rose Street Artists' Market Left: cocktails at Cutler & Co

© Jo McGann / 2020, Cutler & Co

NORTHCOTE

Northcote is part of a string of northside neighbourhoods that have transitioned from sleepy 'burb to gentrified cool. A clear message from this quiet evolution is that Northcote is a staunch supporter of local talent, with many shops and cafes flying the flag for homegrown artisans. The undulating landscape allows for strolls and city views.

nearly 15,000 second-hand vinyls with a sizeable offering of jazz, hip hop and house, along with niche genres like anime soundtracks. *230 High St; www.facebook.com/ rathdownerecords; 11am-6pm Sun-Thu, to 7pm Fri & Sat.*

✪ Palace Westgarth Cinema
The Westgarth is one of the oldest cinemas in Melbourne and officially opened in October 1921 with a screening of *Anne of Green Gables*. Funky, geometric detailing reflects its refurbishment in the art deco era. As well as five indoor screens, there's a cute outdoor cinema behind the bar. *89 High St; www. palacecinemas.com.au/cinemas/ westgarth.*

🔒 Make It Collective
On a street lined with shops that support ethical producers, the Make It Collective's retail outlet celebrates Melbourne-made products: jangly earrings, button brooches and printed purses, plus '70s-style apparel from the retro room tucked down the back. *264 High St; www.themakeitcollective. com.au; 11am-5pm Wed-Fri, from 10am Sat, 10.30am-5pm Sun.*

✖ Top Of The Hill
Good coffee and Reuben sandwiches steal the show at this hole-in-the-wall cafe. The slender store frontage opens up to a large courtyard serving cocktails. A 100-year-old cash register makes paying the bill a highlight. *208 High St; www.facebook. com/208topofthehill; 7am-3pm Mon-Fri, from 8am Sat & Sun.*

✪ Wesley Anne
The Wes is a Northcote institution that celebrates local and touring musicians nearly every night of the week. Retrofitted in a 19th-century church, the cosy pub channels ecclesiastical vibes with candles flickering against brick walls. Most gigs cost zip or less than $20. *250 High St; www.wesleyanne.com.au;* *noon-11pm Sun-Tue, to midnight Wed & to 1am Thu-Sat.*

🔒 Rathdowne Records
When a local music lover started sourcing the odd record to spin in his video store, he didn't anticipate that his musical assemblage would eventually engulf the movie collection. Rathdowne now has

WINDSOR

Windsor hides in the shadow of its pin-up neighbour St Kilda, but its wall-to-wall shops, bars and restaurants along Chapel St make it far from boring. Restless gentrification keeps things novel, while a peppering of thrift shops, nightclubs and dive bars provides solid grounding. From the southern end, the beach is 2km (1.25 miles) away.

reveals a tropical tiki bar adorned with plants and lined with booze. *Boston Sub, 96 Chapel St; www. facebook.com/pg/jungleboybar; 5pm-1am.*

✖ Small Print
The environmentally conscious will delight in this zero-waste pizzeria. Meat and veggie options are available on light, crispy bases and pizzas can be pimped with truffle oil or smoked yoghurt. Nice day? Get a pizza delivered (for free) to the beautiful Victoria Gardens across the road. *388 High St; www. smallprintpizza.com.au; 5-9pm Mon, 4-9.30pm Tue-Thu, to 10pm Fri, 4-9.30pm Sat, to 9pm Sun.*

🏛 Alternating Current Art Space
This small gallery is run by a team of fine-art graduates and provides a public platform for emerging contemporary artists. The area is split into four exhibition spaces, along with the aptly named 'cupboard'. Canvases are switched every few weeks. *248 High St; www.alternatingcurrentartspace. com; 11am-6pm Thu-Fri, noon-5pm Sat & Sun; free.*

✪ Lucky Coq
The Coq is the quirkiest dance floor on the block. All manner of junk hangs from the ceiling and walls – machinery parts, mannequin legs, plenty of cocks (of the rooster persuasion). DJs spin discs behind the busted windshield of a purple truck cabin and the $4 pizzas are legendary. *179 Chapel St; www. luckycoq.com.au; 11.30am-late Mon-fri, noon-late Sat & Sun; free.*

✖ Lady Nelson's Wine + Steak
Limiting patrons to a glass of house wine goes against this lady's philosophy. Instead, 20 domestic and international wines are available by the glass and are switched up every few months. Steak is sourced locally and plated without distraction. Add sides to taste. Staff know their stuff, so

brain-tap for recommendations. *44 Chapel St; www.ladynelsons.com. au; 5-11pm Tue-Sat.*

🍸 Jungle Boy
Seeing a well-heeled crowd step into a sandwich shop fridge may alarm the unversed, but this is one of Melbourne's speakeasy secrets. Rather than a cold room, the door

BRUNSWICK

Melbourne is Australia's live music capital, and if you were to zero in on its core, you'd end up in the city's inner north. Along with neighbouring Fitzroy, Brunswick has long been a magnet for musos and other creatives, and this sentiment is reflected in the suburb's high density of performance venues, generous splashings of street art, and fabulously outlandish fashion sense.

✪ Spotted Mallard

With a name that honours the rare and reclusive, this Brunswick favourite walks a line between grungy and cool and gives a stage to budding local talent.

Musical genres represented are as diverse as the clientele who frequent the venue. Once a month the Mallard shifts focus from music to art when it hosts the Brunswick Artist Market. *314*

Sydney Rd; www.spottedmallard. com; 4pm-late Tue-Fri, from 2pm Sat & Sun.

✪ Howler

A side-street car park by the train tracks generally lacks appeal, but if en route to Howler, it's the gateway to a powerhouse of energy in an old brick warehouse. The leafy, courtyard-style front bar specialises in tacos and tequila, while the band room at the back puts on some of Melbourne's best gigs. Tickets often sell out, so buy ahead online. *7-11 Dawson St; www.h-w-l-r.com; 4-11pm Mon, 4pm-midnight Tue & Wed, 4pm-1am Thu, from noon Fri-Sun.*

✖ A1 Bakery

As you press into Brunswick's northern reaches, the neighbourhood's Middle Eastern flavour becomes more pronounced. Accordingly, A1 is not your typical pie and sausage roll bakery, but a jamboree of falafel, pizza slathered in *labne* (thickened yoghurt) and *zaatar* (a punchy spice mixture). There's nothing frilly about this big canteen-style cafe, so the fact it's perpetually up to the rafters is entirely down to the food. *643-645 Sydney Rd; www.a1bakery. com.au; 7am-7pm Sun-Wed, to 9pm Thu-Sat.*

✖ Beku Gelato

The Bahasa Indonesia name of this gelateria (meaning 'frozen') suggests it isn't your typical ice-creamery. The flavour wheel

MELBOURNE

is Asian-inspired and no-holds-barred, with rotating options including durian, jackfruit, feijoa, wasabi and kaffir lime, along with more mainstream crowd-pleasers like chocolate and Turkish delight. All flavourings are the real deal and everything is made in-house. *171 Lygon St, Brunswick East; 2-9pm Mon, from 4pm Tue-Fri, noon-10pm Sat & Sun.*

✖ Bhang

From the outside, Bhang is little more than a dull glow on a dark street. Step inside and the dim, moody atmosphere continues, but the smell of fragrant curry wafting from the mezzanine kitchen cues a flavourful evening. Indian-style street food dominates the menu, with house specialities served from the charcoal oven. *1/2A Mitchell St; www.eatdrinkbhang.com; 5pm-late Tue-Sun.*

🍷 Noisy Ritual

Proof that wine need not be made alongside hectares of rolling vineyards, Noisy Ritual brings the wine-making process

SYDNEY ROAD STREET PARTY

Every year on a Sunday in March, trams and traffic along Sydney Road are diverted to make way for one of Melbourne's biggest street parties. Eateries shift kitchens to the pavement, bands jam on outdoor stages, and Brunswick's live music venues open their doors for back-to-back performances. Check the Moreland City Council website (www.moreland.vic.gov.au) for dates.

to the city's beating heart. Grapes sourced from all over Victoria are stomped on-site, then end up in wall-to-wall barrels in a relaxed, roomy wine bar. The cellar door experience is amped with live music and platters of locally sourced nibbles. *249 Lygon St, Brunswick East; www.noisyritual.com.au; hours vary.*

🔒 Finki

With a scattering of colourful garb and accessories, shopping at Finki is like walking into a rainbow. The store gives literal meaning to the term local, given the owner makes her own clothing and jewellery in an open workshop out the back. The shop also stocks the lines of other independent designers. *159 Sydney Rd; www.finki.com.au; 11am-4pm Mon-Thu, to 5pm Fri & Sat.*

Top: curries and colour at Bhang
Left: barrels of fun at urban winery Noisy Ritual

© Jake Rodden / 2020, Bhang

© Tajette O'Halloran / 2020, Noisy Ritual

SYDNEY

Sydney impacts instantly with big-name sights, but the urban culture around its characterful central districts is what really seduces the visitor.

Sydney's most interesting neighbourhoods stretch to the east, west and south of the elongated downtown area. These are easily explored by combining public transport with walking or cycling.

To the east of Central Station rises Surry Hills, one of many areas where formerly working-class terraced homes are now highly desirable residences. The locale is a cornerstone of Sydney's contemporary dining scene.

North of here, and easily reached by train, Darlinghurst and Kings Cross are a heartland for the city's prominent LGBT+ community ('the Cross' still conserves a little vice-zone edginess). Beyond here, the Eastern Suburbs offer boutique shopping and a hedonistic restaurant scene. On the coast, the glorious Eastern Beaches run south from Bondi like a string of pearls. Southwest of the centre, the sizeable Inner West consists of a range of characterfully bohemian suburbs with a great cafe, shopping, eating and drinking scene.

SYDNEY

DARLINGHURST & KINGS CROSS

A hub of Sydney's LGBT+ community, this area has seen increasing development at the expense of nightlife in recent years but still pulses with local character. It's a mix of gym-buffed young lawyers and bohemian long-term residents with a villagey feel here that's atypical of central Sydney. Get the train to Kings Cross and wander from there.

🏛 Artspace
Head down the stairs from Kings Cross to waterside Woolloomooloo to find this energetic exhibition space that focuses squarely on avant-garde contemporary Australian and international artists. *43-51 Cowper Wharf Rd Wy; www.artspace.org.au; 11am-5pm Mon-Fri, 11am-6pm Sat & Sun; free.*

🏛 Sydney Jewish Museum
Sydney has an important Jewish history dating back to the earliest days of colonisation. This excellent museum covers past and present but is centred on a powerfully moving exhibition about the Holocaust. *148 Darlinghurst Rd; www.sydneyjewishmuseum.com.au; 10am-4.30pm Mon-Thu, 10am-3.30pm Fri, 10am-4pm Sun; adult/child $15/free.*

🔒 Artery
This friendly spot offers high-quality, ethically-purchased Aboriginal contemporary art, with items starting at very accessible prices (think $35 for an entry-level small canvas). There's also a good selection of gifts, from bags to mugs and mouse mats. *221 Darlinghurst Rd; www.artery.com.au; 10am-5pm.*

✖ Yellow
This restaurant has brought Sydney's vegetarian and vegan dining to new heights with its degustation menus, featuring amazing flavour combinations. There's an excellent wine list courtesy of sister establishment Monopole. *57 Macleay St; www.yellowsydney.com.au; 02-9332 2344; 5-11pm Mon-Fri, 11am-2.30pm & 5-11pm Sat & Sun.*

🍺 Old Fitzroy Hotel
This little backstreet boozer is a world away from the busy Kings Cross strip. It's a charming place, a little bit lost in time, and there's also a grassroots theatre that puts on new Australian plays. *129 Dowling St; www.oldfitzroy.com.au; 11am-midnight Mon-Sat, 11am-10pm Sun.*

SURRY HILLS

Once working-class residences, the terraced houses of leafy Surry Hills are now *de rigueur* addresses for stylish Sydney professionals. Stroll uphill east of Central Station into its sloping streets to find a gentrified good-time world of baristas pushing the boundaries of coffee culture, brunchtastic cafes and avant-garde dining options. Vintage shops and cultural gems round out this intriguing locale.

❌ Dead Ringer

Dedicated to quality food and drink, this innovative good-time venue does delicious bar snacks and sharing platters, as well as pouring intriguing wines and shaking quality cocktails. Head over for meat-free Mondays or very boozy bottomless brunches at the weekend. *413 Bourke St; www.deadringer.wtf; 02-9331 3560; 5-11pm Mon-Wed, 5pm-midnight Thu & Fri, 10am-midnight Sat, 11am-11pm Sun.*

🏛 Brett Whiteley Studio

The tearaway talent of this maverick painter was one of Sydney's brightest artistic moments of the latter part of the 20th century. Here, in a quiet backstreet, you can appreciate his quirky brilliance and get a good idea of him as a person. *2 Raper St; www.artgallery.nsw. gov.au/brett-whiteley-studio; 10am-4pm Fri-Sun; free.*

✪ Golden Age Cinema

This rather lovely basement recreates the glory days of cinema, showing alternative new releases and art-house classics in a sweet little screening room. The bar here is great for a pre-show tipple. *80 Commonwealth St; www.ourgoldenage.com.au; 4pm-midnight Tue-Fri, 2.30pm-midnight Sat, 2.30-11pm Sun; adult/concession $22/17.*

❌ Nomad

Taking influences from around the Mediterranean, this has modern industrial decor but high-quality traditional flavours. Seductive lesser-known Australian wines accompany dishes such as the outstanding vine-leaf-wrapped whole trout. *16 Foster St; www.nomadwine.com. au; 02-9280 3395; noon-2.30pm & 6-10pm Mon-Sat.*

☕ Reformatory Caffeine Lab

With decor and atmosphere straight out of sci-fi dystopia,

SYDNEY

Map labels:

HAYMARKET
Wentworth Ave
Hunt St
Paramount Recreation Club
Golden Age Cinema
Nomad
Harmony Park
Crown St
Oxford St
Zoo Emporium
Taylor Square
Belmore Park
Elizabeth St
Commonwealth St
Hilder Reserve
Campbell St
Flinders St
Riley St
Dead Ringer
Crown St
Bourke St
Frog Hollow Reserve
Albion St
SURRY HILLS
Reformatory Caffeine Lab
Foveaux St
Shannon Reserve
Fitzroy St
Elizabeth St
Fred Miller Park
South Dowling St
Shakespeare Hotel
Devonshire St
Ward Park
Brett Whiteley Studio
MOORE PARK

these guys take coffee very seriously, with exquisitely presented single origins, cold drips and more. *51 Foveaux St; www.facebook.com/ thereformatory; 6.30am-4pm Mon-Fri, 8am-2pm Sat.*

🔵 Shakespeare Hotel

Surry Hills is well stocked with trendy bars, but this traditional pub is a real classic, a no-frills 19th-century beauty with a democratic feel and cheap and tasty bar meals. *200 Devonshire St; www.shakespearehotel.com. au; 10am-midnight Mon-Sat, 10am-10pm Sun.*

🔵 Paramount Recreation Club

This attractive rooftop spot has everything from boxing to yoga through the week. There's also a great cafe downstairs. Book your spot via the Paramount Recreation Club app. *80 Commonwealth St; www. paramountrecreation.club; 6am-8pm Mon-Wed, 6am-3pm Thu & Fri, 6am-2pm Sat, 7am-noon Sun; per class $35.*

SYDNEY MARKETS

Sydneysiders love weekend markets. There are quite a few scattered across the city, all with their own unique vibe. Paddington Markets (www. paddingtonmarkets.com. au) is the busiest, while Glebe (www.glebemarkets. com.au) has a grungier vibe. Bondi (www.bondimarkets. com.au) has laid-back scene while Balmain (www. balmainmarket.com.au) com.au) is untouristy and worth investigating.

🔒 Zoo Emporium

There's a little cluster of vintage shops around the intersection of Crown and Campbell Sts; this is one of the best, with two levels of '70s and '80s glam. *180 Campbell St; 11am-6pm Mon-Wed, Fri & Sat, 11am-8pm Thu, noon-5pm Sun.*

Clockwise from top: Paramount Recreation Club; Dead Ringer; Nomad

EASTERN BEACHES

Bondi is just the first of a string of gorgeous beaches stretching southeast of the city centre. Get away from its famous strip of sand to discover much-loved sea pools, neighbourhood cafes and favourite surf spots. It's where a lot of Sydneysiders are living the dream: jumping in the sea before or after work and lazily brunching the weekend away.

Bronte Beach

This pretty beach is a Sydney highlight, a picturesque crescent of sand between the more famous strands of Bondi and Coogee. The surf is normally pretty gentle, making it good for swimming, and there's a great sea pool. The spacious park is a popular spot for family picnics, while a string of low-key cafes behind the beach has a likeable neighbourhood scene. *Bronte Rd, Bronte.*

Mahon Pool

There's a string of excellent rock pools and sea baths for swimming along this coast and particularly on the picturesque stretch between Coogee and Maroubra. Mahon Pool is a favourite, set in a dramatic rockscape with waves crashing over the edge when the tide is high. *Marine Pde, Maroubra; www.randwick.nsw.gov.au; 24hr; free.*

Little Kitchen

This charming neighbourhood cafe is just uphill from the Coogee strip but feels far away. A husband-and-wife team offer beautifully-presented modern Australian breakfasts and a changing lunch menu. Streetside tables are small but worthwhile if you can deal with the slope. *275 Arden St, Coogee; www.thelittlekitchen.com.au; 02-8021 3424; 7am-4pm.*

Funky Pies

Meat pies are the ultimate Aussie icon but this spot challenges the norm by producing only a range of delicious vegan snacks. Grab a smoothie to wash your pie down and then head straight for some time at the beach. *144 Glenayr Ave, Bondi Beach; www.funkypies.com.au; 0451 944 404; 8.30am-8pm Mon-Fri, 9am-8pm Sat & Sun.*

Gertrude & Alice

A favourite hangout for readers, this second-hand bookshop is a cosy space which also does a nice line in coffee and light meals. Well worth lingering. *46 Hall St, Bondi Beach; www.gertrudeandalice.com.au; 6.45am-9pm.*

EASTERN SUBURBS

The wealthy eastern suburbs run along and south of the harbour and embody Sydney's showy side, where nobody cares how you made it or how you spend it. From the glitzy boutiques of Double Bay and Paddington to the hedonism of boisterous beer gardens and upmarket seafood restaurants, it's a good-time stretch of suburbs that include the city's swankiest residences.

✪ Centennial Parklands Equestrian Centre
Five different riding schools occupy this centre, all offering a horseback circuit around gorgeous Centennial Park. Book ahead; lessons also available. *114 Lang Rd, Centennial Park; www.cpequestrian.com.au; rides $90-100.*

✪ Parsley Bay
This beautiful little beach, bay and park, crossed by a cute bridge, is one of the harbour's finest hidden spots. It's a family-friendly place to relax. *Horler Ave, Vaucluse; www.woollahra.nsw.gov.au.*

✖ Paddington Alimentari
This cafe and delicatessen in the heart of Paddington is a real focus of this eastern suburb. It doles out soul-warming coffee, delicious Italian produce and a feeling that this is the beating heart of the community. *2 Hopetoun St, Paddington; www.facebook.com/paddington.alimentari; 7am-5pm Mon-Fri, 7.30am-4pm Sat.*

🏛 Vaucluse House
This 19th-century mansion offers an intriguing perspective into life for the wealthy in early colonial Sydney. It's set in spacious gardens with a tea room. *Wentworth Rd, Vaucluse; www.sydneylivingmuseums.com.au; 10am-4pm Wed-Sun; adult/child $12/8.*

🔒 Mud
This Sydney ceramics brand has taken the design world by storm with their clean lines and warm monotones. *1 Kiaora La, Double Bay; www.mudaustralia.com; 10am-6pm Mon-Fri, 10am-5pm Sat, 11am-4pm Sun.*

🍺 The Sheaf
The rear garden here is a cracking spot, with upmarket pub food, tasty wines and a convivial atmosphere. *429 New S Head Rd, Double Bay; www.thesheaf.com.au; 10am-1am Mon-Wed, 10am-2am Thu-Sat, 10am-midnight Sun.*

Map of the Eastern Suburbs showing locations including Mosman, Sydney Harbour National Park, Nielsen Park, Parsley Bay, Vaucluse House, Vaucluse, Garden Island, Shark Island, Fort Denison, Clarke Island, Felix Bay, Potts Point, Rose Bay, Double Bay, Elizabeth Bay, Darling Point, Double Bay, The Sheaf, Mud, Bellevue Hill, Rose Bay, Royal Sydney Golf Course, North Bondi, Paddington Alimentari, Cooper Park, Bellevue Park, Blair St, Woollahra, Bondi Park, Moore Park, Centennial Park, Bondi Junction, Bondi, Bondi Beach, Centennial Parklands Equestrian Centre, Tamarama, Marks Park.

INNER WEST

If some parts of Sydney are all about style, the more bohemian Inner West, consisting of a sizeable string of train-connected suburbs stretching west and southwest from Central Station, is more about soul. Urban subcultures, a thriving arts scene and a cornucopia of casual restaurants, cafes, bars and pubs make this the most eclectic, family-friendly and intriguing of Sydney's central districts.

White Rabbit

Tucked away behind the architecturally impressive Central Park complex near Central Station, this innovative gallery of Chinese contemporary art is a genuine eye-opener. Expertly-curated exhibitions are always intriguing, entrance is free and you can do tea and dumplings in the foyer cafe. *30 Balfour St, Chippendale; www.*whiterabbitcollection.org; 10am-5pm Wed-Sun; free.*

Mitchell Road Antique & Design Centre

The Inner West is dotted with vintage and antique shops, particularly in Newtown, but it's difficult to beat this enormous collection of retro curios. It's a surefire way to make you feel older, but there's some engagingly offbeat stuff here and waves of nostalgia are guaranteed. *17 Bourke Rd, Alexandria; https://mitchellroad.wordpress.com; 10am-6pm.*

The Lansdowne

Sydney's live music scene may be pretty moribund by world standards but a few venues are beginning to pop up again. The reopened Lansdowne is kicking things along with bands most nights upstairs and an old-school Inner West vibe in its downstairs pub. *2 City Rd, Chippendale; www.facebook.com/thelansdowne; noon-3am Mon-Sat, noon-midnight Sun; approx $20.*

Carriageworks Farmers Market

The heritage-listed former railway workshop of Carriageworks is now a versatile and innovation-packed performance and exhibition space: check out what's on while you're in town. Inner Westies flock to the Saturday farmers market, where produce from around the state is sold at cheerful stalls. *245 Wilson St, Eveleigh;*

www.carriageworks.com.au;
8am-1pm Sat.

🎵 Lazybones Lounge

Groove the night away in this wonderfully louche upstairs space. Come early for food and live music or roll in after midnight, hit the cocktails and dance to funk and jazz fusion. *294 Marrickville Rd, Marrickville; www.lazyboneslounge.com.au; 7pm-midnight Mon-Wed, 5pm-3am Thu-Sat, 5-10pm Sun.*

⛳ Holey Moley

A quirky activity on the busy King Street strip, Holey Moley offers 18 holes of crazy putt-putt golf. Many of the holes are a tribute to the venue's former life as a rock pub. *387 King St, Newtown, www.holeymoley. com.au, noon-midnight Mon-Fri, 11am-midnight Sat & Sun; per 9 holes $18.*

🍴 Gigi Pizzeria

There's a great range of vegan eateries on this block and this pizzeria is one of the best. Authentic Neapolitan crusts and

BRING YOUR OWN BOOZE

The numerous restaurants of the Inner West cross Asia from Turkish to Thai and from Japanese to Lebanese; they offer Sydney's best-value eating scene. Many of them are 'BYO', which means stocking up on wine (sometimes beer) at a nearby bottle shop before entering. A small per-person corkage fee will be charged but it's a welcome relief from the city's often-extortionate wine lists.

delicious meat-and-dairy-free toppings are on offer, as well as scrumptious desserts. *379 King St, Newtown; www.gigipizzeria.com. au; 02-9557 2224; 6-10.30pm.*

Clockwise from top: pre-golf cocktails at Holey Moley; White Rabbit's chic galleries; Mitchell Road Antique & Design Centre

Thorndon

Wellington

Mt Victoria &
Oriental Bay

WELLINGTON

New Zealand's cool little capital rests its reputation on its coffee culture, boutique bars, movie-making and infamous umbrella-shredding gales.

While the weather is often less than ideal, it's a widely observed truism that Wellington on a good day is hard to beat. Positioned on a dramatic harbour within a ring of rugged hills, Wellington city centre is compact and eminently walkable, and most travellers gravitate there for good reason. If you want to follow a different path and still be within walking distance, take a stroll out to the city-fringe suburbs – each of which has its own distinct personality.

To the north, Thorndon is one of Wellington's oldest residential suburbs, with Victorian houses and a scattering of important cultural sights. To the southeast, Mt Victoria offers dining, theatre, cinema and outstanding views – while neighbouring Oriental Bay is the city's beach and beloved promenade. It's also worth checking out hip Aro Valley and student-filled Kelburn, to the west. Anywhere else you want to explore is an easy bus ride away.

WELLINGTON

THORNDON

A short stroll north of the CBD, historic Thorndon abuts two of the city's most popular sights – the New Zealand Parliament buildings and the Wellington Botanic Gardens – but there's plenty more to uncover. The heart of the neighbourhood is the Tinakori Rd shops to the northwest of the motorway, where there's a compact stretch of pubs, cafes and restaurants.

🏛 Old St Paul's

Although Thorndon is home to two hulking cathedrals, it's this cosy wooden church that truly delights. Built from warm-hued native timbers in the Gothic Revival style in 1866, it served as the Anglican cathedral until the 1960s when it narrowly escaped demolition. *34 Mulgrave St;* *www.oldstpauls.co.nz; 10am-5pm; free.*

🏛 National Library of New Zealand

Call into this esteemed research library to visit He Tohu (the Signs), a fascinating showcase for three of New Zealand's nation-building documents: the Declaration of Independence of the United Tribes (1835), the Treaty of Waitangi (1840) and the Women's Suffrage Petition (1893). An engaging lesson in New Zealand history awaits. *70 Molesworth St; www.natlib.govt. nz; 9am-5pm Mon-Fri, to 1pm Sat; free.*

🏛 Katherine Mansfield House

During her childhood, New Zealand's earliest literary star lived in this two-storey wooden house, which is now a museum devoted to her life and works. *25 Tinakori Rd; www. katherinemansfield.com; 10am-4pm Tue-Sun; adult/child $8/free.*

✖ Hillside Kitchen & Cellar

Casual brunches give way to highly creative multi-course vegetarian and vegan degustation dinners at this meat-free restaurant celebrating the best local produce. *241 Tinakori Rd; www.hillsidekitchen.co.nz; 04-473 7140; 8.30am-2.30pm Sun, 11.30am-2.30pm Mon, 11.30am-2.30pm & 5.30-9pm Tue-Fri, 8.30am-2.30pm & 5.30-9pm Sat.*

🏛 Bolton Street Cemetery

Fans of Gothic gloom will find a lot to love in Wellington's oldest European graveyard (dating from 1840). Look out for the homoerotic memorial to early Labour leader Harry Holland. *Bolton St; https:// boltoncemetery.org.nz; 5am-10.30pm.*

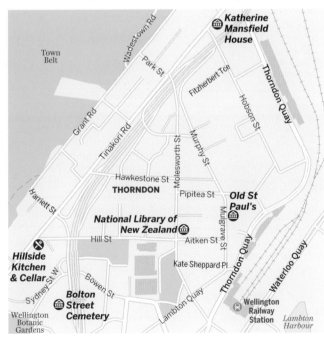

MT VICTORIA & ORIENTAL BAY

Can any other capital city lay claim to a swimmable sandy beach as close to its city centre as Oriental Bay is to Wellington? Stretching back from the tree-lined waterfront is the residential suburb of Mt Victoria, at the base of the mountain of the same name. Its compact grid of narrow streets includes lots of lovely old wooden houses.

Mt Victoria Lookout

You can drive or take the number 20 bus most of the way up, but the best way to explore hidden corners of the neighbourhood is to puff your way up through the residential back streets to Mt Victoria's 196m (643ft) summit. The views over the city and harbour are an apt reward. *Lookout Rd.*

Ortega Fish Shack

The name doesn't do justice to the quality, reputation or the premium prices at this excellent seafood restaurant. The casual Mediterranean vibe reflects the seasonal approach to the menu, which also features fine cuts of meat and fantastic desserts. *16 Majoribanks St; www.ortega. co.nz; 04-382 9559; 5.30pm-late.*

Mt Vic Chippery

While Ortega is perfect for a special occasion, this neighbourhood fish-and-chip shop is an everyday treat – and it's just across the road. *5 Marjoribanks St; www. thechippery.co.nz; 04-382 8713; noon-8.30pm.*

Embassy Theatre

With Sir Peter Jackson and Weta Workshop based in the city, Wellington likes to dine out on its movie-making credentials – and this restored art deco cinema is one of the most elegant places in 'Wellywood' to catch a flick. There's an excellent cocktail bar, too. *10 Kent Tce; www. embassytheatre.co.nz; 3pm-late Mon-Fri, 10am-late Sat & Sun.*

Capitol

Our favourite weekend brunch spot in Mt Vic is this Italian restaurant within the Embassy

Map labels: Lambton Harbour, Chaffers Marina, Freyberg Pool & Fitness Centre, Te Papa, Oriental Bay, Oriental Bay, Cable St, Wakefield St, Chaffers St, Waitangi Park, Oriental Pde, Prince St, McFarlane St, Hay St, Tory St, Allen St, Blair St, Roxburgh St, Hawker St, Pallser Rd, BATS, Mt Vic Chippery, Capitol, Ortega Fish Shack, Charles Plimmer Park, Mt Victoria Lookout, Alpha St, Embassy Theatre, Majoribanks St, Tennyson St, Lorne St, Kent Tce, MT VICTORIA, College St, Vivian St, Elizabeth St, Cambridge Tce, Brougham St, Queen St, Austin St, Pirie St, Town Belt

Theatre building. In the evening, the delicious seasonal fare is the perfect conclusion to a movie-based date – although Capitol can get loud. *10 Kent Tce; www. capitolrestaurant.co.nz; 04-384 2855; noon-3pm & 5.30-9.30pm Mon-Fri, from 9.30am Sat & Sun.*

🏛 BATS

Not-for-profit BATS has a reputation for staging some of Welly's most edgy theatre and comedy. Lumen bar is good for a drink, whether or not you're attending a show. *1 Kent Tce; www.bats.co.nz; 5-11pm.*

GET OFF THE ROAD

While it's well known that the creative energy behind the *Lord of the Rings* and *The Hobbit* movies emanated from Wellington, many presume that the filming was all done elsewhere. However key scenes were filmed on Mt Victoria itself, including the famous 'get off the road' scene, where the hobbits hide from the Nazgûl.

🜨 Freyberg Pool & Fitness Centre

Aside from being a very cool example of 1960s architecture, this waterfront complex has a 33.5m (110ft) heated indoor pool and a well-equipped gym. *139 Oriental Pde; www.wellington. govt.nz; 6am-9pm.*

Clockwise from top: dish at Capitol; Ortega Fish Shack; expansive views from Mt Victoria Lookout

AUCKLAND

Straddling two harbours, 50 volcanoes and 50-plus islands, New Zealand's biggest and most cosmopolitan city is uniquely gifted.

AUCKLAND

While the Central Business District (CBD) has its attractions, any Aucklander will tell you that the city's real appeal lies in the surrounding suburbs. Walk west and you'll reach Ponsonby, with its namesake thoroughfare lined with restaurants, bars and boutiques. Head south through Myers Park to gritty Newton and the famously hedonistic K' Rd strip. To the east, the city straightens its tie in plush Parnell.

A walk to these city-fringe neighbourhoods is inevitably uphill, as their main streets follow the ridges of old lava flows. Thankfully they're all connected by the InnerLink bus, which loops around from the city centre every 10 to 15 minutes.

North of the CBD is Auckland Harbour, which opens onto the glorious island-dotted Hauraki Gulf. Ferries depart every 15 to 30 minutes on the 12-minute jaunt to Devonport on the North Shore, a pretty beachy village bookended by a pair of volcanoes.

PONSONBY

Immediately west of the inner city, this formerly working-class neighbourhood of tightly packed wooden Victorian houses (known in New Zealand as villas) is now the city's most fashionable dining and drinking precinct. Fancy homeware and designer boutiques – including local big-hitters Karen Walker and Zambesi – fill the gaps between bars, restaurants and churches on the long Ponsonby Rd strip.

✖ Ponsonby Central

Fashioned from a former calendar factory at the centre of Ponsonby Rd, this popular complex comprises a cavalcade of goodness: a produce market, homeware shops, cafes, a cocktail bar and a brilliant selection of restaurants (most notably Blue Breeze Inn). *6 Brown St; www.ponsonbycentral.co.nz; 09-376 8300; 8.30am-10.30pm Sun-Wed, to midnight Thu-Sat.*

✖ Ponsonby Village International Food Court

Auckland loves its Asian-style food halls, and this brightly lit first-floor place is one of the most appealing. Come here for good quality but inexpensive curry, noodles, kebabs and pasta. *106 Ponsonby Rd; www.ponsonbyfoodcourt.co.nz; 11am-10pm.*

🍺 Hoppers

Craft beer and gin are the main poisons at this hip garden bar, tucked away in a former stables courtyard behind a Victorian-era shop. Fairy lights, tasselled lamps and potted palms add a quirky charm, while a retractable roof makes it an all-weather proposition. *134 Ponsonby Rd; www.hoppersgardenbar.co.nz; 4pm-late Mon & Tue, noon-late Wed-Sun.*

✖ SPQR

The designer-sunglasses crowd slurp oysters and champagne at the prized outdoor tables. Inside, the burnished copper bar and rough concrete walls are the backdrop to some of the city's best Italian food, like Roman-style thin-crust pizza. *150 Ponsonby Rd; www.spqrnz.co.nz; 09-360 1710; noon-late.*

✖ Sidart

Auckland's most experimental restaurant showcases mini masterpieces of culinary artistry from a perch at the rear of an old movie theatre, with large windows showcasing the city skyline. Foodies: check out the 'Chef's Table' experience on the website. *Three Lamps Plaza, 283 Ponsonby Rd; www.sidart.co.nz; 09-360 2122; noon-2.30pm Fri, 6-11pm Tue-Sat.*

NEWTON

Bisected by a motorway in the 1960s, this city-fringe neighbourhood gravitates around two main thoroughfares: bohemian Karangahape Rd (known universally as K' Rd) and traffic-clogged Symonds St. Once the city's red-light district, K' Rd is now an artsy shopping strip by day and one of Auckland's prime party destinations at night. It's also the hub of the city's LGBT+ scene.

St Kevin's Arcade

The undisputed focal point of K' Rd, this 1920s shopping arcade contains a bit of everything that people come to this part of town for: vintage clothes, second-hand books and records, good food, coffee, booze, live music and an alternative vibe. At the rear, leadlight windows frame extraordinary city views and stairs head down to pretty Myers Park. *183 Karangahape Rd; www.stkevinsarcade.co.nz; 7.30am-midnight Sun-Tue, 7.30am-4am Wed-Sat.*

Wine Cellar & Whammy Bar

Tucked away under St Kevin's Arcade, this conjoined duo revel in their gloomy grunginess, as befitting the strip's edgiest live music venues. Gigs and DJ sets carry on at Whammy until 4am on weekends. *183 Karangahape Rd; www.facebook.com/WineCellarStKevins; 5pm-midnight.*

Lovebucket

Craft beer and quirky cocktails are the hallmarks of this stylish bar, hidden at the rear of the K' Rd Food Workshop complex. DJ sets and live music loosen things up on Fridays and Saturdays. *309 Karangahape Rd; www.lovebucket.co.nz; 4pm-late Tue-Sat.*

Shanghai Lil's

Louche in the extreme, this cocktail bar exists within an explosion of chinoiserie: curtained day beds, carved couches and giant Ming-style vases. The music lurches between live jazz sessions and gay pop hits. *335 Karangahape Rd; www.facebook.com/lilsponsonby; 5pm-1am Wed & Thu, to 3am Fri & Sat.*

Madame George

Down the seedier end of K' Rd, unassuming Madame George serves sophisticated cocktails and contemporary cuisine to foodies

FREEMANS BAY — CITY CENTRE — Hopetoun St — Greys Ave — Myers Park — Pitt St — Beresford Sq — Howe St — Hopetoun St — Lovebucket — Eagle Bar — Wine Cellar & Whammy Bar — Shanghai Lil's — Artspace Aotearoa — Family Bar — St Kevin's Arcade — Caluzzi — Karangahape Rd — Coco's Cantina — Galatos St — East St — NEWTON — Madame George — Gundry St — Ian McKinnon Dr

in the know, putting foraged seasonal produce to imaginative use. *490 Karangahape Rd; www.madamegeorge.co.nz; 5pm-late Tue-Sat.*

✖ Coco's Cantina

Regulars sidle up to Coco's streetside tables to sip wine in the afternoon sun. Others head inside to tuck into delicious plates of simple, seasonal Italian fare. They also come to see and be seen; for all its celebrated informality, this is one of the chicest spots on the strip. *376 Karangahape Rd; www.cocoscantina.co.nz; 09-300*

LGBT+ K' RD

Although modest for a city of its size, K' Rd is the closest thing Auckland has to a gay village. Key venues include Shanghai Lil's, unpretentious Eagle Bar (259 K' Rd) and, directly across the road, big brash Family Bar (270 K' Rd). Then there's Caluzzi (461 K' Rd) – a dedicated dinner-and-show restaurant with riotous drag-queen waitresses.

7582, 4pm-late Mon-Thu & Sat, from noon Fri.

🏛 Artspace Aotearoa

For over 30 years this gallery has been a bastion for challenging contemporary art, usually of the conceptual variety. Quality varies but it's free and thought-provoking. *L1, 300 Karangahape Rd; www.artspace-aotearoa.nz; 10am-6pm Tue-Fri, 11am-4pm Sat; free.*

Top and top left: Artspace Aotearoa's enriching spaces Below: vintage style with a view at St Kevin's Arcade

PARNELL

East of the city centre, well-heeled Parnell's reputation is more 'hip-replacement' than 'hip' but it's home to the Auckland Museum, has a good selection of accommodation, and its steep back lanes are crammed with charming Victorian houses. If the hills get too much, excellent bus and train connections will get you where you want to go.

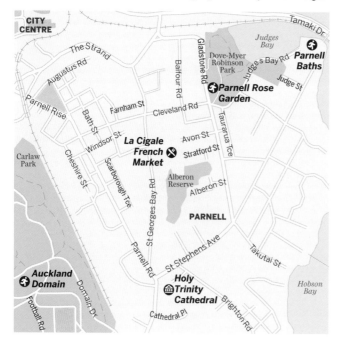

elegant Bishop Selwyn Chapel, completed in 2016. The rose window by English artist Carl Edwards is especially noteworthy. Better yet is gorgeous St Mary's Church next door, built in the Carpenter Gothic style in 1886 and boasting attractive stained-glass windows. *446 Parnell Rd; www.holy-trinity.org.nz; 10am-3pm.*

✪ La Cigale French Market

It's open through the week as a cafe and shop selling imported French kitchenware, cheese and wine, but this *cigale* (cicada) really jumps during its weekend markets. Stalls sell all manner of epicurean delights, from fresh fruit and cheeses to cut flowers and chocolates, while the tables inside are piled with patisserie. *69 St Georges Bay Rd; www.lacigale.co.nz; 9am-1.30pm Sat & Sun.*

✪ Parnell Rose Garden

This pretty formal garden is at its most fragrant and colourful from November to March. While you're here, take a walk down through the mature trees to Judges Bay, where there's a popular swimming pontoon. *85-87 Gladstone Rd; free.*

✪ Parnell Baths

A 1950s mosaic mural provides a striking backdrop to this open-air saltwater swimming pool. *Judges Bay Rd; www.parnellbaths.co.nz; 6am-8pm Mon-Fri, 8am-8pm Sat & Sun Dec-Apr; adult/child $6.40/free.*

✪ Auckland Domain

While the neoclassical Auckland Museum steals the show, there's lots to uncover in the 80 hectares of surrounding parklands, including native bush, sculptures, a band rotunda, duck ponds and Auckland's most overlooked volcano, the remains of Pukekaroa. Don't miss the Wintergardens, with their Edwardian glasshouses, sunken pool and bush walk. *Domain Dr.*

🏛 Holy Trinity Cathedral

Although this hulking Anglican cathedral is a disconcerting mishmash of competing styles, some of the individual elements are lovely – particularly the

DEVONPORT

A short hop by ferry from central Auckland, the affluent suburb of Devonport is liberally strewn with grand Edwardian wooden villas and punctuated by two volcanic cones. Despite the distinctly South Pacific landscape there's something of the English village about Devonport. Pubs, cafes and restaurants line the Victoria Rd strip, while pretty parks and churches pepper the back streets.

Above: Devonport's blue views

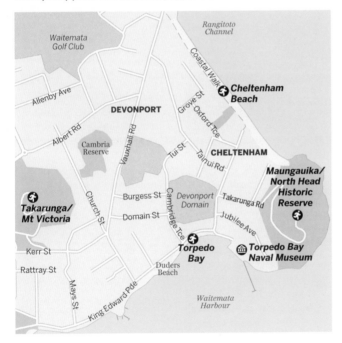

the northern head of Auckland Harbour. It was fortified during the 1880s, and visitors can wander through tunnels to a well-preserved gun battery. A tiny beach is tucked away at its northern edge. *Takarunga Rd; www.doc.govt.nz; 6am-10pm.*

✪ Cheltenham Beach

The first of Auckland's sandy North Shore beaches, Cheltenham could hardly be more picturesque – with Maungauika at one end and a backdrop of mature pohutukawa trees blazing red in summer. Straight ahead, the graceful slope of the volcanic island Rangitoto provides the essential Auckland view. *Cheltenham Rd.*

✪ Takarunga/Mt Victoria

Devonport's loftier volcano reaches 87m (285ft) and it, too, is riddled with military tunnels; one bunker is used as a live-music venue by the Devonport Folk Club. It was once an important Māori pā (fortified village) and the remains of terracing can be seen as you take the 10-minute walk to the summit. *Kerr St.*

✪ Torpedo Bay

Locals swim sheltered lengths at this little sandy harbourside beach. At low tide it's a better bet than the ocean beaches. *King Edward Pde.*

🏛 Torpedo Bay Naval Museum

The navy has had a presence in Devonport since 1841. Its history is celebrated in this fascinating little museum, which emphasises the stories of individual sailors. *64 King Edward Pde; www.navymuseum.co.nz; 10am-5pm; free.*

✪ Maungauika/North Head Historic Reserve

The clue is in the name: this 50m-high (164ft) volcano forms

SOUTH AMERICA & THE CARIBBEAN

LIMA

Hidden between Lima's pre-Columbian ruins, Spanish colonial mansions and shiny modern towers are world-class culinary and cultural marvels waiting to be discovered.

V isitors once bypassed Peru's capital city for the Andean wonders of Cusco, gateway to Machu Picchu. Then came the 2010s, when a globally-recognised culinary revival in upmarket Miraflores and a thriving arts scene in bohemian Barranco helped put Lima back on the tourist map. The former district has a clutch of fine-dining options listed by the World's 50 Best Restaurants organisation, while the latter pairs its own award-winning restaurants with chic modern art galleries and eclectic pisco bars.

Snarled traffic in this bone-dry metropolis of 10 million people remains an enduring problem. However, getting from central Miraflores to southerly Barranco along the Pacific coast is a relative breeze thanks to manicured cycle lanes and seaside walking paths. These two adjoining neighbourhoods form the focal point for most visits to the city, with Miraflores luring families and Barranco attracting both moneyed millennials and fashion-conscious posh-packers.

LIMA

MIRAFLORES

Modern, confident and mannered, Miraflores is the face Lima wants to show to the world. Most tourists base themselves in this ritzy seaside enclave to take advantage of its hip hotels, lively culinary scene and leafy parklands. There are more cycle lanes here than anywhere else in Lima, and walking along its surprisingly lush coastline is a must for any visitor.

⊗ Ceviche Row

If there's one dish that's come to define Peruvian cuisine abroad it's ceviche, a tangy plate of raw fish 'cooked' in lime juice. The best exemplars are found along Avenida La Mar, the city's veritable ceviche row. Restaurants run the gamut from award-winners like La Mar to more casual

neighbourhood dives such as Barra Mar. *Avenida La Mar.*

☕ Neira Café Lab

Ask a Limeño where to get the strongest Peruvian coffee and they'll send you to this four-table dive where baristas whip up classic espressos or trendier V60 pour-overs. There's also a cold

brew with passion fruit and mint-like Peruvian herb muña. *Enrique Palacios 1074; www.facebook. com/neiracafelab; 8am-9pm.*

✈ Playa Mahaka

Conveniently located along the Miraflores coastline, this bite-sized beach is the perfect spot for beginners to test their surfing skills with consistent year-round breaks and several agencies offering lessons, rentals and wetsuits (like English-speaking Pukana Surf School). *Espigón Miraflores (in front of La Rosa Náutica); www. pukana-surf.com.*

✈ El Malecón

Three kilometres (1.9 miles) of parks, gardens and green spaces on the cliffs overlooking the Pacific Ocean, El Malecón's a favoured strip for morning strolls and evening bike rides. Sights include the Parapuerto kiosk, launching ground for urban paragliding tours, and Parque del Amor, home to artist Victor Delfin's larger-than-life statue El Beso (The Kiss). Miraflores Coast.

🔒 Mercado No 1 de Surquillo

Technically outside of Miraflores in neighbouring Surquillo, this market is the most exciting in the area for native Peruvian products. Lunch stalls like Cevichería El Rey Luchin are legendary among residents, while visitors stock up on organic Andean grains, coffees and chocolates at the special Bioferia section on Sundays. *Paseo de la Republica, Block 53; 8am-4pm.*

BARRANCO

Barranco sprouted in the 19th century as a beach destination for Lima's aristocracy, but has since merged with the greater city. Unlike its flashier neighbour Miraflores to the north, it maintains a more historic feel with palm-lined, exceedingly walkable streets. Most of the old mansions, which arose during the prosperous Guano Era, are now bars, hotels or stores with sherbet-coloured facades and verdant patios.

🏛 Amaru Casa Cultural

This historic mansion aims to stimulate right-brained visitors with its myriad cultural offerings. You can order a herb-infused beverage at the medicinal bar, sample Peruvian coffees at the cafe, purchase paintings in the art gallery or browse the curated selection in the small bookshop. Speak a little Spanish? Sign up for lessons in art, flamenco, ballet, theatre, yoga or Quechua. *Jr Sucre 317; www.amaru.cc; 10am-10pm.*

❌ La Bodega Verde

Limeños laze away long afternoons over organic coffees in the plant-packed patio of this lush oasis near Puente de los Suspiros. Join them in the act by reading a good book, tackling some emails or perusing the small gallery space here, which has artwork for sale from young Lima painters. Veggie ceviches, açai bowls and gluten-free baked goods round out the health-conscious menu. *Jr Sucre 335a; www.facebook.com/labodegaverde; 8am-10pm.*

🔒 Dédalo

Your one-stop shop for alpaca shawls, Inca-inspired jewellery or designer artisan goods, such as ceramics and wood-carved bowls. There's also a gallery space near the back that leads out to a leafy patio cafe serving fresh-pressed juices, lattes and craft beers. *Paseo Saenz Peña 295; www.dedalo.pe; 10am-8pm Mon-Sat.*

🏛 Microteatro Lima

Soak up the artistic spirit of Barranco at this bar-cum-performance space with a rotating roster of original works. Shows last no more than 15 minutes and take place in a 15-sq-metre room with a capacity for, you guessed it, 15 people. Most are in Spanish, but the vibe is so electric that you never get too lost in the action. *Ayacucho 271; www.microteatrolima.com; from 7pm Thu-Sun.*

LIMA

Ayahuasca Restobar

This always-bustling bar lies within the rooms of an 1870s-era mansion and is the spot to order pisco cocktails flavoured with endemic Amazonian fruits. With its funky furnishings and fairy-tale lighting, you don't even need the namesake drug to feel intoxicated by the psychedelic vibe. *San Martin 130; http://ayahuascarestobar.com; 6pm-3am Mon-Fri & 8pm-3am Sat.*

© Juan Napuri / Alamy Stock Photo

Mérito

Lima is full of larger-than-life restaurants helmed by star chefs who trot around the globe. Humble Mérito is not one of them. Its artistically plated dishes look and taste like they belong in the city's finest establishments, but they have price tags that even backpackers can splurge on. The wood, stone and adobe interior echoes the food's earthy authenticity. *Av 28 de Julio 206; http://meritorestaurante.com; 01-277-1628; 7.30-11pm Mon-Sat.*

Vernácula

Whether you're on the hunt for

THE BRIDGE OF SIGHS

The small wooden bridge known as Puente de los Suspiros (Bridge of Sighs) is Barranco's most famous landmark. Legend has it that first-time visitors who cross its 30m (98ft) span without taking a single breath are granted one wish. Of course, you'll have to fight past street performers, canoodling lovers and selfie-takers to make it in time!

Peruvian pop art or a dress inspired by the vibrant patterns of Andean textiles, this beloved concept store delivers quality goods with a strong local identity. Stick around on Friday and Saturday nights for live music in the downstairs bar, where string lights paint a soft glow on the fashionable beer-swigging crowd. *Ayacucho 269; www.facebook.com/vernaculaconceptstore; 11am-8pm Tue-Sun, bar to midnight Fri & Sat.*

© Efrain Padro / Alamy Stock Photo

**Above: colourful streets and windows in Barranco
Left: the bridge of legend, Puente de los Suspiros**

El Vedado

Old Havana

Havana

HAVANA

The 500-year-old Cuban capital is revived with creative entrepreneurs, inventive cocktails, cutting-edge art and classic cars.

HAVANA

Havana is on the cusp of a new revolution. Entrenched in 60 years of socialist rule, her spirited citizens were handed the keys to a more independent future almost 10 years ago when ex-president Raúl Castro loosened rules on private enterprise. Many of Havana's two million souls set about opening restaurants, funky cafes, boutique stores, art spaces, plush B&Bs, and running tours, transforming the 500-year-old city. While enrichment is still a dirty word in Castro's Cuba, and some private trade criss-crosses the boundaries of these new business rules, Havana is an urban maze of doors leading to newly forged secret worlds. Explore colourful Old Havana on foot; it's noisy and gritty, save for pockets of gentrified squares and streets, and it's almost dead after midnight. Further west along the coast is el Vedado, a neighbourhood of wedding-cake mansions, art spaces, bars and clubs. Walk the wide, tree root-wrecked pavements, and hail cabs for outlying areas.

EL VEDADO

El Vedado is a chequerboard of mid-19th-century streets dissected by leafy boulevards, stuffed with the best homes sugar profits money could buy for Havana's upper classes: Hispano-colonial mansions with gardens, wraparound terraces and ornate railings. These were later joined by Mafia-built hotels and casinos on the coast. Today, a swathe of el Vedado's smart villas host fashionable bars and cultural venues.

⊗ Grados
Chef Raulito Bazuka revives old recipes at his home-restaurant. Bazuka created an avant-garde *The Matrix*–themed food and theatre experience mixing bent cutlery, TVs and chilling performance in spring 2019. Next up? Brewing beer, and a new venture challenging culinary norms in Cuba. *Grados, Calle E 562 e/ 23 y 25; www.facebook. com/restaurantegrados; 7833-7882; 12.30-3.30pm & 7-10.30pm Wed-Sat.*

🏛 Jardines de la Tropical
Entangled in the trees of Havana's riverside forest is the 1904 playground of Cuba's La Tropical Brewery. Socialites would dance under the Dream Hall and listen to the piano in the mini Alhambra Palace. You can still order a beer from the bar at the back of the Hansel and Gretel–style chapel. *Calle Rizo y Final, entrance from Avenida 51, 7886-1767.*

🏛 Hotel Nacional Tour
The storied 1930s Hotel Nacional hosted the US Mafia's 1946 roast flamingo and manatee dinner as Lucky Luciano and Meyer Lansky hatched their sin city plans for Havana. During the hotel's daily history tour, learn about mafia mischief, climb one of the hotel towers, and descend into tunnels dug out of caves during the 1962 Cuban Missile Crisis. *Calle 21 y O; www.hotelnacionaldecuba.com; 7836-3564; 10am daily; CUC$5.*

⊗ Salchipizza
The unsigned bakery of repatriated Cuban Alberto González Ceballos offers bread (fruit, maize or gluten-free) with beetroot butter, white truffle, fried duck and quail eggs, and mischievous conversation. *Calle Infanta 562 e/ Valle y Zanja; www.facebook.com/pg/ Salchipizza; 5281-8792; breakfast 9-11am Tue-Sat; CUC$7.*

🏛 Cementerio Cristóbal Colón
Seek out the exquisite art-deco *pietà* by Rita Longa, the René Portocarrero gold mosaic inside the Raúl de Zárraga tomb, the pawn on 1920s Cuban world chess champion José Raúl Capablanca's grave, and a René Lalique art-deco mausoleum. *Calle Zapata y 12; 7830 4517; 8am-5pm, CUC$5.*

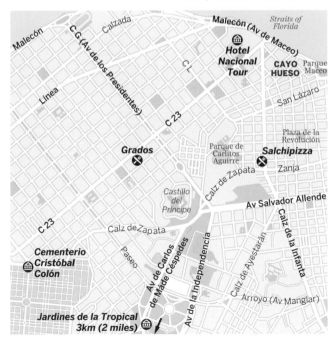

© Julian Peters Photography / Shutterstock

OLD HAVANA

Old Havana is an Andalucía architectural transplant, bulging with muscular fortresses and baroque churches. Fountains tinkle and half-moon stained-glass windows lure visitors who puff hand-rolled cigars, admire sea salt-battered architecture in gelato-hued classic cars, and tour Ernest Hemingway drinking holes. After those, walk the pot-holed streets looking for the odd sign or doorway ajar to creativity within...

🏛 Bacardí Building & Café

The black and golden-hued art-deco former Bacardí HQ soars above the edge of Old Havana with its ziggurat tower topped by the rum's iconic bat motif. Its 12-storey facade is embedded with bronze bats and giant Bs in the ironwork. A glazed frieze of nymphs by American artist Maxfield Parrish is best photographed from the fifth-floor terrace of the nearby Hotel Plaza. The wood-panelled and decorated mezzanine bar recently reopened. No Bacardí, though, is served! *Avenida de Bélgica 261 e/ Empedrado y San Juan de Díos; cafe 9am-4pm Mon-Sat.*

🏛 REX Duplex Theatre + Neon Center

Technically three blocks beyond the fringe, this resurrected venue celebrates Havana's vintage neon heritage. Artist Kadir López, along with Cuban-American Adolfo Nodal, restorer of Los Angeles' neon lights, are repairing more than 200 neon signs. The REX hosts an exhibition of lights and a neon boneyard. A cafe, shop and art gallery are due to open in November 2019. Neighbourhood neon tours shine a light on López's Habana Light Neon + Signs project. *Boulevard San Rafael 161 e/ Industria y Amistad; www. smore.com/396zx; noon-10pm Thu-Tue.*

🏛 San Isidro Distrito de Arte

Cuba's most famous pimp Alberto Yarini was gunned down in the louche lanes of southern Old Havana in 1910. Today the sons of Cuba's most famous actor, Jorge Perugorría, are reviving the area with Miami's Wynwood in mind: walls are painted by Cuban and foreign street artists, two galleries showcase contemporary artists, community fiestas and block parties are celebrated, while a new restaurant and Hotel Yarini were on the verge of opening when we last visited. *Calle San Isidro & around; http://galeriatallergorria.com.*

Map labels: Malecón, San Lázaro, Tacón, Arte Corte, Parque Anfiteatro, Bahía de la Habana, Av Carlos Manuel de Céspedes, Plaza 13 de Marzo, Consulado, Aguiar, HABANA VIEJA, Bacardí Building & Café, O'Reilly, El del Frente, Villegas, San Pedro, Paseo de Martí (Prado), Parque Central, Av de las Misiones, Lamparilla, San Rafael, REX Duplex Theater + Neon Center, Capitolio Nacional, El Café, Plaza del Cristo, Brasil, Clandestina, Muralla, Villegas, Parque de la Fraternidad, Máximo Gómez, Agramonte, Av de Bélgica, Luz, Acosta, Suárez, San Isidro Distrito de Arte, Leonor Pérez, San Pedro, Estación Central de Ferrocarriles (Central Train Station)

© 2020, Clandestina

🏛 Arte Corte

A bar-filled alley in northern Old Havana is home to street murals and a grass-roots project, Arte Corte, which trains up young unemployed hairdressers, bartenders and manicurists for free. Get a free chop at No. 11 (9am to noon from Monday to Friday) and tour the project and the atmospheric living barber's museum. Dining at El Figaro in the enlivened alley supports Arte Corte. *Calle Aguiar e/ Peña Pobre y Avenida de las Misiones; https:// artecorte.org.*

🔒 Clandestina

Ever since Idania del Río and Leire Fernández launched Cuba's first fashion brand in 2015, and later its first online clothing store, their funky colourful totes and tees, emblazoned with nuanced slogans, have been must-buys for souvenir hunters. Through fashion they regularly make fun of Cuba's lack of wi-fi, money and everyday conundrums. *Calle Villegas 403 e/ Teniente Rey y Muralla; https:// clandestina.co; 10am-8pm Mon-Sat, 10am-5pm Sun.*

SMOULDERING PARTY SCENE

HAPE Collective, born in an era of hope after Barack Obama restored US diplomatic relations in 2015 after 54 years of stalemate, aims to push musical boundaries and encounters. The international team of fun invites Cuban DJs and foreign musicians to rock disused rooftops and quirky plots (like Jardines de la Tropical) where the musically curious flock to thumping parties through Havana's humid nights. Each new party address is kept a secret until a day or so beforehand; keep an eye on www.facebook.com/ hapecollective.

✴ El Café

Once a chef and barista in London, industrial engineer-turned-chef Nelson Rodríguez Tamayo runs this small, appealing refuge. From the perfectly poured latte to the sourdough, eggs and avocado, this hidden cafe down 'Bitter Street' nails breakfast, brunch and lunch like no other. We've seen travellers so overwhelmed with what's chalked up on the blackboard that they've ordered the protein platter and the sweet pancakes for breakfast. *Calle Amargura 358 e/ Villegas y Aguacate; www. facebook.com/elcafehavana; 7861 3817; 9am-6pm.*

✴ El del Frente

Artist-turned-chef José Carlos Imperatori, who created a gin bar in a tiny building, expanded the cool factor with this unsigned terrace bar just opposite. The cocktails are a knockout (piña coladas are huge), best ordered with moreish ceviche-topped *tostones* (fried plantain) on the rooftop. *Calle O'Reilly 303 e/ Habana y Aguiar; www.facebook. com/pg/BarEldelFrente; 7867-4256; noon-midnight.*

**Top: Clandestina's hip garb
Below: rainbow-coloured
buildings in Old Havana**

© MMaurizio De Mattei / Shutterstock

Chacarita   Palmero

Almagro   **Buenos Aires**

San Telmo

BUENOS AIRES

Beneath the surface of Buenos Aires' sophistication and fading grandeur lies a passion that finds expression in its vibrant neighbourhoods.

Buenos Aires is divided into neighbourhoods that burst with personality, and the city's residents, known as *porteños* (people of the port), identify strongly with their *barrio* (neighbourhood). Connected by buses, the subte (underground) and cycle lanes, each *barrio* has its own distinct flavour. For chic boutiques, fashionable restaurants, cocktail bars and expansive parks, try Palermo, a large neighbourhood north of the city centre. San Telmo, just south of the centre, contains some of the city's oldest buildings. Its history as an immigrant neighbourhood – home first to wealthy colonialists, then penniless new arrivals – is reflected in its antiques stores and gritty atmosphere. West of the city centre, residential *barrio* Almagro gives a taste of middle class *porteño* life, with elegant cafes and a thriving theatre scene. To stay ahead of the curve, look to up-and-coming Chacarita, west of Palermo and full of street art, vegetarian food and edgy new restaurants.

PALERMO

Known for its shops, upmarket restaurants and lively nightlife, Palermo attracts the city's well-heeled media types and young professionals, who live in modern apartment blocks and sip flat whites. The neighbourhood parks are perfect for jogging, rollerblading and people-watching, and a network of cycle lanes makes this large *barrio* easy to navigate on two wheels.

✪ Café Vinilo

Tap into the local music scene at this fabulous venue that slips under most visitors' radar. From the authentic Monday night *milonga* (tango dance night) to concerts most nights by tango orchestras and a host of other talented musicians, Vinilo is a favourite live music venue for those who know it.

Gorriti 3780; http://cafevinilo.com. ar; 8am-1am Wed-Mon.

🍸 Verne Club

Step behind the velvet curtains to reach a dimly-lit space with dark wood accents and a Jules Verne theme. Owner Fede Cuco is considered the city's top mixologist. Sample his creations and sign up for a cocktail-making masterclass led by Cuco himself. *Medrano 1475; www.vernecocktailclub.com; 9am-2am Sun-Thu, to 4am Fri & Sat.*

✖ Perón Perón Restobar

The political legacy of Juan and Eva Perón is celebrated at this excellent restaurant, which is popular with Perón's supporters. The interior – a shrine of Peronist memorabilia and graffiti – is a tribute to the couple and the food more than lives up to the setting. *Carranza 2225; www.facebook.com/PeronPeronOficial; 011-4777-6194; 7pm-midnight Mon-Thu, to 1am Fri & Sat.*

✪ Hipódromo Argentino de Palermo

For many visitors to Palermo, the historic Hipódromo Argentino remains hidden in plain sight. It's free to go inside, and spending a few hours at the races offers a taste of glamour, whether your eyes are on the tracks or on the colourful characters in the grandstand. *Av del Libertador 4101; www.palermo.com.ar.*

🏛 Vuela el Pez

Behind a nondescript door and up a narrow staircase is this cultural centre and arts space that shuns the mainstream in favour of alternative ideas and forms of expression. There's always something interesting to pick out of its varied programme of art exhibitions, live music, plays, poetry readings and debates. *Av Córdoba 4379; www.facebook.com/vuelaelpez; 8.30pm-midnight Sun & Tue-Thu, to 5am Fri & Sat.*

Map labels: Perón Perón Restobar, PALERMO, Guatemala, Angel Justiniano Carranza, PALERMO HOLLYWOOD, Av Juan B Justo, PALERMO VIEJO, Hipódromo Argentino de Palermo 1.5km (1 mile), Ecoparque de Buenos Aires, Plaza Italia, Av Santa Fe, PALERMO SOHO, Plaza Palermo Viejo, Av Scalabrini Ortiz, Verne Club, Costa Rica, Salguero, Av Córdoba, VILLA CRESPO, Vuela El Pez, Gorriti, Av Medrano, Café Vinilo, Mario Bravo

ALMAGRO

Located right in the middle of Buenos Aires and within easy reach of almost everywhere in the city by subte, bus or bike, Almagro is a residential neighbourhood that exudes a combination of timeless tradition, youthful enthusiasm and everyday life. Its leafy streets are home to a thriving arts scene, a number of atmospheric cafes and some excellent local restaurants.

⊗ Las Violetas

Almagro's *señoras* (that is, women of a certain age) have been meeting at this elegant cafe for milky coffee, *medialunas* (croissants) and gossip since 1884. The stunning stained-glass windows and marble floors date from the 1920s. Come for *merienda*, the Argentine version of afternoon tea; crustless sandwiches and pastries will be served with considerable pomp by a bow-tied waiter. *Av Rivadavia 3899; www.lasvioletas. com; 011-4958-7387; 6am-1am.*

🏛 Señor Duncan

It doesn't look like much from the street, but this renovated old house hosts storytelling events, open-mic nights, salsa classes, swing dancing, jazz bands and more. La Casa del Señor Duncan has the atmosphere of a bohemian house party and attracts a friendly crowd. Ring the doorbell to get in. *Rivadavia 3832; www.facebook.com/ seniorduncan; 7pm-2am Sun & Mon, to 3am Tue-Thu, to 4am Fri & Sat.*

⊗ Dumbo

One legacy of Italian immigration to Buenos Aires is the city's outstanding gelato. Hidden among the big-name chains are those rarer, more precious gems: independent, neighbourhood *heladerías* (ice cream parlours) with queues around the block. Dumbo has been selling artisan ice cream, made on site, since 1942. Try the *dulce de leche* (caramel); locals insist it's the best in the city. *Av Rivadavia 3929; www.heladosdumbo.com. ar; noon-1am Sun-Thu, to 2am Fri & Sat.*

✪ El Boliche de Roberto

Early in the evening this small bar full of dusty bottles seems like a regular, old-time neighbourhood saloon. But once the tango musicians arrive,

Map labels:
Av Córdoba
El Camarín de las Musas 🏛
ABASTO
Bulnes
Gallo
Museo Casa Carlos Gardel ✪
Mercado de Abasto
Jean Jaurès
Av Corrientes
Flower Stalls 🔒
Plaza Almagro ✪
Sarmiento
ONCE
El Boliche de Roberto ✪
Juan D Perón
Av Díaz Vélez
Bulnes
ALMAGRO
Las Violetas
Dumbo ⊗
Señor Duncan 🏛
Av Boedo
Av Rivadavia

take out their guitars and begin to sing so beautifully you'll get goosebumps, it's clear that this place is something special. It's a neighbourhood secret almost too good to share. *Bulnes 331; www.facebook.com/elbolichederobertoOK; 4pm-3am.*

🔒 Flower Stalls

Wander two blocks east of Plaza Almagro and you'll notice the sweet scent emanating from buckets of colourful roses, hyacinths and tulips outside a series of independent flower shops and stalls. When the Almagro flower market closed in 2002, these *florerías* (flower sellers) stayed on. Look for them on Acuña de Figueroa and on Sarmiento, between Av Medrano and Gascón. *Cnr Sarmiento & Acuña de Figueroa, hours vary.*

🏛 El Camarín de las Musas

Almagro has a thriving alternative theatre scene with some worthwhile productions – if

---

PARKLIFE

Plaza Almagro is a grassy square at the heart of the neighbourhood. Most residents live in apartment blocks: Plaza Almagro is the *barrio*'s communal backyard and a place for older gentlemen to play chess, children to let off steam and groups of friends to gather. On the weekends leading up to February's carnival, local troupes practise here.

---

you know where to find them. Start by checking out the programme at El Camarín de las Musas, an intimate venue that stages contemporary dance performances as well as plays. *Mario Bravo 960; www.elcamarindelasmusas.com; 10am-midnight Mon-Thu, to 2am Fri & Sat, 5pm-midnight Sun.*

⭐ Museo Casa Carlos Gardel

On a residential street in the Abasto area is legendary tango singer Carlos Gardel's former home. It's now a small but worthwhile museum where you can hear all of his recordings. In the surrounding streets, keep a look out for a number of murals and mosaic images of the local icon in his signature fedora hat. *Jean Jaures 735; www.buenosaires.gob.ar/museos/museo-casa-carlos-gardel; 11am-6pm Mon & Wed-Fri, 10am-7pm Sat & Sun; AR$50.*

Top: signs in Buenos Aires
Left: smooth moves from the city's tango dancers

CHACARITA

Get here quick: Chacarita is a *barrio* on the up. Still a little sketchy in parts, the neighbourhood's leafy streets hide a number of highly-rated new restaurants as well as classic old bars. Easily walkable, this compact neighbourhood is a short bus or taxi ride from Palermo's nightlife and a 20-minute trip from the city centre on the subte line B.

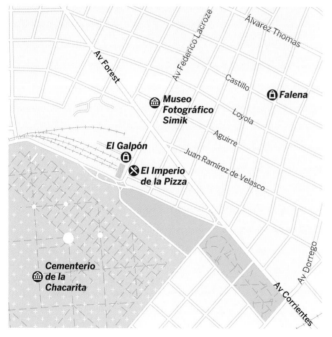

in the know come here for organic wine, artisan beer, vegetarian pizzas, fruit, salad, bread, meat and more. *Av Federico Lacroze 4171; http://elgalpon.org.ar; 9am-6pm Wed & Sat.*

🔒 Falena

On a quiet residential corner, the exterior brick walls of this 1930s building give no hint as to what lies inside. Ring the doorbell for admission to an entrancing space. Light spills in from an internal patio with bench seating and plants; inside there are squishy sofas, bookshelves and a wine bar. Heaven. *Charlone 201; www. falena.com.ar; 2-9pm Tue-Sat.*

❌ El Imperio de la Pizza

Avenida Corrientes has a number of classic pizzerias; skip the more famous places near the city centre and head instead to El Imperio, a charmingly kitsch, neighbourhood joint that's been serving up doughy, greasy pizza pies since 1947. *Av Corrientes 6899; www.facebook.com/ elimperiodelapizza; 5am-1am Sun-Fri, 24hr Sat.*

✪ Museo Fotográfico Simik

Inside an eccentric neighbourhood cafe, this so-called photography museum contains the extensive camera collection and assorted photography memorabilia of Alejandro Simik. Best of all, there's live music every night from Tuesday to Sunday. *Av Federico Lacroze 3901; www. facebook.com/MuseoSimik; 7am-midnight Mon-Sat.*

🏛 Cementerio de la Chacarita

Recoleta Cemetery is one of the city's most visited sights, but few tourists make it out to the larger, equally atmospheric Chacarita Cemetery. Here you can visit the mausoleum of tango singer Carlos Gardel; a statue of the crooner can usually be found holding a cigarette, kept lit by local taxi drivers who come to pay their respects. *Av Guzmán 680; 7.30am-5pm.*

🔒 El Galpón

Hidden at the end of an unpromising cobbled lane is a rustic yellow shed that hosts a twice-weekly cooperative farmers market specialising in organic and agroecological produce, natural soaps and beauty products. Locals

SAN TELMO

Located near the port of La Boca, San Telmo is where many newly-arrived immigrants set up home: the mansions of the wealthy later became tenement housing for the poor. Pretty, cobbled Calle Defensa has a high tourist footfall, but much of the *barrio* remains working class and down-to-earth. The neighbourhood is easily walkable and close to the city centre.

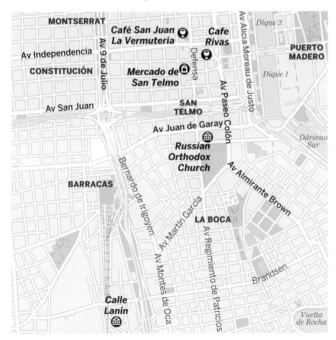

🏛 Russian Orthodox Church

Despite its distinctive bulb-shaped domes and gold crosses, Buenos Aires' only Russian Orthodox church is surprisingly easy to miss among the buildings on Av Brasil. There's a good view of the light-blue, gold-studded bell towers from the banks of Parque Lezama. Few visitors venture inside, but the church is open to guests on the second Sunday of the month at 3.30pm (admission AR$50). *Av Brasil 135; http://www. iglesiarusa.org.ar.*

🏛 Calle Lanín

Just outside San Telmo, in the *barrio* of Barracas, the residents of cobbled Calle Lanín have decorated their houses' outer walls with murals and tile mosaics, transforming the quiet street into a living gallery of public art. *Between Calles Brandsen & Suárez.*

🍸 Café San Juan La Vermutería

If you like vermouth, don't miss the small but exceptionally well stocked *vermutería* (vermouth bar) inside Café San Juan. Try the *aperitivo de la casa*, a very local combination of Cinzano, Cynar and Fernet with soda, accompanied by exquisite tapas from chef Lele Cristóbal's kitchen. *Chile 474; www.facebook. com/CafeSanJuanOficial; 6.30pm-midnight Tue-Sun & noon-4pm Sat & Sun.*

🔒 Mercado de San Telmo

Not to be confused with the famous Sunday open-air *feria* (street fair), San Telmo Market is a vibrant indoor market in a gorgeous 1897 building. Locals still shop here for fresh fruit, meat and cheese, though traditional vendors are joined by third-wave coffee shops and high-end bakeries. *Bolívar 470; http://mercadosantelmo.com.ar; 8am-8.30pm.*

🍸 Cafe Rivas

Idyllically located on a cobbled San Telmo corner, Cafe Rivas is the kind of place that sucks you in and consumes your day. Equally good for a morning coffee as for an evening cocktail, this elegant bar has an immaculate wooden interior that oozes timeless charm. *Estados Unidos 302; www.facebook.com/ caferivas; 9.30am-1.30am Tue-Sat, 11am-8pm Sun.*

ARTS & CULTURE MUSIC & FILM SPORTS & LEISURE EATING DRINKING SHOPPING

Santa Teresa &
Lapa

Rio De Janeiro

Botafogo &
Urca

Ipanema &
the Lakeside   Copacabana

RIO DE JANEIRO

A city of golden beaches, samba-fuelled nightlife and forest-fringed neighbourhoods, Rio offers a mesmerising backdrop for urban exploring.

J ust inland from the crashing waves of Rio's famous beach 'burbs Ipanema and Copacabana, you'll find eye-catching boutiques, buzzing nightspots and cafes, and lesser-known spots to enjoy the tropical scenery – including a saltwater lagoon and a clifftop park with panoramic views. .

A short metro ride north of Copacabana, Botafogo is a creative eating and drinking hub, home to artisanal bakers, craft brewers and easy-going live music joints. Nearby Urca feels like a coastal village with its tiny beaches and waterfront strolls. Further north, the nightlife epicentre of Lapa draws music lovers, who converge on the samba clubs and vibrant bars. Lapa lies at the base of hilltop Santa Teresa, a bohemian enclave of artist studios, eclectic shops and places to eat.

Rio's neighbourhoods are ideal for walking, and you can generally zip between areas using Rio's efficient metro. There's also a bike-sharing service (Bike Rio).

COPACABANA

Though a popular tourist destination, Copacabana has some appealing local haunts that draw *cariocas* (Rio residents) in the know. There's no better place than down in Copacabana for doing yoga out on the water (on a stand-up paddleboard), catching sidewalk samba jams or enjoying ocean-side drinks far from the maddening crowds. Break up long stretches of this 4km (2.5-mile) seaside 'hood by biking or using one of four metro stations.

Café 18 do Forte

Hidden inside the Forte de Copacabana, this outdoor cafe offers fabulous views across the expanse of Copacabana Beach. The shaded tables make a fine spot for coffee, craft beers by Rio brewer Praya, and snacks. You'll have to pay at the entrance gate (R$6), but the secret terrace is worth it. *Praça Coronel Eugênio Franco, off Av Pasteur 520; http://cafe18doforte. com.br; 10am-8pm Tue-Sun.*

Bip Bip

This tiny storefront in Copacabana transforms into a memorable live music space six nights a week. The formula is simple: a long table, where musicians drop by to jam, a fridge full of beer in the back (help yourself then pay the guy at the table in front), and a samba-loving crowd that sings along. *Rua Almirante Gonçalves 50; www. facebook.com/barbipbip; 7pm-midnight Sun-Fri.*

Bairro Peixoto

Copacabana's traffic-clogged avenues are a world away from this serene mini-neighbourhood with its tree-lined plaza, playground, park benches and tables where locals gossip. Come on Wednesdays for the open-air market, when you can find mangoes, papaya, custard apples, passion fruit and more. Watch for marmosets up in the trees. *Praça Edmundo Bittencourt.*

Universo Paddle Surf

One of the best ways to appreciate Copacabana's tropical backdrop is from the water. Join the SUP (stand-up paddleboard) crowd off the south side of the beach. Universe Paddle Surf is one of a few outfitters with gear (around R$60 per hour). They also do SUP yoga at sunset. *Posto 6, Copacabana Beach; 21-98269-5109.*

Gilson Martins

Across from the beach, Gilson Martins sells colourful accessories emblazoned with the Brazilian flag and silhouettes of Christ the Redeemer and Sugar Loaf Mountain. Bags and wallets use recycled, sustainable materials. *Av Atlântica 1998; www.gilsonmartins. com.br; 10am-6pm Mon-Sat.*

Map labels:
Bairro Peixoto
R Tonelero
Siqueira Campos
Gilson Martins
R Constante Ramos
Av Atlântica
Copacabana Beach (Praia de Copacabana)
R Bolívar
Cantagalo
BAIXO COPA
R Miguel Lemos
Morro do Cantagalo
Bip Bip
Atlantic Ocean
Ipanema/ General Osório
Universo Paddle Surf
R Francisco Sá
Café 18 do Forte
Av Rainha Elizabeth
Ponta de Copacabana

IPANEMA & THE LAKESIDE

Between the Atlantic and a sparkling lake (Lagoa), this upscale district houses boutiques, bars and cultural centres. It comprises four districts that grew together: Ipanema, Leblon, Lagoa and Gávea. There's metro access but you'll want a bus or taxi for Gávea and northern Lagoa.

🍫 Chocolate Q

This tiny store in Ipanema stocks delectably dark chocolates that are beautifully packaged and sustainably sourced from a single producer in Bahia. You can also arrange a tasting (the 'Chocolate Q Experience'), where you'll learn the fascinating story of the revival of an old cacao plantation as you munch your way from medium to dark perfection. *Rua Garcia D'Ávila 149, Ipanema; www.chocolateq. com; 10am-8pm Mon-Sat.*

🍸 Palaphita Kitch

Perched on the edge of the lake, this open-air spot is great for a sunset cocktail. Bamboo furniture, flickering tiki torches and views of towering peaks beyond Lagoa make a fine setting for creative drinks and snacks, including dishes made with Amazonian ingredients. *Av Epitácio Pessoa, Lagoa; http:// palaphitakitch.com.br; 6pm-midnight.*

🛍 Maria Oiticica

Inside an ultra-modern shopping mall in Leblon, Maria Oiticica

sells one-of-a-kind earth-friendly jewellery and handbags, made from Amazonian seeds, plant fibres and even tree bark. The colourful necklaces, bracelets and earrings make wonderful conversation pieces. *Shopping Leblon, Av Afrânio de Melo Franco 290, Leblon; 10am-10pm Mon-Sat, 1-9pm Sun.*

🌳 Parque da Catacumba

Just off a busy road on the eastern side of Lagoa, this little-known park has a short but steep trail that takes you up through Atlantic rainforest to a lookout high above the lake. From the 130m (427ft) perch (the Mirante do Sacopã) you'll have a mesmerising view over Ipanema, Leblon and the lush hillsides surrounding the lake. *Av Epitácio Pessoa, Lagoa; 8am-5pm Tue-Sun; free.*

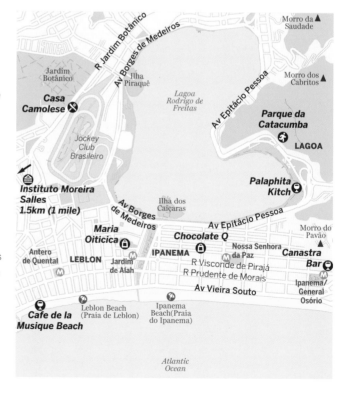

✖ Casa Camolese

Inside the Jockey Club complex, the Casa Camolese is equal parts restaurant, deli, microbrewery and live music space. There's creative bistro fare (try the paprika-dusted octopus) and the outdoor tables overlooking the track are the place to be on clear nights. Jazz concerts (and the occasional burlesque show) happen in the intimate downstairs den known as Manouche. Reserve ahead for dinner and performances. *Rua Jardim Botânico 983, Jardim Botânico; www.casacamolese. com.br; 21-3514-8200; noon-midnight.*

♨ Canastra Bar

A short stroll from Praça General Osório, Canastra draws a wide cross-section of Rio society, who come for sangria and Brazilian wine (really!) along with delicious small plates. Tuesdays are extremely popular – the lane in front transforms into one big street party – it's also when fresh oysters from Santa Catarina are available. You can escape the crowds in the tiny, speakeasy-style bar hidden downstairs. *Rua Jangadeiros, Ipanema, 6.30pm-1am Tue-Sun.*

BEACH KIOSKS

A quintessential part of Rio's beachfront, the *quiosque* (kiosk) is an informal stand that doles out beer, caipirinhas, *agua de coco* (coconut water) and other cold drinks. Most have tables and chairs for prime gazing across the shore. In recent years, a few upscale kiosks have opened, including Cafe de la Musique Beach (www.facebook.com/cafedelamusiquebeach, Av Delfim Moreira, 8am-10pm) in Leblon, which serves excellent cocktails and good Brazilian fare, and has live music on weekends.

🏛 Instituto Moreira Salles

Surrounded by the Tijuca Forest, this beautifully located cultural centre hosts thought-provoking exhibitions, concerts and film screenings. It's set in a former 1950s home that's a jewel of Brazilian modernism. Admission to exhibitions is generally free. *Rua Marquês de São Vicente 476, Gávea; www.ims.com.br; 11am-8pm Tue-Sun.*

Clockwise from top: Instituto Moreira Salles; green coconuts for sale; iconic Ipanema Beach

© Robert Polidori / 2020, Instituto Moreira Salles

© Colors Hunter · Chasseur de Couleurs/Getty Images

© lazyllama / Shutterstock

BOTAFOGO & URCA

Botafogo has undergone a creative renaissance in recent years, with art-filled cafes and bars sprouting like wildflowers along the leafy streets. You can easily stroll between Botafogo's indie cinemas, outdoor music joints and beer-centric places to eat, but you'll need to hop on a bus or a bike to reach Urca, which hides a short but scenic walking trail skirting the coastline.

espressos, açaí and waffles by morning, or curries and cocktails later in the day. After sunset, a pre-party crowd arrives, with jazz trios on Tuesdays and DJs on Thursdays. *Rua Fernandes Guimarães 66, Botafogo; http://colab-rio.com; 10am-1am Tue-Sat.*

Pista Cláudio Coutinho

A favourite place for strollers and joggers in Urca is this little-known 1.2km (0.75 miles) trail that skirts along the forested base of Morro da Urca. Come in the morning or late in the day for the best chance to see small troops of marmosets skittering through the trees. *Off Praia Vermelha, Urca.*

Estação Net Botafogo

When the weather sours, rainy-day escapes include this three-screen cinema near the Botafogo metro station. Independent and cult films are screened, and it has a cosy cafe and bookshop at the entrance. Before or after the movie, grab a bite on restaurant-lined Rua Nelson Mandela, a few steps away. *Rua Voluntários da Pátria 88, Botafogo; www.grupoestacao.com.br.*

Fuska Bar 2.0

Grab an outdoor table on the footpath and let the night unfold at this laid-back spot on a bar-lined corner of Humaitá. There's always a fun crowd, and the unfussy setting makes the perfect backdrop to samba and other sounds. Live music Thursday to Sunday nights. *Rua Capitão Salomão 52, Botafogo; www.facebook.com/fuskabar2.0; 8am-3am Tue-Sun.*

Slow Bakery

Blazing new trails in bakery-challenged Rio, this hipster-loving cafe and *padaria artesanal* (artisanal bakery) turns out beautiful loaves, pastries and cakes, along with some of the best toasted sandwiches in Rio. The sunny space with its chunky wooden tables is great place to linger over a meal or good coffees and refreshing slow brews – perfect for hot days. *Rua São João Batista 93, Botafogo; www.theslowbakery.com.br; 9am-7.30pm Tue-Fri, to 3pm Sat.*

CoLAB

An inviting gathering place for Botafogo's creative types, CoLAB plays all the angles: stop in for

SANTA TERESA & LAPA

The vintage tram from downtown rattles over the Lapa Arches and into the cobblestone streets of charming Santa Teresa. Here old mansions have been transformed into studios, while bars and boutiques cater to the creative residents. Downhill from Santa Teresa, Lapa is famed for its samba clubs, though it's also home to one of Rio's best jazz clubs, as well as a fabulous monthly antiques fair that doubles as a street party.

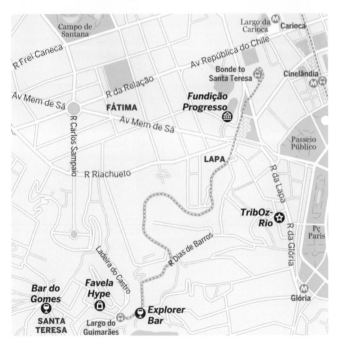

🚇 Explorer Bar

A pretty terrace strung with fairy lights sets the scene at this captivating cocktail bar on a hill. Make an evening of it ordering tasty Mediterranean small plates or heartier dishes like fish with black rice and *farofa* (made from cassava flour). *Rua Almirante Alexandrino 399, Santa Teresa; www. explorerbar.com; 5pm-midnight Tue-Fri, from 2pm Sat & Sun.*

🚇 Bar do Gomes

Black and white photos and antique cabinets give this den a bygone air. Going strong since 1919 and officially named Armazem São Thiago, locals call it Bar do Gomes (after a previous owner). Join young and old over ice-cold *chope* (draft beer). *Rua Áurea 26, Santa Teresa; www.armazemsaothiago.com.br; noon-1am.*

🔒 Favela Hype

Santa's prime destination for fashionable wear both on the street and at the beach. There's also a tiny restaurant and bar tucked in the back, and the whole space transforms into a live music den on Saturdays (from 8pm) and Sundays (from 4pm). *Rua Paschoal Carlos Magno 103, Santa Teresa; www. facebook.com/favelahypeoficial; 11am-10pm Tue-Sun.*

🏛 Fundição Progresso

This former foundry plays a pivotal role in the Lapa arts scene, hosting socially minded exhibitions and running courses in dance, percussion and capoeira. It's best known for its varied music and theatre. *Rua dos Arcos 24, Lapa; www.fundicaoprogresso.com.br; 11am-8pm Mon-Fri, noon-11pm Sat.*

✪ TribOz-Rio

Devoted exclusively to jazz, Trib-Oz is reminiscent of intimate jazz dens in NYC, set in a beautifully converted house in the southern fringes of Lapa. No talking during sets. Reserve ahead. *Rua Conde de Lages 19, Lapa; www.triboz-rio. com; 6-8pm & 9pm-1am Thu-Sat.*

ACKNOWLEDGEMENTS

Secret City

April 2020

Published by Lonely Planet Global Limited

CRN 554153, www.lonelyplanet.com

Printed in China

10 9 8 7 6 5 4 3 2 1

ISBN 978 17886 8916 8

© Lonely Planet 2020

© photographers as indicated 2020

Cover illustration: Big City Collection © Franzi draws,
www.youworkforthem.com

Managing Director, Publishing Piers Pickard

Associate Publisher Robin Barton

Commissioning Editors Dora Ball, Anita Isalska

Editor Anita Isalska

Art Director Daniel Di Paolo

Layout Kerry Rubenstein

Picture Research Lauren Marchant

Proofreading Lucy Doncaster

Print Production Nigel Longuet

Cartography James Leversha, Wayne Murphy

Written by Isabel Albiston, James Bainbridge, Ryan ver Berkmoes, Abigail Blasi, Claire Boobbyer, Celeste Brash, Austin Bush, Lucy Corne, Peter Dragicevich, Ethan Gelber, Bridget Gleeson, Sarah Hedley Hymers, Carolyn Heller, Sandra Henriques Gajjar, Anita Isalska, Mark Johanson, Ria de Jong, Anna Kaminski, Lauren Keith, Thomas O'Malley, Emily Matchar, Emily McAuliffe, Rebecca Milner, Meher Mirza, Catherine Le Nevez, Oda O'Carroll, Lorna Parkes, Veronika Primm, Leonid Ragozin, Charles Rawlings Way, Nora Rawn, Andrea Schulte-Peevers, Helena Smith, Regis St Louis, Andy Symington, Caroline Veldhuis, Mara Vorhees, Jennifer Walker, Hahna Yoon, Karla Zimmerman.

Lonely Planet Offices

STAY IN TOUCH lonelyplanet.com/contact

Australia

The Malt Store, Level 3,
551 Swanston St, Carlton, Victoria 3053
T: 03 8379 8000

USA

Suite 208, 155 Filbert St,
Oakland, CA 94607
T: 510 250 6400

Ireland

Digital Depot, Roe Lane (Off Thomas Street)
The Digital Hub,
Dublin 8, D08 TCV4

UK

240 Blackfriars Rd,
London SE1 8NW
T: 020 3771 5100

MIX
Paper from
responsible sources
FSC
www.fsc.org   FSC™ C021741

Paper in this book is certified against the Forest Stewardship Council™ standards. FSC™ promotes environmentally responsible, socially beneficial and economically viable management of the world's forests.